D0975673

CONNECTING LAW
AND SOCIETY

CONNECTING LAW AND SOCIETY

An Introduction to Research and Theory

ROBERT L. KIDDER

Temple University

Prentice-Hall, Inc., Englewood Cliffs, New Jersey 07632

Library of Congress Cataloging in Publication Data

KIDDER, ROBERT L.
    Connecting law and society.

    Includes bibliographies and index.
    1.–Sociological jurisprudence.   I.–Title.
K370.K52 1983   340′.115   82-20411
ISBN   0-13-167809-4

Editorial/production supervision by Joyce Turner
Cover design: Jeannette Jacobs
Cover photo: Robert L. Kidder
Manufacturing buyer: John Hall

© 1983 by Prentice-Hall, Inc., Englewood Cliffs, New Jersey
07632

All rights reserved. No part of this book may be
reproduced, in any form or by any means,
without permission in writing from the publisher.

Printed in the United States of America

10 9 8 7 6 5 4 3 2 1

ISBN 0-13-167809-4

Prentice-Hall International, Inc., *London*
Prentice-Hall of Australia Pty. Limited, *Sydney*
Editora Prentice-Hall do Brasil, Ltda., *Rio de Janeiro*
Prentice-Hall Canada Inc., *Toronto*
Prentice-Hall of India Private Limited, *New Delhi*
Prentice-Hall of Japan, Inc., *Tokyo*
Prentice-Hall of Southeast Asia Pte. Ltd., *Singapore*
Whitehall Books Limited, *Wellington, New Zealand*

TO LOUISE, GRAHAM, AND CHARIN,
AND THE KIYOSHI IKEDA COHORT:
TWO WELLS THAT NEVER RUN DRY.

CONTENTS

PREFACE

When people try to deal with some chronic problem or solve some puzzle about the world around them, they sometimes begin by breaking their subject down into different parts. They try to isolate separate operations, concepts, or objects and concentrate on the workings of those segments. The history of invention, of human ingenuity, is often a history of such sub-dividing of concepts, objects, and processes. As parts of the whole become identified, scrutinized, manipulated, and altered, specialists assume authority over those parts, and the parts themselves are then subjected to further sub-division. You can see this process in the history of medical science, for example, or the histories of metallurgy, astronomy, agriculture, and aviation. You can also find it in the history of social innovations, such as banking, the entertainment industry, labor unions, and nursing homes.

In many such histories, however, there is evidence that the benefits of innovation are achieved at the cost of minor or major disasters not foreseen by the innovators. The solution of one problem precipitates new ones. On the technological side, think of the consequences of nuclear energy, thalidomide, the automobile, and saccharine. Think also of social innovations such as home mortgages, singles bars, mail-order merchandising, and police. Whenever an innovation produces new problems, there is a suspicion that the innovators were too narrowly focused on the *parts* with which they were tinkering, and lost sight of the *whole* picture.

Law has been one such area of innovation. For centuries people have been inventing, changing, and discarding laws and legal systems in the hope that particular social problems could be resolved. Rules developed by early societies in the context of everyday problem-solving have yielded to the rise of law as a self-consciously separate social institution. The growing separation between law makers and enforcers and the rest of society has been paralleled by the rise of legal studies which treat law as a separate, unique human activity. Like other areas of specialization, law has taken on the trappings of high technology, with the associated mysteries of "technical details" presided over by experts.

This book is about a valuable move backwards. The study of law and society has developed as an antidote to the trend toward separating law from the social settings in which it is created and operates. Why is there a need to "connect law and society?" The move toward treating law as a separate, specialized activity has produced legal "reasoning" based on distorted and poorly supported assumptions about the events in society and their relationship to law. As law has been isolated, its ties with other events and institutions in society have become obscured. People from various social science backgrounds have become persuaded that we need a more careful reckoning of law's place in society. Some have pursued this work as a way of bringing about reform through law. Others expect their research to expose the illegitimacy of the legal enterprise.

You will see the different directions from which social scientists have approached law. You will see some of the history of those approaches. You will also find yourself confronting opposed interpretations of much of the research which has been produced by this law and society movement.

The ultimate destiny of law and society studies is unclear. In recent years it has provided sparks for a rapid expansion of research problems and vigorous debate. Throughout the book you will see both the concrete results of research and how the results affect the status of those debates. You will not be told which position is correct. Instead, you should be provided with concepts and questions to help you enter the debate as an informed participant. You should find reason to question at least some of the things you consider obvious about law. You should discover why you believe certain claims about legal institutions and why those beliefs are solid or shaky. As with any good sociological enterprise, this book should help you see how you and your immediate social world fit into the pattern of law and society connections.

One way of doing this is to show you how law is handled in other societies. I make many comparisons among legal forms in different societies, and for that reason, have not packed the book with American cases or American examples. You will see law happening in India, Japan,

Lebanon, Mexico, and China as well as West Virginia, Boston, Wall Street, and Southern California. You will see it in complex industrial societies and in simpler agrarian settings. You will be familiar with some of the cases described, unfamiliar with others. You may finish the book with more questions than answers. If so, the book will have served you well. Too much about law has been so obscured for so long that most people do not even know what questions to ask.

In trying to integrate a rapidly growing and diversified field such as law and society, it is difficult to identify and thank all those who contributed to the making of a book such as this. There are literally hundreds of people whose work influenced my thinking in ways that affect the final product. Many authors whose work I have cited here spent time helping me to be sure I was not misrepresenting their work. But I owe special thanks to those who first pointed me in the direction of law and society, either through personal support or their "being there" with interesting material, ideas, and questions when I was searching. These include Kiyoshi Ikeda, William Evan, Richard Schwartz, and Marc Galanter. Thanks also to Richard Abel, William Felstiner, Bliss Cartwright, June Starr, and Dan Lev for their help in reviewing my work over the years. In particular, I was lucky to have the help of Fred DuBow, Craig McEwan, and Louise Kidder who patiently and thoroughly reviewed various versions of the manuscript. Thanks also to Martha Davis and Daniel Tompkins for keeping me straight about interpretations of classical Greek and Roman civilization. Thanks to Peter Rigby and Peter Severeid whose colleagueship at Temple has helped strengthen this book and sustain its author. For their patient support and efficient assistance, my thanks to the Prentice-Hall staff of Susan Taylor, Barbara DeVries, Richard Kilmartin, Joyce Turner, and Edward Stanford. And for their dedicated professional skill and integrity, my thanks to Donald Black, Center for Criminal Justice, Harvard Law School; David Bordua, University of Illinois-Urbana-Champaign; Edith E. Graber, Washington Univeristy; Allan Horwitz, Rutgers University; James Inverarity, University of Minnesota; and Jon Simpson, University of Massachusetts. Their help was invaluable in revising the manuscript.

Finally, my thanks to several cohorts of Temple students in Sociology 270 whose reactions and good questions have helped me to develop my thinking about law and society connections and whose comments improved the manuscript.

R.L.K.

CONNECTING LAW
AND SOCIETY

1

INTRODUCTION: CRISES IN SOCIETY AND LAW

City on fire!
Rats in the Streets
And the lunatics yelling at the moon!
It's the end of the world! Yes!
City on fire!
Hunchbacks kissing!
Stirrings in the graves
And the screaming of giant winds!
Watch out! Look!
Crawling on the chimneys,
Great black crows screeching at the
City on fire!
City on fire!
City on fire!*
(From the musical *Sweeney Todd*, words by Stephen Sondheim)

These words were written in our own times. They capture the crazy truths seen by nineteenth-century English lunatics as they bolt to freedom from Bedlam, their asylum, and race through London's streets. We feel their contemporary passion because we ourselves seem to be trapped in a world

*From the musical, *Sweeney Todd*, words by Stephen Sondheim. © 1979 Revelation Music Publishing Corp. & Rilting Music, Inc. Lyrics reprinted by special permission.

in crisis. We have seen our cities literally burning. We have also watched them be consumed by a slower, more mysterious "fire." Confusion all around us makes us wonder what ever happened to the "good old days." Our papers give us only the cold comfort of knowing that nothing seems to work any more, that people have gone crazy, that "the powers that be" cannot cope. Our televisions give us a daily glimpse of events that would have been "unthinkable" just five years ago. We are in shock.

In the midst of this general sense of crisis lurks a more specific, and perhaps more frightening, specter. A legal system and set of laws, which we thought to be a weapon against crisis, begins to show signs that it is part of that crisis. Crime seems rampant, but the police and the courts do nothing. Police blame the courts, and judges blame the police or the taxpayers. Everyone seems to be passing the buck to some other part of the system while agreeing that the faith we place in *The Law* is "unrealistic." Meanwhile people live in fear, turning their homes into fortresses and killing each other with guns bought for "protection."

Other crises swirl like "giant winds" through the precincts of law. Lawyers seem to be "butting in" everywhere, taking over and stirring up more trouble than they settle. The big battles in professional sports no longer happen on the field. They are fought in boardrooms and courtrooms, where lawyers wheel and deal over free-agent clauses, hardship waivers, and contract concessions. We see lawyers leading strikes where we were hoping to see ball games. Why do lawyers interfere with children learning in school, nurses tending patients, or air traffic controllers guiding jumbo jets? We see doctors, dentists, and architects raising their fees so they can pay for malpractice insurance. Lawyers seem to be everywhere inventing problems, pitting people against each other, destroying traditional values and relationships, and getting rich in the process.

What is worse, when ordinary people find themselves in situations where they need legal help, they cannot afford it, and they would not know how to find it if they could. Somehow, with all the visibility of the legal profession, lawyers still seem to live and work in a rarefied atmosphere of high finance which makes them rich, invisible, and unaffordable to people who really need them.

Television's fantasy world gives us mixed messages about all this. During prime time we see that Perry Mason (or his more recent counterparts) is always there to defend the innocent and bring justice to the guilty. We see that the police are quick, efficient, noble, and law abiding, and that they "get their man." During certain television hours crime does not pay. But then comes the news, and we are bombarded by evidence that law in the real world is better symbolized by either the bumbling *Keystone Kops* of silent movie fame or by a Mr. Hyde making forays from Dr. Jekyll's office in City Hall.

We pass admirable laws, trying to control some excess by business, industry, or local government. We set up agencies to protect our environment, regulate commerce, protect consumers from exploitation, save us from managerial recklessness in the nuclear industry, and protect our minorities from attack and exploitation by local bigots. But when we look closer, at the actual use of those laws, we find serious lapses in the work done by those agencies. Too often it looks as if the agency designed to regulate has actually been taken over by the targets of regulation.

In our major cities, odd combinations of insurance, banking, and tax laws combine to make arson so profitable that "fires of suspicious origin" no longer seem the least bit suspicious. Unless it is proven otherwise, we have come to assume that the arson industry has struck again.

The more legal force we bring to bear on "the drug problem," the more available drugs seem to become. When laws could not stop gambling, we saw the paradox of government becoming one of the biggest gambling operators in the United States—in the form of lotteries. Decades of new laws were our answer to the decay of cities and the blight of poverty. Years later urban renewal looks to many people like a disguise for urban demolition. Public housing, instead of solving problems of poverty, appears only to have consolidated them in towers of rage and misery.

Until the early 1950s people would not openly acknowledge a prosecutor's willingness to plea bargain with a defense lawyer in order to get a conviction on reduced charges. Justice was not supposed to be "for sale" in the courts. Today the people who run our justice system not only admit their involvement in plea bargaining; they actually endorse it as the only effective way to handle the crime "explosion." It looks as if the criminals are winning simply because there are so many of them.

Around the world, the picture looks equally grim. Everywhere we hear of "terrorists" kidnapping, bombing, sniping, and bringing general mayhem to industrial societies. Ambassadors ride in armored limousines. Their embassies get seized and transformed into bastions of rebellion. The protocols of international law lie smoldering in the ashes of government-backed "take-overs." When Americans try to condemn others for lawlessness, they stumble over "secret" documents published as paperbacks and sold in supermarkets. They tell a tale of decades of American lawlessness, of "covert operations" conducted by leaders who were supposed to be defenders of the law.

An American president says he is above prosecution because of "executive privilege." Then he announces that he is "not a crook." But he resigns in disgrace. And his successor uses the law to pardon him of crimes he "did not commit." Is this a triumph or a defeat for law? We cannot even agree.

Nearly three decades after the United States Supreme Court declared segregated schools to be unconstitutional (*Brown* v. *Board of Education*), the nation continues to stumble over this issue. Is not the Supreme Court the final arbiter of our laws? Are we a nation of law-abiding citizens? How can our actions since 1954 fit with such an image? Yet if we play games with the Court's rulings, what do we have left to protect us from our own worst tendencies? Or was the "Warren Court" a freak, a temporary leftward drift which empowered misguided men to abuse the law? With either interpretation, our faith in the Court as the bedrock upon which our laws stand is shaken by unresolved controversy, and we look for alternatives.

If courts and presidents are so fallible, how do we know what the law is? If we cannot know what the law is, how can it help us? Why do we so often turn to it for answers? Why, for example, would people actually try to pass laws defining when life begins or banning the sale of handguns? What good can such laws do? What good can any law do if people are determined to resist or corrupt it?

If you recognize these sentiments, even if you do not share them, then you can understand something of the origins of studies in law and sociology. Some people react to an air of crisis by denying its existence. Some bemoan crisis, hoping a champion will come along and set everything right. Some suddenly discover the comfort to be found in a new religious movement which claims to offer salvation, a way out. But others start looking more closely at the wounded beast to try to understand how it has worked in the past and to try to cure it of its ills.

It is this last reaction which initially motivates many, though not all, of those who study the sociology of law. Some enter from outside the law's ranks, because they see some critical social problem and wonder why law has been either unable to solve it or involved in creating it in the first place. Others come from within the system, having seen firsthand some gap between the professed objectives of lawmakers and the practical, everyday effect of their work. From both sides come people wondering whether the law can be used to bring about a significant degree of social progress, a real increase in social justice, a decrease in tyranny.

The movement toward a sociological approach to law began with the crisis of industrialization in the nineteenth century. Out of the turmoil of urbanization, industrialization, and the collapse of older social orders came a small but prolific series of observers who tried to make sense of the momentous changes taking place. Men like Karl Marx, Georg Simmel, Max Weber, Alexis de Tocqueville, Sir Henry Maine, and Émile Durkheim looked carefully at law as one of several institutions which they needed to understand if they were to explain what the old order had been, why and how it was changing, and what the new order was likely to be. To them, modern law, like the steam engine, the factory, and the industrial city, was both symbolic of, and a vital element in, modern society.

Among early social scientists, then, law occupied a spot at the center of their concerns. Among legal scholars of that period, there was considerably less interest in the problems of the "real world." Their research and debate was primarily concerned with ensuring that all laws were logical, consistent with each other, and "sensible" from the narrow perspective of the elite which ran the legal profession. Their concern with the philosophical rigor of legal reasoning is sometimes called *legal formalism*.

However, the growing influence of social science began to make itself felt even within the insular circles of legal scholarship. One example came to be known as *sociological jurisprudence* (Pound, 1921, 1943). It was a critique of conventional legal scholarship on the grounds that good law could not be made without knowing the *social context* in which it was to operate. Advocates of this position argued that legal formalism, without sociological information, would produce distortions and social disruption, no matter how logical and integrated the laws might be with each other. They were aware of sociological evidence that industrial societies were changing rapidly, that major institutions such as the family, religion, politics, and the economy were experiencing crises which were destroying established standards and producing major new patterns of relationships. They argued that the law should be made into an instrument which could deal effectively with those new patterns.

Another group, known as *legal realists*, took a different approach. To them, the major question was: "How are the laws actually being applied? What is their real effect?" (Frank, 1950; Llewellyn, 1960, 1962; Holmes, 1968). Antitrust laws may be written with the tightest possible logic in order to curb "big-business" abuses. But how are they applied "realistically"? If lawyers and judges act in such a way that antitrust laws are only invoked against union organizers, and if their only effect is to break up unions, then the *real* law is antilabor rather than antibusiness. Similarly, if capital punishment is used only on black convicts, then the *real* law is biased even if the lawbooks say there must be no discrimination. Legal realism thus differed from sociological jurisprudence in that it focused on the *implication* of laws, while sociological jurisprudence operated on the assumption that the *content* of laws could help improve social reality. Realists held that the content of laws was insignificant compared to the actual decisions made by enforcers and judges. To them, law could only be used to help society if reformers worked to improve the processes by which laws become "real" in the hands of legal administrators. Law, to them, would be of no use in dealing with the crises of industrialism unless the entire legal process could be understood.

Despite their differences, both sociological jurisprudence and legal realism represented a significant movement away from legal formalism toward a more practical approach to law. It was a start, from within the legal community, toward seeing legal issues as sociological questions demanding factual research. It was a constructive rejection of legal formalism's ostrichlike "head in the sand" attitude toward rapid social change and the imperfections of legal administration.

As these movements were developing among legal scholars, anthropologists were beginning to bring back from distant cultures the message that there are many other viable ways to organize law in society besides our lawyer, judge, and legislator system. Their broadening perspectives on the potential for legal variation fed into the thinking of legal realists, while legal realism stimulated anthropologists to abandon narrow Western notions about law. People began to see in these alternatives some hope that the "craziness" of twentieth-century social upheaval—world wars, drastic depressions, new and unpredictable political orders—might have some order in it which could be harnessed to the desire for reform and social progress.

Following a lull during and after the Second World War, the pace of legal sociology began to pick up. A new generation of both scholars and activists turned their eyes to law as both a source of social problems (for example, laws enforcing racial segregation or sexual inequality) and a resource for eliminating those problems. The Warren Supreme Court stirred up both controversy and research, with decisions aimed at (1) ending public school prayer and segregation, (2) insuring that police practices protect Constitutional rights to a fair and speedy trial, and (3) guaranteeing rights against self-incrimination, unreasonable searches, and unjustified imprisonment. Such decisions raised hopes for greater equality of opportunity among some and fears of greater chaos among others. Consequently, there arose a movement to see what effect all those "radical" court decisions were having.

At the same time, the nation's political climate encouraged policy analysis. Government in general was developing New Deal policies under such progressive names as "The New Frontier" and "The Great Society." Legislation created protection for the voting rights of blacks, increased welfare protection for the poor and aged, programs to cool off the overheated racial passions of the great cities, assistance for people paying medical bills, legal advice and counsel for poor people, and a host of other measures to eliminate serious social problems. Regulation of business and industry increased, as people looked to government to guarantee safe working conditions, clean air and water, safe travel, honest business practices, and other conditions for the good life. *The Law* was being treated as a major instrument for social change. With each such program, there was strong incentive among both proponents and opponents to evaluate its effectiveness. Some researchers were just curious. Others wanted to prove either the value or the futility of such programs.

But the process of researching these very practical, "realistic" questions repeatedly reinforced the conclusion that broader issues were involved, issues which had been raised by the earlier pioneers of social science but which needed new answers in view of new evidence and changed social realities. Hence while some still ask very practical questions about the strength or weakness of the law's impact on particular problems, others have become involved in trying to understand how law as a social institution works. They want to know what legal systems in general accomplish, given that their official pronouncements often do not match the reality of their effects. From such questions, it is not a very large step to the more general question of why societies have legal systems, what conditions lead to the development of law in a society, and why societies differ so greatly in the ways they handle what we call "legal" questions.

It is this broader view which I bring to you in this book. The roots of this book lie deep in the soil of malaise, unrest, and the feeling that our city, our civilization, is "on fire" and needs a dose of the right kind of law to at least control the fire. But the underlying message is that we cannot understand either the fire or the structure which it seems to be destroying unless we step back and look at the broader picture. You will see that while some legal sociologists may agree that the law is like the liquid coming out of the fire hoses, they do not agree on whether that liquid is water or gasoline. They do not even agree that what the fire produces (smoke, ashes, mayhem) is worse than what it destroys. What starts out seeming like a simple set of policy questions ends up driving us to a reexamination of our most basic assumptions.

If we want to know what effects particular laws have, for example, we discover that our answers founder on the treacherous uncertainties flowing around our fundamental assumptions about what law is. What is there about law which makes it different from other human activity? Does law contain some unique ingredient which we cannot find in other institutions? If so, what is that ingredient and how does it work in society? If not, why do we put so much faith in law as a source of protection or social reform? Such questions are the basis of chapter 2, in which we examine people's attempts to find a useful *definition of law*.

Social scientific research on law has led to some remarkable discoveries about the varieties of legal or social-control systems to be found in other societies or in other historical eras. We now know that many people in the world do not have legal systems like our own. So we ask where law systems come from, why they develop in some societies and not in others, and how life is possible in societies which lack some or all of the practices which we call *law*. Chapters 3, 4, and 5 present three different approaches to questions about the *origins of law*. The assumptions and interpretations of each approach differ substantially from the other two. In choosing among them, we must go beyond the simple expression of our aesthetic or political preferences. Each approach has practical, as well as theoretical, implications which relate to the policy-oriented questions people ask about law.

Applying these different approaches to actual research programs in law and society, we find one characteristic division between studies which look at law as initiated from the top among lawmakers and those which see law as originating from below, among ordinary people and their organizations. Chapters 6 and 7 contrast this division. Chapter 6 introduces the *top-down* approach: the study of *legal impact*. When legislators or judges issue rules or decisions for others to follow, the effects of those actions vary. Some researchers ask simply whether the action had its intended effect. Others look for side effects, unanticipated consequences of legal action. Still others have found that such apparently straightforward questions cannot be adequately answered without a much deeper analysis of the entire process of law making, enforcement, and citizen response.

Chapter 7 presents the *bottom-up* approach in the study of legal methods of *dispute settlement*. Disputes arise among ordinary people who then seek ways to resolve them "successfully." We find that legal methods for handling such conflict constitute only a few of the great variety of alternatives which people pursue. The existence of those alternatives and their relationship to legal methods raise difficult factual and theoretical questions when we try to understand the history of particular disputes and the role that law plays in them. As in chapter 6, when we pay close attention to a seemingly straightforward process, we find it laced with connections to other processes which we cannot afford to ignore. We find that whether we enter the field with top-down or bottom-up thinking, the accumulated research evidence forces us to look for a total picture incorporating both perspectives.

Chapters 8 and 9 deal with this problem of integration in more detail by focusing on two areas of particular interest in recent law and society research. Chapter 8 discusses the meaning of *legal modernity* as it relates to current campaigns to simplify Law. Today's crisis of confidence in law has led some people to long for the good old days when law was simple and justice swift. Proposals to simplify law, to return power to "the neighborhoods" or "the community" and take it away from lawyers, judges, and bureaucrats who have allegedly made such a mess of things, have gained considerable momentum. Chapter 8 presents the characteristics of modern law and compares efforts around the world to simplify or decentralize the legal process. It looks at the meaning of, and prospects for, these initiatives as seen from the three "origin of law" perspectives and from both top-down and bottom-up viewpoints.

The *legal profession* holds center stage in chapter 9. As one of several occupational groups working at the core of established legal institutions, the legal profession plays a key role in determining legal outcomes. This chapter focuses on stratification within the profession and between the lawyers and others in society. It compares the histories of ranking systems which have arisen within the American profession and elsewhere. Then it addresses the dominant issue in this field: What is the effect of professional stratification on the delivery of legal services or the accessibility of justice to those who need legal help? The chapter goes beyond this question, however, to explore the most recent changes in the profession, as a way of beginning to predict future developments.

In chapter 10 I return to a basic, abstract set of issues which have sometimes been ignored in the social scientific study of law. I look at the work of social psychologists, who tell us that the answers to many of our most basic questions about law are to be found in the psychological processes which occur in all humans. Where does law come from? Perhaps from a basic human motive to give and receive justice. How does a society manage to rein in and channel the random energies of its newcomers? Perhaps through a series of mental "stages" of development which lead to moral maturity. We also find that some social psychologists reject such arguments because they fail to account for facts discussed in the earlier chapters of this book. Can psychology help us understand the social complexities of law? You be the judge.

Every book has its "slant," and this one is no exception. You will find in each chapter a representative selection of studies done in that area. I believe they are fairly presented. But they are not exhaustive of all studies you could find on each subject. Rather, the chapters are meant to give you a feel for the way in which the "problem" in legal sociology has evolved and for the strengths and weaknesses of different positions as they stand today. My own preference among the several perspectives presented here is for *critical* theory, discussed most fully in chapter 5.

I say this not in an attempt to sway your judgment, but to forewarn you. My purpose is to help you link your own personal experiences and attitudes to a wider awareness of the great variety of things legal. By your use of this book, you should become competent to debate on the major issues which challenge today's legal sociologists. Of course that means that you should be able to pick apart your author's favorite outlook with as much skill as you bring to all other views. I tell you where I stand in the debate. You must judge for yourself, using both this book and the many books and articles which stand behind it.

At the very least, when you have done working with this book, you should be able to do more than shrug your shoulders and go along with the crowd of those saying: "There ought'a be a law," or "Bring back the good old days," or "How come the law doesn't work anymore?" I cannot promise that you will be able to solve the crises, to put out the fire. But you will have a better understanding of what is burning, and why.

REFERENCES

FRANK, JEROME   (1950), *Courts on Trial: Myth and Reality in American Justice*, Princeton: Princeton University Press.

HOLMES, O. W.   (1968), *The Common Law*, London: Macmillan.

LLEWELLYN, KARL   (1960), *The Common Law Tradition: Deciding Appeals,* Boston: Little, Brown.
LLEWELLYN, KARL (1962), *Jurisprudence: Realism in Theory and Practice,* Chicago: University of Chicago Press.
POUND, ROSCOE   (1921), *The Spirit of the Common Law,* Boston: Marshall Jones.
POUND, ROSCOE   (1943), "Sociology of Law and Sociological Jurisprudence," *University of Toronto Law Journal,* 5 (pp. 1–20).

CASES CITED

Brown v. *Board of Education,* 349 U.S. 294 (1955).

2

LAW DEFINITIONS AND THEIR CONSEQUENCES

In the previous chapter, I used the term *law* loosely in the various ways people usually use it. Ours being a time when "law and order" has become a widely debated issue, where the nightly news routinely reports *law* violations and the actions of *law* enforcers, we don't often consider that people may mean different, perhaps even contradictory, things when they use those terms. Like death and taxes, we take law for granted. We are also inclined to think that, like death and taxes, law is an inevitable feature of human life, that we would have chaos without it.

Most people seem to assume that *law* means rules made by elected officials and enforced by police and courts. The notion that rules must have popular approval reflects the democratic philosophy which people also take for granted when thinking about law. But there is such variety in the use of the term, that we must ask: Are they talking about the same thing? If we look beyond our own shores at the great variety of social forms elsewhere, that question becomes even more insistent. Anthropologists, missionaries, diplomats, and even casual tourists bring us stories of law unlike anything we have experienced here. So different are some of these practices that we soon reach the outer boundaries of our commonsense notions of law. We then enter the province of this chapter—deciding what should and should not be included in a definition of law.

Section A of this chapter samples some of the many ways *law* has been used as a description of social events. Section B then shows how social scientists and legal scholars have wrestled with the problem of finding a definition of law which makes sense out of the chaos described in Section A. Throughout this chapter, look for ways in which each definition not only narrows the range of social events treated as law, but also exposes its author's basic theory of the relationship between law and society. Seeking "the perfect definition" of law in sociology has not produced agreement, but it has improved the clarity with which rival scientific positions are stated. As in any social science, sociologists' definitions of terms set limits on their ability to digest observed facts. You will see that each definition presented here opens some doors of inquiry while closing others. But without a definition, we would have to abandon the study of law (assuming it nonexistent) or conclude that law is everything. Or we could muddle along using unspoken, unrecognized definitions whose logical contradictions and hidden assumptions would defeat our desire to clarify the operation of legal institutions in society.

Besides the academic need for clarity of definitions, there is a more personal reason for pursuing this elusive concept. Each of us faces his or her own dilemmas in choosing whether or not to challenge authority when we think it is wrong. The way we perceive those dilemmas and respond to them may depend on the way we define the nature of authority and our relationship to it. Clarity of language focuses both understanding and action.

SECTION A—COMMON-SENSE MEANINGS OF LAW

If you ever studied physics or chemistry, you probably encountered several "laws" about motion, energy, heat, or light. These laws told you that whenever certain conditions were met, you could expect certain things to happen. Put water into a container with two connected chambers, and the levels of liquid are the same in both chambers. Change the temperature of a gas and the pressure also changes. Throw a rock out of a window and the "law" of gravity tells you where it will go.

You may also have heard similarly phrased "laws" about people and group life. Murphy's law, for example, says that if anything can go wrong it will. Parkinson's law (Parkinson, 1957) says that the more people you assign to a job, the more "necessary" work they will invent to keep themselves busy. Like laws of physics, these statements summarize our belief that certain relationships produce inevitable results.

But you have also encountered laws which did not always predict outcomes. We are told, for example, that Moses went up on the mountain and watched as laws were miraculously carved in stone. They told his people not to steal, commit adultery, or covet a neighbor's wife. We do not assume, as we do in physics, that such laws describe what always happened among the Israelites. The Ten Commandments are not descriptions of actual behavior. They are directives, commands. In fact, we suspect that they were written in stone because some members of the group were violating them.

So the law as commandment is clearly different from a law which describes an invariant relationship, as in physics. But isn't it interesting that both cases are described as involving *law*? Is this just linguistic coincidence? We will return to that question after considering other variations in the use of the term.

Consider the "law of the West": the law of the Lone Ranger, of John Wayne, of Matt Dillon, of Wyatt Earp, or of "Wild Bill" Hickock. "Around here, pardner, I am the law." Legend says that these heroes of frontier justice patrolled the West with their bullets and an undying sense of justice and virtue. We are told that Wyatt Earp, by himself, made Dodge City safe for civilization. These stories show *law* reaching as far as the lawman can make it. Law and the gun and a vague sense of righteousness become unified. Unlike Moses, the lawmaker of the West makes law for each occasion. He is not tied to stone tablets or other written codes. But like Moses, the cowboy lawman is driven by a sense of divine justice. He is the agent of an ideal.

Such ideals are lacking in the case of what some call the "*law* of the jungle." Stripped of all justifications and elaborations, the law of the jungle is simple: The strong shall dominate the weak. If you have what I want, I take, unless you can stop me. Whoever has superior fire power, more wealth, leadership charisma, or brute strength will dictate what others will do. Conformity comes from fear and the desire to appease. Survival depends on alertness to the changing tides of power, the capricious whims of the powerful. The only rule in this kind of law is "look out for number one." Some see this as the underlying principle of all human interaction, including all other forms of law.

In contrast, think about what happened when nine volunteers in a nutrition study were voluntarily locked into a small apartment for three months (Weyrauch, 1971). The experiment was testing space-program techniques for feeding, organizing, giving medical care, and communicating with astronauts in actual long-distance flights. It was also designed to identify which subjects could tolerate such confinement and how they would handle cooperation and conflict problems. To one trained observer, an important outcome of the experiment was what he called the "law and constitution of a small group." Nobody in the group wrote down rules or acted as judge or cop or rule interpreter. But systematic recording of trainee behavior showed that an *unspoken* body of rules developed during their confinement. No one outside ordered the trainees to follow these rules. Nor did they hold meetings to create them. But they acted as though the rules existed. The rules could be identified by negative reactions when a trainee broke them. Because trainees seemed to agree about the rules, the observer concluded that law had been established and was governing their behavior.

Each of the previous examples, though noticeably different from the others, has a clear, uncomplicated vision of what law is and how it works. But the debate is not that simple. Think for example of the policeman who patrols the waterfront in New York City and directs traffic when ocean liners are loading or unloading hundreds of passengers and their luggage (Lobenthal, 1971, pp. 20–31). Yellow lane markers and "No Parking," "Three Minute Parking Only," and "Passenger Parking Only" signs declare the *law* as laid down by the New York City government. But the policeman routinely grants parking privileges in "no parking" spaces, selectively allows brief parking in "tow away" zones, and warns cars away from legal parking spaces informally "reserved" for longshoremen who, while the policeman winks and looks the other way, enforce their "rights" by breaking windows and slashing tires on "unauthorized" vehicles. Expediency and the balancing of conflicting interests govern the policeman's decision. He knows from experience how to keep traffic moving and to minimize tensions in crowded situations.

Is this law the same as the Lone Ranger's? The policeman seems to be inventing law on the spot. His "law" is more real than the official city ordinances. He enforces or disregards them at his own convenience. So some element of the Lone Ranger seems present. But something more than just his gun stands behind his decisions. He wears a uniform and a badge. These hint that, though he seems to take law into his own hands, there may be limits to his discretion other than his personal ability to intimidate. People comply with his commands partly because of the uniform. Without it he would look like a derelict or a deranged sufferer of delusions of grandeur. Without it, his use of a gun would quickly spark multiple alarms about a "man armed with a deadly weapon." The uniform promises *limits* on the man's discretion.

Watergate stirred many debates. One of the most important dealt with this issue of limited discretion. Some say that Watergate proved that law is whatever the politicians can get away with. Others say that Watergate was the proof that our legal system works, since it showed that even the president is not above the law.

The issue here is the same as in the case of the waterfront traffic police officer. Is *law* the ideal which applies to all or is it whatever "the authorities" do in practice? When a police officer tells you to park in a tow away zone, what makes the command law? Most people assume that if the officer tells you to park there, you can legally do so. But what is "the law" when a police officer takes a bribe to protect a prostitution ring? Maybe we can dismiss this as simply the deviation of an individual "bad apple." The act is, we could say, clearly illegal because it is isolated, deviant. But suppose the whole police force is involved in such dealings. Frank Serpico (Maas, 1973) was an undercover narcotics detective working for the New York City police force when he discovered that hundreds of police and government officials were involved in the sale of narcotics. What did he discover about the "real law" of New York? Does the fact that the Knapp Commission investigated these charges and instituted major reforms alter your opinion about the "real law" of New York? If drug marketing was a systematic practice of hundreds of authorities for many years, what definition of law gives us the greatest understanding of the New York narcotics law situation?

Law in Other Cultures

The examples used so far should be familiar to you. As different and even incompatible as they are, all are quite common ways of thinking and speaking about law in Western societies. But our selection grows even more varied if we look beyond our own everyday experiences to law in non-Western societies.

In northern Canada, Eskimo tribes do not normally have "laws" or law enforcers. There are no chiefs or judges, soldiers or police, lawyers or authorities. Is there law? Anthropologists who have studied these tribes think so (Hoebel, 1954; Rasmussen, 1927). One expression of Eskimo law is the "song duel." When one man feels cheated or wronged by another, he composes songs loaded with insults against his opponent. He and his rival then confront each other, with everyone in the village present. They sing their insults while weaving and dancing in front of each other, and to emphasize their jibes they butt heads. The songs not only insult, they demand justice in the conflict. Audience reaction is so important that some men hire well-known composers to write their songs for them. No one is found guilty or innocent or forced to pay an opponent. But public exposure to ridicule seems to provide the community with a means of adjusting relationships when they are disrupted by conflict. Because this is accomplished, anthropologists have treated the song duel as an example of law.

If you find the song duel difficult to swallow as law, consider the work of a "native doctor" in Kampala, the capital city of Uganda. A father brings his sick infant daughter to the native doctor for healing. He tells the doctor that his recently divorced wife's dead uncle may be responsible for the infant's illness, because there is ill will between his former wife and him. For a fee the native doctor performs a ceremony in which he goes into trance, allows the soul of the dead uncle to enter his own body, and then debates with the father and former wife the issues that led to their separation. When the soul of the dead uncle is satisfied that the issues have been aired and his niece's actions justified publicly, it returns to the dead and the ceremony ends. When the child recovers from her illness, all agree that it is because the dead uncle has been satisfied (Rigby and Lule, 1972).

You may think that law and medicine are two entirely separate activities. But to many Ugandans, health and interpersonal harmony are directly linked, so that when a conflict goes unresolved bad health is thought to be a result. Given these beliefs, it makes sense to treat what we would call a medical problem as though it were what we would call a legal problem. Thus law becomes a service performed by a doctor in consultation with dead spirits.

A village in Lebanon has a system of law based on bribery and influence (Nader, 1965). Since no one in the village has enough power to impose settlements when fights erupt between the two main factions in town, each side takes its case to court. But neither side expects impartial justice. Instead they offer bribes to influential politicians who use family ties, friendships, or other methods of influence to sway the judge's decision in their direction. The side which offers the most attractive bribe to the most influential politician wins. But no one considers these bribes immoral or illegal. They are accepted as the only way to maintain order between the two town factions. Given their problems, bribery and influence is the law they live by.

In Western societies, modern law is supposed to be rational and scientific. We celebrate heroes like Sherlock Holmes, Kojak, or Quincy, who use logic, intuition, alertness, and modern science to "crack" criminal cases by producing undeniable evidence of guilt. We are strongly committed to the search for technological breakthroughs, such as the lie detector, blood-type analysis, handwriting analysis, fingerprint identification, and voice-print analysis, all of which are expected to stamp out crime.

But in other societies, much swifter techniques are thought to produce even more reliable proof of guilt. In Liberia, for example, a knife is heated in fire and then pressed against a suspect's skin. If it burns him, he is guilty. Similar techniques abound in anthropological literature. People are bound hand and foot and thrown into rivers. Those who drown are thought guilty. Poison is given, and those who do not vomit enough to save their lives are guilty.

While we might be inclined to dismiss these techniques as superstitions, we should recognize that our own law contains dubious beliefs and methods for defining legal truth. When we swear witnesses on a Bible before their testimony in court, we echo the beliefs of Massachusetts settlers who looked for divine evidence against witches in their midst. We denounce the use of torture to extract confessions, yet we continue to debate whether or when police have a right to use force or other strong measures of interrogation. We place great trust in the *eyewitness*, though our research tells us that such witnesses are not reliable. Do our unstated definitions of law lead us to exaggerate the differences between our own practices and methods such as the hot knife in Liberia?

Other Faces of Modern Law

Now shift gears and think of an entirely different type of law. Think, for example, of the law which makes low-cost home mortgages available to American veterans. The Veterans Administration collects and distributes large sums of money, identifies eligible recipients, and provides for inspection and approval of houses for sale. Or think of the law which empowers the president to make money available to victims of floods, tornadoes, riots, volcanoes, or crop-damaging hailstorms. What do these have in common with Moses' commandments, or the New York waterfront policeman, or the hot knife against flesh?

We also have laws which define when a couple can claim to be legally married, what people must do to be sure their property is distributed as they wish after death, and what people must do to make certain that promises made in a business deal are kept. But many of these laws have never been voted on by a legislature or approved by a referendum. They are what we call *common law*. That is, they are practices which legal authorities sanction because other earlier authorities sanctioned them, or because the practice seems reasonable or normal among people in the surrounding society. For example, in one Wisconsin county, authorities insist that no legal document is valid unless a fountain pen was used to sign it rather than a ball-point pen (Simonette, 1963). No one knows why such a rule exists, and it has never been voted on or even written down. But if you want the law's help in that county, you'd better not use a ball-point pen. What does this *common law* have in common with the Eskimo song duels or the policeman on the waterfront?

The variety of things called law is too great to squeeze into this one chapter. But there are two types of law which we need to examine before we move on to systematic social scientific definitions. One is the much debated international law. The other is the law of a tyrant such as Hitler before and during World War II.

International law is a term widely applied to certain relationships between nations. What happens, for example, when a murderer escapes from France and is found to be living in Mexico? By international law, the Mexican government may be obliged to capture the murderer and return him to France. Regular procedures are established through treaty for such extraditions. Another example concerns fishing rights and the rights to natural resources in the oceans. Who owns the oil found in the bed of the

North Sea? How close can Soviet fishing trawlers come to the fishing beds of Massachusetts? What kinds of nets are "legal" and which cause so much trouble they are "illegal"? Or think of international liability. Who pays whom in damages if a Mexican oil well in the Gulf of Mexico leaks so badly that it ruins resort beach business in Texas? What responsibility does anyone have if a piece of an American satellite drops in a populated area of Singapore, killing people and damaging property?

These are all questions of international law, but they are beyond our scope here. Our question is: Is international law really law? What happens if a nation decides to thumb its nose at these agreements? Suppose the Mexican government tells the Texas resort owners to clean up the mess themselves. Who will make them do otherwise? Who, in other words, enforces these laws? There are no higher authorities to force compliance. This was most obvious in the predicament faced by the U.S. government when its diplomatic staff was taken hostage in Tehran. Not only was there no means of enforcing what the United States took to be international law, but there was no consensus about whether there existed an established method for determining whether Iran had violated that law in the first place. The Americans were left with the choices of getting allies to exert economic and diplomatic pressure, using their own military force unilaterally, or using their economic power. In other words, the situation hinged on which side had greater power to coerce.

Some observers see no reason to call such a situation law (Williams, 1945–1946). They argue that with no enforcement mechanism, this system is nothing more than a dressed up version of "might makes right"—the law of the jungle. They say, in other words, that international law does not differ from international relations without law. We shall see later in this chapter how others challenge this dismissal of international law.

Our final example concerns Hitler's rule of Germany. Hitler's rise to power involved several violations of existing German law. Once he took over the government, he instituted many changes, including systematic campaigns against Jews and other minorities, the establishment of separate police forces under his direct control, the elimination of democratic procedures, and the secret violation of international treaties. The courts became a tool of his policies, carrying out unprecedented procedures against citizens who displeased the Führer.

Was Hitler's dictatorial rule an example of law? Or was it nonlegal tyranny? After the war, hundreds of Germans were prosecuted by "war-crimes" courts, which accused them of obeying "illegal" orders. The Nuremberg principle (Smith, 1977; Maser, 1979), established by these tribunals, says that people can be found guilty of crimes against humanity even when they are obeying "laws" of their governments. Law in this case is defined as being superior to the commands of a national government.

Notice that the Nuremberg prosecutors did not attack Germans for carrying out *unpopular* policies. There may have been a majority of Germans in favor of Hitler's commands. But they were treated as criminals because they had violated what the winners of the war called "higher principles."

The revolution which drove the Shah out of Iran took a different stand. Hundreds were executed for having obeyed the Shah's "illegal" orders. But their crimes all related to the idea that the Shah had worked against the people, that his regime was contrary to the popular will. At least some leaders of the revolution thus linked law with popular legitimacy— government must serve the interests of the people in order to be legal.

The Iranian Revolution quickly became entangled in the complications of that doctrine. Who was the revolution? Religious leaders? The intelligentsia with Western educations? The business community? The Marxists? What was the popular will? Some in the revolution argued that the Shah erred because he deviated from divine law, as given to the prophet Muhammed. Others charged that he enriched his own small circle of supporters and enslaved everyone else. So there was an alliance of supporters of natural or *divine law* and supporters of *popular law*. But the alliance was riddled with contradictory demands. Holy men demanded compliance with divine law, but divine law is not necessarily any more popular than the Shah's.

Are these examples from international war and revolution simply additional instances of "might makes right"? Was Nuremberg law or just a smoke screen of pious phrases disguising allied revenge on the defeated Germany? However you answer, you should notice that the core of the debate centers on the definition of law. Each side in these examples wanted to call its own actions law. Whether divine, popular, or humane, *law means legitimacy* in these debates. It means that your actions are demonstrably right. The opposition threatens more than your own well-being. They threaten righteousness through transgression of LAW.

SECTION B—HOW SOCIAL SCIENTISTS DEFINE LAW

The previous section is a sampler of ways the term *law* has been used. For casual conversations, and even for the heated presentation of opinions, we can sometimes do quite well without definitions of the terms we use. But sociology is an activity which demands more careful, more systematic use of terms. And the pressure for clarity felt by sociologists weighs equally on anyone wishing to systematically study law's relationship to society. If we are to escape the special blinders which grow around our minds as we become acculturated, then we must try to expose fully the meanings of the words we use. Once we have exposed those meanings, we find many of them incompatible. The goal is a consistent definition purged of illogical, incompatible elements.

As you will see, where social scientists have failed to identify the exact meaning of the term *law,* they have fallen into heated debates among themselves and with other specialists because they were actually speaking of different things. Settling the question What is law? will not end debate over the place of law in society. But the more attention law has received as a social process, the more its students have felt the need to develop more precise definitions.

One word of warning: Do not expect to find a final answer here to the question What is Law? The need to be precise about the term does not mean that there need be one, universally applicable definition. Different studies require different definitions. The variety of definitions is a direct product of competing theories about law in society. What matters is that in any attempt to study or debate the place of law in society, users of the term law make very clear just how they are using that term. Telling you which definition to accept would be like telling you which religion to practice. In the definitions that follow, look for the ideological assumptions and implications of each rather than the one "true" definition, because choosing a definition is like choosing a design for a car. Each advantage gained from one design sacrifices some other attractive feature. The definitions which follow are an improvement over the chaotic taken-for-granted meanings we sampled earlier in the chapter. But each has characteristics which make it both more and less useful than the others.

Law as a Modern Process

Let's begin with definitions that are closest to our usual ways of thinking about law. Donald Black gives one of the least wordy definitions.

> Law is governmental social control . . . the normative life of a state and its citizens. (1972)

Though simple, this definition is carefully worded to exclude "nongovernmental" social control. Black sees law as a special form of social control which only developed with the growth of nation-states. So he wants to reserve the term for that stage of socio-political development. In the earlier example of the astronauts in training, their "small-group law" would not qualify as law under Black's definition. He would argue that the small group had developed a set of rules and informal social controls, but not law. For him, law is a special form of social control, involving governments, definitions of citizenship, and formality. As he sees it, law has its own special consequences, which must be understood separately from other means of social control. What happens in a small group, like the order found in primitive or ancient social groups, may be analogous to law, but it is not law.

A second definition which also sticks close to common sense is Oliver Wendell Holmes's statement that

> The prophecies of what the courts will do in fact, and nothing more pretentious, are what I mean by the law.

Somewhat like Black's definition in its equation of law with modern legal institutions (the courts), this statement shows Holmes's concern with being "realistic" about the law. He wanted to challenge what he considered unrealistic theories of law which paid no attention to the actual decisions made by judges. He insisted that if judges systematically ignored either those theories or specific written laws, then it makes no sense to call them law. If a particular society's judges decide, for their own reasons, that two plus two equals five, then the law of that land is that five is the answer, even if mathematicians and legislators disagree.

Notice that Holmes's definition is also a brief description of the way he thinks law works in society. He believes that judges hold the key to real law because of their power to decide cases. Later in the book, we will examine his evidence for such a claim along with the extensive research which challenges his position.

Both Black and Holmes give us definitions that limit law to the modern, complex societies we know best. States, governments, and the kinds of courts Holmes speaks of are all features of societies like the United States.

Law as All Forms of Social Control

In stark contrast to Black and Holmes, Malinowski, widely recognized as one of the first anthropologists of law, developed the following definition to organize his studies of society in the islands of the South Pacific:

> Law is a body of binding obligations regarded as right by one party and acknowledged as the duty by the other, kept in force by the specific mechanism of reciprocity and publicity inherent in the structure of society. (1926, 1961)

Malinowski's island cultures had almost none of the elements of modern states. There were no legislature, bureaucracy, police, or courts. Yet he felt compelled to call what he saw on those islands law. It was law because people organized their lives in compliance with identifiable rules. It was law because, when someone violated a rule, routine actions of others made it clear that the violation would have to be rectified. And it was law because it kept those societies from disintegrating into the "bands of lawless savages" which missionaries and travelers of Malinowski's day thought they saw in such societies. By defining law this way, Malinowski was able to dignify illiterate island cultures and show that order is possible without modern legislatures, police, prisons, and courts.

He also helped open our eyes to the intimate connections between law and social process by pointing out the dependence of law on "reciprocity and publicity inherent in the structure of society." This set him apart from many who held law aloft as something separate, autonomous, an activity of experts using esoteric language. Law, he said, is the ordering principle of society, and it is done by everyone in society. I obey a law not only because I fear prison or a fine. I obey because if I did not, the balance of "trade" (economic, social, emotional, and political interaction) between myself and others would be upset. Others would begin to cut me out of their "trade" and I could become so isolated that life as I know it would become impossible for me. So I conform.

Notice again that Malinowski's definition, like Black's and Holmes's, spells out the basic elements of his theory about how law works in society.

Law and Authorized Physical Force

If you look back at the three definitions given so far, you may notice that none of them make specific mention of the need for physical force. Force may be implied where law is defined as "governmental social control," but such definitions do not insist on it. E. Adamson Hoebel, an anthropological student of various nonliterate societies, sided with many others who do insist that without physical force there is no law. Hoebel's definition is carefully worded.

> A social norm is legal if its neglect or infraction is regularly met, in threat or in fact, by the application of physical force by an individual or group possessing the socially recognized privilege of so acting. (1954)

For Hoebel, the essence of law lies in the orderly, authorized use of force. There is, of course, plenty of disorderly physical violence, but it is not law. Johnny takes Billy's toy away so Billy beats up Johnny. Harry seduces Jim's wife, so Jim shoots Harry. India's army occupies land claimed by Pakistan, so there is war.

But what happens if a Comanche brave steals a horse from another member of the hunting band? According to Hoebel, the tribe authorizes the victim to punish the offender. But the victim's revenge is not like the violence mentioned in the previous paragraph, because here the violence is sanctioned by the group. This key ingredient of sanctioned violence is the same as we find in the case of police authorized to "shoot to kill" in American cities, or jailers authorized to forcibly imprison offenders.

Hoebel's definition also incorporates that concept *social norm* which has been dear to the hearts of sociologists for decades. Many consider it basic to all legitimate sociological theory. *Norm* usually means two things: (1) a behavior pattern is typical in a certain group—it is normal, a part of routine life; and (2) the behavior pattern is routine or normal because people have *learned* that they are *obliged* to conform to it, that they *ought* to choose normative behavior. So, when Hoebel defines law as a special species of social norm, he is telling us that law, like other social norms, places demands on people to make choices of action they otherwise might not make. How do we know that a person's behavior is the product of a social norm? How do we know, for example, that when people walk into a bank and *do not* rob it, they are making a choice to obey the law? We draw that conclusion by reasoning that if each person acted in his or her own *self-interest*, ignoring the law, he or she would use any means available, including armed force, to get as much as wanted.

Hoebel's definition fits law into a model of society which includes many kinds of social norms, most of them nonlegal. This means that most social norms are backed by something other than physical force. These other factors could be the elements of "reciprocity and publicity" mentioned by Malinowski. But although they agree about the importance of these factors, Hoebel parts company over the issue of physical force.

Finally, notice that Hoebel deals with Holmes's demand for realism by adding the word "regularly" to his definition. A norm is not legal if it is ignored by those who could use force to enforce it. Old-fashioned laws, forgotten but still on the books, are no longer laws, because no one threatens to, or uses, force to assure compliance. In similar fashion, legislatures may pass laws which judges and police choose to ignore. Campbell and Ross found that when Connecticut's governor ordered license suspensions for all speeders on Connecticut highways, state police made a widespread but unauthorized reduction in arrests for speeding because they were not convinced that most speeding violations were serious enough to justify loss of license (1968). So, while traffic continued to speed along, arrest rates for speeding declined so sharply that the governor thought his crackdown had actually slowed most traffic to legal limits. To Hoebel, the unenforced crackdown would not be law, whereas the Manhattan waterfront policeman's on-the-spot rules are law.

Law, Coercion, and Specialization

No sociological text would be complete without some mention of Max Weber. In the case of law, this mention is mandatory, since Weber took great pains to include law in his general theory of society. His definition of law may leave you breathless if you try to say it aloud, but it is loaded with carefully chosen words. It may sound to you like a wordy version of

Hoebel's definition, but it contains some subtle differences which show a different conception of law. Weber says,

> An order shall be called law where it is guaranteed by the likelihood that (physical or psychological) coercion aimed at bringing about conformity with the order, or at avenging its violation, will be exercised by a staff of people especially holding themselves ready for this purpose. (1954)

The first difference to notice is Weber's "special staff." This is *not* the same thing as Hoebel's "individual or group possessing the socially recognized privilege of so acting," though there is some overlap. When Weber speaks of a special staff, he means persons who specialize in law work, people to whom the authority to enforce orders has been delegated, who occupy official positions in an organization for law enforcement, such as judges, police, labor arbitrators, student judicial boards, and church councils on religious discipline. Weber thus uses his definition to exclude much of what Hoebel would call law, since few nonliterate societies reach the point where they develop such organizations. Weber and Hoebel share the belief that *delegated authority* is a basic feature of law. But Hoebel includes a much lower level of formality than does Weber. Like Black, Weber sees law as a modern development. Therefore Weber would not see Hoebel's Comanche brave as an agent of law, nor would he call that form of social order legal.

But while Weber excludes some social forms included by Hoebel, he also includes others which Hoebel cuts out. Weber speaks of both psychological and physical coercion. By including psychological coercion, Weber expands the realm of law to the activities of many kinds of groups in modern societies. When a university expels a student for cheating on an exam, or when a church punishes a wayward priest by sending him to a remote jungle mission, these punishments do not involve even the threat of physical violence. So, for Hoebel they are not law. But for Weber they are. In Weber's definition, private associations can make *law* even though they have not been granted the right by the state to use physical violence. Weber's definition thus permits discussion of *legal pluralism*, that social condition in which persons may be faced with competing legal demands or opportunities because of involvement in overlapping associations.

But wait, you say. How can associations successfully obtain compliance with rules if they cannot intimidate with threats of violence? Isn't force the ultimate underlying motivation? The answer, to Weber, is obvious. The student wants to graduate. The priest seeks the salvation which his church promises. The fraternity member seeks approval and comradeship, and the baseball player wants the chance to play and be applauded. The bank teller wants a steady income and promotions. Social life, in other words, is loaded with incentives which can be manipulated to assure conformity with rules.

Weber's definition of law, unlike Hoebel's, recognizes these other kinds of incentives. Even the law administered by the state and courts does not rely exclusively on physical coercion. Patriotism, economic incentives, and participatory goals are all used, as Weber's definition brings out, to obtain conformity with laws. Ostracism, ridicule, and shunning can also be used in some social situations as a means of avenging a rule's violation.

Before we go on, let's look back at the definitions presented so far. Weber, Black, and Holmes treat law as a modern form of activity—a special means of producing social order associated with complex societies using organized methods of enforcement. Weber is both more explicit and more inclusive than either Black or Holmes, since he treats nongovernmental groups as having law, and he sees judges as only one kind of special staff involved in law work. Weber sides with Malinowski against Hoebel concerning the issue of physical force. Neither of them agrees with Hoebel's insistence that physical force distinguishes law from other methods of social control. But Weber differs from Malinowski by emphasizing the role of the "special staff." Most of what Malinowski saw in the South Pacific was not law by Weber's definition because it did depend only on "reciprocity and publicity" built into everyday life—there was no special staff to make sure that rules were obeyed.

Law as Justice

If you look back at the previous pages, you will not find a single definition of law which mentions justice. Isn't that strange? Don't we often speak of law and justice as though they mean the same thing? Don't irate citizens castigate the law when it deviates from the paths of justice? All of the previous definitions treat law as a device for producing social control. Except for Malinowski's, the definitions treat law as something done by selected members of society to all others *in the name of order*. They all conspicuously avoid dealing with the issue of justice.

Philip Selznick and others of the so-called Berkeley School of the sociology of law consider justice to be at the very center of any adequate definition. They would ask, for example, whether Hitler's extermination of Jews should be called an example of law in action (Selznick, 1961; Nonet, 1976; Nonet and Selznick, 1978). They point out that if we define law as "governmental social control," we cannot then distinguish between legal and illegal acts of government officials. Without some treatment of the justice issue, we would have to accept as law a police officer's arbitrary back-alley beating of a homosexual, a judge's demand for a bribe in return for a favorable decision, a judge's preference for hanging blacks while only jailing whites for similar offenses, and Richard Nixon's claim that the presidency put him above the law and made his Watergate actions unreviewable. As Selznick states the case

The essence of legality lies not in the exercise of power and control, but in the predictable restraint on those using that power. (1961)

Selznick and his colleagues demote the social-control aspect of law, which is so central to our previous definitions, by saying that we can take for granted that in any society some people will exercise power over others. Leaders, authorities, "men of influence" are to be found in all societies at all times. But *how do they rule?* That is the question of law. If there are no restraints on their powers, then there is no legality, no law. To the extent that they must conform to rules which restrain their use of power, there is more law.

Law is not an either-or situation. It increases and decreases as changes in society increase or decrease the arbitrariness of "the authorities." In general, the development of modern liberal nations like the United States represents, to Selznick, an increase in legality. But unstable social conditions can produce quick reversals, as in the case of Hitler's Germany, Idi Amin's Uganda, or Pinochet's Chile.

While legality is a prerequisite for justice, it has not been able to guarantee justice in modern society. Leaders can perpetuate social injustices such as racism, sexism, and poverty by indiscriminately enforcing laws whose effects reinforce those inequalities. To achieve law's inherent goal of justice in modern societies, therefore, the creation and application of laws must be made flexible, so that law can be *responsive* to specific instances of injustice. But such flexibility is precarious—it holds the danger that the discretion it offers to authorities will allow them to be arbitrary. Debates over "affirmative action" and "reverse discrimination" take place on this knife-edge between arbitrariness and responsiveness.

Law, then, is an organized way to produce justice. To Selznick, it is impossible to understand the relationship between law and society if you leave justice out of your definition of law. It is impossible because it is the ideal of justice which activates law and makes it more than just one more nasty struggle for power. Says the Berkeley School, if you do not compare the social reality of law with legal ideals, you cannot understand what produced that social reality.

Like Weber, Selznick denies the centrality of physical force in law. Like Weber, he sees legality as a feature of private associations as well as the state. If you take an exam and a professor who dislikes you gets you expelled from the university on false charges of plagiarism, there is little legality. But if the professor must defend his charge before a committee which also offers you the chance to present your case, and if you then have the right to appeal the committee's decision to a higher university board of review, then there is more legality. But the legality lies in the fact that no one individual has the *arbitrary power* to ruin your future.

To sum up, the Berkeley School's position is that the ideal of law may be achieved or lost under various forms of social organization. You may be the most powerful ruler in the world, and you may be able to coerce conformity with your orders by using police, torture, judges, and prisons. But your rule will not meet the standards of legality unless the rightness of your orders and judgments can be challenged and reviewed by others with power independent of yours. Justice is not simply the result of passing judgments. It is a term we use for right judgments. And law is concerned with producing justice.

Law as Procedural Justice

Professor Lon Fuller once wrote a parable (1964) which helps to illustrate the kind of position taken by Selznick, while placing even greater emphasis on the notion of law as a special set of procedures. Fuller tells of a kindly young king, Rex, who wants to end the troubles of his subjects by giving them the best possible legal system. So he begins by abolishing all existing laws and courts and hearing disputes and legal problems himself. At the beginning he hopes that by deciding cases he will be able to compile a list of principles which can become new laws. He soon becomes frustrated, like his subjects, by his inability to discover any consistent principles in the decisions he has made.

From that point on, his experiments lead to one failure after another. He adopts a code of laws, but keeps them secret from his subjects. That fails. He adopts laws which demand actions from his subjects which they could not possibly perform. That also fails. In all, he fails to make law in eight ways.

EIGHT WAYS TO FAIL

1. Failure to create rules—all issues decided on *ad hoc* basis.
2. Failure to publicize rules people are expected to obey.
3. Retrospective legislation—threatens all existing rules with later nullification and fails to guide people's actions.
4. Failure to make rules understandable.
5. Contradictory rules.
6. Making rules requiring conduct beyond the powers of the affected party.
7. Changing rules so often that people cannot adjust their actions to fit.
8. Failure of congruence between rules as announced and their actual administration.

What Fuller shows with this parable is that *law* as he defines it—"The enterprise of subjecting human behavior to the governance of rules."—is a difficult achievement, a condition which can easily be destroyed even by well-intended but unreasonable orders. To achieve law, leaders must avoid those eight pitfalls suffered by Rex. The social scientific claim which grows out of this view shared by Fuller and members of the Berkeley School is that societies which avoid those eight pitfalls, which in other words achieve law, have a better chance of survival and stability than those which try to maintain *order without legality*. As they see it, the key to long-term social stability is the development and maintenance of legality.

Law as the Denial of Justice

While Selznick and others see law as the achievement of justice, Howard Zinn takes just the opposite view. To him, law exists to defeat justice. His view of law is summarized as follows:

> Law is a conspiracy against human values; an implement to frustrate the natural tendency of people to act justly. (1971)

To Zinn, law is a modern, sophisticated form of tyranny. Arguing directly against the kind of position held by Selznick, Zinn says there is no ethical content to the rule of law. Governments do whatever they please. They enforce laws they choose to enforce against whomever they wish. If they choose to enforce loitering laws against blacks but not whites, for example, then that is the law, regardless of what written laws may say about equal enforcement of laws.

Law is not, as Selznick puts it, only that which is ideal. To confuse law with justice is to commit propaganda, because it glosses over the reality of law's operation in society.

What is that reality? To summarize what we will study in greater detail in later chapters, Zinn shares with others the view that the purveyors of the "rule of law" (including those who share Selznick's view) have used it to suppress the cultures, values, and community structures of natural human groups. This has been done in the pursuit of power and wealth. It results in a world of conflict where we no longer even recognize that people have a natural tendency to act justly toward each other. If there is justice in human relationships now, it happens only sporadically and *in spite of the law* rather than because of it. Law enslaves people by pitting them against each other in artificially contrived conflicts. Law is part of the problem, not the solution.

Recall that Malinowski's definition of law served to dignify the social order of the preliterate societies he studied. Zinn's definition dignifies those societies in just the opposite way, by saying that they lack law. To Zinn, law is not a proud achievement. Rather, it represents the defeat of humane social forms, a tyranny masquerading as liberty. Anarchy, the absence of law, is true liberty because it conforms to our true nature as humans.

At this point you may be saying to yourself, "That's ridiculous. Everyone knows there must be law of some kind. People don't just naturally treat each other justly. What about robbers, rapists, tax cheaters, and embezzlers? You can't just let them go. It's a dog-eat-dog world." Zinn's reply to you would be that what you take to be "human nature" is in fact a product of the type of society we all live in—a society dominated by the "rule of law." He takes the position that law cancels other influences on people— influences that would get them to act justly toward each other. It is the law you think of as protecting you which actually produces robbing and raping, cheating, and embezzling, because it is one of the major devices used to fit people into alienating, unsatisfying roles in modern society.

Law as Normal Social Process

Zinn's last idea is shared by Linda Medcalf, who arrived at her definition of law from research which, to her, confirmed many of Zinn's arguments. We will discuss her research later, but her position is different from any of the others presented here. To Medcalf

> Law is not some "thing," an entity unto itself to be studied in isolation. . . . Law is best understood as a human activity, a set of relationships between humans and between humans and their world. (1978)

She takes this position because she sees our thinking about law as having fallen into a trap. The trap is that we have concretized law. We have come to think of law as something real, a thing autonomous and separate from people and their interconnected lives.

We think this way for complicated historical reasons. Medcalf, like Roberto Unger (1976), says that law has become a modern substitute for gods or spirits, whose existence has fallen into doubt and whose authority has disappeared from political life. With church and state separated, and science and rationality taking over as the dominant ideology, the name of God carries little weight in a world of secular politics. To fill the void left by this loss of religious mystery, we have elevated LAW to a level of mystical significance.

Medcalf's definition shows her belief in the need to demystify law. She wants to treat it as a process like other social processes which can be studied and modified. To her, the other definitions in this chapter perpetuate the notion of law as a thing, a lofty presence separate from the people doing it. She understands law as a process of interaction—people acting and reacting toward each other.

Medcalf's perspective is a direct attack on the idealism of liberal democratic definitions such as Selznick's. She rejects the argument that law is an ideal of neutral, unbiased rule application. She insists, rather, that law is what people do with and to each other *in the name of law*. But her definition is also a rejection of anarchism, since she acknowledges that, in the name of law, we find both tyranny and resistance to tyranny. Law may not be the liberal ideal of neutral justice, but neither is it the all-conquering weapon of an irresistible conspiracy against human values. It is not an end product of any kind, but rather a process with identifiable characteristics and consequences.   •

Law as Custom Reinstitutionalized

I have mentioned several times in this discussion that each of these definitions reflects its author's ideas about the place of law in society and the way to go about studying that relationship. Let me be more specific by presenting a debate in this field which turns on the relationship between definition and analysis. Look back at Malinowski's definition for a moment. Recall that it treats almost any mechanism of social balance as law.

Another anthropologist, Paul Bohannan, thinks Malinowski, by being so all-inclusive, has sacrificed the ability to understand how law comes into existence, as distinct from custom. Bohannan's definition of law openly doubles as a statement of his basic theory of law in society:

> Law is custom recreated by agents of society in institutions specifically meant to deal with legal questions. (1967)

Notice that this definition describes a process by which law is created. Law is not just a set of commands backed up by sanctions. Nor is it, as Malinowski states, simply a set of shared feelings about what is right and wrong. Bohannan criticizes Malinowski for confusing *custom* with *law*. He says the process identified by Malinowski is only custom, which, however effective it may be in maintaining preliterate social order, is a prelegal stage of social development.

Law begins to develop only when some aspect of custom has become unable to maintain social solidarity. So law always appears later in social history, after a society's institutions (such as family, religion, and economy) have existed for some time with only custom, not law, as their prime regulator. When law develops, only certain aspects of custom get carried over into it.

Why isn't law as defined by Malinowski adequate? Bohannan states that as social conditions change, conflicts arise with the potential for destroying whole social institutions rather than just the individuals involved in the dispute. People discover that this threat is reduced if someone *outside* the institution steps in to handle the conflict. Outsiders are less of a threat because they are free from partisan identity in the conflict. Taking a dispute to outsiders introduces the thinking of "cooler heads," who can apply society's beliefs about right and wrong more objectively than could the disputants. These outside agents also work to sharpen and clarify the often vague definitions of right and duty which are typically found in the unwritten rules of custom. Custom depends on potentially unreliable, imprecise mechanisms such as learning by example, enforcement by persuasion, shaming and ridicule, and interpretation by biased parties to a dispute. Custom is therefore especially vulnerable to becoming ineffectual when faced by conditions, such as population increase or migration, which reduce shared understandings in simple cultures.

Both custom and law are stages of development in Bohannan's scheme. Custom develops when isolated norms in a group become *institutionalized* (that is, those norms become the basis for regular operation of such institutions as family, religion, or politics). Law is a later development made necessary by the growing inability of custom to support those institutions. Law *reinstitutionalizes* the norms of custom by stating them more exactly (so there will be less chance of disagreement over what they say) and by putting their application into the hands of special agents who supervise their use. By creating a separate legal institution, disputes can be "disengaged" from the institutions threatened by them and cooled down by objective application of rules, and the disputants can then be peacefully "reengaged" in the protected institutions.

Malinowski, says Bohannan, fails to recognize this process of *reinstitutionalization*. By making the distinction, Bohannan supports Black's position that law (as governmental social control) is a central social element in processes which increase social complexity. He joins those who treat law as the outcome of specific patterns of social development. He also agrees that law is a distinct operation in society, a special form of social control.

SUMMARY

In later chapters, we will see that social scientists are not united in their views about the social significance of law. They do agree that "pure legal scholarship" (the attempt to understand law through study of the language and logic of written statutes and judicial decisions) cannot clarify the everyday operation of the "living law" (Ehrlich, 1936). But their different approaches to social scientific theory produce conflicting interpretations of law. These conflicts may not begin with their definitions of law, but the definitions distill those differences for quick comparison.

If you define water as a chemical combination of hydrogen and oxygen, while I say that water is a basic weapon against fire, our perspectives may differ but they are compatible. But if you claim that UFOs are the paranoid delusions of emotionally unstable people, while I call them visitors from outer space, our perspectives differ so much as to be incompatible. Certainly they show that we disagree about what should be studied.

You would conduct psychological tests on people who claimed to have seen UFOs while I would develop ways to observe and measure UFOs.

In the same way, the differing definitions of law in this chapter are more than just different views of the same thing. They are sometimes incompatible. Adoption of one perspective points the way to one kind of research or action agenda, itself quite different from those you might adopt with other definitions. You may deal with the same facts as your critics, but you will organize them in very different ways. And you will probably even seek new facts considered irrelevant by those who reject your definition. So as you read farther in this book about research on law, always keep in mind the limitations of each study's perspective.

We began this chapter with a smorgasbord of "commonsense" images of law. We saw how different, and often incompatible, they can be, even though people rarely think about the inconsistencies. If social scientists have not reached agreement on a single definition of law, their debate can at least warn us that common sense is not all that sensible. By attempting to define law, we confront inconsistencies and can then begin debating real issues rather than semantics.

As identified in this chapter, issues of active debate include

1. The equating of law with administrative complexity. Is law present in simple societies, or does it develop as an aspect of increasing complexity?
2. The equating of *law* with the control of *physical force*. Can law operate without force, through consensus, persuasion, social pressure? Or are these only secondary features of a system which must ultimately rely on force?
3. The equating of *law* with *practice*. Is law only what legal actors do, or does it include statements about what they are supposed to do (theory)? Are dead-letter laws law?
4. The relevance of *justice*. Is law a system designed to achieve justice, or are law and justice independent issues? Or is law a system designed to systematically defeat justice?
5. The *uniqueness* of law. Is law a distinct, autonomous, social process performed by specialists, or is it produced by all members of society in the course of their everyday lives and relationships?

Another way to summarize the issues involved in defining law is to identify *continua* of opposing elements which some or all of the definitions presented here address. The following list summarizes eight such continua:

No Specialization	Specialization
Other Incentives	Physical Force
Arbitrariness	Due Process
Injustice	Justice
No Custom	Custom
Actual Practice	Ideal
State's Rule	All Rules
Law as Object	Law as Process

APPLYING WHAT YOU KNOW

To see whether you have understood the differences among the definitions of law in this chapter, take the two questions presented at the end of the first part of this chapter and show how opponents of each definition would respond to them. The first question was whether or not Hitler's actions in Germany were law. The second was whether international law is really law.

In Table 2.1 I have located each author of a definition by whether his or her answer to the two questions is yes or no. First look at the table and see whether you agree with this classification, based on what you have read in the chapter. Then read the explanation which follows.

TABLE 2.1

AUTHOR	WAS HITLER'S RULE LAW?	IS INTERNATIONAL LAW LAW?
Black	Yes	No
Holmes	Yes	No
Malinowski	Yes	Yes
Hoebel	Yes	No
Weber	Yes	?
Selznick	No	?
Zinn	Yes	Yes
Medcalf	Yes	Yes
Bohannan	Yes	?

Explanation of Table 2.1

Only Selznick and the Berkeley School would say that Hitler's actions were not law. Because of the arbitrariness of his rule, they would classify it as tyranny incompatible with the ideal of legality. Hitler's rule fits law as defined by Black, Holmes (because German courts ruled as Hitler told them to), Hoebel, and Weber, since all four of these treat law as commands, methods of social control imposed by authoritative bodies. Malinowski would have to agree, since there is nothing in his definition which would allow for distinctions to be drawn between the practices of different modern nation-states. Either they all have law or none of them do. Zinn would say that Hitler's rule was not significantly different from the control imposed by all modern governments. All use law to oppress. Medcalf, viewing law as a particular kind of process, has no means of excluding Hitler from her concept of law. Bohannan's definition would exclude Hitler only if he could show that Hitler's law was inconsistent with, and contrary to, the customs of Germany. But Bohannan's underlying theory asserts that law develops out of custom, so he lacks any other category for Hitler's actions. Therefore they must be law.

Recall that all of these definitions are for the purposes of social science. If you recoil at the thought of Hitler as an example of law, only Selznick offers you comfort within the social sciences. But you can find much more comfort in the realm of jurisprudence, which approaches these questions by applying logic and basic standards of right and wrong to determine the legal integrity of actions. Selznick and the Berkeley School are the only social science advocates discussed here who favor the application of jurisprudential principles in the social scientific study of law.

Turning now to international law, we can see that Black, Holmes, and Hoebel each treat law in terms that are too narrow to include it. Hoebel insists that law is backed by physical force, but the international use of force in most instances is war, not law. The World Court, the League of Nations, and the United Nations have much of the appearance of law. But they lack Hoebel's key ingredient—the ability to enforce standards, agreements, and shared values by force if necessary. Since they are not the equivalent of a government, their actions do not qualify as law in Black's and Holmes's definitions. Malinowski, Zinn, and Medcalf ironically agree that international law is law, though for very different reasons. The reciprocity and publicity, which (aside from armed agression) are the only tools for enforcing international norms and agreements, are exactly the mechanisms Malinowski held up as typifying law. Similarly, Medcalf would see international law as one of those networks of relationships which, because it is operated under the name and in the language of law, is law. Zinn, on the other hand, might see international law as just one more extension of the system of oppression—a broadening of the conspiracy against human values.

Weber, Selznick, and Bohannan present more difficult problems of classification. Weber would agree that where international treaties and agreements are administered by established organizations (e.g., the World Court, the United Nations, perhaps NATO and OPEC), their ability to exert psychological pressure would turn international agreements into law. But other agreements, whose violation can only be met by the pressure of "world opinion" rather than organized pressure, would not be law. Bohannan's definition would make most of these same distinctions. Selznick, however, would ask whether a specific instance of international "law" represented a set of restraints on some otherwise irresistible power, or whether such "law" was actually a means for powerful international interests to secure dominance over the less powerful. He would, for instance, probably denounce as lacking in legality Prime Minister Chamberlain's "appeasement" treaty with Hitler, which allowed Germany to occupy Czechoslovakia. In contrast, he might view a treaty ending international support for white domination of blacks in South Africa as achieving a high level of legality.

This discussion has been based on speculation. These authors have not necessarily stated any position on the two issues discussed here. The purpose of this exercise is to show some of the consequences of adopting one definition over another.

REFERENCES

BLACK, DONALD   (1972), The Boundaries of Legal Sociology, *Yale Law Journal* 81, p. 1086.

BOHANNAN, PAUL   (1967), *Law and Warfare*, New York: Natural History Press.

CAMPBELL, DONALD AND ROSS, H. LAWRENCE   (1968), The Connecticut Crackdown on Speeding, *Law and Society Review* 3, p. 65.

EHRLICH, EUGEN   (1936), *Fundamental Principles of the Sociology of Law*, (W. Moll, Transl.) Cambridge: Harvard University Press.

FULLER, LON   (1964), *The Morality of Law*, New Haven: Yale University Press.

HOEBEL, E. ADAMSON   (1954), *The Law of Primitive Man: A Study in Comparative Legal Dynamics*, Cambridge: Harvard University Press.

LOBENTHAL, JOSEPH   (1971), *Power and Put-On: The Law in America*, New York: Outerbridge and Dientstfrey.

MAAS, PETER   (1973), *Serpico*, New York: Viking.

MALINOWSKI, BRONISLAW   (1926, 1961), *Crime and Custom in Savage Society*, London: Routledge.

MASER, W.   (1979), *Nuremberg: A Nation on Trial*, (Richard Barry, Transl.) New York: Scribner's.

MEDCALF, LINDA   (1978), *Law and Identity: Lawyers, Native Americans, and Legal Practice*, Beverly Hills, Calif.: Sage Publications, Inc.

NADER, LAURA   (1965), Choices in Legal Procedure: Shia Moslem and Mexican Zapotec, *American Anthropologist*, 67, p. 394.

NONET, PHILIPPE   (1976), For Jurisprudential Sociology, *Law and Society Review*, 10, p. 525.

NONET, PHILIPPE AND SELZNICK, PHILIP   (1978), *Law and Society in Transition: Toward Responsive Law*, New York: Harper & Row, Pub.

PARKINSON, C. NORTHCOTE   (1957), *Parkinson's Law and Other Studies in Administration*, Boston: Houghton-Mifflin.

RASMUSSEN, KNUD   (1927), *Across Arctic America*, Westport, Ct.: Greenwood Press, 1968 (reissued).

RIGBY, PETER AND LULE, FRED   (1972), Divination and Healing in Peri-urban Kampala, in John Bennett (ed.), *Social Science and Medicine in Eastern Africa*, Kampala: Makerere Institute for Research.

SELZNICK, PHILIP   (1961), Sociology and Natural Law, *Natural Law Forum*, 6, p. 84.

SIMONETTE, J. E.   (1963), THE COMMON LAW OF MORRISON COUNTY, *American Bar Association Journal*, 49, p. 263.

SMITH, B. F.   (1977), *Reaching Judgment at Nuremberg*, New York: Basic Books.

UNGER, ROBERTO   (1976), *Law in Modern Society*, New York: Free Press.

WEBER, MAX   (1954), *On Law in Economy and Society*, Max Rheinstein, (ed.), New York: Simon & Schuster.

WEYRAUCH, WALTER D.   (1971), The "Basic Law" or "Constitution" of a Small Group. *Journal of Social Issues*, 27, p. 2.

WILLIAMS, GLANVILLE   (1945–1946), Language and the Law, *Law Quarterly Review*, p. 61.

ZINN, HOWARD   (1971), The Conspiracy of Law, in R. P. Wolff (ed.), *The Rule of Law*, New York: Simon & Schuster.

3
THE ORIGINS OF LAW: CUSTOM

Where does law come from? Why has it developed into a separate social form? What keeps it the way it is in a given society? Why does it vary so much from one society to another? These are all ways of asking about the origins of law.

In the next three chapters we will see how these questions have produced three quite different sets of answers. One approach has been to seek law's roots within the *customs* of society. A second view is that law is one element of social *structure* and gets its characteristics from the *functions* it must serve in society. The third perspective sees law as one of many arenas of *conflict* in which established structures tending to favor the "haves" battle against "have nots" who are seeking to improve their status.

Uncompromising advocates of these positions all see their own theory as incompatible with either of the other two. But they do join forces in rejecting the argument that law exists because people have some *biologically* or *psychologically* programmed need for it. They reject such arguments because they do not help us understand why law systems vary so much from one society to another or from one period to another in the histories of societies. Saying, for example, that law is necessary because people are inherently aggressive does not give us any way to explain why some human groups manage to get along with so little legal development compared with other groups.

Some societies show evidence of very complex legal developments. American business, for example, supports a large, differentiated legal profession. These professionals work full time on contract preparation, warranty writing, policy determination in response to dozens of governmental regulatory agencies also staffed by dozens of lawyers, and protection of company interests in lawsuits ranging from patent infringement and copyright violation to product liability and pollution of natural resources. Law is big business in the United States.

Other societies with similar levels of industrial development show much less development in law (e.g., Japan). Conversely, some societies which are "simple" in other aspects of economic and social development have within them the same elements of law as do much more complex societies, and their peoples spend great time and energy pursuing opponents through legal channels (e.g., India). As we look back at American history, or the histories of other societies, we find periods with very little of what we would now recognize as law. We also find practices which now strike us as alien, if not downright perverse (such as the witchcraft trials of Salem, Massachusetts, or the elaborate legal machinery which maintained slavery for more than two hundred years). One reason for the diversity of definitions we sampled in chapter 2 is that law has not been uniformly produced and structured wherever humans interact in groups.

From such observations we begin to see that what we now think of as law has not always existed, and has not even developed to the same extent or in the same direction in all societies. So we ask the question, "What are the social roots of law"?

LAW AS CUSTOM
REINSTITUTIONALIZED

In this first chapter on the origins of law, I will consider the argument that law arises out of custom. Bohannan's presentation of this position was briefly discussed in chapter 2. As he says, law is a restatement of customs. Customs themselves need no enforcement machinery because people learn them so thoroughly through socialization and informal enforcement that they feel the obligation to conform. Law is a restatement of these feelings which gives them the precision needed by rule enforcers who must make enforcement an explicit, public act.

The key idea here is that law is a particular means of expressing values and norms which develop naturally in a society as it wrestles with the everyday problems of group life. A particularly clear description of this process is found in Hoebel's account of the Cheyenne brave, Wolf Lies Down (1954, pp. 18–28). When his horse was "borrowed" without his being asked, as was customary with most Cheyenne possessions, he complained to the chiefs of his society, because without his horse he could neither hunt nor make war. They summoned the borrower, who then apologized to Wolf Lies Down and offered to return the horse. But the chiefs did more than simply settle this one dispute. To prevent similar conflict in the future, they went on to declare a new rule: "There shall be no more borrowing of horses without asking. If any man takes another's goods without asking, we will go over and get them back for him. More than that, if the taker tries to keep them, we will give him a whipping." The chiefs thus responded to the uncertainty caused by one incident by creating a new rule. The law in this case was developed in response to a partial inadequacy in the society's customs. Tribal members share the feeling (custom) that borrowing is normally acceptable. But they see its disruptive effects in the case of horse borrowing because the horse is so central to the role of the brave. The incident produced the need to state their shared feeling explicitly and declare it as a publicly acknowledged rule. The chiefs recognized that it would be dangerous to leave the feeling unstated. The risk of further disruption would be too high. The custom became law because the chiefs assumed the task of enforcing it. Custom becomes law both in the sense of law as a doctrine or rule and in the structural sense (law as a set of procedures [an institution] for applying the rule).

Law vs. Custom: Recipe for Failure?

This theory that law originates in custom includes the assertion that there must be a basic compatibility between law and the customs of the people. William Graham Sumner summarized this thesis in his claim that "Lawways cannot change folkways" (Sumner, 1906). Others have interpreted this as meaning that if anyone tries to make and enforce laws which are contrary to a people's customs, the laws will fail because law only works if it reinforces custom.

Prohibition

For example, reformers in 1919 succeeded in passing the prohibition amendment to the U.S. Constitution. Sale or use of alcoholic beverages was banned. But the failure of that law has become legendary. Massive evasion by ordinary law-abiding citizens, organized criminals, and public officials led to the repeal of prohibition when it became obvious that the law was unenforceable. The "folkway" of drinking alcohol could not be altered by the "lawway."

Mormon Polygamy

Similar failure occurred in the case of polygamous Mormon fundamentalists living in a remote corner of Arizona (Schwartz and Skolnick, 1970). The U.S. Supreme Court ruled in 1896 that Mormons could not practice polygamy. Prior to that ruling, Mormon doctrine ordered Mormon men to marry several wives. After the ruling, the church's spiritual leader had a "revelation" that God no longer commanded polygamy. So the main church went monogamous. But splinter groups refused to accept this switch and have been practicing polygamy ever since, while accusing the main church of heresy.

Because of their practices, one splinter group in Arizona has been subjected to repeated raids and arrests by Arizona state police (Schwartz and Skolnick, 1970, pp. 57–74). The men are taken away to jail and the women and children become wards of the state. Each time this happens, the community comes back together afterward to resume their polygamous lives as before. If anything, police harassment seems to reinforce Mormon "folkway" beliefs that polygamy is God's law. It is the kind of resistance which Sumner refers to when claiming that law cannot change custom.

Soviet Muslim Women's Liberation

The Muslim area of Soviet Central Asia before the Russian Revolution in 1918 was populated by a traditional Muslim society. Women were treated as the property of their husbands. They were confined to *purdah* (severe restrictions which included confinement to the women's quarters and kitchen at home and the wearing of a shapeless gown in public which totally covered all parts of the body). They lacked the right to divorce their husbands, but their husbands could divorce them easily, sending them penniless back to their fathers. These customs, along with the practice of polygamy, put women prior to the revolution in a position of complete economic and social subservience (Massell, 1968, pp. 179–211).

The Bolshevik revolutionaries who overthrew the Russian czar in 1918 wanted to modernize all Soviet society. This goal, they thought, required an attack on traditional values and customs in various ethnic areas, including Muslim Central Asia. They thought law would help uproot the "backward" practices of the Muslims, which were holding them back from "progress."

They planned to use legal devices to exploit the powerlessness of Muslim women. They assumed the women were chafing under the yoke of male domination. By encouraging women to break out of their slavelike status, the planners expected to crack open the solid shell of Muslim custom, making Central Asia ready for industrialization. New Bolshevik laws and courts were created to encourage women to wear Western-style dress, to publicize their disputes against their husbands, to divorce, and to take jobs outside the home, especially in the lawcourts set up to liberate women. Traditional Muslim judges were stripped of their power. Civil rights for women were legislated, and women were hired as judges.

Massell reports that although these laws had far-reaching effects, their impact was not what the Bolsheviks had planned. Women only gradually began to take advantage of the new laws. The more they did, the more men tried to prevent change. In the courts, for example, Moscow-trained judges quickly discovered that they knew so little about local customs that they could not understand disputes or the strategies used by disputants. Muslim men could easily manipulate the outcomes of cases. Female judges had their power usurped by male court clerks, who became the real "power behind the throne." When Moscow tried to remedy these problems, by using local experts as judges and court officers, the "experts" exploited their positions to twist Soviet laws with interpretations which supported Muslim custom.

Outside of court, women in Western dress were attacked while local police officers (Muslim men) looked the other way. As the Bolshevik campaign intensified, women on the streets were raped and murdered in growing numbers, and police and local government officials joined in the attacks.

These reactions show that the Soviet campaign did succeed in disrupting Muslim social order. Thousands of women left their husbands in search of the promised liberation. But without jobs to support them, most were forced into prostitution. Prostitution became epidemic for a period of time in the 1920s. Then, after serving time in these degrading, "temporary" positions, most women fled back to their homes, begging their husbands' forgiveness and returning to their traditional roles.

Massell concludes that, far from revolutionizing Muslim society, Soviet law was transformed into a cover for the maintenance of traditional practices. To put this in Sumner's terms, Soviet "lawways" could not alter the basic direction of Muslim "folkways." They failed to produce the desired social transformation. Those, like Bohannan, who see law as an outgrowth of custom, would explain the Bolshevik failure by saying that laws can only be effective when they reinforce custom, not when they attack it.

Colonial Law in British India

Before the British imposed colonial rule on the Indian subcontinent in the last quarter of the eighteenth century, it was an area with an enormous variety of political and social systems. Kings, queens, princes, and religious leaders reigned over hundreds of small kingdoms and territories. Their boundaries shifted constantly with the fortunes of war and political alliance. Their law systems were as varied and changeable as their boundaries and the personalities of their rulers.

The British take-over began modestly as a simple commercial trade operation along India's coast. But as trade interests grew, British administrative machinery was spread across the land and ultimately ruled most of the subcontinent. The main administrative objective at first was to create and maintain an orderly environment for trade. Later this limited objective grew into a major crusade to maintain Pax Britannica throughout Queen Victoria's colonial empire.

The legal system the British established in India was a replica of England's own. Its courts and administrators were instructed to use the procedures of English common law to maintain the peace. The British explicitly decided to enforce local Hindu and Muslim customs rather than try to change them. Administrators and judges, in other words, deliberately undertook to "reinstitutionalize" local customs into colonial law. First, of course, they had to figure out what local custom was. For this task, they employed local scholars (usually high-caste Brahmins or traditional Muslim Koranic scholars). They relied on these "experts" to interpret ancient scriptures, which they assumed contained written statements about local custom.

The most widely shared interpretation of what happened with British law in India is that it failed spectacularly. Colonial administrators at the time and anthropologists today (Orwell, 1950; Cohn, 1959, 1961; Mendelsohn, 1981) describe major disruption in the lives of ordinary Indian peasants, artisans, and village and regional leaders, as they all flooded into the courts with lawsuits against each other. This unexpected tide of litigation overwhelmed the courts with crushing case loads. Deception and intrigue became the order of the day, as litigants sought ways to manipulate the courts to rule in their favor. Hired witnesses and perjured testimony became the norm. Lawsuits generated countersuits and bizarre convoluted strategies of legal attack. Appeals were commonplace, further clogging the system. People built fortunes by expertly manipulating the courts to award them land held by less clever or less wealthy neighbors. An attitude came to prevail that going to court was like betting on a horse race, and the gamble often seemed worth the risk.

British observers viewed these uses of British justice as scandalous. Many took them as further proof of their conviction that Indians were uncivilized barbarians in need of Britain's refined culture. But to the more objective anthropologist, the Indian response was further proof of Sumner's thesis about lawways and folkways. Supporters of this view (Cohn, 1959, 1961) say that, by imposing British *procedure* on the enforcement of local Indian customs, British courts actually forced a change in the meanings and effects of those customs. They argue that custom is a living, changing creation. They say that the British judges and administrators froze custom at a particular point in time and prevented its changing nature from being expressed in court. Custom as the courts defined it thus became an alien, antiquated, rigidly used cudgel, which bore only superficial resemblance to the often diverse and conflicting beliefs of the many castes, tribes, clans, and regions of India. As a result, real, living Indian custom quickly reasserted itself in the form of the "perversions" to which litigants subjected the British system of law.

So again the claim is that the "lawways" of Britain could not change the "folkways" of India. In this case, the folkways were the ways in which beliefs, norms, and values were customarily developed and put into practice. The lawways were the misguided procedural rules of the British, especially their insistence on looking into ancient scripture for modern custom. Under the very noses of the English judges, the Indians turned the colonial courts into their own system of law.

We will return to these two examples in later chapters, when we consider rival interpretations of what happened in Central Asia and India.

"Living Law" and Cultural Lag

While law may be an expression of customs, laws and customs are normally at least somewhat out of phase with each other. Current law, for example, may forbid use of marijuana. At the time of their passage, these laws might have been consistent with general social norms (Howard Becker's analysis [1963] is that even when first passed, the anti-marijuana laws did not reflect widespread feelings and beliefs about its use. He argues that this legislation was the pet project of a handful of bureaucrats, while most of the population simply had no opinion about marijuana at all). But those standards (or customs) may have changed, while the law remains unchanged. Law in such a case may have originated in the society's customs, but then lagged behind the rate of change in customs. Bohannan argues that laws naturally respond more slowly to changes in moral standards than do customs because it takes extra time and effort among lawmakers to identify cultural changes, agree on their content and desirability, and then communicate those changes throughout the many branches of enforcement so that operations can be changed in an orderly way.

Because of this cultural lag, there is always some degree of tension between law and the customs of a people. Bohannan maintains that this tension should not lead us to think that law and custom have different, contradictory roots. Law is a crystallized and therefore slower-to-change expression of customs.

Ehrlich spoke of this same tension when he advocated research on the "living law" (1936). He attacked traditional legal scholarship for its futile attempts to discover "the law" on any subject by searching ancient legal codes from Rome or Greece. Even if legal scholars tried to apply such codes, they would fail the way the British did in India unless the particular law happened to fit modern practices. Police and other law officials must bend with the winds of change even if the law on the books remains unchanged. Both officials and citizens must make constant adjustments to changes in life-styles and beliefs. At any given moment in history, the "living law" is the rule actually being followed and enforced. Custom outstrips not only ancient legal codes, but also modern legislation. The actual application of the law, the hundreds of decisions made daily by police, prosecutors, probation officers, and citizens themselves, is determined by the ever-changing, adaptive reactions of people to each other and to society's institutions.

To illustrate, think of the law that says all Americans must drive no faster than 55 mph. Whether you drive or not, if you have lived in the United States during the enforcement of this law, you know that the "living law" on speed differs from the law stated on roadside signs. Why don't police enforce the stated limit?

The answer may be similar to what happened in Connecticut after a statewide crackdown on speeders. (Campbell and Ross, 1968). The Connecticut governor ordered automatic loss of license for anyone caught speeding. This drastic measure was different from traditional speed enforcement procedures, and it meant that many people would be seriously inconvenienced by speeding arrests. Did people slow down? According to Campbell and Ross, the answer is no. The governor's order had only one significant effect—police officers reduced the number of arrests they made for speeding. The governor's order was so out of line with people's customary beliefs about what should happen to those caught speeding, and it was so inconsistent with the opinions of police officers, who generally shared the beliefs of the public, that police simply chose not to enforce it. While the governor boasted of sharp declines in speeding arrests, thinking he had actually slowed drivers down, the police were actually just giving out more warnings but fewer tickets to a public that kept on driving at speeds fitting their customs.

It may just be that the switch to 55 mph as a national speed limit violates the customs of too many people, including highway patrol police. Ehrlich would say that the "living law" about highway speeds places the limit somewhere near what it was before the energy crisis became a public problem.

It should not be hard for you to think of other instances where law lags behind custom, where the "living law" deviates from written law. The waterfront policeman mentioned in chapter 2 had developed a whole micro-legal system for dealing with the special problems of his job. Similarly the federal government calls millions of Mexican-Americans "illegal" immigrants because their entry into the United States was not properly documented. Yet law enforcers in areas which rely heavily on immigrant labor often look the other way so employers can get their work done. For years, many states have had "blue laws" which prohibited stores from opening on Sundays. Many stores in these states simply ignore the laws, and when they are fined for staying open on Sundays, both they and the law enforcers look on the fines as a kind of tax rather than a punishment. Customary attitudes toward the meaning of Sunday have changed though the law has not.

Procedure vs. Custom: Restraints on Authority

At this point, it may help to recall Fuller's King Rex, the embattled monarch in chapter 2 who could not seem to make good law. If we compare Fuller's views with the theory that law's roots lie in custom, we find that there is basic disagreement about how to make good law. Fuller's eight principles are all concerned with the *procedures* by which laws are made and enforced. His parable depends on the existence of a population ready and eager to obey the king, if only he could get his law-making act together. Fuller thus implies that Rex could successfully make and enforce just about any law he might fancy, as long as he went about it with procedural correctness (following the eight guidelines).

But the folkways-lawways relationship we have examined in this chapter shows a different source of restraint on lawmakers. Rex, following Bohannan and Sumner's reasoning, could follow all the correct procedures and still fail, because laws that violate custom are resisted with as much ingenuity and zeal as is necessary to preserve those customs. Even the procedural restraints of the British could not stem the tide of custom in India, though the administrators did everything Rex should have done.

Lobenthal (1970) even goes so far as to suggest that American courts are most successful when they do just the opposite of Fuller's prescriptions for Rex. In his first case as a practicing lawyer, Lobenthal had to defend Gardofsky, a man who often drilled holes through his floor so that he could pour water onto the "evil eye" that he felt staring at him from the apartment below. Neither the tenant of that apartment nor the landlady wanted to hurt Gardofsky—they liked him except for his drilling and surveillance. In court, all parties agreed that Gardofsky would spend thirty days under "observation" in the psychiatric ward at Bellevue Hospital. A month later, the judge threatened to return Gardofsky to Bellevue for more "observation" unless he agreed to a compromise plan where he would move to a basement apartment in the same building and stop drilling holes. Gardofsky agreed out of fear of the hospital, not because he thought the "evil eye" was gone.

Lobenthal argues that the judge was able to produce this satisfactory outcome precisely because the law operates in a shroud of mystery which obscures the severe limits on its real abilities and powers, so that outsiders accept its judgments as legitimate and binding. Behind the judge's lofty legal language and his talk about psychiatric observation, and behind the obscure psychiatric reports about Gardofsky's persecution complex, is the basic commonsense conclusion that "Gardofsky [is] nuts" (Lobenthal, 1970, p. 17). In other words, the judge and the psychiatrists used esoteric language and official forms to arrive at the same conclusion that customary beliefs would produce in the general public. The judge had no special power to alter Gardofsky's behavior. But he could bring about a compromise as long as Gardofsky, the landlady, and the other tenant *thought* the judge had special powers.

In other words, Lobenthal directly contradicts Fuller by saying that the *law works best when people don't understand it,* when they are mystified by it, when they think it has powers it in fact lacks. His example also shows a judge disguising with long words and even lengthier procedures the fact that his solution is no different from what existing custom could produce. To say that Gardofsky is "nuts" is to express customary interpretations of his behavior. To move him to the basement requires no degree in psychiatry or lengthy legal training—it is a *commonsense* solution.

Lobenthal's example supports the idea that law is custom reinstitutionalized. Neither the landlady, nor Gardofsky, nor the other tenant could resolve the problem through the use of customary means. When the court did intervene, it succeeded because its solution was compatible with their customary beliefs. And it succeeded in "disengaging" the dispute from the apartment house situation, where other solutions had failed and where the tranquility of the whole house was threatened.

So Lobenthal supports the position that what law must have to succeed is compatibility with custom rather than procedural clarity as prescribed by Fuller for Rex the King.

Problems of Logic: Custom and Japanese Law

As the next two chapters will show, the theory that law arises out of custom has been attacked by, and is inconsistent with, at least two major alternative theories. The full presentation of those alternatives will be made in those chapters. But here let us examine some of the difficulties we face if we try to apply the theory to actual cases.

Harmony and Legal Underdevelopment

Consider the case of Japan. Compared with other industrialized nations, Japan has an underdeveloped legal system. In spite of its rapid and sophisticated development as an industrial giant, Japan has one of the smallest *per capita* legal professions in the world and its few lawcourts get very little business. Put simply, Japanese people very rarely use law (Kawashima, 1963).

These facts need explanation. Everywhere else that heavy industrialization has taken place under conditions of capitalism, law has played a major role in regulating that development, facilitating it, and absorbing the problems created by it. How could Japan do it without law?

One answer is that public disputing and the formality of law are alien to Japanese custom (Kawashima, 1963). For the Japanese, the most important question is: "What will best maintain public harmony?" Their customary answer rejects public lawsuits, which drag conflicts out into the public, emphasize the fact that conflict exists, and prevent reconciliation between opponents. To the Japanese, harmony is best achieved by some form of compromise, some reconciliation. They seek compromise, not justice, because compromise restores harmony to the group which the dispute has disrupted. Over the years, both governmental and nongovernmental methods of reconciliation have been used, with the result that public lawsuits are very rare.

Minamata Disease: A Case Study

Consider the following example and try to imagine how Americans would have reacted to such a situation.

Minamata disease is the name given to symptoms which afflicted residents of a fishing village on the Japanese coast. Men, women, and children over the course of several years began having extremely serious nervous disorders. Babies were born deformed and lived like vegetables. Adults were reduced to paralyzed vegetables, and children grew up with grotesque deformities. The symptoms affected hundreds of people (Smith and Smith, 1975; Upham, 1976).

The mysterious Minamata disease was finally traced to mercury poisoning. A factory dumping waste into the bay where the villagers fished had put so much mercury into the ecosystem that the fish on which the villagers survived were all heavily contaminated. The Chisso Chemical Company was unmistakably responsible.

Under similar circumstances, wouldn't we expect Americans to head straight for the lawyer's office to file suit? Kawashima thinks we would. But in the village of Minamata, the residents declined for years to become involved in lawsuits, preferring instead to rely on the good faith of the company to "restore the harmony" by compensating them for their suffering. Even when encouraged by outraged observers to seek legal assistance to demand more adequate compensation from the company, most villagers continued to avoid the legal route. They seemed to prefer quiet suffering to public confrontation.

It is this kind of avoidance of legal remedies which Kawashima has in mind when he argues that Japanese custom retards the development of law. We can summarize his position by saying that Japanese law is "underdeveloped" when compared with other industrial nations, because Japanese custom requires people to seek nonlegal remedies for their disputes. They avoid law because they don't like it. To them it is unnatural, immoral.

Are Japanese Customs Unique?

There is a major weakness in the approach described above. It lies in a major unstated assumption that other cultures where lawsuits are more common instill beliefs and values which encourage public disputing and thus lead to a greater degree of legal development. If custom does determine the size and form of legal systems, then we ought to find enthusiastic support for courts and lawsuits in those cultures where suing is frequent and law work is big business. Two such societies are the United States and India.

Are Americans and Indians trigger-happy about invoking the law? Perhaps not. If American endorsement of legalism exists anywhere, surely it is in the world of business executives, whom we assume to be heavy consumers of legal services.

American Business Practices

But Stewart Macaulay found that business people routinely ignore the legal technicalities in their contracts and the advice of their lawyers (1963). To be sure, they do routinely use lawyers to write those contracts and advise them on business decisions. But they much prefer to sidestep legal jargon and deal with each other directly. When a contract says, for example, that the agreement is void if a supplier fails to deliver by a certain date, buyers rarely insist on the letter of the contract or demand damages for failure to deliver. Instead, they make phone calls, mail letters, or send telegrams, without even asking their lawyers' advice. What they seek is to negotiate a compromise on the delivery date.

Macaulay says that businesspeople avoid legal formality as much as possible because it is "bad for business." They look on people who demand strict contractual compliance as untrustworthy. To be "one of the gang" in the business community, it helps to show your contempt for lawyers and their inflexible, uncompromising technicalities. Trust comes from knowing that the other side in a deal wants to continue doing business and must therefore "be reasonable." Being reasonable means being agreeable to compromise. Each kind of business has its own customs which define how far a businessperson must go in being reasonable. Throughout the business world, then, deals are made which purposely demonstrate an acceptable level of distaste for lawyers and strict legal procedure.

Ross made a similar discovery in the American insurance industry (1970). When someone tells a large insurance company that he or she is not satisfied with a settlement being offered in an automobile accident case, we might expect resistance from the insurance company. Surely the company would call in its lawyers and insist on giving no more than the law allows in such cases. We expect, in other words, that an impersonal, profit-seeking organization would rely heavily on lawsuits to protect its profits.

Instead these companies routinely avoid legal involvements by paying claimants *more* than the law requires. To most claims adjusters working for large companies, litigation is a last resort, an option that should be avoided if at all possible. So strong is their incentive to stay out of court that they bend the law to meet the demands of unsatisfied claimants. In *behavior*, then, they are similar to the villagers of Minamata.

Does this mean that they have the same customary preference for harmony found in Japan? Yes and no. They do have a desire to avoid overt conflict. But their reasons are very practical. Their jobs and their chances for promotion within the company depend on their ability to achieve *quick* settlement of claims. Large numbers of unsettled claims are costly to the company because they require continued processing costs and their uncertain outcomes mean reduced ability to predict future financial status. So company management would rather secure quick settlements with overgenerous payments than insist on *justice* and exact enforcement of the law in court.

Reactions to Tragedy in West Virginia

American working-class communities have also seemed very "Japanese" in their reactions to lawyers and courts. When coal miners in West Virginia were hit with a disastrous flood caused by the collapse of a recklessly built coal mine refuse dam, their losses in terms of property and lives were comparable to the Minamata disaster. The negligence of the mining company was plain to see. But the miners and their families showed great reluctance to becoming involved in a public confrontation with the company (Erikson, 1976). Many at first found it easier to accept the company claim that the flood had been an "act of God," and they resisted believing the clear evidence that the company had knowingly allowed the hazardous dam to form because it took care of its refuse problem cheaply. Assuming that the company would "take care of its people," most of them waited patiently for evidence that the company would rescue them.

Only when it became clear that the company would not take responsibility was there any shift in their attitudes. Then, and only then, could some of them be persuaded *by outside public-interest lawyers* to join in a prolonged lawsuit which was finally settled in their favor. Among those who did not join, there was criticism of the litigants. Many of them continued to endure the inadequacies of federally provided mobile homes and unreconstructed communities for years after the flood, and the fatalism with which they accepted their losses was often an exact replica of the statements made by victims in Minamata.

Thus, in the heart of America we find people with the same preference for compromise which Kawashima claims to be a determining factor in the low levels of legal activity in Japan. American business leaders and coal miners say the same things as Japanese villagers—that compromise is better, that lawyers are troublemakers, that people who insist on their *legal* rights are troublemakers and cannot be trusted.

This similarity raises doubts about using Japanese *custom* to explain the absence of legal development in Japan. Even though American business executives prefer the same way of solving disputes, they are surrounded by, and deeply involved with, the lawyers and legal procedures which contradict their preferences. Somehow, in America customs have not been enough to prevent the growth of law. If custom is more resilient in Japan, why?

The answer, whatever it is, cannot be that American businesspeople, insurance claims adjusters, or coal miners are rare exceptions in American society. A moment's reflection should be enough to make you realize that the Japanese preference for harmony is not much different from the preferences many of your own friends and neighbors show. Seeing a lawyer to write a will or conduct the purchase of a house may be quite common. But the preference to avoid hassles by becoming involved in official legal disputes is also common. The much disparaged comment "I don't want to get involved" shows this avoidance. Most people seem to share a feeling that public disputes are demeaning, unrewarding entanglements.

Think of the sighs of relief we hear when a divorce is uncontested. Dragged into court, a contested divorce makes everyone uncomfortable because all the charges and countercharges, the frustrations, and the anger are made public so that they must be dealt with by friends, neighbors, and relatives. We don't seem any more anxious to "air our dirty linen in public" than the Japanese. We have a similar contempt for people who cannot handle such problems discreetly. Dragging a dispute into public represents a kind of failure.

Custom vs. Practice in India

Earlier in this chapter, I described the flood of Indian litigants to British courts in colonial India. Their behavior could not be more different from the Japanese. But is it adequate to say, as have anthropologists who see law as an outgrowth of custom, that Indian custom differs from Japanese concerning involvement in legal disputes? If you look at what Indians *say* about their litigation, and have said since the courts were established, (see Kidder, 1973) you find them just as convinced as the Japanese that lawsuits are harmful, that compromise is always better, that lawyers are troublemakers, and that people who get involved in lawsuits are either troublemakers or unfortunate victims. The difference between them and the Japanese is not in what they believe or feel about legal involvements. Rather they differ in that Indians often see themselves as having no alternative to litigation. Indian culture is full of sayings such as: "In court, the winners are losers, and the losers are dead." People caught up in lawsuits see themselves as having been "dragged to court" by their opponents.

In other words, there are no notable differences in expressed attitude and belief between millions of Indians, whose actions have led to the growth of one of the largest legal systems in the world, and the Japanese, whose actions have had just the opposite effect. How then can we accept the argument that customary beliefs in Japan keep the law from developing as it has elsewhere? Beliefs and values in India are very similar. Nor are American beliefs and attitudes much different.

Perhaps actions speak louder than words. What does it matter what the Americans and Indians *say*? Just look at what they *do*. Surely that proves their customs are different from the Japanese. Certainly, if custom is to be understood as a source of law, there must be some correspondence between people's actions and the customs they are thought to have. It would make no sense to speculate about custom if this correspondence were not assumed, since custom is, after all, being used here as a theory of behavior which affects the legal forms developed by societies. So it is tempting to look at people's *actions* rather than their *words* as a measure of their customs.

But that temptation can be fatal to the theory that law arises out of custom. A distinctive feature of the customary theory of law is its claim that beliefs and values make a difference, that social forms such as law are molded by those beliefs and values. If you discard what people *say* (as do other theories which we will examine in later chapters) on the grounds that "actions speak louder than words" then you are caught in a dilemma. Either you get trapped in circular reasoning (Is that action customary? Yes. How do I know? Because it is done much of the time. Why is it done much of the time? Because it is customary.) or you are forced back to reliance on what people *say* about their actions.

Japanese Lawsuits: Custom vs. Practice

Suppose that actions do speak louder than words. One of the research problems faced by users of customary theories is that people being studied can lead the researcher astray with statements about their customs which are either phony, irrelevant, or overidealized. The researcher who depends too heavily on such statements may miss important information about the people's actual practices.

Again Japan provides an example of this. In the tragedy at Minamata there is abundant evidence that custom was not the only restraint against filing lawsuits (Smith and Smith, 1975). When the same disease broke out at Niigata, a fishing village quite distant from Minamata, the mercury poison was traced to a factory forty miles up the river. As soon as the source was confirmed, Niigata victims filed lawsuits. In addition, they began hounding the Minamata victims to join their legal crusade. Only after this second epidemic, thirteen years after Minamata knew what had poisoned its waters, did Minamata victims start to file lawsuits.

Why was one set of victims so much quicker to sue than the other? It would be meaningless to claim that one group was more Japanese than the other. They share the same culture, so the difference in their reactions cannot be explained as being caused by cultural differences.

Consider this alternative explanation. The guilty factory in Minamata was the biggest employer in town. People's jobs depended on good relations with the offending manufacturer. Victims, like everyone else in town, had established relationships with the company, either as employees, relatives of employees, or long-term neighbors dependent on company-financed medical clinics, schools, and related social services. Challenging the company with "unreasonable" demands for compensation would mean risking the loss of their benefactor's goodwill. Because the company held its people's trust at the outset of the epidemic, company lawyers were able to exchange quick token compensation to victims for their written promises that they understood there would be no further compensation if in the future they won a lawsuit against the company.

The situation in Niigata was entirely different. The offending factory was neither neighbor nor employer of victims or their friends and relatives. There had been no preexisting relationship between the factory and Niigata. They just happened to be on the same river. Hence the risk of offending the company meant nothing to the victims compared with their outrage at the injustice of their suffering.

Given the same provocation, people sharing the *same customs* took *opposite actions* relative to law. If we stopped our research upon hearing that Minamata victims spoke of "honor, public harmony, and compromise," we would be unable to explain either their actions or those of the Niigata victims. The comparison shows that we must look for other factors to explain law-oriented (and therefore law-producing) behavior. In this example, we have brought in the preexisting networks of influence, obligation, and power as factors explaining the differences between the two villages. The existence or absence of such networks, as we shall see in the next two chapters, has been the subject of much study which downplays the role of custom in the origins of law.

THE PRESUMPTION OF IRRATIONALITY IN CUSTOM-BASED THEORIES

The theory we have been reviewing in this chapter is a special case of the general theory that custom can be used to explain typical behavior in groups. This approach has been used to explain many other social phenomena. For example, some sociologists have tried to explain the intractable nature of poverty by saying that poor people have their own special customs which keep them poor. In the case of rural poverty in poor nations, these customs are identified as superstitions which prevent peasants from adopting modern agricultural methods which would boost their productivity. In American cities, poverty customs include fatalism, inability to defer gratification, and emphasis on values which prevent participation in mainstream American life. So, the theory goes, poor people have children who will also learn to be poor. The vicious cycle of poverty, in this view, is perpetuated by the preservation of poor customs.

All theories which take this cultural approach make the same basic assertion which, as we will see in the next two chapters, is directly challenged by other sociological theories. The assertion is that people make their choices on the basis of learned, but subconscious and irrational, preferences. The preferences can be shown to be irrational because the people holding them cannot convincingly explain how their welfare is improved by making such choices. To the "rational" observer, other choices look more sensible. Look at the "irrational" Indian custom of worshiping cows, for instance. While people starve, cows which serve no productive purpose are allowed to wander anywhere, eating large quantities of scarce food. This behavior must be due to an irrational custom, the theory would say, because it is not rational to let people starve. Or look at the example in this chapter of the "irrational" Japanese fishing villagers who rejected the rational advice of others that they ought to sue the chemical company. Saying that Japanese custom prevents the development of law is saying that Japanese people *en masse* make "irrational sacrifices" of their own self-interest because they do not want to suffer the shame that comes with violating custom. Were they rational, they would seek every cent of compensation, every iota of money owed them, every right guaranteed them. Of course, if they did this, the effect of their actions would ultimately be the growth of a more highly developed legal system.

Likewise, to say that Indian peasants flocked to the courts because public disputing was customary (Cohn, 1959, 1961) is to say that it would often have been in their interests to stay out of court. Advocates of theories based on custom have pointed out that Indian lawsuits have often wiped out the fortunes of families "dragged into court." If, as researchers assumed, lawsuits cost families far more than they could possibly recover even if they won their suits, then the behavior would have to be described as being shaped by irrational customs. How could such behavior be thought rational?

Much of early anthropology consisted of recording "odd customs" and marveling that people could be so blind to the unreasonableness of their ways. Later, however, customs took on a more rational appearance when systematic research began showing how customs fit together to give a society the coherence it needed to survive. People might not understand how their customs contributed to their group's well-being. They acted as they did because they "had always done it that way." In that sense, their behavior could still be called irrational. But the anthropologist's broader view, based on a kind of social Darwinism, could grasp the survival value of customs integrated into a group-based world view. The inherent irrationality becomes a liability when the group's environment changes, rendering traditions obsolete. Irrationality impedes the development of appropriate new responses.

In its purest form, then, the theory that law originates in custom depends on one's acceptance, as an article of faith, that a society's law and legal system looks the way it does because its people are "inscrutable," wedded to unique customs which we can describe but not explain as rational. Japanese law is what it is, following this reasoning, because Japanese people act Japanese. This, of course, does not explain why Japanese law differs from law in other industrialized societies. It is just another way of saying that it does. If we leave our attempts to understand the origins of law at this level, we are forced to abandon the use of comparisons between different societies as evidence, because the differences we find have no meaning beyond the raw fact that societies differ. We would have abandoned the attempt to explain why they differ by agreeing that irrationality neither demands nor supports further explanation.

In the two chapters which follow, we will see how other students of law in society make use of the comparisons between societies. We will see that they insist on going beyond the raw facts of behavior differences in search of the reasons for those differences. And we will see that because they do so, their work produces rival answers to the basic question which introduced this chapter: "What are the origins of law?"

CONCLUSION

Our inquiry into the origins of law as a feature of societies around the world is based on rejection of the commonsense belief that humans are by nature aggressive and contentious and therefore in need of regulation. We adopt the position that it is no more natural to have laws, lawyers, courts, and police all around us than it is to have locks on doors, flush toilets, a two-party political system, or Monday night football. If some people can live without all the trappings of what we call law, why can't we? What do we gain from it all? By what process did the present system come into existence?

When we reject "human nature" as an explanation, we are making a choice. We are rejecting one possible definition of law, namely that law is "any system of control which restricts and channels human instincts for aggression and conflict." Sociology of law has not explored that approach because it seems unable to illuminate the very differences between legal systems which social scientists seek to understand. If human nature is so monolithically aggressive and competitive, why have different groups in human history produced such widely differing ways of "doing law"? Why, in fact, do some observers come to the conclusion that many human groups have no law whatsoever?

A group's customs are taught by one generation to the next. How particular customs come into existence is a subject for research and sometimes multiple rival explanations. One kind of explanation, *structural-functionalism,* will be our main concern in the next chapter. But it is important to understand the difference between explaining behaviors as the product of custom and explaining custom as the product of some prior process such as social structure. Custom, as a theory of behavior, differs from all other sociological theories because it depicts people as programmed carriers of demonstrably irrational cultural lessons which restrain their ability and willingness to adopt "progressive" changes. The only thing "sensible" about custom (and it is an important antidote to the image of irrationality) is that when enough people follow it, the group they belong to may have a better chance of survival in a stable environment than when everyone pursues only his or her own self-interest.

What is true of customary theories in general is true of custom seen as the root of law. The most practical implication of the theories presented in this chapter is that lawmakers must keep themselves carefully attuned to "grass roots" opinion and practice lest they make laws which run against the grain of society's customs. This is a very democratic position, because it implicitly denies that the power to make and enforce laws can be successfully separated from the general public which must decide whether or not to obey. Where custom becomes transformed into law, the lawmakers and enforcers are seen as fellow passengers on a spaceship with an automatic guidance system: The gyroscopes of custom will pull the ship back on course no matter how hard individual tyrants or groups of politicians try to alter its course.

The threats to this theory lie in a cluster of assumptions and circular reasoning: (1) the necessary assumption that the primary evidence for a people's customs must be found in what they say when explaining their actions; (2) the false assumption that because behaviors and institutions differ between two societies, those two groups must have different customs (as measured by what they say); and (3) the resulting circular logic of trying to explain behaviors and institutions with a concept (custom) which users carelessly define as including the behaviors and institutions they are trying to explain.

Social scientists who have developed the theory of custom as the source of law rely heavily on careful records of people's explanations and justifications for their actions. Like all social researchers, they face the problem of reconciling apparent contradictions between people's actions and their words. Saying that this method flirts with the trap of circular reasoning does not mean that people's words should be ignored when we conduct research on their legal practices. But it does mean that we need a theory which can explain the relationship between their words and their actions without becoming circular. Both *structural-functionalism* and *conflict theory* (explained in the next two chapters) try to make that connection.

APPLYING WHAT YOU KNOW

When judges in American and English courts are faced with cases where the stated laws are not completely appropriate, they may call upon a doctrine of rationality to help them decide. The "reasonable man doctrine" gives the judge leeway in applying laws which might otherwise produce injustice. The "reasonable man" is an abstraction. It consists of the judge's notions about how a normal person in society ought to think when faced with dilemmas or choices which might have legal consequences.

For example, suppose you are taking a test and in the middle of it your professor sees that you have placed your answer sheet in plain view of another student. Since you are an outstanding student and the other student is on the verge of flunking, your professor accuses you of helping the other student. You both fail.

Assuming that you know you were not trying to help the other student, you appeal. In your hearing, the judge finds you guilty even though there is no specific rule saying that you must not allow your answer sheet to be placed where it was. You are presumed guilty because, says the judge, any "reasonable student" should know that, given the academic pressures on students and the rewards to be gained from cheating, putting a probably correct answer sheet where it could be seen invites cheating. In other words, the judge calls on the "reasonable man doctrine" to fill in for the lack of exact proscription in the rules.

This doctrine has received careful attention from legal theorists and has been considered a distinguishing feature of Anglo-American legal tradition. So it was with surprise and delight that the legally trained anthropologist Max Gluckman suddenly recognized the "reasonable man" in the opinions of tribal judges in Africa (1963). His first discovery of this reasoning among the Barotse led him to search for, and find, similar principles of justice in many other settings.

His conclusion that the same legal doctrine can be found in two entirely different societies raises interesting questions relative to the material we have examined in this chapter. Suppose that you are the anthropologist and that you record a trial in which a man is accused of murder. The only evidence introduced is the fact that the man allowed the victim's prayer beads to fall into a fire. As "everyone knows" in this tribe, the burning of prayer beads destroys a man's will to live. So allowing the beads to burn was equivalent to letting the man drown. When a tree branch later fell and killed the victim, the murder was complete even though the murderer was visiting another village at the time.

You find, therefore, that the judge condemns the accused murderer because he assumes that the accused is a normal "reasonable" member of the tribe. He should "know" that his actions would cause a tree branch to fall and kill the victim. Therefore he is guilty.

I have deliberately chosen an example in which I assume that you will find such thinking "unreasonable." You probably would reject the connection between prayer-bead burning and tree-branch falling as superstition. But is the judge's conclusion a "reasonable" one? If you assume the truth of the kinds of beliefs which are customary in the tribe, then the judge's decision does come to resemble the American judge's reliance on the "reasonable man doctrine." Gluckman did not mean to say that he accepted all of the beliefs of different African tribes as reasonable in the sense of being believable. But he did hold that the acts of judges working within those belief systems had the same basis in reason as the decisions of good English judges.

How can a judge's decision be both reasonable and unreasonable at the same time? Relate this question to our discussion of the relationship between custom and irrationality. Where do we place Gluckman's conclusion that the "reasonable man" is to be found in a wide variety of societies with divergent customs? How does the "reasonable man" relate to the social scientist's attempt to use custom as an explanation for the origins of law? Whose customs are operating when a judge invokes the "reasonable man" to decide a case?

REFERENCES

BECKER, HOWARD S.   (1963), *Outsiders*, New York: Free Press.

BOHANNAN, PAUL   (1965), The Differing Realms of Law, *The Ethnography of Law*. Supplement to *The American Anthropologist*, 67, Pt. 2, pp. 33–42.

CAMPBELL, D. AND ROSS, H. L.   (1968), The Connecticut Crackdown on Speeding, *Law and Society Review*, 3, p. 55.

COHN, BERNARD   (1961), From Indian Status to British Contract, *Journal of Economic History*, 21, p. 613.

COHN, BERNARD   (1959), Some Notes on Law and Change in North India, *Economic Development and Cultural Change*, 8, p. 79.

EHRLICH, EUGEN   (1936), *Fundamental Principles of the Sociology of Law* (W. Moll, Transl.) Cambridge: Harvard University Press.

ERIKSON, KAI T.   (1976), *Everything in Its Path*, New York: Simon & Schuster.

HOEBEL, E. ADAMSON   (1954), *The Law of Primitive Man: A Study in Comparative Legal Dynamics*, Cambridge: Harvard University Press.

GLUCKMAN, MAX   (1963), *Order and Rebellion in Tribal Africa*, New York: Free Press.

KAWASHIMA, TAKEYOSHI   (1963), Dispute Resolution in Contemporary Japan, in A. T. von Mehren (ed.), *Law in Japan: The Legal Order of a Changing Society*, Cambridge: Harvard University Press, p. 41.

KIDDER, ROBERT   (1973), Courts and Conflict in an Indian City: A Study in Legal Impact, *Journal of Commonwealth Political Studies*, 11, p. 121.

LOBENTHAL, JOSEPH   (1970), *Power and Put-On: The Law in America*, New York: Outerbridge and Dientsfrey.

MACAULAY, STEWART   (1963), Non-Contractual Relations in Business, *American Sociological Review*, 28, p. 55.

MASSELL, GREGORY   (1968), Law as an Instrument of Revolutionary Change in a Traditional Milieu: The Case of Soviet Central Asia, *Law and Society Review*, 2, p. 178.

MENDELSOHN, OLIVER   (1981), The Pathology of the Indian Legal System, *Modern Asian Studies*, 15, p. 823.

ORWELL, GEORGE   (1950), Shooting an Elephant, in Walter Blair and John Gerber (eds.), *Repertory*, New York: Harcourt Brace Jovanovich.

ROSS, H. LAWRENCE   (1970), *Settled Out of Court: The Social Process of Insurance Claims Adjustment*, Chicago: Aldine.

SCHWARTZ, RICHARD AND SKOLNICK, JEROME   (1970), *Society and the Legal Order* New York: Basic Books.

SMITH, W. EUGENE AND SMITH, AILEEN   (1975), *Minamata*, New York: Holt, Rinehart & Winston.

SUMNER, WILLIAM G.   (1906), *Folkways: A Study of the Sociological Importance of Usages, Manners, Customs, Mores, and Morals*, Boston: Ginn.

UPHAM, FRANK   (1976), Litigation and Moral Consciousness in Japan: An Interpretive Analysis of Four Japanese Pollution Suits, *Law and Society Review*, 10, p. 579.

4

THE ORIGINS OF LAW: STRUCTURE

In the previous chapter we looked at law as an outgrowth of custom. Keep in mind that this perspective is one of several explanatory traditions in the social sciences and, like any such tradition, it is an overview which tries to make sense of all we have learned, both through systematic research and casual observation, about law. Also, like any tradition, it has its supporters and detractors, its strengths and weaknesses.

One of the strengths of the theory that law grows out of custom is that it brings out some of the weaknesses in those philosophical theories which ignore the social origins of law. For example, it directly challenges the *natural-law* theories which hold that laws either come directly from the word of God or are inevitable rules made in harmony with the nature of things. It also challenges the belief that might makes right, or in other words that laws and law systems are simply the creations of those with power in society. And it strongly criticizes the belief of some legal scholars that laws are inevitable conclusions reached through the process of reasoning and pure logic. Each of these alternatives is a belief system about law which does not stand up well when submitted to careful research, especially research comparing law systems in different societies.

But we also saw in the previous chapter that custom-based theories by themselves have several problems. While they try to locate law's origins in social facts, they leave many unanswered questions and unexplained negative evidence.

An alternative sociological orientation has been applied to this question of law's origins, and the answers from it often contradict those based on custom alone. In this chapter we will be considering the origins of law as seen from the perspective of *social structure,* the analysis of society as a system with systematically structured needs for the preservation of organized activity.

Structural explanations for the origins of law and legal system claim that legal forms are the result of the *structure of relationships* existing in the larger society and within the legal system itself. This means that patterns of exchange, differences in power and wealth (especially the way in which people from different ranks relate to each other) methods of production and distribution, and organizational relationships among institutions other than law all contribute to the kind of legal system a society has. As the structuralist sees it, society is like a complex engine or a biological organism. Its parts are all interrelated, interdependent. Failure of one may produce decay or destruction of others. If one part fails, it must either be repaired or replaced by some other part which will accomplish the same vital task. People acting out their roles within society's many different institutions are the interchangeable parts or cells with which the organism maintains itself.

What does all this mean when applied to real cases? Later in this chapter we will try applying structural analysis to some of the cases presented in chapter 3. We will also discuss the frequently made argument that structure and custom are compatible ingredients in a single perspective. But let's start with some straightforward structuralist examples.

EARLY STRUCTURALISM: SPECIALIZATION AND POPULATION GROWTH

A classic example of structuralism is Durkheim's claim that modern legal systems are an inevitable result of the *division of labor* (1893, 1933). Durkheim argued that society is only possible if certain mechanisms are created and maintained to keep people together and cooperating. As he said, society is a fragile creation, constantly threatened with disintegration by forces within and outside itself. Societies differ according to the kinds of challenges they face to the preservation of solidarity.

The biggest difference is between ancient and modern societies. In ancient times, societies were simple collections of people who shared living spaces and worked side by side at identical tasks (such as hunting, fishing, or gathering roots and berries). Social order under these conditions could be preserved by "mechanical solidarity." Since everyone knew every other member of the society and worked at the same tasks in the same places, each member learned the rules, the customs, the "law" of the group by simply absorbing the everyday actions of fellow members. There was no need for courts, lawyers, judges, or other legal forms because whenever a rule or custom was violated, the whole group would immediately know about it and act to avenge it. *Revenge,* said Durkheim, was the primary goal of primitive law. Violations of custom threatened the "sacred" order of the group. Gods might be angered by rulebreaking, and angry gods could be a threat to the whole group, not just the offender. To rectify the sacrilege, the violator was made to suffer.

Law was simple in such societies because the structure of relationships was simple. Since everyone did the same work, shared the same experiences, and knew everyone else, their law could be simple, swift, and direct.

Why did things change? Why can't we get along now with the same kind of law? Are we so "civilized" now that revenge is an emotion we no longer feel? That seems unlikely if we consider the popular call for law and order and a return to the good old days when justice was "swift and firm."

Durkheim said that *population growth* created a crisis of social solidarity which led to the kind of law we now think of as normal. As populations grew, existing resources and ways of using them became inadequate. Land became scarce, food and water supplies could not keep pace, and the materials for making the tools of survival began to run low. To compensate, people began to *specialize* in the kind of work they did. Like biological organisms seeking new, unoccupied niches for survival in a crowded ecosystem, people worked out specialties which took them out of the competition for overused facilities or resources. By specializing, they could produce needed objects or services more efficiently. *Efficiency* and *reduced competition* compensated for the survival problems which had arisen because of overcrowding. Durkheim called this increasing practice of specialization the *divison of labor.*

But specialization forced changes in the way other things got done. First, it reduced the degree to which all members of society shared the same experiences. A basket maker might come to see the world as a set of problems surrounding the search for materials, techniques for preparing them, and ways to sell them. A barber in the same society would have a very different daily routine, working always in the presence of men, for example, rather than alone or with women, and depending not on knowledge of nature (to find good reeds for baskets, for example) but knowledge of people for success.

Durkheim held that these differing daily routines created by the division of labor led to differing beliefs, values, and interests and therefore to a diversity of norms. With increasing diversity of experience, norms became less sacred. The barber just could not get as excited about a crime committed against a basket maker, unless it happened to be the kind of crime which could happen to anyone. It was no longer like in the old days of mechanical solidarity where every member of society would feel threatened by any norm violation because everyone was in the same position as everyone else. Declining consensus about norms pushed societies in the direction of justifying norms as "practical" rather than righteous. The sanctity of law became difficult to sustain.

As this desanctification of "law" progressed, the functions of law changed. The needs of people in newer, more differentiated societies were not for revenge in defense of the sacred. Rather, economic specialization, the division of labor, created a new need for *coordination,* management. Without coordination of the various specialties, none of them could survive. This is obvious today in such operations as an auto factory. The subcontractor who produces plastic turn-signal lenses goes out of business unless General Motors regularly buys them. General Motors comes to a halt if the subcontractor falls behind in production. Both of them depend on the trucking contractor and the teamsters' union to make sure that the lenses get to the assembly plant on time. The law of contract monitors these mutually dependent relationships so that the chains of interdependence do not break. Also, the law of contract emphasizes agreement and performance on a practical basis, rather than revenge. To Durkheim, contract law typified all that is different between modern and ancient law.

In modern society, then, group solidarity is preserved by the *differences* between people. Where ancient society could have mechanical solidarity because everyone was the *same,* modern society had to develop *organic solidarity,* a new type of social cement which worked because of the *differences* created by the division of labor. Law developed as a means of preserving organic solidarity. To be effective it must abandon ancient demands for revenge, repression, and strict control. Instead, it must work to coordinate interdependent relationships, either by providing efficient ways of reestablishing relationships that had been disrupted by dispute or norm violation, or by developing mechanisms to prevent disruption and dispute from happening.

So, in place of the *repressive law* typical of ancient or primitive societies, we now have *restitutive law,* or law which functions to repair disrupted relationships, to maintain organic solidarity. (Later structuralists have concluded that Durkheim, working with inadequate information, got his analysis backward [Schwartz and Miller, 1964]. Most later anthropological evidence supports the view that primitive or early societies relied mostly on restitutive law, while repressive law has appeared only in modern, more complex societies.) We find restitutive law dominating the time and attention of our legal system. We see it in contract law; the law of torts (e.g., laws concerning who shall pay in the event of personal injuries); labor law; laws about patents, copyrights, libel and slander; constitutional law; and the historical trend toward the separation between civil and criminal law. Accompanying the increased complexity of society, we have increasingly complex legal institutions. Their complexity is created by the need for efficient maintenance of "organic" harmony.

Notice how this theory differs from explanations based on custom. The legal systems of ancient societies with mechanical solidarity did have automatically enforced customs. But modern law could not be predicted from those customs. People were forced by the pressure of survival problems to abandon those customs in favor of a more efficient system. Within our own smaller groups in modern society we can still experience mechanical solidarity based on repressive "law." A college fraternity, for example, may inflict swift, repressive justice on a deviating member. But most such groups give us only partial support. We cannot count on them for our survival. We need ways of cooperating with others whose customs may be very different from our own.

In our society, for example, business tycoons, athletes, authors, and politicians must depend on truck drivers whose language and habits may be "unacceptable" at the country club. Similarly, the career of a wild, free-spirited rock superstar may rise or fall on the decisions of business-minded managers and order-loving computer specialists. So, we reserve our customs for use within the small groups we belong to. At the same time, we give allegiance to, and count on the support of, the more remote, but efficient, restitutive law of the state. State law, and the particular devices used for applying it, cannot be just an elaboration of our group customs because too many *competing customs* exist. Instead, our law is formed around the need to reconcile diverse customs and interests.

A variation on Durkheim's structural theory can be seen in Simmel's discussion of the origins of law. *Simmel* (1893, 1955; 1903), like others, saw custom as an earlier method of social control which gives way to law. Like Durkheim, Simmel saw *population pressure* as the chief force leading to the move from custom to law. But unlike Durkheim, Simmel considered the process to be a simple question of numbers. Wherever large groups are in need of coordination, according to Simmel, law is the only means of maintaining control, because custom controls by the pressure of public opinion, which loses its effectiveness in large groups. It fails for very simple, pragmatic reasons. Where large numbers are involved, communication is slower and less complete, people cannot know or recognize all other members of the group, and where a task must be done by the group, it becomes numerically impossible for all members to participate in the decision making and direction of the task's execution. Given these problems, large social units are more likely to have formal legal systems operating in place of custom.

ELEMENTS OF MODERN
STRUCTURALISM

Structuralism has developed a substantial list of revisions and additions to the first efforts of the classic theorists. Some of these later developments build on the early theories, using more sophisticated methods for testing structuralist propositions. Others extend the structuralist mode of thought to accommodate the more accurate and detailed information gathered by anthropologists.

In this section, we will sample some of the issues which modern structuralists have addressed. As you will see, while they can all be classified as users of structural analysis, their conclusions are sometimes at odds. Structuralism is a large umbrella sheltering people with a wide variety of sometimes conflicting interpretations.

Interaction Density

Durkheim and Simmel's early structuralism has stimulated more recent attempts to sharpen and elaborate the prediction that population size leads to legal formalization. One effect of population increase is an increase in the "density of interaction" (Mayhew, et al., 1976a, 1976b, 1972). To understand what this means, think of a cocktail party. Let's say that it begins with just two people, a host and hostess, before the other guests arrive. At this moment all interaction takes place between the two of them. When a third person arrives, the possibilities for interaction multiply rapidly. Now there can be interaction between host and guest, hostess and guest, host and hostess, and between any two of them interacting as a pair with the third. When the fourth person enters, the multiplication effect becomes even more pronounced. Of course, by the time the party is in full swing, the density of interaction will have taken a giant leap from its modest beginnings. If you think of each possible interaction as a two-way arrow between actors, "interaction density" means the number of such arrows you could draw for a given situation. If we assume that any one of those interactions holds the potential for both cooperation and conflict, we can see that as our cocktail party grows from, let's say, two to thirty people, the potential for cooperation and conflict rises from one (the arrow between host and hostess) to a number much larger than thirty. For any number of people, the number of arrows or the density of interaction can be calculated by a simple mathematical formula.

Since this potential for cooperation and conflict rises so much more rapidly than the population itself (in mathematical language, population is an arithmetic function while interaction density is a geometric function), population growth produces an accelerated need for administrative coordination if there is any task the group must get done. The more people there are, the harder it becomes for any of them to keep informed about who each member is, what each one is doing, how each one feels about other members, the group, and the group's actions. So there is a growing need for coordinators—administrators who do nothing but furnish the integration which has been threatened by increasing population. This reasoning leads to the prediction that the number of administrators in a given social unit will increase *more rapidly* than the population of the unit itself, and that the *rate* of increase in administration can be precisely calculated as a mathematical function of interaction density.

Research on various organizations bears out this prediction, showing that the numbers of administrative personnel can be predicted quite precisely from a logarithmic function based on this interaction density model. That is why, for example, a large university has a *greater percentage* (not just a larger number) of administrators and a budget more heavily weighted toward administration than does a small college, even though both institutions do the same job.

The most important point for our discussion here is that much of this administrative work is what we have come to call *law*. If we assume that legal institutions exist as a means of coordinating the diverse actions and purposes of people in society, the interaction density model predicts that legal institutions will grow more rapidly than the society's population. A study of the American legal profession found that it had in fact outstripped the rate of American population growth (Meyers, 1975). More important, however, is the almost perfect fit between the actual rate of increase in numbers of lawyers and the rate predicted from the interaction density model. These results fit with Mayhew and Levinger's demonstration that violent crime in the United States also increases at a predictable rate that is faster than the rise in population.

Notice how thoroughly irrelevant the issue of society's customs is to this discussion. To the militant structuralist it does not matter what the society's customs may be. If its population increases, it will have no alternative but to create mechanisms to coordinate the increasing diversity which goes with growth. Those mechanisms are law or other activities which augment law as social coordinator (such as dictatorship, psychiatry, religion, mandatory school attendance, or organized sports).

To summarize the structural position as described so far, there are certain hard realities facing any collective activity, whether it be a university, a little-league organization, a city, or a nation. These realities are the numerical limits on our ability to interact with other members of the group, time limits on our ability to communicate, and limits on our capacity to process information about other people (just imagine trying to remember the names of each of the thousands of citizens who write suggestions and complaints to the White House each week). Our organized activity, if it is to be protected from chaotic directionlessness, must reflect these hard realities. So, as populations in need of coordination become larger, the demand for *law* in place of custom as a type of coordinating tool increases.

Before we proceed, you should be warned that interaction density theory is, like many theories in economics, based on the assumption of *ceteris parabus*. That is, it predicts that population growth will increase the size and formality of legal institutions *unless* the society manages to invent alternatives to accomplish the same task. This escape clause is a structuralist's way of handling evidence that populations of similar size (e.g., the United States and Japan) may differ drastically in the size of their legal institutions. If people can organize their collective activities in alternate ways, they may be able to avoid the disorganizing effects of population growth without resorting to law. Can you see why this escape clause opens the door for advocates of custom as the basis of law?

Collective vs. Private Ownership

The *ceteris parabus* disclaimer in the previous paragraph takes on added importance when we find two groups with similar population size but different levels of legal development. One set of factors which can modify the effects of population size involves the way in which property ownership and productive labor are organized. These factors were discovered in a study of two communal settlements in Israel in the early 1950s (Schwartz, 1964).

One of the communities was a *kibbutz* in which everything was shared on an egalitarian basis. Members lived in community-owned housing, dined together in communal dining rooms, treated all possessions as belonging to everyone, used communal bathing and toilet facilities, and placed their children in communal nurseries and schools where all children were raised by community teachers and nurses. Most important, all work was shared by all members. The farming and maintenance jobs were rotated so that everyone had the experience of working at all jobs (remember what Durkheim [pp. 60–62] said about the effects of shared labor).

The other community was a *moshav*. Here the land was owned communally, and much of the farm machinery was also shared. But the crops were grown privately, each family working its own separate land and prospering or failing according to its own actions. In addition, living arrangements were private. Each family had its own separate house, often set quite far from other farms, and meals and child rearing were private family responsibilities. Household items and luxuries were private property.

Aside from these differences, the two communities were very similar. Both were founded by Eastern European settlers in 1921. Both shared similar allegiances to Israeli political parties. Both were engaged in raising the same kinds of crops on about the same amount of land with the *same size populations.* Given these similarities, Durkheim and Simmel would both probably agree that law in both communities should be very similar.

But it was not. The moshav developed a *formal* legal system while the kibbutz did not. The formal law which developed on the moshav was centered around its *judicial committee,* a separately constituted permanent committee charged with enforcing the community's rules. It had the power to hear complaints by members against each other and to enforce rulings by invoking community-approved sanctions. It operated according to written procedures and enforced a set of written rules. No such committee or set of rules and procedures existed on the kibbutz. Such differences are the cause of our basic question: What is the source of legal development?

The structuralist looking at these differences finds an answer in the differences of organizational structure between the two communes. Because the moshav treated the *family* (rather than the commune as a whole) as the unit of production, domestic care, and child rearing, it was forced to develop legal formalities which the kibbutz *did not need.*

Life on the kibbutz showed what the moshav had sacrificed for family privacy and individualism. Because of the intense daily contact with all other kibbutz members, no one could stray far from group norms without immediate, direct, personal sanctions from other members. Since kibbutz life meant always working and sharing with others, each member could be subjected to a rich variety of subtle and not-so-subtle scoldings and punishments. Ridicule, a raised eyebrow, public criticism, "the silent treatment," denial of small informal personal privileges, and reduced cooperation on work projects could all make life miserable for a nonconformist. No special committee was needed for these actions. Only the least sensitive person could fail to comprehend the rules which the group shared, even though they were never written down or even formally articulated.

On the moshav, by contrast, the daily routine was with family. Contact with other members was less frequent since each family was practically self-sufficient. So it was possible for moshav members to develop their own interpretation of community rules without knowing whether others shared their interpretation. Behavior of doubtful legitimacy could pass unnoticed by other members. Rule violations could go undetected for longer stretches and the identity of offenders could be disputed. It also became possible for dissidents, because of their self-sufficiency and seclusion, to ignore public opinion without suffering round-the-clock hostility from everyone in the community.

None of these forms of dissidence and deviance could develop or fester in the glare of shared activity on the kibbutz. In the rare case where the kibbutz endured the persistent misbehavior of a dissident, the problem lasted only because that person had the rare capacity to withstand a withering blast of continuous face-to-face criticism and defamation.

A formal judicial committee with written rules was created in the moshav because its system of private ownership and enterprise made informal methods weak. The kibbutz, like the moshav in most other respects, had a system of organization which made formal law unnecessary. Structuralism says that the legal form of the moshav was made necessary by the need for coordination of a more complex social form which lacked the means to maintain social control more simply. As in most structural theories, the evidence here is used to show that facts of structural organization made the birth and growth of formal law necessary. Moshav custom did not differ greatly from custom on the kibbutz when the two communes were started. But the interconnectedness of organizational characteristics made law on the moshav inevitable. Notice that while this is a structuralist analysis, the results indicate a weakness in those structuralist theories which treat population pressure as the primary cause of law. Remember that the populations of both communes were the same.

This analysis also directly challenges the view that law is a restatement of customs. The moshav's judicial committee actually had to establish community norms because the organization of the community hobbled the development of custom. However, the two kinds of analysis do converge in their agreement that the formality of law becomes necessary when informal custom cannot cope with social disorder.

Perhaps, as you read this, you have already noticed that the narrowly based research results on two Israeli settlements can be extended to broader predictions. If private initiative and ownership produce a need for law in the moshav, perhaps there is a more general rule that systems organized around private initiative and enterprise have a greater need for law than those which emphasize local collective organization, such as in Japan, China, or the Soviet Union. Perhaps this is why the legal establishment in the United States is so much larger than in those more collectivized societies. Such a conclusion may be premature and oversimplified, but it shows the kind of direction in which your thinking might point if you adopt the structuralist perspective.

Levels of Societal Complexity

One aspect of structure which has fascinated social scientists because of its effects on many important institutions is the degree of *complexity* found in different societies. Structuralists see history as a series of developments which increase the levels of complexity in societies around the world. Our world today, with its complex system of industrial production and mass marketing, with our use of insurance, large governmental bureaucracies, mass communication, and high-speed transportation has more *complexity* (in the sense of more intricate linkages between a larger variety of social activities and structures) than ever faced the members of an Amazon rain forest tribe. Societies with money, written language, job specialization, and private property are considered more complex than those without (Schwartz and Miller, 1964). Structuralists usually treat the growth of societal complexity as a process of evolution (e.g., see Lenski and Lenski, 1970). In this sense, they see human societies similarly to the way biologists view more complex organisms as later, more sophisticated developments from simpler plants or animals. Like animals and plants, social complexity is seen as the result of adaptation to a changing environment.

Structuralists apply this kind of reasoning to the growth of law, linking it to the growth of structural complexity in other areas of social life. One way to do this is to compare societies at different stages of development. In one study of sixty-five societies around the world three legal forms (mediation, police, and lawyers) were found to develop in a predictable sequence as societies become increasingly complex (Schwartz and Miller, 1964). The simplest societies have none of these legal forms. They seem to operate like the kibbutz without any separate control mechanisms. Those with somewhat more complexity have *mediation only*. By mediation, we mean the use of some third party who helps to maintain communication between two disputants so that they can find some common ground for resolving their dispute. The next level of complexity typically combined *mediation* with some kind of *police force*. And the level above that in complexity had all three legal forms: *mediation, police* and *lawyers*. Most important for structuralist theory was that no society had just police or just lawyers without the "earlier" legal forms. Societies seem to be forced by some *structural imperative* to develop legal forms in a limited sequence from earlier to later forms.

To structuralists, this result supports an evolutionary theory about legal development in general. The theory is that legal characteristics develop cumulatively *in a particular order* because they are created by problems arising from growing societal complexity. In simple societies, no law is needed. Slight increases in complexity create a need for mediation. Then comes a need for police, and finally lawyers become necessary. Each step is a response to the inadequacy of previous arrangements. The inadequacy is created by increasing complexity.

Form vs. Function

So far in this chapter we have examined those structural conditions which are said to produce development of or variation in legal forms. But we need to remember that although two societies may have similar legal forms, such as a particular type of court or police force, they may make very different uses of those forms. One society may use police as a domestic intelligence network to prevent political opposition, while another may use police mostly as guardians of property. A divorce court in New York City may serve as a rubber stamp for requested divorces, while a court with the same title in a small town in western New York may act as marriage counselor and mediator in attempts to ward off final divorce. A small-claims court in Chicago may serve primarily as a collection agency for businessmen who use it routinely, while a downstate small-claims court may operate mainly in service to ordinary people seeking swift, inexpensive solutions to small but annoying disputes (see, for example, Yngvesson and Hennessey, 1975).

So, in asking our basic question—what are the origins of law—we need to recognize that law is a process of interaction between formal institutions and practices on the one hand and the responses of people to those formalities on the other. Our question then becomes What determines the form of the relationship between formal institutions and the people they are meant to control?

Evidence from Mexico (Nader and Metzger, 1963) directly illustrates part of the contention that population pressure alters the type of law operating in society. At the same time, this evidence demonstrates the application of structuralist analysis to a case where people use a single legal form in opposite ways. In two Mexican towns with the same system of community courts governed by the same formal state laws, the actual function of the courts was very different because of structural differences between the two towns.

In town A most family quarrels did not reach the courts. Husbands and wives tried to resolve their differences by appealing to family elders. The elders normally stepped in and exercised their authority to force both sides to settle. They imposed penalties and issued commands and were usually obeyed without question. The only disputes which ended up in court were those where reconciliation was considered impossible and the opponents wanted to use the publicity of court procedure to announce a separation of husband and wife and to impose restrictions on their search for new spouses.

Disputes in town B, by contrast, wound up in court whether disputants sought reconciliation or separation. Use of the court in town B was much more common than in town A because of structural conditions caused by population pressure. When a mine near town B closed around 1900, town B's population nearly doubled because mining families moved in to take up farming. This growth had three main effects on legal development there. First, it brought people to town who were separated from their extended families. While the elders of extended families in town A were the major deciders in domestic quarrels (grandfathers, senior uncles, and brothers were all present and could lend their weight to decisions made), town B immigrant families could not be directly monitored by such elders, so their disputes often had no family forum for resolution. Second, the *increased size* of town B brought it to the attention of state authorities and church leaders who became interested in increasing their influence there.

Both church and state campaigned to have town residents make their marriages both sacred and legal. Consequently, when marital disputes arose, church and state were immediately assumed to have an interest in the outcome. Town A, by contrast, basked in its isolation from such outside interference. Most of its marriages were neither consecrated nor legal. Because of its small, stagnant population, there was little outside pressure to change this.

Third, and most important, the population growth in town B increased the pressure on farmland. It became increasingly difficult for a family elder to offer his sons farmland adjacent to his own. Sons were forced to go farther afield to set up their own farms. The result was a reduction in the influence of the elders. They could no longer hold out attractive inheritances as an inducement for a son's obedience. Nor could they keep a close eye on the behavior of their offspring because the move to new and more distant farmlands removed them from easy view "right next door." This meant that disputes could become more intense, facts more debatable (who hit whom first, has the husband been habitually staying out late at night, are the children well-fed), and mutual insults more irreconcilable before other family members learned about them. As a result, family elders had reduced power to impose their rulings on rebellious offspring. The courts became an important alternative to disputants. Women could no longer count on fathers-in-law to force wayward sons back into line. So the authority of law increased as that of the elders decreased.

In this example, we see *population pressure* producing structures of family relationships which are more *privatized,* as in the Israeli moshav. The result is more actual reliance on formal legal institutions, as in the moshav. In theory, both towns had the same court system. But in practice the courts served very different functions in the two towns because of the structural differences created by the population growth in town B.

Multiplex vs. Simplex Relationships

Advocates of structural theories have found the distinction between *multiplex* and *simplex* relationships useful. *Simplex* relationships are those contacts people have with each other which occur for very limited, specific purposes (Gluckman 1969). When we have a simplex relationship with someone, we speak with him or her only about one topic, and we have no other reasons for interaction. Examples would be a customer getting movie tickets from a ticket seller, a person getting a telephone number from an operator, or a student taking a course from a professor. In each case, the interaction may involve only the practical business of completing the specific transaction.

Simplex relationships are efficient. When you want a quick lunch, you go to the fast-food counter and give your order. You don't ask how the waitress's mother is feeling after her operation, you don't pull out pictures of the wedding you attended, you don't discuss your tax returns and how much you should deduct for travel expenses, and you don't discuss the latest entries in the "Top Forty" listing of popular records. You know what people in the line behind you would say if you did talk about such things. You also keep silent because you probably don't know the waitress—you are strangers so the transaction is brief and limited. Because it is, the fast-food place can serve billions of hamburgers at lower cost and more rapidly than your friendly neighborhood delicatessen, where food is not necessarily the only link between you and the proprietors.

In contrast, think of a relationship you might have with Uncle Fred. Uncle Fred is either your maternal uncle or an avuncular friend in your neighborhood. You trust him as a reliable financial advisor, the holder of a mortgage on your home, a partner in a business venture with you, godfather of your oldest son, leader of the political party dominant in your neighborhood, your family doctor, and the person with whom you share valuable tickets to professional football games or ballet performances. On top of all that, he also runs the delicatessen where you go for refreshment.

By now, you may be thinking, "Yuchchch—who could stand being so tied up with one person? And besides, it's dangerous to mix so many relationships together." If you react this way, it is probably because *multiplex* relationships like this are not as common in modern society as they once were when all societies were less complex. For us today, living in a complex industralized society, *simplex* relationships are much more typical because most of the tasks done by people for each other have become specialized. Financial advising is one specialty, doctoring another, mortgage lending another. In simpler societies, such tasks are all intermingled with complex kinship ties. So people living in simpler societies are more likely to be involved in multiplex relationships.

How does this connect with law? The basic structuralist position is that *a decline in the frequency of multiplex relationships increases the necessity of using law for social control.* (see Black, 1976, pp. 41–48). Structuralists reason that multiplex relationships give people multiple sources of control over each other. If, for example, you had all those connections with Uncle Fred, then whenever a disagreement arose between you, or whenever either of you wanted to get the other person to do something, you could each gently remind the other of all the rewards stemming from your joint ventures. No other person could easily take the place of either you or Uncle Fred in the relationship, because you each occupy a special *combination* of positions in relation to the other. If you got into an argument over the mortgage, for example, your anger and urge to retaliate against Uncle Fred would be tempered by your recognition that overreaction could cost you your family doctor, entertainment partner, son's godfather, and favorable standing in the local political party.

Contrast that with the simplex relationships where, if disagreement arises, the limited nature of the relationship offers few resources for resolving the problem. Since there is only one narrow aspect of the relationship which matters to either side, disagreement can easily lead to the breakdown of the relationship. Where you or your uncle could call on mutual acquaintances from the church, the social club, the party, the family, or the neighborhood for support and understanding, people in simplex relationships have no allies except in the law. Law becomes the substitute for all those informal incentives which people can offer in multiplex relationships. Therefore, where social structure is dominated by simplex relationships, law becomes formalized and increasingly occupies a dominant position in society.

Functional Alternatives: Avoidance and "Lumping It"

Structuralism thus shows conditions which *could* produce legal development. But the theory also says that alternatives can arise in a society if they fulfill the same function as law. In simplex relationships, for example, disagreement can lead to "avoidance" or "lumping it" (as in the expression "like it or lump it") rather than law (Felstiner, 1974). Modern society is full of people who often just "lump it" when they feel cheated or wronged by others. Others often find it less costly (both economically and psychically) to simply walk away from a claim and avoid their opponents altogether. Such responses are less possible in multiplex relationships because to end a relationship over one issue would mean ending the relationships in all those other activities also shared. Since avoidance is too costly in disputes involving multiplex relationships, people in such relationships rely primarily on mutual acquaintances to bring peace. Hence, in simpler, poorer societies where multiplex relationships predominate, we find that mediation is widely relied upon for dispute settlement.

What about disputes in complex, rich societies like the United States? Here, where simplex relationships are the norm, we find ourselves forced to choose between suing or "lumping it." Simplex relationships do not put people into positions where they can be effective as mediators. Like the elders in Mexican town B who lost control over their families, we have all lost the interconnected means of influencing each other if a relationship hits a snag. So if we cannot afford to lump it when, for example, the landlord shuts off the heat during the winter to save money, our only recourse (aside from violence) is an adjudicated lawsuit where a judge uses impersonal rules and police enforcement to resolve a dispute which festers because less formal methods do not exist.

Structures of Conflict and Alliance

Another structuralist distinction which concerns the growth of law is that drawn between *factionalism* and *pluralism*. A comparison of a factionalized Lebanese town and a pluralistic Mexican village shows how the difference can produce major differences in legal structure (Nader, 1965).

In the Lebanese town, everyone belonged to either of two factions. The split between the two sides was almost complete. Members of faction A would not intermarry, trade, worship, or associate with anyone in faction B. Hostility did not always characterize their sharing of the town, but whenever a dispute arose between members of the two factions, there was no way to settle it within the town. If the dispute pitted two members of the same faction against each other, elders of the faction could usually intervene and resolve the problem. But no elder in town was trusted enough to resolve disputes between the factions, because every elder was identified as a faction member.

The result was that when, for example, a man from faction A was caught hiding a goat belonging to a man in faction B, the two sides appealed to influential politicians and judges *outside* the town to "fix" the problem for them. Their technique for "fixing" was to use either bribes or the demand for favors done on the basis of family ties. Whoever had more of this kind of influence usually won the case.

Contrast this dependence on outside "lawmakers" with the system of internal mediation maintained in a Mexican village. The key difference between the Lebanese and Mexican villages was that the Mexican village was not structured into two factions. Instead, its people had crosscutting or *pluralistic* ties to each other. Each individual had family ties with one group, religious ties that included some others, social ties including still others, age group and economic ties which involved even other villagers. The result was that each person had some regular interdependence, if not with everyone else in the village, then at least with groups including everyone else. As a result, disputes usually involved people who had existing ties between them which they wished to preserve. This pluralistic structure provided multiple sources of incentives to resolve disputes quickly and agreeably. So the Mexican village had developed no system of reliance on law outside its limits, as had the Lebanese village.

Pluralism is a structural feature related to multiplex relationships. Both terms refer to multiple linkages binding people together and providing them with the means and motives to resolve conflicts in a way which will preserve those relationships. But multiplexity and pluralism refer to different levels of structure in a community. Pluralism or factionalism refer to patterns of relationships *between groups*. Within those groups, we may find either simplex or multiplex relationships. In the Lebanese village, for example, members of faction A could handle their own disputes without external help because they had multiplex relationships among themselves. Factionalism cut them off from having such relationships with faction B members.

INEQUALITY, JUSTICE, AND LAW: STRUCTURAL ANALYSES

Up to this point we have discussed structure as though it consisted only of interrelationships between different social roles, held together by the need to respond to threatening environmental conditions. But structure has another meaning in sociology. To many sociologists, structure means first and foremost the differentiation of society into *unequal classes*. Structure means the organized pattern by which privilege, power, and wealth are unequally distributed. Sociologists with this perspective see the concepts of structure and law coming together in questions such as whether poor people receive equal treatment at the hands of legal authorities, or whether poor people have as much access to lawyers and courts as do wealthier citizens. Related to these theoretical questions are the more practical ones: What can be done to give poor people greater access to legal protection? Can law be used to help poor and powerless people gain a greater share of the wealth and power in society? How can the poor be protected from abuse at the hands of legal authorities?

Poverty and Access: Structures of Legal Need

One major question concerns *access*. American law has often been charged with ignoring the legal needs of the poor. High fees keep lawyers' services out of reach. Without access, poor people must therefore be experiencing the denial of justice.

Research on this question shows that the picture is more complicated. A survey of Detroit residents asked what kinds of people used lawyers most often and for what purposes (Mayhew and Reiss, 1969). As expected, poor people were less likely to use lawyers. But the reason was not that they could not afford to pay. Instead, poor people make less use of lawyers because their poverty keeps them from becoming involved in those activities where lawyers can be helpful. People most often use lawyers to deal with problems associated with private property ownership. The buying of a house is one example. Writing of wills is another. The legal profession is prepared to deal with property-related matters and is therefore of little use to people who cannot afford ownership.

The survey thus supports the argument that the structure of inequality in the United States produces different patterns of demand on the legal system. The kinds of problems poor people have do not receive the legal system's attention. Where such problems have been addressed, they generally do not make lawyers' services relevant.

Once again, then, we have the argument that structure determines legal forms. In this case, the structure of poverty and wealth are held to have produced legal forms which are preoccupied with problems of private property. This preoccupation in turn serves to perpetuate the irrelevance of the law to poor people.

Poverty and Access: Structured Advantages in Courts

In the Detroit study, we see one application of structural analysis in which structure means inequality. However, even among those who share this approach to the meaning of structure, there is disagreement over the interpretation of research results. For example, another interpretation of the Detroit data might emphasize the fact that poor people have certain distinct disadvantages when involved in lawsuits. The court process favors *repeat performers* over *one-shotters* (Galanter, 1974). *One-shotters* are people who hardly ever get involved in formal legal proceedings. If they do become involved, the intricacies of the system are a complete mystery to them. They do not know what to expect, whom to contact, or how to interpret what is happening around and to them. Even more important, their concern is only with the specific case which brought them to court. They don't care what happens to others with similar cases. They want only quick justice so they can get back to *normal* life (meaning life without legal entanglements).

Repeat performers play the law game very differently. For them, involvement in formal legal proceedings is part of normal living. Their activities and interests are such that they expect to have to deal with courts and lawyers regularly. One result is that they become much better informed about how things work in law and at court. They develop "inside" contacts among the many bureaucrats who operate the courts. They learn the special esoteric language of the law (see O'Barr and O'Barr, 1976) and are therefore not so easily intimidated by lawyers throwing around big words. Probably the most important contrast with the one-shotter is the repeat performer's *long-range perspective* on the significance of cases. No single case totally concerns the repeat performer, as it does the one-shotter. An insurance company, for example, deals with thousands of claims each year. In contesting any one of those claims, the company is less concerned with the money it will have to pay out than with the *legal precedents* which might be set by the case, or with the company's on-going relationships with court workers, judges, and lawyers with whom they must routinely deal year after year (see Ross, 1970). The company can afford to "lose" cases here and there if by doing so it preserves its long-term good reputation in the courts and if its actions preserve a pro-company set of legal precedents. To one-shotters with claims against the company, the lawsuit's outcome is all that matters because they are not trying to lay the groundwork for future legal action.

Repeat performers also have the advantage of being able to budget their resources for legal combat. Legal expenses do not come as a fiscal shock to their operations. They can adopt a cost-effectiveness attitude toward each case rather than the one-shotter's typical "all or nothing" pursuit of total victory. When repeat performers encounter a case with high potential for long-range damage or advantage, they can spend much more than the case is "worth" by itself. The Ford Motor Company, for instance, spent millions defending itself against a criminal liability charge that its Pinto automobiles had caused unnecessary deaths because of defectively designed fuel tanks. The legal fees were paid willingly because Ford executives knew that if they lost, they faced hundreds of similar claims which would rock the company's treasury. The one-shotter does not have this same incentive to spend beyond what the case might recover.

For all these structure-related reasons repeat performers have a strong competitive advantage over one-shotters. Since wealth is associated with being a repeat performer, the "haves" do usually win over the "have nots" in court. Poorer people, being more likely to be one-shotters, may be making a very sensible choice to avoid involvement with formal law. Against a seasoned landlord, for example, the inexperienced tenant suing in rent courts may have as much chance of success as a soldier told to fight a battle with a wooden sword.

Notice that this conclusion differs from one saying that poor people get less justice because "money buys justice" or because "might makes right." There is always the possibility that poor people or other one-shotters can become repeat performers and that wealthy people may find themselves in the position of one-shotters. Various native American tribes have recently become repeat performers through their on-going legal attempts to have ancient land right treaties enforced (see Medcalf, 1978). A large number of black homeowners in Chicago banded together and collectively overcame some of the disadvantages of one-shotter status by barraging the courts with challenges to the grossly overpriced and misconstrued home-buying contracts they had signed (see Fitzgerald, 1975). Wealthy families are sometimes impoverished when they become embroiled in lawsuits over the distribution of a dead relative's estate. While they may be sophisticated repeat performers in other areas of law, inheritance battles put them all in the one-shotter status. So wealth alone does not a repeat performer make. The advantage goes to anyone or any group whose structural position makes involvement in formal legal action a routine pattern.

STRUCTURE VS. CUSTOM:
COMPARING PREDICTIONS

I have argued throughout this chapter that structural theories on the origins of law make different assertions than we find in theories based on custom. Chapter 3 showed several of the custom-based explanations. Let's try applying structuralist reasoning to examples introduced in chapter 3.

Japanese Litigation

Recall the case of mercury poisoning in Minamata, Japan. Remember that the Minamata residents avoided legal action for years before any of them filed suit. The Niigata victims, in contrast, went immediately on the attack through law. So public and "unJapanese" was their reaction that they actually goaded some Minamata victims into joining them in litigation. We examined this case because the contrast between the two reactions throws doubt on the theory that antilitigious Japanese customs keep people away from legal institutions.

How would a structuralist approach the same case? One way to look at the two villages is to say that in one, Minamata, legal action was *not needed*, while in the other, Niigata, it was. This reasoning is like the structural explanations for differences between the two Israeli settlements and the two Mexican towns. In Minamata, the victims were all closely associated with the factory that caused the poisoning. Many worked for the company, while the rest were involved in a local economy which directly depended on the factory. Because their relationships with the company were close, both physically and socially, the differences between victims and the company could be managed through informal methods. Since most of the town's social services (schools, medical services, welfare, marriage halls, etc.) were provided by the company, victims were probably involved in multiplex relationships with some of the company's managers. Town-company relations, because they had years to develop before the tragedy, could adequately compensate for the disruption caused by the poisoning.

But in Niigata, no multiplex relationships existed between victims and offender before the poisoning. Since Niigata was forty miles from the offending factory, there were no preexisting ties which could be relied on to settle the disruption. Niigata had even less connection with the polluting factory than the Lebenese villagers in faction A had with their rivals, faction B. So the victims were left with no structural alternatives. Law was the only option.

If we must choose between customary theories and those based on social structure, this Japanese case seems to give greater support to structure as an explanation. Japanese custom would not predict the Niigata reaction. The contrast between Niigata's and Minamata's social structure might.

Muslims and Soviet Law

Chapter 3 also described two cases where custom appears to have defeated incompatible law. The Muslim reaction to Bolshevik legal reforms seems to support the theory that law arises successfully only out of custom, since it shows that law designed to change custom failed. But a structuralist would approach the case differently, perhaps emphasizing that the reforms actually did find favor with thousands of women, and that they did produce massive disruption in Muslim society. Why did the reforms ultimately fail? As a structuralist, you might argue that they failed because the Bolsheviks neglected to create adequate *structural alternatives* for the women who sought liberation. Muslim custom triumphed because in terms of social structure it was "the only game in town" for most women. Had there been adequate development of economic institutions which women could have used to support themselves without dependence on their male-dominated families, then Bolshevik legal reforms would have prevailed instead of becoming a false front for continued Muslim custom.

Colonial Law in British India

What about the British attempt to impose their law on India? Wasn't the distortion of the British legal process evidence of the force of Indian custom? As a structuralist, you might answer that the use of courts in India was a reflection of structural conditions in British-Indian colonial society. You might point out, for example, that the British did more than simply introduce a method for settling disputes. They forced people to think about land in ways that had not existed before (Mendelsohn, 1981). They required villages, for example, to clarify who owned which land, so that they could develop a systematic procedure for taxing the land. They declared certain village leaders landlords and made them responsible for collecting taxes from everyone else in the village. Prior to British rule, land ownership had been vague if not nonexistent. Land was used by peasants to grow their family's food. But it was not "owned" in the sense that one family could buy or sell a field. Use of land fluctuated according to family influence, size, and need. and control of land varied from one region to another.

As a result, when the British introduced the notion that land had to be owned, they precipitated a scramble for ownership and it was this scramble which flooded the courts with litigation. Because land-use relationships (structure) had been vague and unstable before the British came, Indian use of British courts and law became just another expression of this structural instability.

In other words, the British did not simply introduce a set of legal practices incompatible with Indian customs. They actually altered Indian social structure by changing the rules by which things got distributed, and by becoming a new element in that system of distribution. The vagueness and flexibility of Indian custom was not simply clarified when the British tried to give it legal force. The legalization of Indian custom was tailored to the needs of British administration as a powerful new element in Indian society. Indians found that they had no choice but to adjust their actions to this new element.

The British brought several changes which might also have contributed to structural change. Their railroads, highways, and telegraph system linked areas together which had previously developed in isolation. Their demand for raw materials (minerals, cotton, jute, tea, and spices) brought many areas of India into the colonial market economy where money (rather than barter) was the medium of exchange and where land began to be treated as a commodity with market value. India also became a huge market for the excess productivity of Britain. The economics of the colonial relationship were such that Britain depended on India as a market for British production.

Instead of saying that the Indians turned British courts into just another expression of Indian custom, the structuralist might say that what happened in those courts was a predictable product of new structures of economic, political, and social activity. Even though the British thought they were reinstitutionalizing Indian customs, their pervasive economic and political presence in India created structural changes which swept away the very customs they sought to enshrine in law.

SUMMARY

The structuralist explains law and legal forms as being the necessary result of the way a social unit is structured. Structuralists assume that, in order for the social unit to survive and operate, it must have regular ways of absorbing and defusing the structure-threatening danger of conflict. So, when structuralists compare different legal systems, they explain differences in their development of formal law as being the result of differences in social structures.

Where social and economic activity is structured in a way that creates frequent or interconnected reciprocal relationships which people expect to rely on in the future, law tends to be "underdeveloped," informal, mediational, or even nonexistent. Where specialization or other conditions isolate people, reduce or depersonalize their interdependence, or offer them a variety of new ways to pursue their goals, then conditions for informal maintenance of order are not good. In place of those informal methods, formal law develops.

If, in the development of formal law, there come to be patterns of inequality in its use or administration, the inequality is a direct result of inequalities in the society which produced that legal system. Even a legal system founded on principles of equal justice for all will operate with a bias in favor of those in society who are favored by higher positions in its structure. This bias will be explainable not as a simple extension of customary bias into the legal system, but as the result of the strategic advantages available to the "haves" from their positions in structures outside the legal system.

Structuralists may not agree with each other about particular explanations of law forms. They may differ over which structural features are relevant. They may produce conflicting theories about which combination of structural characteristics produces which type of legal form. But they agree that structure is the place to look for an explanation. They agree that explanations based on custom, on variations in culture between groups, are fundamentally misguided because they can ultimately be reduced to the uninteresting tautology that "people are different because they are different."

It would be misleading to portray social science as split into two unyielding factions, the structuralists and the advocates of custom. Many would argue that we need to consider both structure and culture in constructing a complete picture of any social system (e.g., see Simpson and Yinger, 1965, ch. 1). They say that unless custom and structure are compatible with each other, the social instability that results from incompatibility leads to changes that achieve compatibility. So, they say, in examining the rise of a phenomenon such as law, the only way to fully understand its origins is to understand the ways in which both custom and social structure contributed to it.

But purists who argue for structuralism hold that the study of custom can only show us how a given society does things, not why. They say that custom does not produce the pattern of interaction we see in a society, that custom is that pattern of interaction. So, they argue, we have to look beyond the pattern to find out why it exists and why it changes the way it does. When we look beyond the pattern, we find environmental conditions (such as population growth and changes in climate) and structures of organized reaction to those conditions. What pushes people to act in certain ways and build particular institutions is not just the momentum of custom but the fact that those customs help reinforce the ability of the group to cope with its environment.

As we will see in the next chapter, sructuralists find themselves now challenged by conflict theorists, who reject the fundamental assumption that law or any other social institution comes into existence because society needs it. Conflict theorists hold that this structuralist assumption puts them into the same bag of errors as the culture theorists.

REFERENCES

BLACK, DONALD   (1976), *The Behavior of Law,* New York: Academic Press.

DURKHEIM, EMIL   (1893, 1933), *The Division of Labor in Society,* New York: Free Press.

FELSTINER, WILLIAM   (1974), Influences of Social Organization on Dispute Processing, *Law and Society Review,* 9, p. 63.

FITZGERALD, JEFFREY   (1975), The Contract Buyers' League and the Courts: A Case Study of Poverty Litigation, *Law and Society Review* 9, p. 165.

GALANTER, MARC   (1974), Why the "Haves" Come Out Ahead, *Law and Society Review* 9, p. 95.

GLUCKMAN, MAX   (1969), Concepts in the Comparative Study of Tribal Law, in Laura Nader (ed.), *Law In Culture and Society,* Chicago: Aldine, p. 349.

LENSKI, GERHARD AND LENSKI, JEAN   (1970), *Human Societies: An Introduction to Macrosociology,* New York: McGraw-Hill.

MAYHEW, BRUCE AND LEVINGER, ROGER   (1976a), On the Emergence of Oligarchy in Human Interaction, *American Journal of Sociology,* 81, p. 1017.

MAYHEW, BRUCE AND LEVINGER, ROGER   (1976b), Size and the Density of Interaction in Human Aggregates, *American Journal of Sociology,* 82, p. 86.

MAYHEW, BRUCE; LEVINGER, ROGER; MCPHERSON, J. M.; AND JAMES, T. F.   (1972), System Size and Structural Differentiation in Formal Organizations, *American Sociological Review,* 37, p. 629.

MAYHEW, LEON, AND REISS, ALBERT   (1969), The Social Organization of Legal Contacts, *American Sociological Review,* 34, p. 309.

MEDCALF, LINDA   (1978), *Law and Identity: Lawyers, Native Americans, and Legal Practice,* Beverly Hills, Calif., Sage Publications, Inc.

MENDELSOHN, OLIVER   (1981), The Pathology of the Indian Legal System, *Modern Asian Studies,* 15, p. 823.

MEYERS, T. D.   (1975), *The Formalization of Interaction and the Distribution of Lawyers in American Society,* Doctoral Dissertation, Temple University, Dept. of Sociology.

NADER, LAURA   (1969), Styles of Court Procedure: To Make the Balance, in Laura Nader (ed.), *Law in Culture and Society,* Chicago; Aldine.

NADER, LAURA   (1965), Choices in Legal Procedure: Shia Moslem and Mexican Zapotec, *American Anthropologist,* 67, p. 394.

NADER, LAURA AND METZGER, DUANE   (1963), Conflict Resolution in Two Mexican Communities, *American Anthropologist,* 65, p. 584.

O'BARR, WILLIAM AND O'BARR, JEAN   (1976), *Language and Politics,* The Hague: Mouton.

ROSS, H. LAWRENCE   (1970), *Settled Out of Court: The Social Process of Insurance Claims Adjustment,* Chicago: Aldine.

SCHWARTZ, RICHARD   (1964), Social Factors in the Development of Legal Control: A Case Study of Two Israeli Settlements, *Yale Law Journal,* 63, p. 471.

SCHWARTZ, RICHARD AND MILLER, JAMES   (1964), Legal Evolution and Societal Complexity, *American Sociological Review,* 70, p. 159.

SIMMEL, GEORG   (1903, 1955), *Conflict and the Web of Group Affiliations* (Kurt Wolff and Reinhard Bendix, Transl.) New York: Free Press.

SIMPSON, GEORGE E. AND YINGER, J. MILTON   (1965), *Racial and Cultural Minorities* (Third Edition) New York: Harper & Row, Pub.

YNGVESSON, BARBARA AND HENNESSEY, PATRICIA   (1975), Small Claims, Complex Disputes: A Review of Small Claims Literature, *Law and Society Review*, 9, p. 219.

5

THE ORIGINS OF LAW: CONFLICT, THE CRITICAL PERSPECTIVE

Custom and social structure, as we have seen, share a common intellectual tradition in the social sciences, though they represent rival ways of explaining the origins of law. Both of them share honors as targets of what has come to be known as the *critical* (or *conflict*) *perspective*. The most important feature of this third perspective is that it denies the claim that law develops where other social mechanisms have become too weak to maintain social integration. Challenging this passive evolutionary view (the law filling a vacuum), the critical perspective views law as a device actively developed by powerful elites in society to establish and maintain their dominance over other classes.

As you will see in this chapter, the critical perspective emphasizes *conflict* and *power* as the decisive features involved in the formation of law. It focuses on inequalities developed or maintained by laws and legal institutions. Hence, critical studies often deal with the experiences of the poor and the powerless as victims of law, though critical theorists try to deal with law in all its activities and forms.

POWER, CLASS DOMINATION, AND LAW: HISTORICAL EXAMPLES

Poachers and the Black Acts

To give you an idea of the critical perspective in action, let's look at some English legal history as seen by critical theorists. One major factor in the development of the English legal system was the struggle which took place over *enclosure* and its attendant practices. Enclosure was the process of fencing off and guarding lands as *private property*. To us, this may not seem like a very drastic measure, but to English peasants and other poor people, it was a major change in the way people organized their chances for survival. Previously, land had been the object of complex patterns of use within feudalistic networks of rights and obligations. Enclosure was a move to terminate those feudalistic relationships, converting land from a "sacred trust" of the lord into a marketable piece of property.

As part of this general campaign by landholders against the landless, a series of laws was passed, beginning in the late seventeenth century, which attempted to reserve for owners the right to hunt game on their private lands. Deer, squirrels, rabbits, and wild fowl, which had been the legitimate quarry of anyone who could manage to kill them wherever they were found, suddenly became "protected." Only the aristocrats, the barons and dukes and other landowners, were permitted to shoot such game.

E. P. Thompson has described in great detail the struggle which resulted from this aristocratic drive to increase control over vital natural resources (1975). Resistance to enclosure had already developed before the attempt to prevent hunting. But the antihunting laws brought the resistance to a head and organized it. Groups, known as "Blacks" (because they blackened their faces for camouflage) developed ingenious techniques for tracking and killing game, despite the best efforts of hired estate guards. Much to the distress of the aristocrats, the poacher's efforts proved alarmingly successful. In response, landowners promoted a succession of laws, known as the Black Acts, which were designed to stamp out poaching and deer hunting. These laws made such acts punishable by death, and they even made it a capital offense to be found with a blackened face.

Thompson found that the laws and the various courts set up to enforce them had only spotty success in capturing and prosecuting the Blacks. To the Blacks, indeed to peasants generally whether they practiced poaching or not, hunting was a God-given right which their ancestors had practiced and which they felt entitled to practice. Their custom was being directly attacked by the laws of the aristocrats. So they fought back. The struggle over poaching went on for decades.

Over time, however, the nature of the struggle shifted. The whole class structure of British society was in the process of deep change. The aristocracy, whose wealth and power came from land, were losing power to a new class who got their wealth from control of industrial production and commerce. These new middle classes, flushed with the success of their business ventures, began to demand and get increased political power. One of their targets for change was the whole legal apparatus of the antipoaching laws. Being landless themselves, they were barred by these laws from hunting. But hunting in England had come to symbolize prestige, leisure, and power, and the middle classes wanted to clothe themselves with such symbols. They sought reform so that they could join the aristocrats in shooting game for sport (Howkins, 1979).

Throughout the nineteenth century they succeeded in passing reform laws which opened the shooting of game to "everyone" (Howkins, 1979). But, at the same time, the laws they passed placed new restrictions (requirements for hunting licenses and permission from landowners to shoot on their land) which had the effect of continuing to exclude the rural poor from legal hunting. During this period the economic health of the rural poor had been deteriorating because by then methods of farming were eliminating steady farm jobs, leaving only seasonal work. The new laws, if obeyed, would have cut off one important source of food, for the poor hunted only for food, not for sport.

The amount of poaching which persisted in spite of these laws fluctuated with the farm labor seasons, because most poaching was simply a continuation of the ancient custom of supplementing meager diets with whatever squirrels, rabbits, and small birds could be found. For decades, regardless of the law's content or the judges' commands, the poor hunted small game and flaunted their "criminal" violations in front of judges, "legitimate" middle-class hunters, and landowners alike. The laws and the courts proved ineffective, even when the middle classes retaliated with increased penalties and severer methods of enforcement (including the use of newly formed police forces and laws allowing "stop and frisk" searches for tools and weapons used in poaching). But the battle continued as a stalemate throughout the nineteenth century.

Here, then, is an example where the laws were a direct attack on, rather than a means of support for, custom. People who chose to follow their customary hunting practices were redefined as criminals. Critical theorists see this as a clear contradiction of the notion that laws simply give formal expression to existing customs. For generations of poor people it became *customary* to flout the law.

This example also challenges the structuralist's claim that structural conditions *necessitated* the formation of courts and laws to regulate private property. Recall Schwartz's conclusion (chapter 4) that the institution of private property on the Israeli moshav *created* unstable conditions which necessitated legal formalization. In England, by contrast, the decisive factor was not the change in relationships brought about as an unforeseen by-product of a widely supported shift to private property. Rather, private property is a system of unequal privilege aggressively promoted by one class for its own advantage. Legal institutions develop as one type of device by which that class can expand its pressure on the poor to cease their customary behavior. How different, then, are the structuralist and conflict explanations for the apparent affinity between law and private property. And how different, therefore, their explanations of the origins of law and legal institutions.

Crime, Labor, and Vagrancy Laws

A second example of the critical perspective comes from a study of the history of *vagrancy laws* (Chambliss, 1964). In this history, we see how the content of a single law changes in response to the changing identity and interests of the dominant class in society.

Vagrancy laws, which modern American police have found useful in keeping derelicts and "weirdos" off the streets and away from the "nice" parts of our cities, trace their history back to the bubonic plague (the Black Death) which swept England in 1348. It wiped out half the nation's population, plunging England into severe economic crisis, since so much of the labor force was destroyed.

The aristocrats on their large estates had already begun to feel the labor pinch, because new industries in the towns were siphoning away the cheap labor needed to run the estates. The ". . . vagrancy statutes were designed for one express purpose: to force laborers (whether personally free or unfree) to accept employment at a low wage in order to insure the landowner an adequate supply of labor at a price he could afford to pay" (Chambliss, 1964, p. 69). The first vagrancy laws required every "able-bodied" person to work at pay rates which prevailed *before* the epidemic. They forebade workers from seeking higher wages or better-paying jobs. To support these rules, people were also forbidden to give alms to "able-bodied beggars," the purpose being to put them back to work.

Stiff as they were, these original vagrancy laws had little of their intended effect, since judges did not enforce them regularly. The reason for this legal dormancy is that the emergence of English society from feudalism had already gained too much momentum. The demands of the growing industrial sector for *free labor* (workers free to move to the best-paying jobs) overrode the interests of the landowners. As this shift of power accelerated, a corresponding change took place in the focus of the vagrancy laws. While they retained mention of punishing persons who did not appear to have an "honest job," the emphasis had shifted to the term "honest." Job holding came to represent honesty, and vagrancy laws were reworded to deal with a new class of full-time felons. Leaders of commerce found that trade was being threatened by thieves, highwaymen (remember Robin Hood?), and vagabonds. They tried to use the vagrancy statutes as a way of clearing the trade routes for safe commerce. Charges of vagrancy enabled the merchant class to imprison a "suspicious character" even if they could not prove actual commission of a crime. Later, the laws were further amended to attack various kinds of fraud which harmed commerce by sowing the seeds of distrust among merchants.

Vagrancy laws were thus part of a new social class's campaign to establish favorable conditions for their own climb to power. The laws were at times actively enforced against "criminal elements" because they gave enforcement authorities great leeway in deciding who should be treated as vagrant. But the shift in emphasis from labor to criminality was a direct reflection of the triumph of a new ruling class over the old elite. The history of these laws does not indicate that they arose out of some *custom* (such as the idea that it is good to work), or that they changed in response to changing customs. Rather, they were established by one elite trying to preserve its waning power, and they were taken over by another elite to consolidate its growing power.

Critical theorists would reject the structuralist interpretation that by protecting commerce and industry, the laws helped protect society as a whole by preserving "the balance." Like the Black Acts and other anti-poaching laws, the vagrancy laws were an expression of the struggle between rival class interests. As such, they promoted imbalance and conflict.

REJECTING CONSENSUS

A general characteristic of the critical perspective is that it challenges assumptions of consensus which are fundamental to theories based on custom and social structure. When, for example, Bohannan speaks of law as a way to "disengage" trouble cases from threatened social institutions (see chapters 2 and 3), he implies that the social stability maintained by this process helps everyone. He may not deny that class differences exist. But he sees law as a system which protects the well-being of all members of society by protecting society's institutions. Similarly, when structuralists speak of the organizational problems produced by private property land use, or the inevitable consequences of population growth, they are saying that these changes create conditions which threaten the fabric of society itself and therefore the well-being of everyone. So, they say, when custom or peer pressure prove inadequate, people wisely submit themselves to a more effective guarantee of social tranquility: law.

Law as Promoter of Conflict and Inequality

Austin Turk lumps all customary and structural theorists into a single category: the *moral functionalists* (1976). They are wrong, he says, because they define out of existence some of the most important social scientific questions we can ask about the law. All of the theorists in chapters 3 and 4 start by assuming that law is a social invention whose key function is to *reduce* conflict, to stabilize social relations. So they all define the "law problem" as a question of *how* the law enters into unstable situations and restores stability. None of them asks the question about which critical theorists are most skeptical: Does law stabilize and reduce conflict, or does it instead destabilize social relations and stir up conflict?

Where does law come from? Moral functionalists look to those conditions which cause instability (weakening custom, population growth, private property) and describe law as a device for restoring "the balance." Critical theorists look for major conflicts in society and find that law is one of several tools developed by classes of antagonists, not to "restore a balance" but to promote their own interests over other classes of antagonists. At different times they may find conflict just as necessary to their cause as is tranquility at other times. So law may be used to stir up conflict as much as to quell it. Certainly the English middle class did not use the antipoaching laws to calm the ruffled feathers of the rural poor. Rather, they used law in a decade-long struggle to reduce the share of the commonwealth available to poorer people and to affirm their superiority over the declining aristocratic class.

Why Not Brute Force?

While critical theorists thus attack the consensus model of society implied in customary and structuralist theories, they have had to deal with the nagging fact that consensus so consistently *appears* to be an objective of legal systems. If the wealthy class wants to dominate the poor, why use law? Wouldn't armed troops force compliance? Doesn't law diminish ruling-class power by giving judges and rules some power to thwart illegal plans? With English poachers, for example, why didn't the aristocrats just shoot them?

Early Marxist theory has been criticized for failing to deal with these questions (Sumner, 1979, ch. 8). Promoting the theory that law was a tool for domination, early Marxists, and even some of more recent vintage (e.g., Quinney, 1974), tended to ignore or deny evidence that law provides a way for lower classes to *resist* efforts of other classes to dominate them. They ignored what more recent critical theorists call the law's *ideological role* in promoting class domination. Law does more than simply reinforce the ruling class's grab for power. It contains the language of universal justice, *consensus*—the notion that law is for all the people, because such language helps the ruling class expand its network of alliances against threats to its control. The promotion of the "rule of law" dampens the resistance of poorer classes by obscuring the real, imbalanced consequences of the system.

Stanley Diamond sees law as a more effective tool for domination than the simple use of brute force, because the law incorporates elements of diverse customs into its system of rules, thereby deceiving people into believing that the law supports their interests (1971). In Diamond's view the evil genius of modern law is that it has grown by "cannibalizing" the customs of smaller groups (tribes, feudal estates, churches, ethnic groups). By this he does not mean that the makers of modern law set out single-mindedly to destroy local customs through blatant domination (as the Bolsheviks tried to do in Central Asia [see chapter 3] or as the Nazis tried to do in Europe). Instead, law has grown by isolating fragments of various local groups' customs and transforming them into justifications for the centralization of power.

Centralization, the growth of the modern nation-state in conjunction with corporate forms of industrial production, is synonymous with the growth of modern law. Law is the method of domination under modern political conditions. Law's growth has been achieved by destroying the separate power of those local groups (tribes, classes, villages, ethnic groups, associations) whose customs stood in the way of "progress." Their customs have been cannibalized to give the tinge of legitimacy to laws which were designed to disempower such groups.

The driving purpose behind this perverted use of custom was the creation of a compliant, available work force for industry. Direct attack on customs would only provoke massive resistance such as we saw in Soviet Central Asia. But by making the law appear to include the customs of various groups, the ruling class could defuse much of their organized resistance.

Conflict theorists focus particular attention on laws which most Americans consider to be sacred—laws, such as the Bill of Rights, which guarantee *fundamental freedoms* to *individuals*. This approach is one of the cleverest deceptions of the system. By insisting that individual rights receive priority in laws and legal procedures, modern law strips away the authority of leaders within all those local groups whose separate autonomy once stood as a barrier to the consolidation of power in the hands of the new ruling class. Legal guarantees of individual liberty, while seeming to protect the individual from all the antiquated tyrannies of our benighted past, actually strip us of all protection from the state's tyranny. This paradox results from the fact that the flow of authority from the local group to the state destroys those local social units which could protect the individual from state domination. For example, the tribal chief loses authority when members of his tribe can challenge his decisions by appealing to national courts where their *individual rights* as *citizens* (not just tribal members) are the only issues the judge will consider. The elders in Mexican town B (chapter 4) saw their authority slip away in the face of state judges and laws which rebellious sons and daughters could turn to as an alternative.

Cloke summarizes this perspective as follows:

> Through the individual incident or transaction, law makes individuals the basic unit of any case. . . .The persons who are normally engaged in legal controversy are separated out from the mass of people by the legal process and made to look special; and each case is made to appear different from others . . . social struggles and political movements are splintered into their individual components and prevented from making any stronger or more collective statements than might be made by any of the individuals involved. . . (1971, p. 69)

Modern law allows the owners and managers of industrial corporations to hide behind the myth of the "corporate person" (which makes the corporation rather than the people who run it responsible for any damage it might do to customers, neighbors, or society as a whole), while the same legal system, using the theory of individual rights matched by individual duties, refuses to support the angry black ghetto resident's claim that his participation in a riot is a legitimate *collective* response of his group to its suppression *as a group*. The law caters to the collective needs of business leaders and Wall Street investors, while rejecting the same collective theory when applied to blacks in American society. Black tenants who cannot get the landlord to fix a furnace may be suffering the winter's cold because they are black and cannot get better housing. But the law provides only an individual route (sue the landlord) for eliminating the problem. The legal approach ignores the root of the problem. Any black who chooses that route will thus be diverted into squandering time and money on an irrelevant lawsuit which cannot alter the basic problem. To the extent that other members of that group are similarly diverted, the group will be effectively fragmented and unable to mount a collective movement against its collective problem.

A recent stark example of this fragmentation occurred in nazi Germany. The government openly encouraged German children to spy on their parents and report disloyalty to the police. Nazi political ideology justified such intrusions into private relationships as serving the greater glory of the "German race," a muddled hybrid myth which appealed to people's local associational loyalties (custom) but harnessed them to the central political goals of Hitler's state.

Conflict theorists believe it mistaken to think that Hitler's methods were a freak occurrence. They see Hitler's methods as a logical extension of the modern trend toward the "rule of law." The intrusion of law to override the loyalties of customary groups is the essence of law's development over the past few centuries.

Let's compare conflict theory on the relation between custom and law with the custom theory of chapter 3. Both note that much of the law's language reflects the ideas of custom. But custom theorists say that legalization is a way of guaranteeing that those customs will be obeyed. Conflict theorists reply that the customary content in law is a smoke screen for the emasculation of the very groups which developed those customs. It is naive to think that just because modern law contains statements of customs, it must be a way of shoring up the authority of those customs. A custom written into modern law codes is a custom stripped of its traditional context and used like a prostitute to lure traditional groups into the marketplace consciousness and activity of modern capitalism. Law does not clarify what people are required to do. Rather it obscures, because people cannot possibly keep up with the complex development of laws made and enforced by remote politicians and bureaucrats. This is what other conflict theorists mean when they say that *law mystifies class relationships*—it hides the facts of exploitation (Sumner, 1979, p. 250). Where custom does rule, people have a much clearer idea of the behavior required of them because custom cannot operate unless everyone knows the rules. No separate enforcer stands ready to mobilize rules people don't understand.

We have, then, one answer to the dilemma of consensus (the charge that if critical theorists are right about law being used to dominate, they cannot explain why the law gives protection to the poor and powerless). Law is frequently more effective and efficient in supporting domination than is brute force, though ruling classes use either tool when it suits their needs.

Turk has organized this argument into a statement about five kinds of power which an established legal system can give to those who control it (1976, p. 276). *First,* law takes from others the power to use *physical force,* violence, to get their way. It gives that power to those who control the law, including not just police, judges, and prison wardens, but also those civilians who can regularly enlist the law on behalf of their claims. *Second,* it gives *economic power* to those who control it because it creates a system of rewards and punishments for economic activity. Tax and property laws in particular channel economic decision making according to the preferences of those who control the system. *Third,* the legal system gives *political power.* It supports certain political structures and their norms over others. Law and politics are intimately joined as mutually reinforcing methods of control. *Fourth,* the legal system provides an *ideological environment* which helps promote compliance. The existence of law becomes an unquestioned aspect of people's social reality. Like death and taxes, people come to believe that law is inevitable, indispensable. This underlying belief promotes a general "adherence to the ground rules of conventional politics" (p. 281).

This is why we have been encouraged to feel loyalty to "our country," "mein Führer," "the motherland," or "mankind," rather than to "us hill-billies," or "us good ole boys," or "the Godfather."

Fifth, says Turk, the law provides *diversionary power.* It gets people involved in one set of activities and concerns (e.g., lawsuits and legal reform movements) rather than others which might better promote their interests. In the midst of India's campaign for independence from Britain, for example, Mahatma Gandhi called for a boycott of English courts because he was convinced that his people's energy and time were being wasted in lawsuits against each other when their real hope for improvement lay in driving the British out of India.

To summarize the critical perspective thus far, critical theorists see law as a special method of social control. It is not found universally in human society, but is rather created during identifiable periods of history by classes seeking to consolidate their power over other classes. To those critical theorists who trace their thinking in part to the theories of Karl Marx (which make up some but not all of the field), law is part of the process by which excess wealth becomes unequally distributed and thereby stimulates actions to preserve those inequalities.

CONFLICT AMONG ELITES: IS
THERE A RULING CLASS?

The struggle for power and wealth has not produced uniform results in all societies. The pattern of legal development in a given society is a result not only of campaigns to dominate but also of efforts to resist domination.

Critical theory has been criticized for oversimplifying the notion of the "ruling class." Complex societies have various elite groups who do not necessarily have compatible interests and values. They may actually be in serious conflict with each other over who should rule and whose values should prevail.

Who rules in the United States for example? There are, of course, the Duponts and Rockefellers, the "Boston Brahmins," and the WASP elite. But we also find power centers in the universities (e.g., Henry Kissinger), churches, religious movements (e.g., Jerry Falwell, Reverend Moon, the Maharishi Mahesh Yoga, Billy Graham), mass media (e.g., editors, TV network directors), organized crime, mass movements (e.g., Martin Luther King, Equal Rights Amendment leaders, the ecology movement), and ethnic groups (e.g., the Jewish and Hispanic lobbies). Obviously, these different groups are not always united in their actions—often they are locked in conflict with each other. In the case of the antipoaching laws in England, we saw two elites (the aristocracy and the new, industrial middle class) struggling with each other for control. If law expresses the will of the ruling class, what happens when the ruling class itself is fragmented?

The Witchcraft Business in England and Europe

In Europe this struggle centered for some time around accusations and trials for witchcraft (Currie, 1968). Continental legal action against witchcraft differed significantly from actions taken in England. The differences were a direct result of differences in the ability of elites to achieve absolute power.

In England, witches were almost always "found" to be women, often widows, of lower-class origin. They were propertyless outcasts even before anyone accused them of practicing witchcraft or making pacts with the devil. Most often their accusers were also lower class. The English legal system actually fostered the temporary growth of a marginal profession in the identification and testing of witches (English law made proof of any crime, including witchcraft, dependent on witness's testimony, not confessions. So a class of "professional witnesses" arose claiming the ability to identify, through secret methods, true witches). Throughout England's history, only five to six hundred persons were put to death as witches.

How different it was in continental Europe. There hundreds of thousands of confirmed witches were put to death. Most of them first confessed to their crimes. And large numbers of them were neither poor nor women. Often they were the cream of the aristocracy. Conviction as a witch meant the complete loss of all the witch's family wealth. Witches' abundant lands and movable wealth typically went to the officials who condemned them.

Because church law on the Continent required that witches confess before being found guilty, torture was used with almost no restraints. Torture produced a steady flow of confessions, which helped to convince the general populace that witchcraft was a serious problem. It also produced a rising tide of denunciations—the naming of a confessed witch's accomplices. So the flow of witches to the stake, property to the new church-state ruling class, and power to the central political authority grew from a trickle to a flood as each witch confessed the sins of two or three others.

Witchcraft became such a major industry in continental Europe, according to Currie, because continental law was a repressive system with few of the restraints found in English law. The restraints put on authorities in England, on the other hand, made the "witchcraft business" much riskier, less profitable, and therefore uninteresting to potential accusers.

Currie does not explain why Continental and English law differed. But we may have already seen the answer in our discussion of the Black Acts and reactions to antipoaching laws. The English elite may have been more fragmented, riddled with dissension, than the church-backed elite on the Continent. The development of repressive legal style on the Continent involved the activities of self-interested dominant classes who manipulated local populations with appeals to their fears. They grew even richer and more powerful on the proceeds thus "liberated." Presumably some combination of events prevented officials in Britain from creating a similar gravy train for themselves.

The State as a Rival Class

Critical theorists have recently tried to answer the criticism that they ignore the heterogeneity of elites in modern society—that their view of the "ruling class" is naively simplistic. One answer is to say that the state (and therefore the law), which early ruling classes created to advance their own interests, has taken on a life of its own (Althusser and Balibar, 1970; Hirst, 1976). By setting up a separate legal institution run by independent specialists, the economic "ruling class" has created a kind of Frankenstein for itself—a force able to operate *to a certain extent* independently of the economic elite. The state becomes able to exploit conflicts between different factions of the ruling elite and does so to retain its own independence. Thus it becomes one more contestant in the never-ending struggle to control.

A second answer is to say that the solidarity of the ruling class itself is a difficult achievement, since complex economies offer so many opportunities for treachery in the search for personal advantage. Law may be the ideology giving the ruling class power over others, but it also provides a means of stabilizing relations among ruling-class factions. It is a set of agreements, alliances, which maintain that class's domination over others in society (Hunt, 1978).

One striking feature of this argument is that it looks as though critical theory is sneaking structuralism in the back door to shore up a shaky argument. If law can *function* to preserve ruling class solidarity, why isn't it equally valid, as the structuralists in chapter 4 were saying, to hold that law preserves the solidarity of all of society, that just as law helps structure the elite, it structures society as a whole?

The critical theorists' response is that the moral functionalists ignore the extensiveness of struggle between different classes and the extent to which law has played a role in generating conflict as well as calming it.

CONFLICT, REFORM, AND DOMINATION

The class conflict expressed in most legal activity is sometimes obvious, sometimes subtle. When Hitler ordered the extermination of all European Jews, the raw class conflict was obvious to anyone who ignored nazi efforts to use bland, bureaucratic language and procedure to clothe their actions in the ideology of law. To Americans it is not very difficult to see the class domination expressed in the repressive "apartheid laws" of South Africa.

We view as ludicrous their claims that such laws merely preserve the customs of the different racial groups "sharing in the South African economic miracle." And we might not find it hard to agree with a critical theorist's claim that the laws of slavery in the United States before 1863 were repressive and exploitative.

But critical theorists hold that these same processes operate wherever modern legal systems operate. Where you think you see law protecting the poor, or the downtrodden, or "human dignity," say critical theorists, you are probably missing certain key ingredients which transform limits on power into added fuel for the central powerhouse.

In this section, you will see how the critical view reinterprets four examples of reform: child labor laws, anti-corruption reforms of police departments, protection of American Indians from White exploitation, and the furnishing of aid to "underdeveloped" societies.

Child Labor Reform: Building Monopolies

As "everyone knows" today, children go to school and only "greedy monsters" would try to put them to work in factories or mines or at other menial jobs. But today's protection of children is the result of a long, bitterly fought battle during the late nineteenth and early twentieth centuries. Before the passage of child-labor laws, which effectively barred employers from using children, American industry thrived on their cheap labor. But reformers campaigned for years against the illiteracy, ill health, hopelessness, and moral degradation produced by these employment practices. Support for reform was considered "radical" in some quarters (a University of Pennsylvania professor, Scott Nearing, was fired because of his vigorous support of the reform movement). But reform was promoted as common decency by its many active supporters.

Moral functionalists would probably say either that such laws simply reinstitutionalized the strong American custom of protecting children and promoting family life or that by passing such laws, the American legal system was rectifying some structural imbalance. Surely any decent American ought to feel revulsion over the specter of little children sweating away twelve hours a day in some horrible sweatshop, ruining their health and never learning to read or write.

But according to Platt the campaigns to institute these child-labor reforms (and by implication much of the legislation since then aimed at regulating working conditions for American laborers) had more sinister sources of support, which fits the critical theory perspective (1977, p. xxi).

A widespread, but largely unreported, effect of these laws was that they drove out of business those smaller factories and commercial establishments whose survival depended on cheap child (and female) labor. Many of the leaders of the child-labor reform movement were wives of prosperous business leaders, and the campaign was well oiled by donations from those bigger industralists who stood to gain from a reduction of competition from smaller factories. This apparently benign reform movement fit in nicely with the monopolistic motives of large-scale producers, who saw the legislation as a means of increasing their control over competitive markets. Reform laws promoted monopolization of American industries by driving numerous small competitors out of business.

Note that Platt does not accuse all reformers of harboring these devious motives. Conflict theorists say that the genius of law as a tool for the promotion of class interests is that it does enlist the support of many who misunderstand its effects. When law "cannibalizes" a custom, such as the sanctity of childhood and family, it exploits our custom-based sentiments, to gain our support for actions serving hidden well-organized interests.

Police Reform: Building Centralized Control

Serpico, the story of the New York policeman who "single-handedly" exposed the multimillion dollar involvement of hundreds of New York police officers and administrators in illegal drug selling (Maas, 1973), is supposedly a story with a happy ending. The scoundrels were exposed, the Knapp Commission systematically investigated the crimes, and the New York police force was supposedly purged and reorganized so that such massive abuse would not recur.

But the history of police reforms in the United States suggests that the Serpico incident is just a reincarnation of events which have recurred on a regular twenty-year cycle since police were first introduced into American life in the nineteenth century (Sherman, 1974). All major American cities have gone through these twenty-year cycles. Each period of corruption is interrupted by a politician or politicians who launch a vigorous, well-publicized campaign to "throw the rascals out" and cleanse the police force of the stench of bribery, favoritism, extortion, and official misconduct. Once the reforms have gone into effect, police officers and administrators are prosecuted and many go to jail, are fined, and resign in disgrace. Then the political climate begins to cool, and everyone expects the reform procedures to insure police purity.

But new forms of corruption replace the old. New patterns of individual deviance combine with new methods for organized wrongdoing, and the city is soon "back to normal." After about twenty years of normalcy, the city is hit with another reform campaign.

However, though this looks like a revolving door (corruption in and corruption out), the effect of the reforms is to alter the nature of policing and its relationship to politics in the city and across American society.

These cycles produce a steady trend toward tighter, more centralized control of police work. Early police forces put officers in neighborhoods, where they became regular members of the local scene. Their police authority stemmed from their ability to personally dominate others. They became easily recognized local leaders whose whereabouts, personal habits, and policing methods were generally known. They could impose swift "justice" on local juveniles without ever reporting incidents to higher authorities. They had, in other words, plenty of discretion left to them in the way they ran their "beats."

Of course, this autonomy also created particular kinds of opportunities for corruption. Police could become involved in protecting illegal operations because their presence and silence could be counted on. In the normal course of daily routines, they could become receivers of routine "favors" (e.g., free meals at local diners) in exchange for the kinds of favors they could give because of their authoritative positions. Surveillance and supervision of their behavior was difficult. More importantly, the arrangements they made in their territory, while they contained elements of "improper" behavior, often created stable, "peaceful" conditions because of the proximity and speed of "curbside justice."

Reforms have eliminated this kind of policing in the United States, though it still typifies urban police work in Japan (Bayley, 1977). How different is the life of the modern American police officer who cruises his patrol sector by car, unrecognized by most residents and on call constantly by radio from central police headquarters, where supervisors and computers handle much of the decision making. Police communications, the switch from foot to car patrols, the consolidation of authority into a chain of command, the centralization of police precinct headquarters, and the removal of most of their discretionary authority—all of these moves can be traced as much to the campaigns against corruption as to the "war against crime." Technological innovations, especially in communications and their systematic linkage to computers, have contributed to this trend. But the drive to make use of these inventions has regularly come from the pressure to centralize authority.

Ironically, this stripping away of the patrol officer's authority has been accompanied by a persistent drive to "professionalize" the police. Police academies have been created to take the place of on-the-job training, which typified earlier police work. An ideology of professionalism has come into vogue, supported by books, speeches, and grants from federal agencies. Officers are encouraged to "improve" themselves by taking college courses and earning degrees (some cities now require college degrees as a condition of employment). This campaign reflects, in part, the theory that corruption is caused by "rotten apples in the barrel"—random individual police officers with inadequate training and indoctrination. The result has been that as police become better trained, their authority to make decisions has been reduced, taken over by central police and political administration.

This analysis thus redefines the significance of police reform movements. Reform does not eliminate corruption or reduce crime. Rather it eliminates competition in the marketplace of police corruption (like legitimate police work, corruption becomes centrally controlled). But more significantly, reforms relocate decision-making power away from local neighborhood social networks and into bureaucratic offices controlled by political elites. Reforms thus contribute to the struggle between centralized authority seeking to dominate and local neighborhood groups trying to retain their solidarity and separate identity. In the name of treating "all men" as "created equal" and therefore deserving of "impartial justice," local neighborhoods are stripped of an important authority figure (the foot-patrol cop) who was part of the local system of neighborhood authority. In return, people find themselves being watched by anonymous patrol cars and "professionals," who deal with them not as community members of Flatbush, or Lincoln Park, or Kensington, or "little Italy," but as *citizens, individuals,* part of the mass with their own personal problems, psychological characteristics, and legal difficulties. In combination with other forces working against the solidarity of the neighborhood, police reform has thus contributed to the demise of neighborhood *custom* and the rise of distant, depersonalized, more powerful, central government.

As the two previous examples illustrate, *reform* may be an effective disguise for the promotion of dominant class interests. Reforms create the illusion of progress toward shared goals while disguising new methods of domination and exploitation. Law is an ideology, a system of beliefs and values which serve to mobilize different groups within complex societies (Sumner, 1979, ch. 8).

"Protection" for American Indians: Disguised Exploitation

Sometimes reform is used alternately with more overt methods of domination. In the case of the Potawatomi tribe of northeastern Kansas, the story is a dreary sampler of the different "legal ways" in which white land speculators and railroad developers used the United States Bureau of Indian Affairs and the courts to strip the tribe of its treaty-guaranteed lands (Forer, 1979). The story revolves around government manipulation of tribal authorities, the alternate granting of autonomy and its withdrawal, as internal factionalism was stirred up and exploited by outsiders interested in the tribe's wealth. "Tribal constitutions," which guaranteed "individual rights" similar to those in the United States Constitution, led to individual challenges against tribal authority. They opened the tribe's collective wealth to fragmentation and tempted individuals to sell. They also drove a wedge between tribal leadership and members, because outside government authority always stood ready to side with the individual against the chiefs.

As in the case of police reform, government policy alternated between reform (support for tribal autonomy, cultural preservation, and self-determination) on the one hand and unchecked opportunism (the attempt to root out Indian "separatism" through cultural and economic assimilation) on the other. Regardless of intent, both kinds of policies had the same result: loss of Indian lands to white business and governmental interests, and decaying authority within the tribe.

Even today, Indian tribes which have become active in lawsuits to force return of lost lands and hunting and fishing rights find that the law designed to help them actually forces them into ways of thinking and relating to each other which destroy their separate cultural identity and social viability (Medcalf, 1978). Even sympathetic "movement" lawyers who take the Indians' side and fight vigorously for their rights have the effect of forcing Indians to frame their claims and define their intertribal relations in terms that are acceptable to the white man's courts. They must therefore abandon patterns of collective ownership and tribal governance in favor of individualized, rationalized definitions of rights. They are forced, in short, to develop the white man's "rights consciousness," which emphasizes marketplace thinking about property, contractual agreements, and individual as opposed to collective rights. Unless tribes are willing to define themselves as corporations engaged in a business venture, the law will not accommodate their collective traditions. But as corporations, they are subject to business regulations, accounting requirements, and procedural standards like those the law demands of General Motors.

So the best-intentioned efforts of lawyers working to reform the government's treatment of American Indians have the effect of driving tribal members into the control system of the modern marketplace power system. Reform legislation guaranteeing "Indian self-determination" has actually produced even more pressure for "dispersal, urbanization, and cultural asborption of Indian tribes" (Forer, 1979, p. 91).

Aid to Underdeveloped Societies:
Preserving Central Control

Critical theorists often link the American Indian experience to *Third World* exploitation in general. *Third World* is a term critical theorists use to mean the societies called "underdeveloped" by the "moral functionalists." The ravages experienced by American Indians are part of a worldwide pattern of domination in which law plays a key role. The elements of this process are

. . . the cultural, commercial, and military penetration of native territories; the destabilization of traditional native societies and governments by encouraging factionalism and/or manipulating existing factionalism; the creation of surrogate native governments; the domination of surrogate governments through a trustee, protectorate, or "sphere-of-influence" relationship; the institutionalization of this relationship through a system of treaties, law courts and civil service; the resocialization of the native population to acceptance of the authority of these institutions as well as the authority of the colonial and native police and military power to suppress overt resistance to this authority; and the rationalization of the total process on grounds of racial superiority, Christian imperative, economic progress, national interest, mutual self-interest, law and order—in a word, on grounds of "civilization." (Forer, p. 92)

Forer thus supports a recent development in critical theory: a perspective on underdevelopment known as *dependency theory*. Dependency theory argues against the traditional American liberal program to give economic, military, or intellectual aid to underdeveloped societies, because such aid merely increases the control the givers have over the recipients. Dependency theorists argue that aid is based on a faulty theory of the origins of underdevelopment.

Dependency theorists (Wallerstein, 1974; Frank, 1979) say that underdevelopment in Third World societies (places like India, Ghana, Bolivia, Afghanistan, and Albania) or "backward" regions of "advanced" societies (e.g. Indian reservations, rural Mississippi, West Virginia mining regions, northern Maine) is *not* mere backwardness stemming from a late start at modernization. Third world people are *not* just "living in the past" the way they did centuries ago. They are *not* made poor by backward beliefs, traditions, or superstitions. And their hope for rising out of poverty does *not* lie in reliance on American ingenuity, aid, or investments to "propel them into the twentieth century."

They are, rather, a vital part of the twentieth century. Their condition is the result of their forced submission to outside control. They are the *peripheral* (or satellite) economic servants to the *central* (or metropolitan) controllers who dominate a *worldwide economic system*. Peripheral societies serve the centers by providing cheap raw materials and labor. The Philippines send mahogany; Jamaica sends bauxite; Liberia sends rubber; India sends jute, tea, and spices; Cuba used to send sugar. All send their natural wealth to the industrial and commercial centers (the United States, Japan, Germany, France, England, and the Soviet Union) where the consumer products sold around the world are produced. The products are marketed from the center toward the periphery. Third World nations thus help absorb excess production and keep profits from slipping.

Peripheral societies cannot develop their own industry to become self-sufficient because any attempt they make gets beaten down either by the higher efficiency of existing industries at the center or by political domination, which either directly forbids such development or writes tax and trade laws which squeeze peripheral competition out. Center industrial giants have a tremendous competitive edge because of their high volume of business, established purchasing and marketing systems, monopolistic control over their markets, and cooperative government tax and tariff policies.

You might think that the discovery of new natural resources in an underdeveloped nation would help it, would improve the living conditions of its citizens. But dependency theorists show that such discoveries typically increase poverty in the periphery while increasing wealth and power in the center. This happens because the extraction of the resources requires re-organization of the native population. People are converted from simple farmers into miners, plantation workers, coolies. Families break up, and traditional methods of mutual support are lost as men leave home to work in the mines and plantations for wages. Wages are the only means they have to pay taxes imposed by governments friendly to the mine or planta-tion owners. Wages also buy the finished products which they have learned to want from the center. But the wages are not adequate to support fami-lies. Migration is also forced on people when lands are consolidated into plantations, or taxes are raised above the ability of small, "inefficient" farms to pay. Peripheral society becomes overburdened with drifters—people cut loose from family, clan, or tribe, and totally dependent on occasional wage labor for survival. Their numbers insure a steady supply of cheap labor, but their labor becomes increasingly unneeded as technology developed at the center devises labor-saving extraction techniques. The smartest and best-trained natives migrate to the center, where their train-ing will pay off in useful, lucrative jobs. Their work then adds to the center's control of this worldwide process rather than the independent development of their native lands.

A dependency theorist might look at the differences between legal development in Japan and in India as further support for dependency theory. India, which was dominated by England for nearly two centuries, today suffers as one of the poorest of the Third World nations. Yet it is saddled with one of the most highly "developed" legal systems in the world. Japan, on the other hand, was one of the only regions of Asia which was never ruled or controlled by colonial powers. Japan also shows much less legal "development" than India. Dependency theorists would see India's legal system as part of the apparatus by which India's resources were har-nessed to the service of the British Empire. Japan's isolation, on the other hand, furnished it with the protection it needed to become the only major industrial power in Asia.

Dependency theorists thus conclude that when America exports grain, or jet fighters, or lawyers and legal codes as aid to Third World nations, the most predictable effect will be the further impoverishment of those nations and their increased dependence on the center.

COMPARING PREDICTIONS

The critical perspective gets its name because it is a criticism of customary and structuralist explanations of law. Let's look back at some of the analyses presented in chapters 3 and 4 to see how critical theory might assess those studies.

British Colonial Law in India

We have already seen that critical theory directly attacks the ideas in customary theory about "double institutionalization" and the idea that custom and law must be compatible. But what about India's reactions to English colonial law? Don't they support Bohannan's case? From the critical perspective, the British treatment of India is a perfect argument for rejecting Bohannan and all other advocates of the customary perspective. Critical theorists classify British law in India as a key element in the dependency process described above (see Mendelsohn, 1981). They emphasize that Britain turned India into a massive supply base for British industry "back home" in England. The flow of raw materials from India to Britain, and of finished products from Britain back to India, was partly sustained by legal measures which were never mired down in the endless delay and deception which native Indians experienced when they went to court. Laws were passed, for example, outlawing the use of Indian cotton in Indian spinning and weaving factories. Indians were required to send their cotton to England, and then buy their cloth from English producers. The effect, of course, was to stifle the growth of what would have been a naturally profitable indigenous industry. Similar regulatory laws affected the use of most of India's other known natural resources and cash crops.

Critical theorists might argue that the "failure" of British law—the flood of litigation and the crass, unprincipled manipulation of procedural safeguards about which British administrators publically lamented—was actually a key element in Britain's successful strategy for controlling a huge non-British population. British rules about clarifying property ownership, imposing taxes to support colonial administrative work, and particularly about upholding "ancient custom" in the courts had a *diversionary* effect. Such strategies *deflected* Indians from attacking the British colonial system, which was systematically altering social relationships in support of the empire. Instead, people by the millions began using legal weapons to attack each other, leaving the British in a position to thrive on the fragmentation created by this native response. Law in India *created* conflict. The methods introduced by the British, including their insistence that they only wanted to enforce native custom, created a demoralized population, divided against itself and unable to resist the perversion of its customs in the hands of British, or British-trained Indian, judges and administrators.

In other words, critical theorists would say that British law in India was a great success, and that administrators' lamentations about the "perversions of British justice" being committed by Indians were nothing more than crocodile tears disguising the basic satisfaction of British rulers with the functioning of their empire. The pattern of *divide and rule*, though on a much grander scale in India, is much the same as the one used by the American government in dealing with native Americans (Forer, 1979).

Japanese "Harmony" and Elite Domination

In chapter 3 I also discussed the mercury poisoning case in Minamata and its possible application to the claim that Japanese law is "underdeveloped" because public law is contrary to Japanese custom. Chapter 4 contains a structuralist criticism of this customary theory. But the critical perspective challenges both those approaches to the events in Minamata. A critical theorist would give far greater weight to the dominant power position of the chemical factory in Minamata than do customary or structural theorists. Critical emphasis would be put on the fact that the company controlled the economic destinies of most of the Minamata victims, while the Niigata victims had means of support well insulated from attack by the factory that poisoned them.

The dependence of Minamata victims is more than the power-neutral network of multiplex relationships which structuralists would invoke as an explanation. Multiplex relationships imply nothing about the relative power of participants to force compliance with their wishes. In Minamata the chemical company engaged in deception, blackmail, and organized violence to reinforce the fear people already felt for their livelihoods and well-being. A company doctor who made the first discovery of the link between the company's waste disposal and the mysterious disease was silenced. His research materials were hidden, he was reassigned to other work, and when he continued to speak out about the problem, he was fired and defamed by the company (Smith and Smith, 1975, pp. 122–125). The company knew about the connection between its mercury refuse and the disease years before it made any public moves either to alert the community or alter its production process.

As public charges began to surface and evidence of community support for the victims grew, the company used other tactics. Rumors spread easily about the closing of clinics and schools if the company were "forced" to give substantial compensation to victims. Those with jobs in the company had good reason to fear and reject victims as pariahs, since the company made it clear that open sympathy for victim's grievances would result in loss of job. A group of demonstrating victims was invited into company offices for negotiations and then savagely attacked by "guards" and union members organized by company management (Smith and Smith, 1975, pp. 94–95). (The American journalist-photographer who was investigating these events received such a serious head injury in this attack that he had permanently impaired vision and nonstop head pains for the rest of his abbreviated life.)

The critical theorist would therefore explain the Minamata conformity to Japanese "custom" as a perfectly rational response to a position of powerlessness. Passivity does not signify consensus. It does show fear and submission.

While we don't have room here to attempt a full-scale theory of Japanese legal underdevelopment from a critical perspective, there is one additional twist to the Japanese story which should be mentioned. The apparent "underdevelopment" of Japanese law is a post-World War II condition. Before that war, rates of litigation and the size of the legal profession were both substantially larger (Haley, 1982, pp. 140–145). The dramatic decline in Japan's legal establishment may be the result of a campaign organized in the 1920's and 1930's to substitute enforced conciliation for adversarial litigation. According to one account (Haley, 1982) forced conciliation was imposed on many areas of Japanese legal action by a government bureaucracy dominated by those favoring neo-Confucian collectivist values as opposed to Western liberal legal rights for individuals. For a time, the introduction of conciliation actually increased the number of people pressing legal claims, because it opened up an additional avenue for action. But for some reason, legal actions of all kinds withered away with the onset of war and never returned to their previous levels.

Muslim Responses to Soviet Law

Now let's consider the Soviet use of law in Central Asia. In chapter 3 this case looked like a victory for custom over alien law. After all, even with full military and police enforcement, the Bolsheviks failed to effect major changes in Muslim society.

Or did they? the critical theorist might ask. Consider this alternative view. They did succeed in producing major disruptions in Muslim society. Thousands of women accepted the opportunity opened to them and left home. Major conflict was created in the area by enactment and enforcement of Soviet laws. But conflict was the Bolshevik goal, not harmony and balance. If they did fail, the failure lay in their inability to contain the conflict and channel it in the direction of modern economic activity. Massell makes it clear that they did fail in that respect. But it is a failure resulting from Bolshevik lack of economic resources, not the weakness of law in the face of Muslim custom. The Bolsheviks had the *political* power to alter laws. But the local population did not depend on them for economic well-being. So the Soviets could not manipulate the most important ingredient in the kind of power (economic) which critical theorists say lawmakers must have to make law a useful addition to the arsenal of power.

Conflict in the Division of Labor

Turning now to Durkheim's structuralism, we find a critical chorus of denunciations. Even some structuralists (e.g., Schwartz and Miller, 1964; Dubow, 1973) have pointed out that Durkheim's depiction of primitive societies as *repressive* does not fit with more recent anthropological evidence that most such societies rely almost exclusively on *restitutive* social control measures such as mediation, while modern societies use the repressive institutions of prisons, police forces, and secret intelligence systems. So Durkheim has been knocked around even by structuralists who share his general perspective.

But critical theorists deliver what they consider the knockout punch when they charge that Durkheim ignores clear evidence that specialization and inequality go hand in hand. Jobs don't just get divided up into specialties. Administrators aren't *needed* to coordinate the work of all these specialties. Rather specialization and the growth of separate classes occurs because some groups establish domination over others by controlling the excess wealth which is produced by these more efficient methods. Specialization gives a competitive edge to those who control the productive process. So *specialization increases inequality*. Dominant classes use law as one way to guarantee that they can continue to exploit those who have less of the excess wealth. Because they control the producing processes in society, they increase the amount of specialization *at their convenience* when it promises to increase their wealth and power (see Braverman, 1974).

Law in Israeli Communes

Critical theorists reject the basic premise presented by structuralists in chapter 4 that certain forms of organization *necessitate,* or inevitably push a group toward, the use of legal formality. To use the Israeli commune study as an example, critical theorists might take two approaches. One would be to deal with the evidence at the level of the communes themselves. If the moshav moved toward legal formalization, a critical theorist might say, it did so because some faction within it (pehaps the same faction which successfully convinced the commune to operate on a private-property basis) saw some advantage for itself in establishing the judicial committee and writing up a code of rules. The advantages would probably lie in the differences of wealth created by differential success among separate farm families. Critical theorists would look to the rules enforced by the judicial committee, expecting to find evidence that they work to protect the more prosperous and powerful moshav families from acts of frustration or rebellion by the less successful.

Taking a broader view, an alternative critical perspective would be that the differences between moshav and kibbutz are insignificant and don't represent any trend which can be generalized to larger societies. Both communes are small and governed largely by custom, not law. The moshav legal committee is a miniscule move away from custom and control by public opinion. Law is a much more complex process than the mere formalization of a few rules in a small community. Law has developed with the nation-state as part of the historically unique development of capitalism. To equate a moshav judicial committee with the larger development of law as a feature of private-property social systems around the world merely contributes to the legitimization of social inequality (see Quinney, 1974, p. 4) because it equates the *need* for law on the moshav to need for law in complex nation-states. Since law in complex societies supports ruling-class domination, the structuralist position dignifies their domination by calling it *needed*.

Conflict theorists reject structuralist claims that there are built-in, unseen features of social organization which make certain legal forms inevitable. Instead, they argue, the law as we know it today is a product of conscious decisions made by elites to promote and protect their privileges. Nothing happens to make custom "inadequate." Its only inadequacy is that, where powerful elites (e.g., Firestone Tire and Rubber, Alcoa Aluminum) decide to exploit resources they find under the control of "backward" societies (Liberia, Jamaica), native customs do not prepare group members to resist the schemes of the powerful outsiders.

CONCLUSION

One thing about which the conflict theorists and the customary and structuralist theorists agree is that law is not *natural*, an inevitable part of human society, a product of the need to control base aggressive human instincts. Like the others, critical theorists see law as a social product. It is born of specific historical events, and we come to think of it as natural only because our own perspectives are limited by our subordinate positions, which are also the product of those events.

But on almost every other point, critical theorists charge their opponents with naïveté or knowing collusion with sociolegal systems which oppress people and exploit conflict to serve dominant class interests. The history of the law's development is the history of a sometimes rampant, sometimes restrained, drive to consolidate power and control in the hands of privileged classes. If lawmakers have trouble defeating the force of custom in smaller groups, it is only because the ruling class has not mobilized its economic strength effectively to overcome the autonomous authority of customary leaders. Custom never becomes "inadequate" to control behavior in customary groups. It is driven out by law when the customary group is forced into submission to the "higher authorities" of ruling classes who get their power by dominating many such groups.

In these chapters on the origins of law, we have seen three rival perspectives. In the chapters which follow, we will be discussing some of the specific research questions which social scientists have been studying. The three perspectives we have discussed so far also apply to these research questions. Often a question is raised by adherents of one position and then reinterpreted by advocates of rival positions. Answering the question Where does law come from? is of course a major accomplishment. But other major questions with only partial connection to this first one have drawn much attention from social scientists.

As you consider these chapters in turn, keep the three major theoretical perspectives in mind. Try to approach the research question from each of the three perspectives. Theory may sometimes seem boring, too abstract, unreal. But without it, you can quickly get lost in a sea of facts, observations, casual opinions, and pseudotheories, which will leave you as ill-informed, confused, and frustrated about the law as when you started. Once you understand the value of theory, you may move on to the even more desirable position of rejecting all three theories we have studied here and developing a new one which better accounts for all the "confusion" we find in discussions about law.

ORIGINS OF LAW: APPLYING WHAT YOU KNOW

While ancient Greek civilization had its problems, every generation since then seems to have found it useful or inspiring to explore the wealth of ideas and practices generated during that era. Among the most remarkable features of Greek civilization was its development of democracy and law. Libraries abound with explanations for the apparently unique level of philosophy, art, literature, and political practice achieved by these ancient people.

Now that we have laid out three basic approaches to the question of where law comes from, you should be able to apply what you have learned to one interpretation of social change in ancient Greece. In particular, try to explain how each of our three perspectives on the origins of law would deal with the growth of law and democracy in Periclean Athens.

E. R. Dodds (1951) describes a series of cataclysmic changes in ancient Greece which not only produced democracy and law but also led to their ultimate demise. He divides Greek history (prior to its final eclipse by the rising star of Rome in the 330s B.C.) into three periods according to the predominant way in which people reacted to violations of rules, values, and norms. The first, or "Homeric" period (prior to 850 B.C.), was a "shame" culture, while the latter two were "guilt" cultures. (The distinction between shame and guilt cultures was borrowed by Dodds from Ruth Benedict's *The Chrysanthemum and the Sword*, 1946.)

In the Homeric period, people lived together in close-knit patriarchal family and communal units. The father's word was "law"—he was the ultimate authority over everyone in his family. Individuality was subordinated to the needs of the family and the community. The only exception to this pervasive collectivism was the encouragement given to father-rulers to be heroic warriors. Aside from this limited expression of individual skill and courage, everyone was bound by the collective obligations of their local ties.

As a result, whenever people behaved in unforeseen ways, violating rules, or insulting elders, or forgetting obligations, others would say that they had been taken over by some supernatural force (*ate*) which made proper behavior impossible. Offenders could say (and believe) that they had been temporarily driven off course by any of a host of supernatural forces. This would not protect them from punishment, but it meant that they would feel only *shame,* not *guilt,* over their misbehavior.

From about 800 to 600 B.C. (the Archaic Age) the Greek *shame* culture changed into a culture obsessed with the idea that misfortune and evil were inherited by later generations because of the misdeeds of ancestors. *Inherited guilt,* not the interference of supernatural forces, came to be seen as the explanation for such social catastrophes as incest, murder within families, and disregard of elders, especially the family or clan patriarch. This period was rocked by great social upheaval: warfare and general social and economic collapse. Archaic Greece went through two hundred years of what we would call depression and war. As a result, family and clan ties were shaken. Patriarchal authority could give little protection against these forces, so it was weakened. Pessimism replaced optimism, while fear, jealousy, envy, and other emotions of desperation produced the belief in inherited guilt.

But out of the chaos of this period arose a citadel of reason, democracy, law, philosophy, art, and especially hope: Athens from about 599 to 323 B.C. As Athens rose to prominence as a military and commercial force, it attracted people from rural areas. Prosperity, power, and new ideas appealed to the adventurous and ambitious. Their migrations, along with the cultural heterogeneity which wars and class battles had produced, led to a loosening of the close family ties which had dominated both the *shame* and *inherited guilt* cultures of the previous two eras. Men in particular began making decisions and behaving in ways which violated ancient tradition and the taboos of their rural homes. Life in Athens left them on their own with few guidelines for behavior, except those offered by the new philosophies of reason. Those philosophies openly called for an end to ancient traditions, religious superstitions, and family obligations. In their place was supposed to step reason, in the form of *new laws* consistent with the *rational* sciences which philosophers were promoting.

This shift produced the second type of *guilt* culture—a type associated with the rise of *individualism* in Greek philosophy, law, and politics. Like people in the previous Archaic Age, Athenians were violating traditional rules, especially those which demanded complete obedience to one's father. But unlike those earlier Greeks, Athenians were stripped of the notion of inherited guilt. They were left with a strictly individualized, internalized sense of guilt. Instead of blaming their ancestors, Athenians could blame only themselves for catastrophes associated with their actions. The new philosophies told them their traditional loyalties to family and clan were "irrational." With the loss of traditional loyalties, therefore, people were left with only the "rational" explanation that they alone were responsible for their actions.

Dodds concludes that in the absence of traditional loyalties, Athenians needed law. Moreover, that law needed to be *rational,* consistent with the new image of the person as a rational citizen of a rationally organized, democratic state. Reason, or understanding, they thought, would bring prosperity and the good life. Failure would be their own fault just as success would be their achievement, not the gift of some remote Olympian god. Education and self-knowledge were the keys, not religion. Since all men were responsible for their own actions, they must all be included in their governance, and judged as individuals.

But Athens never did realize its dream of total reason. Plagues and pestilence, internal dissidence, war, and death continued to shake people's confidence in the power of reason. Perhaps, some thought, the old irrational ways of tradition were best. Perhaps the gods and spirits were angry with them for their arrogant abandonment of patriarchal domination within the family. Thus irrationality warred with rationality, and many of the leading voices of reason, such as Socrates', were forced to recant their teachings, leave Athens in exile, or suffer death. The great republic of political democracy and the rule of law became only a flawed memory, a thing to be fixed up, redesigned, and offered as a dream by Plato in his version of the ideal, *The Republic.*

This, then, is Dodds's account of events in ancient Greece. It is an account of social and legal change. It contains hypotheses about how and why law developed as it did over the centuries. You should therefore be able to use the materials in chapters 3, 4, and 5 to evaluate the adequacy of this account.

How would this account fit, for example, with chapter 3's emphasis on the production of law from custom? Does it support that theory or does it lend more support to chapter 4's account of social structure as the determining factor?

Does Dodds's account give enough information so that you can answer the above questions? Does it allow you to distinguish between social structure and class conflict as rival explanations of legal development? For example, do you know enough about Greek class relationships from this account to assert that class rivalries either do or do not explain the shift from familial customs to Athenian law? What additional information about ancient Greece would you look for if you wanted to develop a well-supported argument for one of the three theoretical perspectives? How would a critical theorist look on Dodds's use of the shame-culture–guilt-culture dichotomy? How does this account fit with Nader's analysis (in chapter 4) of the differences between two Mexican villages? Does the fact that Athenian society was divided between free, voting citizens and slaves with no political rights need to be added to the picture when deciding among the three theories? If so, what change would it make in your assessment?

REFERENCES

ALTHUSSER, L. AND BALIBAR, E.   (1970), *Reading "Capital"* (Ben Brewster, Transl.) London: New Left Books.
BAYLEY, DAVID   (1977), Modes and Mores of Policing the Community in Japan, in Richard Vuylsteke (ed.), *Law and Society: Culture Learning through Law* Honolulu: East-West Center, p. 71.
BENEDICT, RUTH   (1946), *The Chrysanthemum and the Sword,* Boston: Houghton Mifflin.
BRAVERMAN, HARRY   (1974), *Labor and Monopoly Capital,* New York: Monthly Review Press.
CHAMBLISS, WILLIAM   (1964), A Sociological Analysis of the Law of Vagrancy, *Social Problems,* 12, p. 67.
CLOKE, KENNETH   (1971), The Economic Basis of Law and State, in Robert Lefcourt (ed.), *Law Against the People,* New York: Vintage Books.
CURRIE, ELLIOTT   (1968), Crimes without Criminals: Witchcraft and Its Control in Renaissance Europe, *Law and Society Review,* 3, p. 7.
DIAMOND, STANLEY   (1971), The Rule of Law vs. the Order of Custom, in Robert Wolff, (ed.), *The Rule of Law,* New York: Simon & Schuster.
DODDS, E. R.   (1951), *The Greeks and the Irrational,* Berkeley, Calif.: University of California Press.
DUBOW, FREDRIC   (1973), *Justice for People: Law and Politics in the Lower Courts of Tanzania,* Doctoral Dissertation, Berkeley: University of California Press.
FORER, NORMAN   (1979), The Imposed Wardship of American Indian Tribes: A Case Study of the Prairie Band Potawatomi, in Sandra Burman and Barbara Harrell-Bond (eds.), *The Imposition of Law,* New York: Academic Press.
FRANK, ANDRE GUNDER   (1979), *Dependent Accumulation and Underdevelopment,* New York: Monthly Review Press.
FRANK, ANDRE GUNDER   (1967), *Capitalism and Underdevelopment in Latin America* New York: Monthly Review Press.
HALEY, JOHN O.   (1982), The Politics of Informal Justice: The Japanese Experience, 1922–1942, in Richard Abel (ed.), *The Politics of Informal Justice* Volume 2, New York: Academic Press, pp. 125–147.

HIRST, PAUL   (1976), Althusser and the Theory of Ideology, *Economy and Society*, 5, p. 385.

HOWKINS, ALUN   (1979), Economic Crime and Class Law: Poaching and the Game Laws, 1840–1880, in Sandra Burman and Barbara Harrell-Bond (eds.), *The Imposition of Law*, New York: Academic Press.

HUNT, ALAN   (1978), *The Sociological Movement in Law*, Philadelphia: Temple University Press.

MAAS, PETER   (1973), *Serpico*, New York: Viking.

MEDCALF, LINDA   (1978), *Law and Identity: Lawyers, Native Americans, and Legal Practice*, Beverly Hills, Calif.: Sage Publications, Inc.

MENDELSOHN, OLIVER   (1981), The Pathology of the Indian Legal System, *Modern Asian Studies*, 15, p. 823.

PLATT, ANTHONY   (1977), *The Child Savers: The Invention of Delinquency* Chicago: University of Chicago Press.

QUINNEY, RICHARD   (1974), *Critique of Legal Order*, Boston: Little, Brown.

SCHWARTZ, RICHARD AND MILLER, JAMES   (1964), Legal Evolution and Societal Complexity, *American Sociological Review*, 70, p. 159.

SHERMAN, LAWRENCE   (1974), *Police Corruption: A Sociological Perspective* New York: Anchor Press, Doubleday.

SMITH, W. EUGENE AND SMITH, AILEEN   (1975), *Minamata*, New York: Holt, Rinehart, & Winston.

SUMNER, COLIN   (1979), *Reading Ideologies: An Investigation into the Theory of Ideology and Law*, New York: Academic Press.

THOMPSON, E. P.   (1975), *Whigs and Hunters: The Origin of the Black Act*, New York: Pantheon.

TURK, AUSTIN   (1976), Law as a Weapon in Social Conflict, *Social Problems*, 23, p. 276.

WALLERSTEIN, IMMANUEL   (1974) *The Modern World System*, New York: Academic Press.

6

LEGAL IMPACT: DOES LAW MAKE ANY DIFFERENCE?

In chapters 2–5, we drew together many kinds of evidence from a variety of social environments in order to address relatively abstract questions. Much of the work now being done in this field, however, is begun because some practical question needs answering. Should federal law regulate cable television? What will happen if narcotics use becomes decriminalized? If we increase the number of district court judges, can we reduce delay and congestion in the courts? Is there any way to provide greater legal service to middle-income families? If we make those improvements, what effect will they have?

In the next three chapters you will see that, as ample and diverse as these questions have been, we can find important common threads running through them which can help us to organize our thinking about law. Chapters 6 and 7 deal with two major categories of research on law and society: *legal-impact* studies and research on *disputes* and *litigation*. Aside from being generally recognized categories of theory and research, these two subjects display opposite ways of viewing the law.

Legal-impact studies usually ask questions which treat law as a top-down process, while many studies of disputing take a bottom-up approach. That is, in legal-impact studies, the questions begin with the assumption that *lawmakers* and *enforcers* (people at the top) make legal decisions to which others are expected to respond. In studies of disputing and litigation, the focus is on the *law-making potential* within the activities of *ordinary* people in conflict with each other. Law in the impact study is an external stimulus introduced into society by some social-control agent. Law in dispute studies tends to be seen as a set of institutional responses to activities initiated within society by ordinary people.

As you can see, this dichotomy resembles the distinction between structuralism and conflict theory (chapters 4 and 5). Most legal impact research has been conducted with at least vague assumptions, if not outright assertions, that structural principles of analysis best clarify impact issues. Some research on disputing comes more clearly from the conflict theory tradition.

However, you should not exaggerate this distinction. You will see that both subjects, legal impact and disputing, have been addressed from all three theoretical perspectives presented in chapters 3, 4, and 5. The top-down approach to impact studies has been criticized by conflict theorists. The bottom-up approach to disputing has been put to the test and modified in several different ways.

In chapter 8, I review both top-down and bottom-up thinking about proposals aimed at simplifying legal institutions. These proposals, which have recently gained considerable popularity, help us integrate much of the theory and research in chapters 2–7 because they directly address the prospects for legal programs which would buck the tide of modernization. When people propose reforms to "uncomplicate" the law, they directly confront the processes discussed earlier concerning the origins of law. They also face issues of legal impact, and their programs typically involve the creation of simple ways to handle disputes. In chapter 8, therefore, we are saying to ourselves: "Now that we have reviewed what we know about legal processes, what can we say about the probable outcome of a particular family of reform proposals? What kinds of questions should we ask about those proposals? Where should we look for answers?"

INTRODUCTION: LEGAL IMPACT
AND COMMON SENSE

In 1954, when the Supreme Court ruled against segregation in the public schools, [Henry] Luce (the founder and czar of the *Time-Life*, Inc. publishing empire), son of a missionary, was vastly relieved. "Well, that's good," he said to his editors, "that takes care of that problem." As far as he was concerned the problem of race and segregation in America no longer existed. (Halberstam, 1979, p. 77)

With hindsight, it is easy for us to see how naïve and inaccurate such a conclusion could be. With riots in Boston and Miami and continued school segregation a general pattern more than a quarter of a century after the Supreme Court's ruling, it is obvious that even the highest court in the land has limits on its ability to alter social conditions in the United States through law.

But how much do we know about those limits? And how different is Henry Luce from the rest of us when he thinks that once a law is passed or a court judgment is given, people will obey and the problem will be solved? One of the most predictable features of modern journalism is the attention it gives to the passage of laws and the rendering of courtroom verdicts establishing new rules for the rest of us to live by. Each year the causes change. What remains constant is the apparent belief that conditions will improve, life will be better, justice will prevail, if only the law can be changed.

In the late 1970s and early 1980s, for example, great controversy raged over the issue of abortion. The 1973 Supreme Court ruling which "legalized" abortion represented a turning point to many people. Some saw it as a major breakthrough for good sense, civil rights for women, and the abandonment of hypocritical and uneven restraint on people's morals. Others saw it as a major setback for American morality, an expansion of "godless humanism," and an open door for "legalized murder." On both sides there was deep conviction that changes in the law would produce major changes in society. Millions of dollars were spent to oust congressional opponents of "the right laws." Volunteers worked tirelessly to promote passage of legal reform, putting pressure on legislators, administrators, and doctors and hospitals to get the law altered in the desired direction.

These actions and convictions typify many controversies in American life. They also reflect a general tendency to believe that social conditions can be changed if the law is changed.

But can they? And if so, how reliable is law as a tool? Those are the basic questions of this chapter.

LAW AS VACCINE: A MODERN PERSPECTIVE

The question of legal impact is the central concern for many of the social scientists who study law. In a general sense, all social scientific study of law is concerned with the impact question, since all studies attempt to interpret information about the place of law within larger social processes. But many social scientists see the question of legal impact as a special set of issues requiring separate study and separate interpretations.

Most of those who take this approach share a basic assumption that law is like a medical *vaccine*. It is a curative injected into socially ailing institutions to restore their health. As with a vaccine, the critical questions are (1) Does a legal initiative work? and (2) What are its side effects? This position is most often identified with structuralists (see chapter 4), since structural theory tends to treat existing social institutions as organisms in which the parts function to preserve the overall unit. But critical theorists (chapter 5) often adopt vaccinelike views of the law's impact, though they differ from the structuralists in that they see the vaccine as helping to create or sustain a social monster.

Those who study legal impact under the influence of this vaccine model usually conduct their research as follows: (1) They identify a clearly defined legal action with a specific target population; (2) they search for cases where relevant behavior should have changed, testing whether it did; and (3) they try to determine whether the legal action produced the change or failed to produce it.

Looking at law in this way may seem like common sense now. But it is by no means typical of the ways legal actions were evaluated in the past. During the nineteenth century, for example, lawyers and judges carried on their law-making and law-changing work without ever conducting scientific impact studies. When judges ruled that the law should require a particular action, they did so on the basis of their own intuition about what people were like psychologically or what conditions were like economically or socially. They often referred to abstract ideas about how people ought to think and how they ought to make their own decisions. *Utilitarianism* was a general philosophy which informed much of the development of criminal law, for example. It held that people make their decisions about obedience to law according to the balance between costs and benefits of obedience. That is why so much of formal criminal law ranks crimes and assigns greater or lesser penalties. It was assumed that higher penalties would counter the temptation to commit more serious or rewarding crimes. But the assumptions were never put to the test.

Only by screening new law cases brought before their courts could judges evaluate the adequacy of their abstract ideas. But even that meager information was lacking among the legal scholars of the time. They constructed elaborate logical theories of particular legal codes which they proposed to use, not because anyone could show that they worked, but because they were "pure"—all statements in the code fit together logically.

Going back even further, we find periods in history when it simply did not matter whether the law was practical, whether it worked. The law of those times was *sacred* (see Unger, 1976, pp. 47–133). It was decreed by God, through his earthly representatives, the kings or bishops. Under those circumstances, you would not even have dared to ask the kinds of

questions raised in this chapter. You would have been accused of blas-
phemy, or at best irrelevance, if you had asked what effects the law was
having. If it was God's law, the only issue was obedience.

So when we ask today whether a law has an impact, when we see that a
whole research tradition has now developed around getting *scientific* answers to practical questions about the law, we are looking at a peculiarly
modern legal development. It reflects a major change in the way people
think about the law. Law is no longer sacred, a command to be obeyed
unthinkingly. Now we routinely treat it as a tool, an instrument for the fine
tuning of a social machine. If we are to obey it, we must be convinced that it
"works," that it "makes sense," that it is having its intended effects. We
seem to believe that we can discover answers to these questions, and that we
can then change the law to improve its effectiveness. Science, in this case
social science, has become the knowledge system in which we believe.

In the legal-impact study, we have turned science, our most convincing system of knowledge, to questions of law. One of the most celebrated
aspects of the Supreme Court's school desegregation decision in 1954 was
that the judges listened to, and used, social scientific studies showing the
negative psychological impact of segregated schooling on black children.
Since that decision, social scientific analysis has appeared with increasing
regularity in court testimony, legislative debate, and administrative policy
debate. The 1980 census was challenged in court by several large cities,
which claimed that their populations had been undercounted. The loss of
government benefits resulting from such undercounts could be in the hundreds of millions of dollars and have far-reaching effects on the continued
economic health of whole regions. The court battles that raged over the
census were primarily confrontations between social scientists using demo-
graphic information and evidence about effective survey techniques. The
census, as an element of various legal policies, had to undergo strict scientific scrutiny.

IMPACT STUDIES: EXAMPLES

On its face, the legal-impact question seems straightforward enough. Do
laws against murder curtail murder? Does the Supreme Court decision that
police must advise suspects of their rights before interrogation (the famous
Miranda decision) "handcuff" the police for effective crime fighting, as
many police claim? Does a law governing the disposal of toxic wastes and
the release of polluting gases into the atmosphere produce a cleaner, safer
environment? Does a government agency created to regulate the airline
industry result in safer, less costly, more complete air service than before?
Such questions don't appear insoluble. And they are important to many
people, because we spend great amounts of our time and wealth either

trying to make such laws work or finding new ones that will work better. These are the kinds of concerns which have led to a large number of "legal-impact" studies conducted within the framework of the *vaccine* model, which treats law as a curative injected into ailing social institutions to restore social health.

The Unevenness of Impact

One thing which early impact studies showed was the not too surprising fact that sudden legal changes don't always produce the results intended by the judges or lawmakers. The Supreme Court ruled in 1948 that public schools could not be used for religious instruction, since such use violated the principle of separation of church and state. The obvious question is, did public school officials comply with this decision?

Public school responses to the Supreme Court ruling showed that you could find almost any response imaginable if you looked far enough (Patric, 1957). Some schools immediately terminated religious instruction. Others made adjustments so that it would look as though they were complying while they actually continued to give religious instruction as before. Still others totally ignored the ruling and went right on teaching religion as they always had. No single response typified the impact of the Court's decision.

Many impact studies have shown slow and uneven "percolation" of court decisions down through society. We have learned that judicial decrees are only one of many steps which must be taken before most new legal doctrines can begin to correspond with what is actually happening in society.

The Unpredictability of Impact

Sometimes laws which were passed to produce one effect end up having either unintended side effects or opposite effects from those intended. One recent study (Croyle, 1979) compared the rules adopted by state court judges concerning the extent to which manufacturers could be held responsible for injuries caused by their products. In some states, *product liability* was very limited. Manufacturers could only be forced to pay for injuries to the persons who bought the product, not to bystanders or family friends. Other states allowed manufacturers to write their own warranties and ruled that only the terms of the warranties could govern claims against manufacturers. But in other states, judges adopted rules making the manufacturer's liability much more severe. Some held that warranties applied to anyone who was using a product reasonably, whether they had bought it or not. The strictest state courts held manufacturers responsible to anyone injured by the product whether it came with a warranty or not.

One possible side effect of stiff liability laws could be their effects on the amount of insurance coverage manufacturers purchase against liability lawsuits. If manufacturers in the more severe, *strict liability* states spent more on insurance, their products would cost more. A side effect of strict liability standards, then, would be higher costs for consumers. Impact research showed that this is exactly the case. Companies in the strictest states have increased their liability coverage by about 20 percent over the amounts being paid for insurance in the loosest states. A reasonable conclusion from this research is that new liability laws laid down by state court judges have far-reaching effects on prices paid for products and on relationships between producers and consumers.

Looking at criminal law, some researchers believe they have good evidence to support what has come to be known as *labeling theory*. In effect, this is a theory of legal impact, because it argues that people develop criminal patterns of life *after* they have been caught and prosecuted by the criminal justice system and *because* of that process (Becker, 1963; Schur, 1971). Labeling theorists hold that once people have been caught and prosecuted, they begin to think of themselves as criminals and others treat them as such (shunning contact with them and excluding them from "legitimate" work and recreational activities). As a result, criminal patterns are the only ones left open to labeled persons, and their criminal behavior increases.

In a study of shoplifters, for example, juveniles who were caught and prosecuted were measurably more likely to do more shoplifting than were those who admitted having done it and "gotten away with it" (Klemke, 1978). The impact of the law, and of the actions of law enforcers, then, appears to be the opposite of its purpose.

Can Law Change Attitudes?

Some impact studies ask whether changes in the law can produce changes in people's attitudes. This concern goes back to the idea we discussed in chapter 3 that "lawways cannot change mores"—that you cannot change people's ideas, beliefs, and values by force, but must tailor the laws to fit the attitudes they already have.

One of the most worried-about and researched attitudes in the United States is the degree of racial prejudice and hatred in the population. Can legal action change those attitudes? One study asked whether the Supreme Court's 1954 school desegregation decision had produced an increase or decrease in levels of racial tension, prejudice, and hatred (Hyman and Sheatsley, 1964). It is often argued that decisions like this on such a controversial matter simply inflame passions and worsen an already bad situation.

But surveys of attitudes in 1942 before the decision, in 1956 soon after it, and in 1963 showed that racial attitudes became more tolerant after the decision. Expressions of prejudice and hatred declined ᴗver the years. One interpretation is that the Supreme Court's decision, combined with official actions taken by government officials to comply with that ruling, resulted in a general reconciliation in the attitudes of whites toward blacks. The psychological mechanism applied in this case is called *cognitive dissonance*. This theory says that people cannot persist in behaving in ways that are incompatible with their beliefs and values. "Apparently the pattern is that as official action works to bury what is already regarded as a lost cause, public acceptance of integration increases because opinions are readjusted to the inevitable reality" (Hyman and Sheatsley, 1964). If the law prevents people from acting consistently with old beliefs and values, then they abandon the old beliefs and adopt new ones which fit the actions they find themselves doing. This approach thus rejects Sumner's claim that "lawways cannot change folkways." Law can change "folkways" or "mores" through the process of cognitive dissonance.

Impact studies generally follow the pattern we see in these examples. They focus on a limited, specific instance where the law is changed or invoked for specific purposes, and they ask whether that purpose has been achieved. Some also ask whether, like strong vaccines and medicines, legal actions have negative side effects unforeseen by the lawmakers. The studies we have looked at so far in this chapter show both of these concerns. But each of them contains assumptions, and a view of the law's significance, which may make their conclusions unsound. We will return to them after we take a look at some of the basic problems anyone has in trying to measure legal impact.

LEGAL IMPACT: PROBLEMS OF MEASUREMENT

The question of legal impact is basically a problem of explaining behavior. We want to know whether the changes or patterns we see in people's actions can be explained as a response to changes in the law.

Now, imagine yourself sitting high on a cliff overlooking a vast desert. Crossing the desert are two highways which intersect at a point where a person can see twenty miles in all directions. As you watch, a car comes into view and twenty minutes later it approaches the intersection. It comes to a complete stop and then proceeds. As you watch, five other cars, spaced out over a two-hour period, do the same thing. But you notice that cars coming along the other highway go right through the intersection without stopping. What do you conclude? There must be a stop sign on the one highway and not on the other. Your binoculars confirm your suspicion. Cars stop because the stop sign (the law) says they must. You have just observed "legal impact."

Or have you? Is there any other way of explaining why those cars stopped? If there is, then law may not be the decisive cause of the behavioral pattern you have observed.

Obedience vs. Self-Interest

First, ask yourself this: Would I stop like that if I could see for twenty miles on both sides that nothing was coming? Research shows that if you are a typical driver, you probably would not stop under those conditions (Feest, 1968). At most, you would probably slow down and "roll through," stopping just enough to look both ways. As a typical driver, you would stop completely, as the law says you must, only if trees, a hedge, or a hill obstructed your view of the crossing highway, so that you had to stop to be safe. The only other reason for stopping would be if you saw a police car parked near the intersection.

Here, then, is our first major obstacle in answering the question Does law make any difference—does it account for the observed behavior? How can we know that people's actions are a response to law if their behavior also conforms to their own self-interest? Whenever we try to explain behavior as stemming from the operation of a norm, whether legal or not, we must show that the behavior has been channeled away from obviously self-serving behavior toward action which is more socially acceptable.

We would not say, for example, that people are obeying the law if they avoid scaling the outer wall of the World Trade Center in New York because they are afraid of heights, or know nothing about mountain-climbing techniques, or prefer frisbee throwing as recreation. The law may say that it is illegal to climb that building. But we can see that most people don't do it because they are afraid of falling.

To conclude that the law has an impact *because it is law,* then, we must show that poeple are choosing actions which, but for the law, are incompatible with their self-interest. We must show that if people do act in their self-interest in conforming with the law, it is because the law, not other circumstances, has made the action self-serving.

An example which shows these difficulties of interpretation comes from Hawaii. In Honolulu immediately after World War II, a severe housing shortage resulted in the passage of *rent-control laws* aimed at preventing profiteering (Ball, 1960). Landlords who obeyed the law got lower returns on their real-estate investments. To obey the law meant to sacrifice their goal of maximum profits from rents.

The law did not place equal restrictions on all landlords. Three categories of landlords had been created by the law. Rents were frozen according to a schedule of dates based on when the buildings had been built and first rented. In other words, rents were "rolled back" to three different earlier levels. The practical effect of this distinction was the creation of three different levels of restriction on rents. The amount of landlord compliance with these laws was measured by interviewing the tenants. They were asked how much rent they were supposed to pay (by law) and how much the landlord actually made them pay. The amount of compliance with the law varied according to the severity of its restrictions on landlords' profits. The group which showed the highest level of compliance was the group hurt least by the regulations. Landlords most severely restricted by the laws were also the most frequent law violators.

These differences are evidence that the contents of the law can make a difference. But the difference here was not so much between preregulation and postregulation rents as between whether or not landlords who charged the rents they felt entitled to were breaking the law. Those whom the law allowed to charge the highest rents were quite content to obey the law, because to do so was compatible with their self-interest as defined independently of the law. Did the law actually control rents in Honolulu? In other words, did it have its intended impact? A certain percentage of landlords in all three categories obeyed the law. But large amounts of housing remained available to tenants only if they cooperated with landlords by paying extra.

Our first major difficulty in demonstrating impact, then, comes from the problem we have sorting out self-interested behavior from law-following behavior.

Law vs. Morality or Habit

Getting back to our stop sign example, another complication in concluding that the law makes people stop shows up in evidence that people with passengers in their cars stop consistently more often than people driving alone. What does this mean? Are the drivers with passengers trying to be more careful because of their added responsibility? Or are people with passengers in less of a hurry? Perhaps (and here is the rub) people with passengers feel some kind of *moral pressure* on them, either to be more careful, or to obey the law. Another possibility is that people who drive alone are just a different group of people (loners, angry young men, hot rodders, etc.) who have different driving habits.

Feest was not able to test all these variations, but his observations certainly complicate the simple *vaccine model*, which holds that the stop sign, and the law enforcers represented by the sign, make people stop. These observations point out the necessity of considering the *social context* within which the law operates. Does compliance indicate obedience to the law? Or is it produced by the simple compatibility between what the law says and what people customarily do anyway? If a neighborhood stormed city hall after the death of a local child at a dangerous intersection, demanding a stop sign there, how would we explain it when we then observed them stopping at the new stop sign? We would at least have to consider the possibility that they stop because neighborhood morality, and their own inner convictions, make them stop. This problem applies to all impact studies: The behavior we observe might prove that the law is just a symbol restating what people have already chosen to do rather than a "vaccine" which impels them to conform to an unwanted directive.

The effect of passengers on stopping behavior also raises the possibility that people sometimes obey the law *because* it is *the law*—people feel moral (not just legal) pressure to obey laws, and therefore are more likely to do so in the presence of other people, even if those people are not empowered to enforce the law. In other words, the law may have a halo of legitimacy which interacts with public opinion to produce compliance. An alternative to this process is the theory that people only stop because they fear being caught by the police. Careful observation of many law-related situations would be needed to sort out whether people who stop fully, even when there is obviously no cross traffic, do so out of respect for the law or out of fear of prosecution. People may even differ in this respect, some stopping for one reason and others for the other.

Related to this issue of moral pressure is the possibility that a law creates a situation where people feel liberated to do what they could not before. If racial hatred and prejudice create pressure on business operators, for example, to exclude blacks, then a law requiring equal treatment in business places could liberate those merchants who wanted to have the additional business from blacks but feared losing white customers. Such a law could also liberate those who wanted to act decently towards blacks but feared reprisals. In such a case, the law would be having an impact, but our measure of that impact would be complicated by the fact that it produces compliance because it fits with self-interest or moral preference rather than violating them.

Returning again to our stop sign example, another complication is caused by the fact that people may stop at stop signs out of sheer *habit*. They have ridden in cars all their lives. As children, they watched adults stopping. When they learned to drive, they probably began obeying stop signs out of fear, or the desire to please teachers and parents, or some general belief in the need to obey the law. But as people become older, these original reasons may drop away, leaving habit as the explanation. Drivers who stop out of habit would be difficult to distinguish from all others who stop for other reasons.

Obligation vs. Information

Still another complication, connected with the issue of self-interest, is that the stop sign provides *information*. It announces that you are approaching a dangerous driving situation, that highway engineers have studied that place and concluded that you must stop in order to be sure you don't drive into danger.

Some laws are more obviously designed primarily to give information than others. Laws against homicide do give information about what law enforcers will do to you if you murder someone. But their primary purpose is normative—they are made on the grounds that murder is wrong, despicable, and therefore to be punished. But consider legal doctrine which requires cigarette manufacturers to warn you that cigarette smoking is dangerous to your health. Here is a law at the other end of the spectrum. It does not prevent you from making or selling cigarettes, and it permits you to smoke them. But it insists that the message be repeatedly announced. The question is whether a study of the impact of these messages is a study of *legal* impact. While it is government which is producing the announcement, there seems to be an important difference between this kind of "law" and one which punishes lawbreakers. The information function is not much different from the commercial presentation of advertisements for vitamin pills, fire prevention week, or exercise bicycles. We don't even begin to ask whether those messages have "legal" impact.

The problem is that many laws are a mixture of *command* and *information*. Helmet laws not only *inform* people about the dangers of unprotected cycling; they also *punish* people who don't protect themselves. So, when a researcher demonstrates that states with helmet laws have fewer motorcycling fatalities and higher rates of helmet use (Robertson, 1976), the interpretation problem comes in sorting out whether the law had its effect because of its threat of punishment (a true legal impact), because it was the law and the law should be obeyed (also a true legal impact), or because the law alerted people to the dangers of cycling. The informational impact of law is not such a pure case of legal impact, because it is not clear that its effect is any different from the effect we might get from a high-powered Madison Avenue media blitz.

Positive vs. Negative Impact

One last possibility must not be overlooked—that the law will have its impact by tempting people to break it *because it is the law*. This is the opposite of legitimacy. Some people may roll through stop signs just to prove their independence or their willingness to dare. If we can show that they fail to stop where they otherwise would have, then we have shown *negative impact*. During the 1960s and 1970s it was often argued that drug use was increasing *because* the law forbade such use. As a reaction against the Vietnam War and Watergate, the argument went, young people smoked pot and used other drugs. It was a way of symbolizing their denial of legitimacy to the authorities which were responsible for unwanted political conditions. Note that these users were choosing to ignore the informational content of narcotics laws, which claimed that drug use would produce mental and physical health problems. But can we say that they became users because the law told them not to? That is a question of impact.

Stop sign behavior may not strike you as an earth-shaking problem. It is used here to show that even in such a simple legal impact setting, complex problems plague our attempts to measure the law's impact. The same issues arise when we want to know what effect a farm subsidy bill has on wheat production, or whether a gun-control law in a particular city reduces rates of violent crime, or whether a Supreme Court verdict in favor of abortions has any effect on their frequency. Our basic problem is to show either that legal action produces behavior that would not otherwise have happened, or that the behavior commanded by law has not been forthcoming (see Weber, 1962, pp. 3–4, 7, 13, 26). To do so, we must somehow demonstrate that other nonlegal explanations for the behavior we observe cannot better account for that behavior.

Impact Examples: A Second Look

Looking back at the impact-study examples we discussed earlier, we find that they all have difficulties proving their case. In the study of product liability judgments, for example, impact conclusions have been attacked on two grounds, the first of them similar to the issues we confronted with stop signs and the second another kind we have not yet discussed. First, economic decisions, such as whether or not to increase liability insurance coverage, are made on the basis of a host of complicated economic calculations (Rabin, 1979). The law's contribution to those equations is difficult to isolate. Second, the state of the law itself may not be clear.

This second criticism is especially damaging to the conclusion that judge-made law led to higher insurance payments. The research isolated one judicial decision as marking a turning point in court handling of liability suits, arguing that, like a stop sign suddenly posted at an intersection, the decision put a sudden barrier in the path of producers. But the judge who made that decision did so because most courts had already adopted the stricter standards, though they had not stated clearly that their rulings constituted a new legal position (Rabin, 1979). In other words, dramatic legal change was not dramatic at all. Business managers had years of experience adjusting to new judicial positions, and probably also years of opportunity to influence the course of implementation of the new rules through their own actions in legal and political battle. If judicial action produced changes, short-term impact research could not have detected them.

The study showing attitude changes after the Supreme Court's school desegregation decision is weakened by its overreliance on *cross-sectional* data—that is, data from fixed points in time. For one thing, the attitudes of the *same people* were not measured both before and after the Court's decision. Rather, the data came from surveys of randomly sampled populations at three different times. The legal-impact conclusion rests on the assumption that such sampling makes the surveyed populations comparable. The problem is that there are many other things happening to affect a population's attitudes over time besides their experience with the law.

For example, the researchers concluded that the decision had its most noticeable effects on the attitudes of southern whites, who showed the largest amount of attitude change over time. But during this same period, migration of whites from northern to southern states, and blacks from southern to northern states was producing a major change in the composition of the southern population which later surveys sampled. Each subsequent survey of "southerners" included more northern whites than the previous one. Since the data also show that northerners generally hold attitudes more favorable to blacks, this flow of northerners into the south could be the reason that "southerners" appear to be making the biggest attitude shift.

But this research also suffers from its failure to demonstrate that a change in people's attitudes goes along with a change in their behavior. Suppose we found that a whole white population suddenly started *saying* that they loved and respected blacks. And suppose we could demonstrate that the change was produced by a court decision. Would we conclude that there had been legal impact if we also found that these same whites continued to practice discrimination in all the major institutional areas of social life where they had always done so before the court's decision? Is it enough to show that attitudes, as expressed on a survey, have changed? A rival explanation would be that people have simply learned what kind of racial attitudes they are *supposed* to show to strangers asking survey questions. That would be a problem for survey designers.

But the attitude-behavior connection contains an even more nagging problem for the legal-impact conclusion. The problem lies in questionable assumptions about the way major patterns of social life are established and maintained. Even if there were a genuine shift in people's attitudes toward a racial minority, the intricate patterns of social and economic organization in a complex society might prove forcefully resistant to changes which would provide true equality to the minority. The term *institutionalized racism* has been applied to the theory that even people with the most benign racial attitudes participate in the repression of minorities, because their "normal" participation in "normal" institutions preserves the deprivation and exclusion which minorities have traditionally faced. For example, court-ordered school desegregation in major American cities has moved at a snail's pace despite the Supreme Court's directive that it proceed "with all deliberate speed." This happens because institutional patterns of new housing construction and the decentralization of industry away from the older central cities has produced minority-group concentrations in those cities with no nearby white groups to integrate (Yancey and Ericksen, 1979). Whether whites care or not for minority groups and racial equality, whether they are prejudiced or not, their pursuit of economic security and the best housing they can afford produces patterns of residential segregation which are reflected in school populations. Nothing could be clearer than the image of integrated public schools which the 1954 Supreme Court justices wrote into their decision. But the persistence of de facto school segregation, especially in northern cities, decades after that decision attests to the problems we have discussed in trying to measure the impact of legal action. It also highlights the inadequacy of proving that people's attitudes are changed by judicial decrees.

FILTERING AGENTS AND IMPACT MODIFICATION

Researchers who have tried to avoid some of the pitfalls discussed so far in this chapter find themselves trying to understand the *social context* within which particular laws are supposed to have impact. One context is the social world of *law enforcers.* When laws are passed or judicial decisions rendered, police, prosecutors, public defenders, regulatory agency administrators, and private law administrators are among those whose actions affect the way the law really works, the impact it has. *Law interpreters* (lawyers and judges) are a second group making up the context of legal impact. The third general category we will discuss here involves the patterns of social interaction which exist in the general population, especially between members of the *population* most directly *targeted* in the specific laws.

All three of these groups can be thought of as *filters* through which legal changes are processed and modified.

Impact Filters: Law Enforcers

In chapter 3 we saw one good example of law enforcers affecting law's impact. We discussed the state of Connecticut's attempt to crack down on speeding violators by using severe penalties (Campbell and Ross, 1968). The governor took false credit for reductions in the amount of fast driving on Connecticut roads. The reason official records showed less speeding was that state police officers altered their procedures and drastically reduced the frequency of arrests they made after stopping speeders. They issued more warnings and fewer citations because their own views on the legitimacy of the strict new laws, combined with the pressure put on them by outraged, and in many cases influential, guilty citizens, combined to make the new regulation unenforceable.

This study shows that the impact of a law can be strongly filtered through the attitudes, working conditions, and career prospects of those who are charged with frontline enforcement of the law.

Other evidence shows this to be a general characteristic of law enforcement: When laws are made especially severe, they are likely to be less well-enforced than more moderate laws. In England during the eighteenth century, the death penalty was ordered for a long list of crimes including some which were trivial (pickpocketing and petty theft). The result was a drastic decline in prosecutions for those crimes. The decline continued until the death penalty was lifted (Tobias, 1968, p. 199). Malaysia and India show markedly different success rates in collecting income taxes because India's severe tax has produced massive tax evasion in which public officials collude (Myrdal, 1968, p. 2102). Puerto Rican laws against check forgery were at one time so severe that they had relatively little effect (Beutel and Medero, 1967). In four different studies of the effects of sudden increases in penalties for driving violations, Ross found that law enforcers compensated for the severity by reducing their enforcement activity to a level which fit their idea of good law and reduced public pressure on them to a tolerable level (1976).

The process also works in reverse. When laws against homosexuals were rescinded in Colorado in 1972, local police apparently continued to take action against gays at the same rate as before (Ross, 1976, p. 411). The decriminalization of homosexuality was too sudden to accept, both for the police themselves and for many citizens whose opinions influenced the police.

Severity or softness of the law are not the only conditions under which the law's effects are modified by law enforcers. These cases merely dramatize a general fact—that laws are always filtered through complex decision-making networks of enforcers. Because this is true, the impact of particular pieces of legislation, judicial decisions, or administrative orders is apt to be modified in sometimes surprising directions.

Our first impulse is to assume that insurance companies would be as stingy as they could in settling claims. They are, after all, in business to make a profit. They are huge financial institutions—what do they care about the injured individual to whom they owe compensation?

Research on auto accident claim settlements, however, shows that insurance companies normally give out settlements *higher* than the law requires of them (Ross, 1970). The reason involves working conditions and career considerations among claims adjusters at the bottom rung of the companies. The adjusters are like many other people—they want to please their supervisors and get ahead in the company. To do that, they must "clear" their case loads as quickly as possible. It is more important to supervisors to settle claims quickly than to squeeze them down to the lowest possible dollar figure.

Pressure for settlement is strong because whenever a case remains unsettled for any length of time, the chances increase that claimants will get lawyers and their cases will end up in litigation. If this happens, the size of each claim quickly escalates, and the costs of lawsuits to the company more than make up for the small extra payments they might have to make for early, nonlitigated settlements. Claimants might not get any more out of lawsuits than they would by early settlement. But the lawyer's fees, the fees paid by claimants for lawyer-recommended visits to medical specialists and hospitals, fees paid for extra x-rays and blood tests as evidence for the judge, and fees paid for expert witnesses might all end up coming out of the insurer's treasury. Much better to settle quickly and avoid all those extras.

Therefore claims adjusters get the message, in the form of pressure from supervisors, that the letter of the law should be ignored if the company can avoid settlement delays by paying more than the law requires. Adjusters often resent the "generous" settlements they must dole out to "blood-sucking" claimants. But they do it anyway because their futures depend on good work reports from supervisors.

Other research shows similar manipulation of legal rules among public defenders, those lawyers provided by the state for accused criminals who cannot afford their own attorneys (Sudnow, 1965). The defenders' most pressing concern is to maintain good working relations with other court personnel with whom they routinely work, and whose daily decisions could make life pleasant and rewarding or miserable and ineffective for defenders. As a result, the defenders collaborate with prosecutors and judges in developing what Sudnow calls "normal crimes."

"Normal crimes" are not necessarily the things defendants have actually done. They are formula stories which speed up the plea-bargaining process. Since the whole process of prosecution involves bargaining for pleas of guilty, all law enforcers must come to agreements about the "stories" they will put into the official record to explain, for example, why they give a three-year sentence to one burglar and probation to another. As they work together over the years, they jointly develop standard "stories" which make their actions conform with the official laws, even when a defendant's behavior does not fit the "story."

So, for example, a man accused of sexually abusing a small girl might be told by his defender to plead guilty to "loitering around a school yard" even if the crime did not take place near a school. By making this change in the story, the defender can get the defendant a lower sentence, one which is close to what the prosecutor could probably win if the case went to court, and which both prosecutor and defender agree is "just" in the particular case. By agreeing on this standard "story," the prosecutor and defender are abiding by the unwritten laws of their particular workplace rather than the written laws of the state. The formal law makes no such connection between sexual abuse and loitering. But experienced police, prosecutors, and judges would "normally" make that connection. Therefore the defender must define his or her client's crime as "normal" in order to bargain effectively with the enforcers.

The enforcement filter acts not only through the values and career motives of individual enforcers. An important source of modifications on legal impact comes from variations in the way enforcement agencies are organized. Our example here involves the enforcement of *statutory rape* laws.

Statutory rape is the charge made when a male of any age has sex with a female under the age of "consent" (usually around sixteen, but this varies from state to state). The theory is that underage girls are not able to make their own decisions, so any male who has intercourse with them must be "raping" them, even when there is no coercion.

Suppose you found drastic differences in the rates of statutory rape in two otherwise similar American cities. You could conclude that girls in one city are more sexually active than those in the other. Or you might find that the police in one city are more zealous in their pursuit of statutory rapists. Maybe people in the one city are more religiously conservative than in the other, and therefore demand stricter enforcement.

A study which uncovered a situation like this found evidence against both of those interpretations (Skolnick and Woodworth, 1970). In the city with the higher rate of statutory rape, welfare agencies had a policy of refusing medical services or pregnancy advice to "underage" pregnant girls unless they told the police the name of the man who had "raped" them. In most cases, the girls were not willing to name the "rapists" because they did not think of the act as rape. But the welfare-system–police-department link forced them to name names in exchange for needed services. As a result, police had a steady supply of solid evidence against the fathers in these cases, and their arrest rate was high.

In the city with few cases of statutory rape, there was no connection between the welfare offices and the police. Hence, girls could conceal the identities of the fathers, and police lacked the most important ingredient in any legal case against "rapists": an accusing witness (compare this situation with the English witchcraft trials described by Currie in chapter 5).

Behavior of young men and women in both cities was not significantly different. The law in both cities was also basically the same. Furthermore, individual police officers in both cities had basically similar attitudes toward the law and those who broke it. But the organizational differences in the way police departments were or were not integrated with other governmental agencies produced a sharply different pattern of law enforcement.

Impact Filters: Law Interpreters

Law filters through a population in a variety of ways. We have just reviewed some of the actions of law enforcers—police, prosecutors, and public defenders. Lawyers and judges make up a group which acts as *law interpreters*, and their actions can have significant effects on the impact of laws.

One of the United States Supreme Court's more famous decisions banned prayer in the public schools as a violation of the doctrine of separation of church and state. As in its earlier decision against religious instruction (see p. 117), the court seems to have expected their decision to bring an immediate halt to public-school prayer. But court decisions like these meet with a wide variety of responses, including outright resistance and indifference. Impact studies, which tell us only that a court decision has had uneven impact (e.g., Patric, 1957), give us very little insight into the conditions which determine how school districts (or other target populations) will react, which ones will comply and which will resist.

When the school prayer ban was announced, one school district was deeply involved in a debate over the issue (Muir, 1968). The school board's attorney played a key role in directing that school district's response to the court decision. School board members were under considerable pressure to resist the Supreme Court's ruling. Many saw their jobs in jeopardy if they voted to comply with the Court's order to eliminate prayers. Some wanted to introduce nonsectarian prayers as a kind of compromise. Had they responded the way many school boards around the country did, they would have adopted some measure of resistance to the Court's ruling.

But the school board's lawyer played a major role in getting the board to comply with the Court. Because he strongly favored the ban, he had prepared board members months in advance for a court-ordered ban. When it came, he persuaded them to abandon each of the evasions they dreamed up as responses. He also served as a kind of lightning rod to attract the wrath of pro-prayer citizens away from elected board members, since he helped them argue that their hands were tied in the matter. Without the lawyer, the board might have spent years challenging the decision and fighting lawsuits which would have changed the law very little. So the attorney, as interpreter of the law, moved the board in the direction of compliance despite their strong community-based motivation to resist.

The presence of such lawyers on school boards and their inclinations to resist or comply with the Court's decision were variable. This study was not broad enough to show how typical one school board's experience was. A school district in Indiana was probably more typical (Dolbeare and Hammond, 1971). Lacking a lawyer with pro-ban sympathies, the Indiana school board simply preserved the status quo by "allowing" individual teachers to conduct classroom prayers on a "volunteer basis."

The impact of laws, especially those guaranteeing individual rights, can be strongly affected by the economic and social context within which lawyers work. In recent years, the name Ralph Nader has become a synonym for concern about the protection of consumers against fraudulent business practices, unsafe products, and exploitative marketing strategies. He and other advocates like him are seen testifying before congressional committees, touring the country to drum up support for legislation, and publishing consumers' guides on various issues. The law, say consumer advocates, must protect individual consumers against the corporate might of the producers.

But as Ralph Nader knows (1976) and as systematic studies have shown, there is much more to *changing the law* (i.e., changing society through law) than achieving headline-grabbing legislative victories. The Magnuson-Moss Warranty Act of 1975 was a key piece of legislation in the consumer movement. It was supposed to give consumers strong ammunition in the battle against producers who would not give adequate compensation for defects in their products. The impact question is, then, Has the act helped individuals with product complaints? Research results answer "probably not" (Macaulay, 1979). The reason for this lies in the way the law has been handled by the legal profession.

A detailed study of the way lawyers in Wisconsin responded to Magnuson-Moss showed that two years after the passage of the act, almost none of Wisconsin's lawyers knew what it said. Several had never even heard of it. One reason for this widespread ignorance is that it is rarely in a lawyer's interest to learn about a particular body of law unless there is strong potential for monetary payoff in the form of a regular supply of clients with problems related to the law. To become informed about a body of law means investing time and money (money for the periodical notes which lawyers must buy to keep abreast of current developments in judicial interpretations of particular laws). In the case of consumer complaints, most Wisconsin lawyers simply did not get enough business to warrant the effort of learning about laws such as Magnuson-Moss.

Ironically, lawyers representing business clients were generally better informed about Magnuson-Moss than were those who might have been able to develop a clientele among aggrieved consumers, the persons who were supposed to benefit most from the law. Business "compliance" came mainly in symbolic form—notices printed on products pointing out the limits producers put on the warranties they were offering.

Furthermore, Wisconsin lawyers avoid formal use of *any* consumer-protection laws if they can because they want to retain the respect of judges, court officers, fellow lawyers, and potential clients in the business community. They need to avoid the image of troublemaker. They want to be known as reasonable, meaning that they guide their consumer clients into bargained settlements based on "sensible" (not legal) compromises.

Hence, for clients who have consumer complaints, most Wisconsin lawyers act as mediators between consumer and producer or supplier. As mediators, the lawyers try to bring about compromises by getting both sides to be "reasonable" and avoid the excessive costs and emotional stress of courtroom confrontations. But they rarely used the Magnuson-Moss Act or any of a number of other consumer protection laws as a consideration in their bargaining strategies. The laws may in theory have given their clients a number of important rights, but the lawyers either do not know about them or choose to ignore them in the interests of compromise.

Here, then, is a law which was passed with great fanfare in 1975 after much pressure from consumer advocates. Yet it has almost no effect two years later. Lawyers continue to handle consumer complaints as they did before the law's passage.

As Macaulay says,

> We could see most of the individual rights created by consumer protection laws, as well as many other reforms of recent times, as primarily exercises in symbolism. The reformers gained the pretty words in the statute books and some indirect impact, but the practice of those to be regulated was affected only marginally. We can wonder whether those who wrote these reforms understood that the individual rights they had created would be converted into little more than an influence on the bargaining process if lawyers learned about and chose to make use of them . . . reformers are likely to go on creating individual rights which have little chance of being vindicated, and as a result, they may fail to achieve their ends repeatedly. (1979, p. 161) (Used by permission.)

Lawyers are not the only law interpreters who mediate the effects of laws. Judges play an important role in this process. If judging were a clear-cut task of finding appropriate laws and simply applying them to the facts of each legal case, then we could easily eliminate most judges and replace them with computers. But judges in fact engage in a much more complex task which involves, among other things, taking written law and adapting it to the real-life situations brought before their courts.

Because there is room for variation in these interpretations, social scientists have asked whether *nonlegal* criteria ever affect judicial decisions. Do prejudiced judges, for example, hand out stiffer sentences to blacks? Do "hanging judges" differ from others in the severity of their sentences? Are judges influenced by the fact that they must, in some jurisdictions, run for reelection? Do they make their decisions with popular opinion in mind? Are some judges consistently probusiness and others prolabor?

Many studies show that judges are, in fact, influenced by the social environments in which they live and work (Becker, 1966; Dolbeare, 1967; Canon and Jaros, 1970; Gadbois, 1970; Jacob and Vines, 1971; Giles and Walker, 1975; Cook, 1977; Kritzer, 1979). For example, judges who traveled from one county court to another in Iowa handed down consistently more severe sentences in those counties where citizens were publicly expressing strong concern over crime (Gibson, 1980). Their sentences were also more severe if they had, at some earlier time, been defeated in a judicial election. So judges in Iowa had their "ears to the ground" as they heard and decided criminal cases. They were not "slaves to the law." The impact of criminal laws was filtered through their impressions of grass roots opinion.

It is by now generally acknowledged among social scientists that American judicial behavior is some kind of mixture between lofty indifference to outside pressures and crass appeal to popular prejudice or executive influence. But many who have studied the European courts argue that the American pattern, and to some extent the actions of judges in any of the *common law* countries (Britain, Canada, Australia, India, etc.), is unique. They hold that the *civil law* tradition of countries like France, Germany, Belgium, and Holland gives much less leeway to judges than they have in common law nations. Civil law tradition places more emphasis on spelling out all of the law's requirements and consequences in detail, creating a "seamless web" of law in which there can be no doubt about how the law will apply in specific cases (see Merryman, 1969). While there is good reason to believe that civil law systems never achieve their ideal, we can nevertheless see that the common law tradition, with the broad discretion it grants to judges, creates decisional dilemmas which are different from those in more closely regulated civil law systems. As a result, there may be a good deal more nonlegal, external influence over the interpretations American judges give to the laws they are charged with administering.

Considering the public fanfare surrounding many Supreme Court decisions, you might think that they automatically become law in lower courts. Many studies have shown, however, that decisions of the United States Supreme Court receive uneven, sometimes contradictory, treatment once they reach the hands of state court judges (see Wasby, 1970, pp. 196–203). Consider, for example, the reactions of state supreme courts to the 1960 U.S. Supreme Court ruling in *Mapp* v. *Ohio*. This was a case where the Court ruled that when police obtain evidence against a suspect illegally, the evidence cannot be admitted in the trial. If police stop and search a car just because they have a "hunch" or because the occupants "look criminal," they cannot tell a jury that they found stolen property or marijuana or illegal firearms, because they had no legal justification for searching in the first place.

State supreme courts adopted a variety of stances toward this decision (Canon, 1972). The variation came in the ways the courts elaborated the original decision. *Mapp* left many questions unanswered. Could a spouse waive immunity against search, thus leading to the arrest of the other spouse? Could police tramp through yards and peer through windows without violating Fourth Amendment rights? If a car were stopped for a traffic violation, could it be searched for evidence of other crime? Each of these ambiguities created opportunities for the state courts to express their own political and legal philosophies, personal preferences, and pressures put on them by opposing interest groups (e.g., the Fraternal Order of Police, the American Civil Liberties Union).

Reactions to *Mapp* in these courts ranged all the way from total support for the "spirit of the law" to systematic efforts to strip *Mapp* of its effectiveness in actual law enforcement situations. Some courts adopted rules which extended the *Mapp* exclusions. Others used every ambiguity to give search power back to the police. Variations like these probably occurred repeatedly with Supreme Court decisions in the 1960s because the state courts differed widely in their reactions to the "judicial revolution" wrought by the Warren Court's many rulings on behalf of civil rights and civil liberties (Wasby, 1970).

Summarizing the responses of five government agencies (e.g., the Workmen's Compensation Board and the Human Relations Commission) in Pennsylvania to that state's supreme court's rulings aimed at their operations, Johnson (1979) shows a pattern found in many other studies.

> The agencies here read the state supreme court decisions as subjectively as possible, complied as little as possible where the decisions were adverse to their interests, and utilized common techniques of avoidance and relief. . . . Two agencies did not comply because of their limited initial interpretation of the decisions. Another did not comply because enforcement probabilities seemed low. The others did not comply because they had sufficient resources to support a policy of evasion and because the costs to the agency of compliance were simply intolerable (or so they believed). (p. 55) (Used by permission.)

Outside political pressures and individual personality differences are not the only factors which alter legal impact in our courts and administrative agencies. At least as important are the limits imposed by *organizational* characteristics and *imperatives* such as those we saw affecting police work in the statutory rape example above (p. 129).

One way to see what courts do is to study them as a service industry (Friedman, 1967). Like any business, the price of court services is affected by *supply* and *demand* (*supply:* how much of the service can the business provide at any one time, given the size of its staff, its support resources, and its flexibility in adjusting to fluctuations in demand for its services; *demand:* how many people turn to the business for help with their problems).

Rules established by courts always have a dual function: (1) their apparent purpose—that is, the impact which they seem to be designed to achieve, and (2) their effect on expanding, containing, or reducing the demand on the court's services (Friedman, 1967). Courts cannot respond rapidly to sudden increases in demand for their services. There is no ready reserve of extra judges, court clerks, and courtrooms. Therefore when a judge lays down a new rule offering expanded rights or imposing new duties on some constituency in society, an important effect of that rule is the increase it will bring in *demand* for the courts' services. New rules often "open a can of worms" (e.g., the burst of lawsuits inspired by the Supreme Court's school desegregation decision). If courts accepted all possible cases stimulated by such rule changes, they would be so clogged with cases that nobody would live to see the outcome of his or her lawsuit.

Something must happen to put a rein on cases demanding judicial attention. High legal costs are one way to keep court work loads within reason. Courts also take the "can of worms" into consideration when making judgments, sometimes making conservative decisions not because these are most consistent with "the law," but because to do otherwise would create an unmanageable flood of cases which the courts could not handle.

Internal organizational problems like these cause people to work out alternatives to going to court. We saw one example of that in the handling of consumer complaints by lawyers in Wisconsin (pp. 131–32). Another solution among law administrators is to develop *automatic routines* for dealing with legal disputes. We saw one example of this in our discussion of "normal crimes" (p. 128). The amount of pressure on the courts to provide additional services determines how much of this routinization occurs (Friedman and Percival, 1976; Heydebrand, 1977). Some courts actually become transformed into little more than administrative agencies where judges rubber-stamp decisions rather than listening to legal debate (see Yngvesson and Hennessey, 1975, for descriptions of this process in small claims courts; also see Fitzgerald, 1972, 1975, on routine processing of landlords' claims in Chicago's rent courts). Where such routines develop, informal "rules" or routines which court administrators adopt for convenience and efficiency often override the commands of the formal law which they are supposed to be administering.

Judges in courts are not the only persons who do judging work in our legal system. But like judges, other rule interpreters work in environments, and bring preconceptions to their work, which color their applications of law and affect the law's impact.

For example, Congress framed the draft laws to apply uniformly across the country. At the same time, they intentionally kept the composition of draft boards localized so that "little groups of neighbors" could interpret the laws according to local values and social and economic conditions (Davis and Dolbeare, 1968). As a result, a young man who would have received a deferment or classification as a conscientious objector in a liberal district might be prosecuted for draft evasion in another because its conservative members might refuse to accept liberal notions about conscience or the importance of a college education. Decisions made in farm districts differed from those made in industrial areas because of differing needs for young workers. "Influential" people could sway decisions in some areas but not in others. So the nation was a crazy quilt of different interpretations of the law. If you wanted to measure the impact of the selective service act as a whole, or of particular procedural rules, your answer would depend on the local board you chose to study.

The idea that internal organizational features of courts shape their role in modifying legal impact reflects structuralist thinking (see chapter 4). It says that legal impact is modified by the functions being fulfilled by different divisions within the institutions that interpret and administer the law.

Critical theorists (see chapter 5) agree that modification does occur within these institutions. They point out, however, that the beneficiaries of the "filtering" process are usually the "haves" rather than the "have nots" (Galanter, 1974). To critical theorists, it seems obvious that courtroom routines favor landlords, businessmen, and large corporations, who routinely use the courts, over tenants, customers, and individual citizens, who rarely even speak with lawyers, much less find themselves engaged in legal battle. The "haves" are usually "repeat performers." They go to court often, hire the best lawyers available, and become intimately acquainted with court routines, judges, and other court personnel. Since they are often playing for long-range legal advantages, they can afford to spend lavish resources on settlements which preserve favorable court routines. The "have nots," on the other hand, are usually "one-shotters"—people who have never before seen the inside of a courtroom, do not understand court routines, don't even know their own lawyers well, and must aim only for outright victory since they don't have any reason to pursue long-range changes in court routines or rules.

Therefore, say critical theorists, the routines which filter the impact of laws are not the result of impersonal, impartial, structural pressures, and their effects are not impartial. Rather, they favor the wealthy, the powerful, because they are produced by pressures put on the law's interpretative institutions by those seeking to preserve and enhance their power and having the resources to do it.

Impact Filters: Target Populations

In the previous section, we saw that the question of legal impact leads to investigation of the social characteristics, opportunity structures, and organizational processes operating among official law enforcers and interpreters. How they interpret the wording of laws, and how those laws fit into their everyday working decisions, affects the long-term impact of the law.

But the filtering process does not end with the actions of officials. *Target populations,* the people who are supposed to be regulated by particular laws, also modify the law's impact. When we examine evidence of these effects, we are putting to the test, and actually going well beyond, Sumner's abstract claim that "lawways cannot change folkways."

We have already looked in detail at some examples where target populations alter legal impact. The Muslims of Central Asia managed to produce major modifications in the impact of Soviet laws. India's complex population produced massive distortions in the operation of British colonial law.

Closer to home we find that certain kinds of criminal laws produce strong incentives to violate the law. These are laws which prohibit certain kinds of market transactions on the grounds that they are immoral. They include laws against narcotics, prostitution, gambling, abortion, and pornography. In a way, such laws create "crime tariffs" (Packer, 1968, pp. 277–82). They never terminate the trade, they merely tax it. They increase the risk associated with doing business in the forbidden market. They therefore drive up the prices of the service or product, drastically inflating the profits going to those willing to take the risk. Moreover, laws such as those against narcotics lead to the development of crime organizations, which are then in a position to expand into other areas of business, legal or not (Becker, 1963). Where the general population continues to want a certain service or commodity regardless of price, laws banning trade in that area simply raise profits by reducing competition among sellers.

If you combine this "crime tariff" effect with the fact that law enforcers usually reduce their enforcement activity when laws suddenly and severely increase the penalties for criminal acts, you will see that proposals to "crack down on drug pushers and pornographers" with stiff jail terms are likely to be at best ineffective, if not counterproductive, in campaigns to eliminate these kinds of activity.

In an age of social security, food stamps, unemployment insurance, and other forms of government-paid social welfare, a major political question has also been a question of legal impact: If people are provided with "hand-outs," won't these reduce people's willingness to work hard, save, improve themselves, and get off welfare? Many of the laws which are designed to provide welfare assistance have also included "ceiling" restrictions which cut people off from aid if their incomes rise above clearly defined levels. The thinking behind such ceiling limits seems to be that additional aid would be a disincentive to work.

However, studies have shown that it is not at all obvious what will serve as an incentive or disincentive for people. The complication comes from the fact that people are not just lone individuals making isolated decisions. Rather their decisions must be made within a complex of conditions (family, job market, practices of financial institutions, racial and ethnic discrimination, for example) which combine in different ways to put different kinds of pressure on people. Social security regulations, for example, make it more economical for some married couples to divorce, while continuing to live together, because benefits are higher for lone individuals than for persons living as married couples.

In public housing, there is evidence that *income ceilings* (rules forcing families to move into private housing as soon as their incomes rise above fixed levels) have just the opposite of their intended effect. Instead of inducing people to leave, ceilings provide a strong economic motive for remaining in public housing and turning down higher paying jobs (Ikeda, et al., 1964, 1966). If a moderate increase in family income forced a family out of public housing, their net gain might turn into a net loss because of the pricing effects of a private-housing shortage.

Another unexpected effect is that when the most successful families are forced out of public housing, housing projects are regularly deprived of *good role models* (people who have learned how to "make it"). As a result, newcomers have to fend for themselves in learning how to boost their own families to a position of self-sufficiency. Ceiling rules cut them off from contact with people who faced the same kinds of problems and solved them.

In an experiment where low-income housing projects with income ceilings were compared with a project having no ceiling, the "ceiling" projects showed low mobility out of public housing, and interviewers found residents turning down better jobs, lying about their incomes, and avoiding the private housing market because they lacked the skills and the money to make the move (Ikeda et al., 1964, 1966; Lempert, 1967). In the "no ceiling" project, people had an alternative. They were given assistance in the complex work of finding and financing private housing, and they were allowed to stay in public housing while they accumulated sufficient resources to make the move to private housing a secure one. As a result, that project had a higher rate of mobility into private housing. The experiment thus demonstrated that ceilings can work as a disincentive for people caught in the welfare trap.

LEGAL IMPACT: THE QUESTION OF INTENT

So far in this chapter we have seen that the law's impact, if there is any, cannot be studied as though it were a simple response to a vaccinelike injection of reform and regulation. Laws are filtered out through the actions of enforcers, interpreters, and target populations in a variety of complex ways. Whether we are trying to show that a legal command has had its intended effect, or that it has had unforeseen side effects, we find ourselves dealing with a research problem that is much more complex than the vaccine model suggests. Some impact research takes that filtering process into account. But much of it simply ignores such problems, perhaps because much of it is sponsored by agencies which want to show that their policies are having measurable, positive effects.

But we have not yet exhausted our supply of problems with legal-impact research. One of the outstanding assumptions which most impact researchers make, whether they use the simple vaccine model or the more complex filtering model, is that they know the *intent* of the rules whose impacts they are studying. In the case of the school desegregation order, we have to assume that we know the Court's purpose. We assume that they wanted to end school segregation, because that purpose appears to infuse everything they wrote in their opinion. We assume that helmet laws are designed to increase the use of helmets and reduce the incidence of motorcycle deaths.

The problem with these assumptions is that once we look into them, they often prove to be simplistic or plain wrong. We might assume, for example, that the "intent" of lawmakers who put stop signs at intersections is to make people stop and thereby avoid accidents. But suppose we discover that the municipality which made those laws depends heavily on revenues from fines of traffic violators. Suppose further that among police officers, it is common knowledge that certain stop signs are always good for filling ticket "quotas" because they are in such ridiculous locations that nobody would stop for them. Our best guess here might be that the town is a "trap" using traffic laws to keep property taxes down. Certainly such a conclusion would not be obvious if we simply guessed at the intent by reading the law or the sign.

In a previous chapter, we discussed laws supposedly designed to get children out of factories and into schools. We saw that one of the principal effects of these laws was the reduction of competition in industry and the increase of profits to larger industrialists. In the campaign to pass those laws, that outcome was never mentioned publicly as a reason for having the laws changed. No record of congressional debate would include such statements of purpose. But some observers believe that economic warfare against small business was one of the chief moving forces behind the bill (Platt, 1969).

Of course, not everyone who favored child labor laws was a greedy business tycoon. Many other types of people, some motivated by religious or humanitarian purposes, also joined the crusade, and were in fact the most obvious proponents. The point is not that we can always find devious or hidden purposes behind apparently benign law. The problem is that we must sort around among all the supporters (and opponents) of any legal action in search of the "true purpose" of that law. And the "true purpose" is often not one, but a hodgepodge of interests which coincide on some issues and are in conflict over others.

For example, in Brazil nearly 20 percent of the population lives as "squatters" on land owned by the state. This means that they have no legal rights to the land on which their homes are built. The government could, at any time, legally evict them and confiscate anything in their homes. Yet many such squatters have lived that way for two or three generations, and

squatter areas have become full-fledged suburbs of many important Bra-
zilian cities.

Squatters such as those around Rio de Janeiro provide the government with special power *because squatting is illegal* (Santos, 1977). Since the
squatters have no right to be where they are, government does not spend
tax revenues for government services such as sewers, police, courts, or fire
fighting. Furthermore, because they can be thrown out at any time, squatters are vulnerable and therefore more compliant with government orders
which they might otherwise resist. Political independence is sacrificed by
squatters, who fear loss of their homes.

Hence the government preserves a situation of massive lawbreaking,
in part because by doing so it gains control of a significant section of the
population without great expenditures of government resources. Perhaps
the "intent" of the laws which originally created private property, and the
ownership of lands by the government, was to protect certain patterns of
ownership and make available government lands for government-spon-
sored projects. But the reality which has emerged from these laws shows a
very different kind of purpose, which may or may not have existed when
the laws were first passed.

We can see, then, that if a law emerges from a legislature, or a decision is rendered by a court, or a rule is established by a government regulatory agency, its "intent" may be many intents, each interpreted by a different interest group. It may be the product of multiple compromises brought
about momentarily by the ebb and flow of political conflict and competition.

This competition is multiplied by another feature of the legal process
which impact studies often ignore. Laws don't just spring into life like the
stone tablets which Moses found on the mountaintop or the instant justice
which King Solomon handed out to his citizens. Most laws are the product
of ongoing political struggles. As such, they can be thought of not as the
"final word" on a particular question of behavior or social organization, but
rather as way stations or temporary residues of the conflicts which were at
particular stages of development at the time the laws were passed.

For example, the Supreme Court declared abortion legal in 1973. But
that decree obviously did not quell the conflict. Major political forces mobilized to overturn that decision, to obtain a constitutional amendment, to
pressure the court into narrowing the scope of its ruling, to pressure legislatures and lower courts into overriding the upper court's purpose. On the
other side, political groups acted as "watchdogs" to insure that the Court's
ruling was carried out. More than that, they pushed for further reforms in
the direction of women's rights. And remember, all of this political activity
aimed at bending formal law to political purpose went on out in the open—
it was in addition to all of those informal actions which we discussed above
as the "filtering process."

In the case of other laws, the battles that produced them have long since burned out, and their champions have moved on to other, newer battlegrounds or have passed from the scene entirely. Such laws remain on the books but no one cares anymore. Unless some new interest group can figure out a new use for them (for example, see the discussion in chapter 5 about the successive uses of vagrancy laws), they will become shells, hollow reminders of battles now past.

None of these difficulties means that it is impossible to figure out how a particular claim became law, which groups in society succeeded in having their views stated as laws, or what happened in the aftermath of particular legal moves. But they do make the vaccine model of legal impact inadequate. In fact they raise doubts as to whether the study of legal impact can be conducted in any way differently from the overall study of law as a social phenomenon. We may become interested in law as a social object because we have some question about the impact of particular legal actions. But if we take the investigation down the several roads of inquiry described in this chapter, we end up with a full-scale analysis of social and legal processes within which the particular legal-impact question has meaning. To do any less—to try, for example, to measure the impact of a single Supreme Court decision on its "obvious" target—is to act like a blindfolded person trying to understand a rose by feeling the end of one thorn.

Perhaps this is why critical theorists (see chapter 5) have been particularly hard on legal-impact studies (see, for example, Quinney, 1974; and Hunt, 1978). When the impact theorist asks whether a law had its "intended effect," the critical theorist asks, "intended by whom?" and answers "probably by a ruling elite whose intentions are probably not obvious in the wording of the law." As Medcalf argues, law is not a separate moment or thing in social life which can be isolated for study separate from other social processes (1978). Law is a part of the interactions of persons and institutions, but it is never alone and rarely unchallenged. The question, What was a law's impact on society? must be matched by the opposite question, What was society's impact on the law? Both questions must be asked, whether we are studying what is usually assumed to be a *democratic* society where there is supposed to be citizen participation in lawmaking, or what is assumed to be a *totalitarian* society where law appears to be a one-way process of commands backed by force. Even where there is no open political debate, we have learned that the filtering effects of various social constituents make the legal-impact question complex.

We sacrifice accuracy and understanding when we make the mistake of studying law as a vaccine, something separate, a command external to the ongoing processes of society but capable of altering those processes. A law, a judgment, an administrative rule must be seen as a temporary position staked out on some social battlefield. Its meaning, its interpretation, its contribution to the further development of that conflict does not remain static, trapped in the wording of the act or in judicial opinion. The words offer new opportunities to take the law down new, untraveled pathways of interpretation, actually expanding rather than limiting the powers of discretion in the hands of those who know how to invoke, challenge, or deflect the law (Pepinsky, 1976). Thus the importance of a law is transformed by the ways conflicting interests either use or fail to use the opportunities created by the law.

CONCLUSION

I began this chapter by noting that the systematic, scientific study of legal impact was a bold new direction for students of legal matters. It raised questions earlier legal scholars had not thought to ask, or preferred to avoid. It was a program to modernize our understanding of law, to bring it under the scrutiny of newly developed social scientific research methods, and to liberate it from errors stemming from the ill-informed hunches, "common sense," and abstract logic of judges and ivory-tower law scholars. Were it not for the interest which has developed in legal impact, the sociology of law might not now exist as a recognizably distinct subject of study (see Hunt, 1978).

One approach, which developed early and continues to be followed in many studies, treats law like a *vaccine*. The researcher looks at a particular legal doctrine (be it legislation, judicial action, or governmental administrative ruling) and tests for specific predicted effects. The prediction may come either from the researcher's interpretation of the law's "intended effects" or from social scientific theory which points toward possible "unintended" side effects.

Much of what we now know about legal systems we have learned from studies using this vaccine model. This is ironic, because what we have discovered is that the vaccine model badly distorts the reality of legal process. We have discovered a growing list of institutions, processes, and agents which *filter* any legal command, bending, modifying, or deflecting its effects according to the tides of conflict and cooperation among groups interested in, or having to react to, those laws. The filtering process is as much a process of *making law* as is the creation of formal legal commands. The filtering process is an ongoing expression of the same conflicts which moved people to pass a law or go to court in the first place.

Another weakness of the vaccine model concerns the *intent* behind laws. The environment of conflict which leads to the creation of new law may create misleading assumptions about *the* intent behind those laws. The existence of hidden agendas in the actions of lawmakers as well as those charged with law enforcement weakens our assumption that we can know the purpose behind a law just by reading it or by reading news accounts about why it was passed. Laws, which are the creatures of legislative or judicial compromise, may actually represent conflicting purposes, with two or more opposing sides hoping to gain control over the subsequent process of implementation. The vaccine model is weak in these cases because we cannot assume a singular definition of (1) the problem (the "disease" to be treated), (2) the content of the law passed to meet that problem (the nature of the ingredients in the vaccine), or (3) the location in social process where the law should have its effects (location of the disease in the body).

We have seen that conflict theorists attack the vaccine model as an example of wrong thinking among structuralists. They see impact research as an example of the false assumption that anyone (lawmaker, judge, administrator, or social scientist trying to advise lawmakers) can be outside or above the fray of political conflict. They see most legal-impact studies as regrettable examples of a *technocratic* stance, which says that educated specialists can scientifically (not politically) study social problems and develop dispassionate solutions for them the way biologists develop medical vaccines for diseases. They say that social scientists or other "specialists" are no less partisan than any other actors in the arena of politico-legal conflict.

Ironically, some conflict theorists back themselves into the same untenable corner as they accuse structuralists of occupying. They may feel so strongly about the imbalance or inequality built into particular legal situations that they come to assume that they know the "hidden intent" behind laws. With such thinking, they risk the same kinds of oversimplification in the vaccine model which they accuse structuralists of committing.

As helpful as the vaccine model has been in getting us to conduct more careful investigation into the way law works, it must ultimately yield to a more complex view of law as an ever-changing arena of conflict where no single act is either the beginning or the end of the question.

Perhaps, then, the best place to look for evidence on legal process is in the midst of conflict. Many of those who have focused their attention on disputing and litigation have, I said at the beginning of this chapter, taken a bottom-up approach to the study of legal processes. In the next chapter we will see what dispute research is about, and we will weigh its success in surmounting some of the problems we have discovered in the legal-impact approach.

REFERENCES

BALL, HARRY   (1960), Social Structure and Rent Control Violation, *American Journal of Sociology*, 65, p. 598.
BECKER, HOWARD   (1963), *Outsiders*, New York: Free Press.
BECKER, THEODORE   (1966), A Survey of Hawaiian Judges: The Effect on Decisions of Judicial Role Variations, *American Political Science Review*, 60, p. 677.

BEUTEL, FREDERICK AND MEDERO, TADEO   (1967), *The Operation of the Bad Check Law of Puerto Rico,* Editorial Universitaria.

CAMPBELL, DONALD AND ROSS, H. LAWRENCE   (1968), The Connecticut Crackdown on Speeding, *Law and Society Review,* 3, p. 55.

CANON, BRADLEY   (1972), The Impact of the Formal Selection Process on the Characteristics of Judges. *Law and Society Review,* 6, 4, p. 579.

CANON, BRADLEY AND JAROS, DEAN   (1970), External Variables, Institutional Structure and Dissent on State Supreme Courts, *Polity,* 3, p. 175.

COOK, BEVERLY   (1977), Public Opinion and Federal Judicial Policy, *American Journal of Political Science,* 21, p. 567.

CROYLE, JAMES   (1979), The Impact of Judge-made Policies: An Analysis of Research Strategies and An Application to Products Liability Doctrine, *Law and Society Review,* 13, p. 949.

DAVIS, JAMES AND DOLBEARE, KENNETH   (1968), *Little Groups of Neighbors: The Selective Service System,* Chicago: Markham Publishing Co.

DOLBEARE, KENNETH   (1967), *Trial Courts in Urban Politics: State Court Policy Impact and Functions in a Local Political System,* New York: John Wiley.

DOLBEARE, KENNETH AND HAMMOND, PHILLIP   (1971), *The School Prayer Decision: From Court Policy to Local Practice,* Chicago: University of Chicago Press.

FEEST, JOHANNES   (1968), Compliance with Legal Regulations: Observations of Stop Sign Behavior, *Law and Society Review,* 2, p. 447.

FITZGERALD, JEFFREY   (1972), *The Contract Buyer's League: A Case Study of Interaction between a Social Movement and the Legal System,* Unpublished Doctoral Dissertation, Northwestern University.

FITZGERALD, JEFFREY   (1975), The Contract Buyer's League and the Courts: A Case Study of Poverty Litigation, *Law and Society Review,* 9, p. 165.

FRIEDMAN, LAWRENCE   (1967), Legal Rules and the Process of Social Change, *Stanford Law Review,* 4, p. 798.

FRIEDMAN, LAWRENCE AND PERCIVAL, ROBERT   (1976), A Tale of Two Courts: Litigation in Alameda and San Benito Counties, *Law and Society Review,* 10, p. 267.

GADBOIS, GEORGE   (1970), Indian Judicial Behavior, *Economic and Political Weekly,* 5, p. 1.

GALANTER, MARC   (1974), Why the "Haves" Come Out Ahead: Speculations on the Limits of Legal Change, *Law and Society Review,* 9, p. 95.

GIBSON, JAMES   (1980), Environmental Constraints on the Behavior of Judges: A Representational Model of Judicial Decision-Making, *Law and Society Review,* 14, p. 343.

GILES, MICHAEL AND WALKER, THOMAS   (1975), Judicial Policy Making and Southern School Segregation, *Journal of Politics,* 37, p. 917.

HALBERSTAM, DAVID   (1979), *The Powers that Be,* New York: Dell Publishing Co.

HEYDEBRAND, WOLF   (1977), The Context of Public Bureaucracies: An Organizational Analysis of Federal District Courts. *Law and Society Review* 11, 5, 759–821.

HUNT, ALAN   (1978), *The Sociological Movement in Law,* Philadelphia: Temple University Press.

HYMAN, HERBERT AND SHEATSLEY, PAUL   (1964), Attitudes toward Desegregation, *Scientific American,* 211, p. 16.

IKEDA, KIYOSHI; BALL, HARRY; AND YAMAMURA, DOUGLAS   (1964), Legal Interventions, Social Mobility, and Dependence: A Study of Public Assistance in Housing for Low Income Families, Paper presented to the Annual Meetings of the American Sociological Association.

IKEDA, KIYOSHI; YAMAMURA, DOUGLAS; BALL, HARRY; AND LEMPERT, RICHARD   (1966), Regulatory Norms and Occupational Conduct among Low Income Households: A Study of Public Assistance in Housing, Paper presented to the Annual Meetings of the American Sociological Association.

JACOB, HERBERT AND VINES, KENNETH (1971), State Courts, in Herbert Jacob and Kenneth Vines (eds.), *Politics in American States* (Second Edition) Boston: Little, Brown.

JOHNSON, CHARLES (1979), Judicial Decisions and Organizational Change: Some Theoretical and Empirical Notes on State Court Decisions and State Administrative Agencies, *Law and Society Review*, 14, p. 55.

KLEMKE, LLOYD (1978), Does Apprehension for Shoplifting Amplify or Terminate Shoplifting Activity?, *Law and Society Review*, 12, p. 391.

KRITZER, HERBERT (1979), Federal Judges and Their Political Environment: The Influence of Public Opinion, *American Journal of Political Science*, 23, p. 194.

LEMPERT, RICHARD (1967), Strategies of Research Design in the Legal Impact Study, *Law and Society Review*, 1, p. 111.

MACAULAY, STEWART (1979), Lawyers and Consumer Protection Law, *Law and Society Review*, 14, p. 161.

MEDCALF, LINDA (1978), *Law and Identity: Lawyers, Native Americans, and Legal Practice*, Beverly Hills, Calif.: Sage Publications, Inc.

MERRYMAN, JOHN (1969), *The Civil Law Tradition*, Stanford, Calif.: Stanford University Press.

MUIR, WILLIAM (1968), *Prayer in the Public Schools: Law and Attitude Change*, Chicago: University of Chicago Press.

MYRDAL, GUNNAR (1968), *Asian Drama*, New York: Pantheon.

NADER, RALPH (1976), Consumerism and Legal Services: The Merging of Movements, *Law and Society Review*, 11, p. 247.

PACKER, HERBERT (1968), *The Limits of the Criminal Sanction*, Stanford, Calif.: Stanford University Press.

PATRIC, GORDON (1957), The Impact of a Court Decision: Aftermath of the McCollum Case, *Journal of Public Law*, 6, p. 455.

PEPINSKY, HAROLD (1976), *Crime and Conflict*, New York: Academic Press.

PLATT, ANTHONY (1969), *The Child Savers: The Invention of Delinquency*, Chicago: University of Chicago Press.

QUINNEY, RICHARD (1974), *Critique of Legal Order*, Boston: Little, Brown.

RABIN, ROBERT (1979), Impact Analysis and Tort Law: A Comment, *Law and Society Review*, 13, p. 987.

ROBERTSON, LEON (1976), An Instance of Effective Legal Regulation: Motorcyclist Helmet and Daytime Headlamp Laws, *Law and Society Review*, 10, p. 467.

ROSS, H. LAWRENCE (1970), *Settled out of Court: The Social Process of Insurance Claims Adjustment*, Chicago: Aldine.

ROSS, H. LAWRENCE (1976), The Neutralization of Severe Penalties, *Law and Society Review*, 10, p. 403.

SANTOS, BOAVENTURA (1977), The Law of the Oppressed: The Construction and Reproduction of Legality in Pasargada, *Law and Society Review*, 12, p. 5.

SCHUR, EDWIN (1971), *Labeling Deviant Behavior: Its Sociological Implications*, New York: Harper & Row, Pub.

SKOLNICK, JEROME AND WOODWORTH, J. RICHARD (1970), Bureaucracy, Information, and Social Control: A Study of a Morals Detail, in Richard D. Schwartz and Jerome Skolnick (eds.), *Society and the Legal Order*, New York: Basic Books, pp. 458–63.

SUDNOW, DAVID (1965), Normal Crimes: Sociological Features of the Penal Code in a Public Defender Office, *Social Problems*, 12, p. 255.

TOBIAS, J. J. (1968), *Crime and Industrial Society in the Nineteenth Century*, New York: Schocken Books.

UNGER, ROBERTO M. (1976), *Law in Modern Society*, New York: Free Press.

WASBY, STEPHEN   (1970), *The Impact of the United States Supreme Court*, Homewood, Ill.: Dorsey Press.

WEBER, MAX   (1962), *On Law in Economy and Society*, Max Rheinstein (ed.), New York: Clarion Books, Seabury Press.

YANCEY, WILLIAM AND ERICKSEN, EUGENE   (1979), The Antecedents of Community: The Economics and Institutional Structure of Urban Neighborhoods, *American Sociological Review*, 44, p. 252.

YNGVESSON, BARBARA AND HENNESSEY, PATRICIA   (1975), Small Claims, Complex Disputes: A Review of Small Claims Literature, *Law and Society Review*, 9, p. 219.

7

DISPUTES AND LAWSUITS

"The Rockford Files" and "Davey Crockett" were both highly successful American television series. Yet their principal stars, James Garner and Fess Parker, both claim that they were cheated out of their fair share of the profits by the film studios which produced their shows (CBS, "Sixty Minutes," December 7, 1980). Both claim that dishonest accounting procedures picked their pockets to the tune of several million dollars. So they are suing.

For most of us who have never even seen a million dollars, such a dispute seems hardly earth shaking. Millionaires battling millionaires, that's all.

We are more likely to become incensed over the plight of the inventor of the "weed whacker," a weed trimmer which operates by spinning nylon line at high speeds. Soon after he began marketing his invention, several big companies began producing copies without his permission, despite his careful attempt to protect his invention with a patent ("NBC Magazine with David Brinkley," December 5, 1980). So, like the TV stars, he sued. He lost, however, because the judge accepted the argument that his invention was "obvious."

Whether or not we feel sympathy for these people, we should note that their cases were presented on national television networks during prime time. Nor are these isolated instances. We seem to find disputes fascinating even when they do not involve famous television stars. For whatever reason, disputes draw our attention, stimulate our imagination, and provoke discussion even when we are not involved. Disputes and lawsuits are good theater on American television.

According to social scientists, people in African villages (Dubow, 1973; Abel, 1979), Mediterranean societies (Peristiany, 1965; Starr, 1978), and Indian towns (Cohn, 1959; Kidder, 1973) also find them good theater and greatly enjoy themselves when a "good" case is in court. Historians say that our foremothers and forefathers in colonial and frontier America had a similar fascination with lawsuits and used to crowd the courts as observers.

One probable source of this widespread curiosity about disputing as a social process is probably just its intrinsically interesting nature. We like to ponder legal disputes the way some people discuss moves in a chess game or the way "Monday morning quarterbacks" argue about what their favorite team should have done on the weekend. The uncertainty of combat is probably part of the fun. Other elements also seem to contribute: the complexity of alternative strategies and the spectacle of public confrontation in which someone will win and another will lose. Public disputes in our courts promise something we do not usually find in everyday life—definitive decisions supporting one perspective, one set of actions, among the fog of ambiguous situations and choices most of us find ourselves facing the majority of the time. Sports may have become a major industry in the United States for much the same reason—they promise regular answers to the questions: Who is right? Who is the best? Who is the winner? How we long for such answers. How rarely we get them.

However, in the social sciences today, the subject of disputing and litigation has become a major research topic for other, less "natural," reasons. Several lines of inquiry based on quite separate research traditions have converged on a common set of questions and proposed answers concerning disputing. The first of these traditions is the analysis of "games" and strategy by mathematicians, economists, and psychologists. Mathematicians initiated this research in their development of *game theory*. By using very restrictive assumptions about how people will act in artificially created competitive games where choices must be made, game theorists have tried to develop equations which tell how predictable the choices will be and which ones are "rational." Psychologists and professionals who specialize in "conflict resolution" (those, for example, who work as family counselors, mediators, and labor arbitrators) have tried to adapt the game theorists' abstractions to real-life conflict situations. We will examine some of their efforts in this chapter.

A second tradition is one already discussed at some length in this book: the cultural anthropologists' interest in "dispute resolution." Ever since Malinowski uttered the then-astounding claim that "savages" have "law" in the islands of the South Pacific (Malinowski, 1926), anthropologists have treated the handling of disputes as an important piece of information which they should nail down in their ethnographies of exotic cultures. Some have treated disputing as a major focus of their research (e.g., Hoebel, 1954; Gluckman, 1955; Bohannan, 1957; Pospisil, 1958; Nader, 1964, 1969; Gulliver, 1969). We will examine some of their work in this chapter.

The third tradition is the research done on American legal institutions, especially courts, to see whether they are "working" (i.e., are successful) or to figure out how to make them work. This tradition began at a very high level in the system, examining the work of the higher-level appeals courts. But the drive for realism in studies of how courts work quickly led to a focus on lower courts, where much more law is "done" every day, and where, it was assumed, most legal disputes terminated. In these studies, researchers have asked whether the courts provide adequate outlet for the hearing of disputes; whether everyone has sufficient "access" to legal ways of resolving differences; and whether the courts are capable of providing unbiased, helpful, tension-reducing resolutions in the cases they do get. We will also examine some of these studies in this chapter.

As different as these three approaches are, they all arise from a shared concern about the effectiveness or suitability of different methods for settling disputes. While some "pure theorists" in each of the three traditions have studied disputing for purely theoretical reasons, others have used the theory as a basis for proposing reforms in modern legal practices, in order to provide better, more effective, more accessible, more "appropriate" dispute-settling institutions.

Also in this chapter, we will see that some students of disputing have recently taken some elements from each of these traditions and produced a new direction which is meant to eliminate their separate weaknesses. We will see why the study of *conflict resolution* and *dispute settlement* has been renamed the study of dispute *processing*. And we will discuss a sample of the great variety of methods social groups have developed for dealing with disputes in everyday life.

GAME THEORY, BARGAINING, AND STRATEGY ANALYSIS

Mathematical Analysis of Game Strategies

Suppose that you and a business partner have just been arrested. You are charged with tax evasion. Prosecutors take you to separate rooms for questioning. Your financial situation is such that if you both refuse to confess, you will go free. But the authorities offer you both the promise of a large reward if you confess. They also warn you that if you remain silent while your partner confesses, you will spend many years in prison while your partner gets the reward and goes free. If you both confess, you both get a reduced sentence but no reward. What do you do? Can you trust your partner to keep quiet? Should you confess?

You are in the "prisoner's dilemma," one of several decision-making games devised by mathematicians to explore the logic of decision-making situations where the *strategies* of two participants are *interlinked* (see, for example, Rapoport and Chammah, 1965). Several different games have been designed. In each, the interests of two parties are made to depend on the way they combine thinking about their own choices with their expectations about what the other party will choose.

The object of these highly abstract games is to dissect the logical structure of *joint decision-making strategies* in order to pinpoint the best possible strategies for both parties. A dispute can be thought of as one kind of joint decision-making situation. Opponents in a dispute are often as locked into reacting to each other's moves as are two prisoners in the "dilemma." They can both act in ways that either harm both of them, help both, or help one while harming the other. So, while the mathematicians' games are not necessarily formulated as disputes, their analysis may apply directly to the question of how best to resolve disputes.

Taking the prisoner's dilemma as an example, the best outcome from both prisoners' perspectives is for both to remain free by keeping silent. But neither one can be sure that the other will "button up," because both know that the other partner is being offered reward money and threatened with prison, and they had no time before the interrogation to plan a strategy. Therefore, the prisoner's dilemma is an *indeterminate game*—that is, there is no way of identifying the best strategy which both sides can be advised to take. (Notice that the decision is indeterminate as long as we assume pure rationality. In game theory, we exclude irrational considerations such as a personal *moral* conviction that the law or the authorities should be obeyed.)

While some games provide no predictable (or advisable) outcome, others do provide clear-cut "best choices" and therefore are "determinate." There is a difference, for example, between "zero-sum games" and "positive-sum games." In zero-sum games, anything that person A wins must be at the expense of person B. If both players start with ten dollars, for example, then each time the game is played, any money won by A comes out of B's pocket, and vice versa. Look at Matrix 7.1 below.

(B's Choices)

		b_1	b_2
	a_1	0	2
(A's Choices)	a_2	3	−1

(Rapoport, A., 1960, p. 154)

The numbers in the cells of this matrix show the *payoff to player A,* given different combinations of choices between A and B. Player A has two choices (^{a}1 and ^{a}2) and player B has two choices (^{b}1 and ^{b}2). The outcome of the game depends on the *combination* of choices they make. Neither one knows the other's choice before making his or her choice. In this game, if A chooses ^{a}1 while B chooses ^{b}1, both win zero—they break even. But if A chooses ^{a}2 while B sticks with ^{b}1, then A gets to take three dollars away from B. But A is not sure whether to risk choosing ^{a}2 because if B chooses ^{b}2 at the same time, then B would take one dollar away from A (in the matrix, this is noted as -1). Similarly, B cannot decide whether to risk choosing ^{b}2 because if A should choose ^{a}1 at the same time, then A would take two dollars from B.

There is a "maximin" point for A in this game. That is, there is a logical choice A should make if A wants to minimize the chance of losses and maximize the chance of gain. In this game, A's maximin point is choice ^{a}1 because at worst A would get zero, and A could even win two dollars with this choice. But there is no maximin point for B. With either choice B risks losing, but also has a chance of winning. B has no break-even point.

The plot thickens however. The mathematician assumes that A and B are rational seekers after these dollars. Therefore B is assumed capable of recognizing the temptation for A to choose ^{a}1 because it is the maximin solution. Thinking this way, B would choose ^{b}1 because this way B and A both get zero. But if A anticipates B's thinking, then A would switch to ^{a}2 in order to win three dollars instead of zero. If B anticipates this move by A, then B will switch to ^{b}2 and win a dollar away from A. And so on and so on. No matter how much anticipating both sides do, there is no way to discover the one best solution for each—the choice each side is *sure* the other side will make, which would tell that side what decision it should make. So although this is a zero-sum game, it has no solution.

But let us consider another approach. Suppose that, instead of just playing this game once, the two were involved in a hundred games like this. Then according to mathematical calculation, the game does have a solution—strategy can be predicted. In this game, says Rapoport (1960), the best strategy is for A to play ^{a}2 in thirty-three of the hundred games and ^{a}1 in sixty-seven of them. B should split the choice fifty-fifty between ^{b}1 and ^{b}2. Rapoport shows that any other strategy by either of them would end in greater losses for whichever side deviated from the prescribed ratio. As it happens, this game is set up so that, on average, the best B can hope to do in a hundred games is lose an average of one dollar per game. The best A can hope for is to win a dollar per game. Other arrangements of the payoffs could be made which would eliminate this inequality or even shift it in the opposite direction.

The important thing to notice here is that a relationship which was indeterminate when confined to a single trial became determinate when repeated many times. Keep this in mind when you read later in the chapter about social scientific evidence that dispute processing varies significantly depending on whether the disputants are strangers to each other (and therefore do not expect to deal with each other in the future) or are involved in on-going relations which they hope to maintain in the future. Experiments with games show that the expectation of future involvement in the playing of a particular game, combined with the knowledge of an opponent's game-playing "style" gained from previous game trials, has a clear and predictable impact on the choices players make (Rapoport and Chammah, 1965).

In a *variable-sum* game (such as the prisoner's dilemma) the payoffs are arranged in such a way that both sides can come out ahead if they cooperate, and can lose if they don't. In Matrix 7.2 we see the payoffs in one version of the prisoner's dilemma.

Matrix 7.2

	b1	b2
a1	5,5	−10,10
a2	10,−10	−2,−2

If both A and B keep quiet (choosing a1 and b1) both get five (in this matrix, the first number in each cell is A's payoff and the second is B's). But if A keeps quiet (choosing a1) while B confesses (b2), then A loses ten while B wins ten. So there is a temptation for both of them to confess, yet if they both remain "faithful" to a cooperative spirit, they can both win a smaller amount.

The real world is, of course, often more complicated. We make decisions about how to deal not just with one other person, but with many others. Often we join forces with others in relating to "outsiders" or other third parties. Game analysts have therefore broadened their theory to deal with more complex situations. The relations among just three people can be much more varied than between two. As soon as we include three people in a game (or in real life, say some of the theorists) we enter the realm of *coalitions* and *alliances* (Caplow, 1968). The analysis of the game must expand to include all possible combinations of the three actors. A weak party may ally with a strong party against another strong party. Such a game differs from one where all three are of equal strength. As in some dyadic games, there are triadic games that have determinate solutions and others that are indeterminate. Triadic analysis in particular has led to terms like "balance of terror" and "balance of power" because it has been found particularly useful in appraising conflicts between nations and between labor and management in industrial disputes.

(Triadic analysis has also been put to use in psychotherapy. A whole school of psychotherapy [see Bowen, 1978] centers its attention on the "triangles" in which people become entangled and which generate conflict in a person's life. The nature of the triangle is the object of therapy in this tradition. The theory is that if the person can identify the triangle, the inner pain and turmoil of dealing with the conflicting, and heretofore unrecognized, demands coming from the other two points in the triangle can be eliminated. It is worth noting here that psychiatry is a heavily used method of dispute processing in modern societies, though its theories locate many disputes as growing out of internal personal conditions rather than external conflicts.)

Strategy in Real Life: Complexity and Emotion

For many of the mathematicians who developed game analysis, the project was strictly an exercise in mathematical logic. They made no attempt to relate their calculations to real life, except to give some of them real-life names such as "prisoner's dilemma." Others however recognized that the tight logic of the theory held promise of helping people resolve conflicts between themselves. Economists, psychologists, and political scientists began experimenting to see whether real-life conflicts could be understood in terms of payoff matrices, determinate and indeterminate games, and zero-sum or variable-sum conditions.

Some have applied this analysis to the issue of international disarmament (Boulding, 1963). Both nuclear superpowers fear each other. Both see the other as aggressive, powerful, and untrustworthy. So there is temptation to charge ahead in an arms race. But the long-range effects of military buildup damage both sides. It becomes increasingly costly, and it actually increases the danger, since both sides feel pressed to "keep up" with the other. Such conflicts have logical solutions, which are determinable through the kind of game analysis we have been discussing. The way to change the situation is to change the numbers in the payoff matrix (or perhaps only to get everyone to see what the existing payoff values are). Changing the numbers may not be simple, but game analysis tells us how to do it, and also shows us why an arms race is a vicious cycle with no "solution."

One of the most widely recognized methods of dispute settlement is the process of bargaining for compromise. Two neighbors disagree over who has rights to the apples on a tree which sits squarely on their property line. If they follow the "arms race" model, neither one is likely to get any apples. Each side would attack the other if an apple picking were attempted. So the apples rot. Obviously a better solution would be some kind of compromise.

This kind of dispute can be thought of as a *positive-sum game* (Schelling, 1960). If the two sides cooperate, they can each get some apples. But to do so, they must give up their claims to the whole harvest. Compromise does not necessarily mean that each side gets 50 percent of the apples. Other considerations may enter which push the compromise toward an unequal distribution. The problem is that this game involves both cooperation and conflict as motives. Each side wants to get as much as it can without demanding so much that the overall compromise (the cooperative element) is killed and they both end up with nothing.

The real world puts strict limits on the usefulness of game theory. You have seen how complex the reasoning can be when just two players are involved. Triadic games multiply the number of possible combinations of events. Add a few more players and the game becomes impossible for any mathematician to analyze.

Moreover, real-life strategies may be affected by other than rational considerations. Where two sides are very unequal in bargaining power, the weaker party can turn the tables by making an "irrevocable commitment" to only one outcome (Schelling, 1960). By thus freezing the bargaining process with this "unreasonable" rigidity, the weaker party forces the stronger to "take it or leave it," knowing that since the position gives the stronger party some payoff, and since some is better than none, there is a chance that the weaker party will get what it wants. We saw this situation in the embassy "hostage crisis" in Iran. The weaker side (the Iranian revolutionaries) took an extreme position because they had "nothing to lose." They bargained then for concessions that could not have been won any other way. Airline hijackers use this strategy with regular success.

Another real-life complication is that disputes often generate strong emotions. Opponents choose strategies based on their passions rather than their cool calculation of "maximin" solutions. Opponents want to defend their "honor." They want to see "justice" done. They want to expose to the public the "treachery and venality" of their opponent. These desires cannot usually be fulfilled by bargaining for compromise.

In Chicago, for example, Fitzgerald found that a group of home buyers who had been exploited for years by real-estate "blockbusters" (agents who would scare whites into fleeing their homes, buy the houses at low prices, and then sell them to blacks at inflated prices financed by contracts denying them any equity in their homes until the total loan was repaid) rejected several "reasonable" compromises proposed by their opponents because their "movement" had become a cause and they wanted public vindication (1974). Emotional goals such as these are unstable and next to impossible to quantify (see Felstiner, Abel, and Sarat, 1981). So they cannot be reliably used in the analysis of payoff matrices.

The strength of the game-theory approach (and its major weakness, some critical theorists would argue) is that it allows for the exploration of *intrinsic* features of conflict situations. That is, by manipulating the payoff numbers of each game, the game theorist can create different game situations and then arrive at conclusions about how rational players would *have* to play in order to get maximum reward from it. The theory holds the potential, therefore, for pinpointing the reasons why real-life disputes are settled the way they are or why they so stubbornly resist all efforts at resolution. It tells us to look beyond the specific details of particular disputes to discover the strategic details of game types. Once the strategic structure has been identified, we ought to be able to prescribe changes in the payoff structure which would end a deadlocked situation and produce a compromise.

When the leaders of Egypt and Israel, for example, finally began bargaining seriously with each other in the negotiations which resulted in the "Camp David Accords" (1978), a major lubricant in the process was the role of the United States government in changing the payoff structure. Offers of American support to both sides (e.g., the promise of a new air base for Israel to replace one given up in its withdrawal from the Sinai Desert) altered the basic "payoff matrix of the game" and produced the "Camp David miracle."

It is easy enough for the mathematician to juggle the figures in a payoff matrix with a few short instructions to the computer. But the fact that we call the Camp David Accords a miracle should alert us to the difficulties we face in everyday handling of disputes. Conflict can *end* in ways which do not *resolve* the dispute (Boulding, 1963, p. 308–10). One side may choose *avoidance* (see discussion of Felstiner, p. 72). That is, they may simply walk away from a dispute. Instead of playing the game to a conclusion, they decide that *no choice* is better than continuing the dispute. Conflict may also end in *conquest*, where one side uses force to win. This is a special kind of avoidance since it means the forcible removal of one side from participation in the game.

Conflicts are *resolved* only when there is a *procedural* ending to them (Boulding, 1963). The procedure may be *reconciliation, compromise,* or *award*. In reconciliation, both sides are brought back into a cooperative relationship. In compromise, a mediator helps produce a solution satisfactory to both sides but leaving them in a competitive, potentially conflictful relationship (e.g., a contract settlement after a strike). The award procedure occurs when both sides agree to let a third party decide the outcome. Game theory analysis is useful only in cases where one of these three procedural endings is possible.

Another limitation on the solubility of disputes is the degree of centrality of the conflict to a participant's self-identity. Conflicts involving the
core of a person's self-identity are much tougher to resolve than those
where only the *shell* of that identity is at stake. Core values are those which
make up the basis of the person's self-identity. So, for example, if a conflict
threatened the sexual identity of a man, and that sexual identity was central
to the most important roles played by him in his community (as we saw
among the Muslim men in Central Asia in chapter 3), there would be little
chance of resolving that conflict. It could be endable, but only by conquest
or award. And if the opposition were strong enough, it might remain a
stalemate. But if a conflict involved nothing more than a claim to some
property which both sides could afford to lose without damage to their
basic positions in society, then the conflict would be easier to settle—compromise, award, or even reconciliation might be possible.

Another name for this core-shell distinction is the contrast between
conflicts of value and *conflicts of interest* (Aubert, 1969; Eckhoff, 1966). Conflicts of interest are more soluble through the efforts of mediators than are
conflicts of value. Only forced intervention breaks the deadlock in cases of
value conflict. "A conflict about bread is going to be more severe than one
about caviar" (Boulding, 1963, p. 325).

EXPERIMENTAL DISPUTES

The studies we have examined so far in this chapter are projections of
mathematical logic developed through the study of abstract games. They
are one way of discovering the suitability of various dispute-settling mechanisms for disputes with varying characteristics.

Another method for studying these same questions places people in
artificially created disputes where the conditions are manipulated experimentally. The purpose is to discover patterns of disputing behavior by
observing repeated cases of such behavior rather than by trying to deduce
people's choices from mathematical logic.

In one project (Thibaut and Walker, 1975) the object was to provide
people with dispute-settling tools which best fit their situations and preferences. The experiments were designed to discover what kinds of circumstances would lead to what kinds of preferences. Three basic circumstances
were manipulated: (1) the *temporal urgency* people felt (that is, the extent to
which subjects were made to feel rushed about reaching a settlement); (2)
the presence or absence of a *standard* against which to measure the legitimacy of their conflicting expectations (in law, a standard might be, for
example, the definition of anyone under the age of eighteen as a juvenile,
or a doctrine that water with more than five parts per million of some
carcinogen is officially defined as polluted); and (3) the presence or ab-

sence of *outcome correspondence* (correspondent outcomes are those in which both sides *share* the gains or losses that result from their joint activity).

The experimenters created artificial disputes between student volunteers and offered them five different methods for settling the disputes so they could finish their assigned tasks:

1. *Autocratic*—a third party is told the nature of the dispute and decides alone who should win
2. *Arbitration*—a third party hears the dispute, including explanations by both disputants, and decides alone who should win
3. *Moot*—a third party listens to both sides and then the sides must reach an agreement about how to resolve the dispute
4. *Mediation*—a third party hears the dispute, makes suggestions, and then leaves it to the disputants to decide the outcome
5. *Bargaining*—the disputants argue with each other and must reach some kind of agreement by themselves without third party assistance

In order to complete their assigned projects, the students had to resolve the disputes. The conditions of each project were varied experimentally. For instance, some pairs were put under severe time pressure while others were given plenty of time. Some were given a standard, others had none. And some were put in situations where there was outcome correspondence, others were given noncorrespondent conditions.

The results showed that the students had very clear, predictable preferences among the five dispute-settling techniques, depending on the conditions of their disputes. When they were under strong time pressure, for example, they preferred some kind of third-party participation because direct bargaining was too time-consuming. When a standard existed, they also preferred third-party intervention. With it they could avoid the burden of having to invoke the standard themselves. When time pressure and a standard were included together in a dispute, the preference for third-party intervention was even stronger.

Other conditions created preferences for *less* third-party intervention. When there was outcome correspondence in the task but no standard, there was a preference for mediation or bargaining because the problem was resolvable (since there was outcome correspondence), but the absence of a standard meant that the two sides had to reach a consensus on the nature of their task. When relations were noncorrespondent, participants would not care about the "truth" in their situation so long as they could get their way. So people in noncorrespondent relations showed preferences for strong third-party intervention (autocratic or arbitration). Mediation could not satisfy them, because mediation only helps when the main problem is figuring out *how* to create a mutually satisfying solution. In other words, if the problem is a *cognitive* one, a difficulty in getting accurate information as a basis for a solution, then mediation helps. But it does not help if the two sides are trying to make each other abandon their interests in the outcome.

Similar experiments tested the validity of claims about the effects on dispute outcomes of differences between Anglo-American legal practices and civil-law forms in Europe. *Adversarial* procedure, as in the United States and England, is based on the assumption that justice depends on exposing the truth and that truth is more likely to be exposed when two lawyers are pitted against each other on behalf of their opposing clients. So in trials it is the responsibility of the opposing lawyers to dig out evidence, cross-examine witnesses, and bring in supporting witnesses.

Inquisitorial procedures are more common in Europe. There it is the judge who must work to expose the facts. Judges are assumed to be motivated by their commitment to professional excellence and impartiality, not by their partisan commitment to one or the other of the opponents in a case.

Proponents of the adversarial model claim that more facts are found out when opposed lawyers do this work, because they are motivated to find as much favorable information as possible about their own clients, and as much damaging evidence as they can about their opponents.

Law school students were given imaginary law cases and told to prepare their "clients'" cases for trial. The "trials" were conducted under either adversarial, inquisitorial, or mixed procedures. Since the experimenters controlled the information given to the "lawyers" about each case, they could measure how much of it was passed on to the "judge" under each condition. These varying levels of information were their measure of the amount of truth produced by each procedure.

Their results showed that the adversarial system does produce a distinct advantage for some clients under some conditions. The most important condition is the level of the *lawyer's commitment* to the client. Even in the adversarial system, many lawyers develop a *court-centered*, rather than *client-centered*, orientation to their work. This occurs because lawyers who routinely handle lawsuits get to know the court personnel and other lawyers and gradually develop mutual-interest relationships with them which they become reluctant to endanger by being "overzealous" about any one of their clients' cases. To sustain their work-place relationships with people who can make life either easy or stressful for them, some lawyers begin treating their clients as persons whose interests in a lawsuit must be partially sacrificed in order to maintain work-place harmony.

In this experiment, some students were told to go all out for their clients. Others were told to keep in mind the needs of the courts and the need for work-place harmony. The result was that the adversarial system produced more information favorable to clients with originally *weak* cases only when they had *client-centered* lawyers. Under those conditions, the adversarial system was clearly a boon for the underdog. The inquisitorial system did not produce more information under any conditions. The experimenters concluded that the proponents of adversarial procedures are partially right in claiming that justice is better served by the open clash of opposed lawyers, if the lawyer has not been drawn into compromising relationships with courtroom personnel and other lawyers.

All of the research we have discussed so far in this chapter is based on the faith that disputes or conflicts have certain common features which (1) cut across cultural and historical variation, (2) are the same wherever disputes arise, and (3) can therefore be discovered through abstract reasoning and controlled experimentation. These studies have the advantage that the factors thought important in the process can be carefully manipulated and measured in laboratory settings. But they face the criticism that in the real world the processes of disputing are much more complex, that any attempt to generalize from the laboratory to events in the real world risks overstepping the limits of laboratory findings.

Nevertheless, as we will see next, studies of "real-world" disputing have led investigators to conclusions supporting some of these laboratory results. Many "real-world" researchers also share the same faith that underlying principles of dispute settlement can be discovered by comparing the various methods found in the real world and searching for their common features.

CROSS-CULTURAL STUDIES OF DISPUTE SETTLEMENT

Throughout this book, you have seen many examples of anthropological research into dispute settlement. The range of dispute-handling methods which anthropologists have found is too broad to be fully described here. But the examples already given, plus more to be discussed, reinforce the claim of legal anthropologists that, even without courts, judges, and written laws, societies around the world have been extremely inventive in their methods for dealing with conflict.

The Study of Trouble: Hunting for Jural Postulates

As we saw earlier (chapter 2), legal anthropologists, beginning with Malinowski (1926), led a campaign to destroy the ethnocentric notion that if primitive (or "savage" as they were then called) societies lacked the trappings of Western law, they must be lawless, governed by instinct rather than reason or culture. Several anthropologists made it their mission to discover and describe the "legal systems" of non-Western societies. In doing this, they focused on the ways in which disputes in these societies were settled. They discovered practices which, on their surface, seemed different from both Western law and the practices of other non-Western cultures. But beneath the differences, they hunted for similarities. Their concern can be seen in titles such as *Dispute Settlement without Courts: The Ndendeuli of Southern Tanzania* (Gulliver, 1969); *Law without Precedent* (Fallers, 1969); *The Judicial Process among the Barotse of Northern Rhodesia* (Gluckman, 1955); *Kapauka Papuans and Their Law* (Pospisil, 1958).

Ever since Llewellyn (a law professor) and Hoebel (an anthropologist) teamed up to study the law of the plains Indians (1941), some anthropologists have looked to the study of disputes to show how people in a society view the world. Llewellyn and Hoebel advocated the study of *trouble cases,* that is, disputes or disagreements which people could not resolve without bringing them to the attention of the whole group or community. Anthropologists felt that trouble cases could expose elements of a culture's view of the world which are normally hidden when relationships proceed according to routine. In Hoebel's words "The case method (the study of how trouble cases are handled) treats the statement of norms as the end product, not the beginning" (Hoebel, 1954, p. 36). In other words, instead of trying to see what effect norms (rules) have on people's actions, we can study trouble cases in order to figure out how societies adjust their rules to fit changing conditions.

Other anthropologists elevated this approach to a major search for the *jurisprudential principles* (Hoebel called them the *jural postulates*) of the societies they studied. Jurisprudence means the development and critical study of *legal theories* (inclusive logical explanations of the legal procedures and decision-making patterns which prevail in a society). For example, in Western jurisprudence an act is usually treated as criminal only if there is *mens rea*—criminal intent. We would distinguish for example between a person shooting another "on purpose" and one who "accidentally" fired a gun which "happened" to hit someone. So our "legal theory" is that damaging acts are crimes only if they are done "on purpose"—with *mens rea.* Other cultures do not share our theory. Their jurisprudence says that any harm done to another requires punishment, even if it was what *we* would call accidental. This could be because they believe that all harms not otherwise explainable must be the result of witchcraft. Or it could come from a spiritistic belief that all harms must be expiated in order to placate watchful spirits who could harm the whole group if disturbed.

Some anthropologists held that the study of disputes would reveal these patterns of thought even when the people studied did not know that their ideas fit such patterns. Gluckman went on to argue that since Western law had the most mature level of jurisprudential development, anthropologists should try to translate the guiding jurisprudential principles they find in non-Western cultures into the jurisprudential terminology of the West (1955).

He claimed, for example, that "The reasonable man is recognized as the central figure in all developed systems of law, but his presence in simpler legal systems has not been noticed" (Gluckman, 1955, p. 83). The "reasonable man" is an abstraction which has received detailed jurisprudential attention in the West. Judges explain their decisions as being based on what a "reasonable man" would think or do. People pay fines, go to jail, and lose lawsuits if they are found to have acted unreasonably. Gluckman argued that every society where a dispute-settling process could be found also showed clear signs of reliance on the idea of the "reasonable man."

Notice that this search for universal principles of jurisprudence is similar to the claims of game theorists and strategy analysts that their discoveries in laboratories are generalizable to all dispute situations. Other anthropologists charged Gluckman with overstating his case. One charge was that, by trying to force his observations into Western categories, Gluckman was distorting the meanings of legal ideas to the people he was studying (Bohannan, 1965). If we follow Gluckman's lead in applying the "reasonable man" rule everywhere, the rule itself becomes almost meaningless. The variations found in other cultures, even those studied by Gluckman, strip the Western concept of the "reasonable man" of most of its carefully constructed and limited meanings.

While some anthropologists thus sought to show that disputing everywhere has certain basic similarities, others worked to expose the variation, the dissimilarities, among cultures in the ways they handle disputes. Still, they all agreed that earlier notions of "savage lawlessness" were baseless. Their way of destroying such ethnocentric notions was to report and analyze the obviously careful and sensitive thinking which went into the development of rules and procedures in non-Western cultures.

Trouble as Process: Disputing Procedures in Action

While the early emphasis in legal anthropology was thus on the study of "trouble cases," a new generation of researchers criticized the approach for overemphasizing the importance of rules in dispute settlement. Like sociologists who were then attacking lawyers and law scholars for their neglect of the "living law" (i.e., the way rules are actually used, ignored, or modified in the everyday processing of conflictful relationships), anthropologists attacked the "trouble-case" method for assuming that jural postulates actually affect the way people resolve disputes. They were shifting the attention of legal anthropology to the *process* of dispute settlement. They held that in order to understand the consequences of apparently well-established jural postulates, we must look beyond the abstract statements of rules to the actions of people who are involved in apparently rule-relevant situations. How do they act? How do they use the rules that are available? How do they produce changes in those rules? How do various external social conditions affect the process of dealing with disputes? And does the application of a rule have the intended effect?

The effect of rules or jural postulates varies according to the type of dispute-settling process being used. Two main types stand out: *negotiation* and *adjudication* (Gulliver, 1969). Adjudication involves a third party (judge) who has the power to issue binding decisions which disputants must follow. In negotiation there is no third party. The two disputants, along with their supporters and representatives, try to get as much as they can by mustering whatever sources of power they have. Negotiation leads to settlement by compromise, because until such an agreement is reached, nothing happens to end the dispute. In adjudication, the verdict of the judge settles the case. Rules have greater significance in the case of adjudication. Disputants invoke the rules more often and appeal to the judge on the basis of rules, and the outcomes are more obviously shaped by rules. Where negotiation prevails, standards are more vague and flexible because they have no more authority than the two sides are willing to allow them. Notice that this research in the "real world" has produced the same conclusion as experimenters found in the laboratory (see pp. 157–58).

Actual case studies usually show a mixture of negotiation and adjudication, with rules (or jural postulates) alternately being invoked, ignored, or modified as the disputing relationship moves from stage to stage. An adjudicator may require disputants to try to negotiate a settlement. Sometimes a person with the power to judge becomes more of a mediator than a decision maker. In other cases, mediators may develop enough support from others in the group, and perhaps from the disputants themselves, to impose a rule-determined or rule-making decision.

These "real-world" discoveries have led to a shift of anthropological attention from the strictly rule-bound procedures of adjudication toward the broader question of the origins of disputes, their "careers" as they pass through various phases of strategy, and the characteristics of "final settlements." Dispute handling in different cultures is compared in order to find "the common patterns and regularities of interaction between the parties in negotiation irrespective of the particular context or the issues in dispute" (Gulliver, 1979, pp. 64–65).

The point being made by these anthropologists is that the significance of rules cannot be understood if they are made the ultimate object of research. They must be identified, but only because they are one aspect of the negotiating or bargaining process. How they will be used, what their effect will be, and even when or whether they will be used are questions that cannot be answered by simply knowing what the rules are supposed to be.

When rules will be invoked, for example, is not nearly as clear as the rules themselves may sound. If you have ever lived in a small community, you have probably experienced the problematic nature of rule invocation—the fact that people often "look the other way" so they can avoid putting their relationships, traditions, and values to the test. For years villagers in an island fishing community off the coast of Norway had quietly suppressed their concern about the "swimming coach" who taught swimming to their daughters (Yngvesson, 1976). The coach, a man, regularly "assisted" the girls with their showers after their lessons, and everyone in town knew about it. While they did not approve of his actions, it was years before anyone brought the behavior to public attention and called for action.

Similarly, in a small working class community near a major American city, an old man living alone regularly appeared naked on his front porch in the mornings as children passed by going to their bus stop. Everyone in the community knew about his behavior. But when one irate father tried to circulate a petition to have the old man arrested, people called him a troublemaker. No one would sign his petition. They apparently felt that, while the old man was obviously breaking the law, police action would be counterproductive and demeaning to the community.

Cases like these demonstrate the need to identify the place of disputes in the ongoing relations between people. Rule violations, custom breaking, and even harm done to another do not necessarily lead to the kind of public confrontation and rule invocation which we call disputing. Even when disputes occur, we cannot assume that people will fight them out only in court. Disputes have *careers* which only occasionally bring people into formal legal settings. Even when they reach the formal stage, the result is not necessarily dispute settlement. The availability of strategy choices which existed prior to legal action continues to affect the relationship after "final judgment."

Some anthropologists have divided the disputing process into stages, so that they can more closely study the choices people make at each stage and the reasons for those choices. One three-stage typology includes (1) grievance—one person sees a situation as unjust, (2) conflict—that person confronts the offender with a claim of injustice, and (3) dispute—the conflict "goes public" and a third party becomes involved (Nader and Todd, 1978, pp. 14–15). At any of these stages some disputes end, while others persist. Explaining why particular types of disputes or relationships follow predictable paths through these stages has become one of the objects of recent research.

What we are seeing in anthropological studies of disputing is the emergence of a *strategy-oriented perspective*—a view of disputing as an extended "game" in which opponents' strategies lead them into conventional dispute settling institutions, a search for alternative locations for proceeding with the "game," or unconventional ways of using conventional disputing institutions.

Some researchers even refer directly to game theory (Gulliver, 1979). This leads, for example, to explaining the centrality of negotiations in dispute settlement as resulting from the fact that most disputes are *positive-sum* games, in which the solution is being blocked because *information flow* between the two sides is inadequate. Negotiations, especially where a mediator is involved, are the instrument for increasing the flow of information, making it possible for the two sides to *learn how* to settle their dispute.

LEGAL COMPLEXITY AND
DISPUTE SETTLEMENT

We have seen that there has been a convergence between the game-theory–strategy-analysis tradition and research trends in legal anthropology. A third research tradition which has investigated these same issues came to them as the result of asking whether our modern courts adequately serve peoples' needs for effective dispute-settlement methods. Joined in this effort are sociologists, political scientists, law reform specialists, and even some anthropologists who first developed their interest in the processes of disputing in non-Western cultures (e.g., see Nader, 1980).

Courts and Disputes: Is There
Adequate Access?

As a dispute-settling system, American law has been attacked from two contradictory directions. One attack, which appears with impressive regularity in our popular press, declares that we are in the midst of a "law explosion" (Rosenberg, 1971; Ehrlich, 1976; Kline, 1978; Manning, 1979). Critics on this side argue that people are being unnecessarily stirred up by lawyers and assorted rights advocates who take resolvable issues, and sometimes even "imaginary" grievances, and puff them up into major legal confrontations. The result is that the courts become clogged with unimportant issues and cannot handle more important problems. The other result is that we become an overregulated society, with government sticking its nose into all areas of life and offering usually inadequate, incompetent, or irrelevant solutions to people's problems.

From the opposite direction, critics argue that court congestion, delay, and expense make our legal system *inaccessible* to most people and therefore irrelevant in dealing with their disputes. These critics agree with the "law explosion" critics that the courts are congested with case overloads. But they argue that the problems people have are real, not imaginary, and that the plodding, "gentlemen's club" pace of the courts makes them suitable only to the rich.

If your neighbor persistently fills the night air with the blast of amplified music which you dislike, you probably will not take him to court. It would cost too much, you might lose, and no matter what the judge's ruling, the bitterness and friction between you would probably increase. Or suppose a teacher takes a disliking to your child and routinely subjects him or her to psychological abuse (ridicule, sarcasm, punishment for petty offenses, withholding of rewards given to other children, etc.) What will you do if school officials refuse to challenge the teacher or allow your child to transfer? If you are like most parents, you cannot afford to take such a case to court. Similarly, suppose your new car suddenly needs a four hundred dollar repair job, and the dealer refuses to honor the warranty or give you a new car in its place. Would you go to court if your lawyer told you the action would cost at least eight hundred dollars, half of which you would have to pay before any lawyer would even take the case?

Ironically, we know more from anthropological research about how grievances and disputes are dealt with in African villages and Mexican towns than we do about their fate in the United States (Felstiner, 1974; Nader, 1980). Americans may not have access to effective dispute-settling methods like those found in simpler societies. On the other hand, modern societies create relationships which may be easier to break up if disputes arise (Felstiner, 1974). If this is so, then the inaccessibility of courts is not such a problem. An unresolved dispute may be distasteful, but most are not so critical that we cannot just "lump it" and carry on with our lives. As we shall see such a conclusion has both supporters and critics.

Supporting that conclusion is a study of the history of American courts since the mid-nineteenth century (Friedman, 1967). Looking at the courts in one way, we might think that their creators intended us to bring all our disputes before judges, who would settle them according to law. In American history, however, the state has systematically tried to divert trouble cases away from the courts, because the capacity of courts to respond to demand fluctuations is limited.

Courts can be thought of as a service business which cannot react quickly to increased demand by adding personnel or quickening the pace of service. A sudden increase in lawsuits cannot usually be met with the judicial equivalent of Kelly girls, or rent-a-judges. (While Friedman is probably right about this in general, it is interesting to note that the state of California has recently begun allowing wealthy litigants to hire their own judges (usually retired judges with plenty of time on their hands) in order to avoid the delay and expense of regular courts. For a fee of five hundred dollars a day, litigants can literally rent a judge and get a quick trial to settle their differences [*Wall Street Journal*, August 6, 1980, p. 1].)

Beginning around 1850, commercial expansion in the United States put rapidly escalating pressure on the courts. Commercial-sector disputes accelerated. Something had to be done. The options available were

1. Expansion of the courts
2. Routinization and mass handling of commercial matters in court
3. Routinization and mass handling of cases *outside* of court
4. Expansion of a policy to encourage settlements, compromises
5. Development of efficient dispute settlement mechanisms outside the judicial system
6. Adoption of court rules which would discourage litigants from using the courts
7. Making litigation more expensive, to cut down on demand

The first option was never used. The second and third were more common solutions. In court, for instance, practices such as wage garnishment became a routine way of handling the rising tide of suits by businesses demanding payment from customers. The fourth option appeared in the general attitude of court administrators who regularly applauded the value of compromises settled out of court. The fifth solution developed in the form of commercial arbitration.

However, options six and seven also played an important role in protecting the courts. Delay, expense, and congestion played a central role in producing a balance between demand and supply. In effect, court congestion prevented even worse congestion, because people had to think twice before pressing forward with "frivolous" disputes which could be handled elsewhere or by some other means. Expensive justice kept marginal cases out of the courts. Of course, this meant that less wealthy people were more likely to be barred from access to legal remedies, since every procedural rule which complicates or prolongs the litigation process increases the cost of litigation.

The argument here is that high litigation costs *reduce* people's tendency to insist on their legal rights. Expense therefore reduces the frequency of conflicts. Landlord-tenant relationships, for example, are governed by leases that are filled with rights for both sides. But life would be a never-ending lawsuit if both sides insisted on all of their rights all of the time. The relationship becomes tenable in part because each side has "reciprocal immunity"—both have enough rights "in reserve" so that if one side starts insisting on "sticking to the lease," the other can make legally correct counterdemands. Since both sides want to avoid the expense and inconvenience of litigation, they are more likely to settle their disagreement by themselves.

Congested courts may not produce "pure justice" either from within or by their effects on the way people behave outside of them. But the argument here is that no amount of expansion of court facilities could ever be adequate to cope with every instance of conflict which arises in complex societies. Some line has to be drawn separating "serious" disputes from the rest. Expense, congestion, and delay help to draw that line. So we should realistically recognize that these conditions are a *normal, functional* characteristic of judicial dispute-settlement methods.

Others have challenged this conclusion as blind to the harmful effects of unresolved conflict (Danzig and Lowy, 1975). American society, for example, is full of situations where untrained and often reluctant mediators must try to patch up relationships between people who have no alternative because of the inaccessibility of courts. Police often complain, for example, about the amount of working time and personal risk they must invest in mediating family disputes. In Wisconsin, the Department of Motor Vehicles became diverted from its main function of approving and withholding licenses to auto manufacturers and dealers and became instead the main mediator in disputes between them (Macaulay, 1966).

The lack of adequate dispute-settling institutions may produce *social pathologies* costly to both individuals and society as a whole. High job turnover, assaultive crime, wife and child abuse, juvenile delinquency, and emotional instability are all possible consequences of disputes left unresolved.

Heavy demands on psychological and psychiatric services, and on welfare institutions, may be a result. Consider the plight of a Philadelphia policeman who was badly in debt (Stern, 1980, p. 14). Harassment from bill collectors put him into such a depression that he attempted suicide. Only after hospitalization did he discover that he could have escaped his plight much more sensibly by filing for bankruptcy. His ordeal was a clear-cut case where the legal system's remoteness, and the lack of alternative ways to resolve the problem, led to severe personal and social costs.

When people "lump it" rather than complain about shoddy products or services, those responsible for the problem may never learn the consequences of their action. So problems which could be remedied persist and spread. One study showed, for example, that in cases of consumer complaints over products or services, dissatisfied buyers took action in only one-third of those situations where something was wrong with their purchases. Among those who did take action, only about half reached satisfactory settlements. Everyone else just had to lump it.

On the other hand, consumers may do more lumping than necessary because some of the inaccessibility is in their imaginations only (Ross and Littlefield, 1978). A study of complaint-handling procedures of several large merchandisers showed that customers who do complain usually receive at least as much compensation as the law would require, and often quite a bit more.

If both studies are correct, then part of the problem of inaccessibility may be the general dampening effect of delay, congestion, and formality on people's readiness to pursue legitimate grievances. What they might actually find if they did complain could be quite different from what they fear.

Disputes as Process

One thing all of these critiques of accessibility have in common is their grounding in studies which look beyond the formal statistics produced by legal institutions to the ways in which people actually pursue disputes—whether they reach courts or not. These studies complement those anthropological works we have already discussed which emphasize the *process* of disputing—the actions of individuals making choices. They lead to the conclusion that even when people do use courts, their actions reflect opportunities either available to them or blocked off from them because of established practices.

For example, in one study of an ethnically mixed working-class neighborhood in an eastern American city ethnic diversity and poverty prevented neighbors from resolving disputes by informal means (Merry, 1979). Gossip (public opinion) carried no clout because people holding negative opinions were "different" from, and powerless to influence, people who might have been the target of criticism. As a result, people relied heavily on the courts, but not in ways for which the courts were designed. People with grievances against their neighbors filed *criminal* charges against them. Because these were complex disputes involving neighbors who had ongoing relationships with each other, the criminal courts were ill-equipped to settle the disputes. People used criminal charges as a means of harassing opponents. The tension and humiliation of being ordered around by the police and the inconvenience of having to appear at court combined to make the criminal process a relatively effective way to discomfort an opponent.

The courts therefore had become a weapon of battle and did not resolve the disputes. The only true resolutions to conflicts in this neighborhood were accomplished by avoidance—either "lumping it" or having one side in a dispute leave the neighborhood entirely.

Not only do delay and congestion deflect legitimate grievances from the courts, but when people use the courts, the effect may be to increase or transform conflict rather than resolve it.

People use urban courts in India in the same way (Kidder, 1973). Congestion and delay have reached seemingly intolerable levels (for example, in one state the average duration of civil lawsuits, from time of filing until time of final judgment, is *seventeen years*), and people speak of involvement in litigation as similar to slow death. Yet people by the millions are involved in lawsuits. Their disputes keep a large number of lawyers very busy. Many litigants fight court cases for years (in one case, a cloth merchant had been involved in a bankruptcy suit for fifty years and was fighting the grandchildren of the man he had originally been sued by).

Such behavior does not make much sense if we think of the lawsuit only as a form of dispute *settlement*. But if we remember the anthropological discovery that disputing is better understood as an ongoing *process,* Indian uses of the courts become more comprehensible. People in India use the courts as part of overall strategies for dealing with each other in relationships which they expect to continue in the future and which contain elements of both cooperation and competition. Like the "games" of the mathematicians, the strategic development of relationships in Indian communities is complex, long-lasting, and interdependent. The courts are just one of many places (or arenas) in which people seek to maximize their advantages, or minimize their losses, in these ongoing relationships.

The fact that lawsuits last for years reflects the fact that the courts cannot alter the basic competitive-cooperative nature of the relationships which produce the suits. People go to the courts originally hoping for justice and vindication of their views, just as do the American city dwellers who take their neighbors to criminal court. But as in the American criminal courts, the Indian courts cannot impose effective measures to terminate these disputes because they are ill-equipped to deal with the full range of factors around which these relationships and disputes revolve.

The inadequacy of courts stems from the severe procedural limitations characteristic of adjudication. Courts are allowed to address only the "case" presented to them. Cases must be stated in precise, narrow language fitting predetermined legal categories. Judges cannot normally probe a case to discover whether, as is very often the case, it is but a distorted and partial picture of the full range of cooperative and competitive connections between opponents.

People quickly discover that this narrowness can be manipulated to achieve purposes completely hidden from the judge and the official court records. In India, for example, the son of a wealthy family had watched as one of his brothers starved to death. He was himself living off the charity of his lawyer. His poverty was evident despite the fact that he was an owner of factories, warehouses, racehorses, and fine automobiles. In the settlement of his father's estate family members had fallen into an extremely complex set of disputes. The courts had responded by freezing all of his assets for the duration of the various pending lawsuits. The battle had turned into a question of who could wait the longest for the others to die or give up. The courts, with their rigid procedures, were obviously not only failing to resolve these highly counterproductive disputes (all of the factories and warehouses had been closed and sealed by court order), but were also actually being used in a deadly game of "chicken."

Having learned to use the courts in these ways, people find them useful for regulating relationships where levels of animosity are much lower. Again in India, it is not unusual to find two men fighting each other in one lawsuit and allied with each other against some other party in another suit. Suits which are filed as disputes over land use may evolve over time to become used to pressure an opponent to pay a debt. Suits are one way to dun an opponent for payment of dowry in a marriage agreement, even though dowry has been declared illegal by the government. Suits can force an opponent to withdraw as an officer of a politically influential charitable organization. Since all of these issues involve the same people, either simultaneously or over the years, the lawsuit is just one of several situations where each side must cover itself against attack while seeking to maximize its gains.

It would be tempting to conclude that such people are unusually contentious, even to the point of being irrational about it. But a careful look at the way their relationships are organized, at the expectations that are placed on them in their social roles, at the pressures of social change forcing them to adjust to new situations, and at the opportunities available to them shows that their ways of using the courts may make perfect sense, though they bear little relationship to the kind of role the courts are officially supposed to play in the settling of disputes.

This pattern of court use defeats the adjudicatory function of courts. We find that Indians have transformed *adjudicatory* institutions into settings for protracted *negotiations*. The duration of the cases and the strategies and motives which litigants describe for their cases show that *settlement* is not the product of the process. Instead of ending conflicts, the courts give them a special kind of public exposure and treatment which fits into the strategies of opponents in an ingenious variety of ways.

To some, it might be comforting to think that our evidence from India shows these "distortions" of modern Western law because Indians are culturally different from us. But there is plenty of evidence that our American courts play a very similar role. Think again about the evidence that urban Americans use criminal charges as a form of harassment. Then recall that almost all criminal cases in America are resolved by *plea bargaining* (i.e., negotiation over guilty pleas for reduced charges and penalties) rather than adjudication (Feeley, 1979). Combining these two facts, we must conclude that at least some of the business of criminal courts in America represents their use as a scene for the *negotiated adjustment* of relations among neighbors who have no other resource for resolving their differences. Like Indian litigants, American city dwellers find it useful to harass their opponents with court action. As in India, they find such action inconclusive.

Other American courts apparently receive similar treatment. In American *federal* courts and *small-claims* courts, "Litigation is rarely an unequivocal call for judicial action; it is instead frequently intended to promote out-of-court negotiations" (Sarat, 1976, p. 342). Lawsuits rarely go the full route to final judgment. Cases drop out at various preliminary stages as opponents either abandon the combat or move it to other nonlegal battlefields. The fact that the courts have been the scene of battle in particular disputes does not mean that the courts' actions have resolved those disputes. As in any war, the battles which take place in court may influence the future development of both the combat and efforts to end it. But in many kinds of disputes, courts apparently lack the means to perform the kind of social magic their official posture has led people to expect.

DISPUTE ANALYSIS: A BASIS FOR REFORM?

Some people react to these findings by trying to develop reforms which will give people real dispute-settling options, choices that work. They seek ways to "restore the balance" (Nader, 1980) as it is done in Mexican villages and other "non-Western" settings. Others criticize the "need-for-balance" assumption, either on the grounds that society does not operate by maintaining such equilibrium or that inequalities built into society inevitably produce dispute-handling forms which reinforce inequality. Problems with reform proposals even lead to doubt that the term *dispute* can withstand the crossover from simpler to more complex conflict environments without distorting our understanding of modern American conflict relationships.

One source of reform proposals has centered around complaint letters which frustrated Americans have sent to consumer advocate Ralph Nader (Nader, 1980). By the thousands, those letters reveal the tragic waste, suffering, and bitterness pervading American society as a result of unresolved disputes. Because this situation is unstable, there has been a rising tide of efforts to develop dispute-settling measures outside the legal system. These measures include neighborhood justice centers, consumer advocate organizations, media ombudspeople (e.g., radio, television, and newspaper "action lines"), along with more traditional alternatives such as complaint-handling work by members of Congress.

These alternatives, combined with conventional methods, make up an "ecology of dispute processing" in the United States (Galanter, 1981). Formal courtroom adjudication is just one of a host of methods people employ in pursuit of justice. Many of these alternatives are produced by determined people struggling against the tendency of formal law to monopolize the dispute-handling business.

Some social scientists, however, challenge the claim that society has a "need for balance." No court or other dispute-settling mechanism, they say, can produce real conflict resolution (Galanter, 1981). Cooperation and social harmony are not the normal state of society. Disputes and conflict are normal, even necessary, in developing social institutions (e.g., see Coser, 1956). For example, when a group faces opposition from a determined enemy, internal discord diminishes and group solidarity increases. Societies could not survive without the creative force of conflict. If all conflicts were successfully "resolved," the society would be left in a stagnant position with respect to an ever-changing, challenging environment. Nature, they say, does not long tolerate stagnant organisms.

From this perspective, some see the problem of inadequate access to courts and legal remedies as a problem not necessarily calling for reforms in the judicial system. Rather, barriers to access are evidence that prior conflicts have left one group in control of one part of the "ecology of dispute-processing" mechanisms. Since conflict does not end, we know that the closure of access to one means of disputing produces pressure to open new forms of expression. Inequalities in society may become entrenched in the legal system, as anywhere else. But when they do, as in the case of expensive, slow justice in the courts, the fight against them will surface elsewhere, either within the legal system or as alternatives to it.

Others who oppose the "social balance" perspective say simply that the courts promote the interest of the ruling elite which created them (Turk, 1976). Courts cannot transcend the powers which create and sustain them; they cannot "bite the hand that feeds them." So the courtroom ideal of equal justice handed down by impartial judges masquerades the bazaarlike haggling which actually typifies litigation. Where "let's make a deal" justice prevails, as in the courts, the outcome favors the party with the strongest bargaining position and best bargaining skills. The "haves" not only come out ahead in this deal, but they try very hard to insure that lawcourts are the only recourse open to those who would challenge their privileges.

In view of the complications we have discovered in our efforts to understand how disputes get settled, we have learned to be wary of even the vocabulary of dispute settlement. *Settlement* appears to distort what is going on, so we speak of *processing*. But what about the term *dispute*? Remember that the concept *disputing* received much of its social scientific content from both anthropological research and game-theory strategy analysis, especially as applied to practical issues such as labor and commercial disputes. Because of this background, when we use the term "dispute" now, it is hard to avoid implying some of the assumptions which have typified anthropological and applied strategy analyses.

The term *dispute* conjures up images of two parties facing each other with resolvable, but temporarily incompatible, claims. It hints that each side has a "bargaining" position which gives standing to a disputant. It also hints that a feeling of injustice pervades the relationship between the two sides (e.g., see Felstiner, Abel, and Sarat, 1981). Inherent in the way many social scientists use the term is an untested set of assumptions about the emotional climate and resource balance between the two sides.

Because of these connotations, reform proposals based on the transfer of concepts (e.g., Nader, 1980; Felstiner, Abel, and Sarat, 1981) from anthropological studies in non-Western societies to relationships involving individuals or huge corporations in the United States face some major problems of distortion. Can concepts (e.g., *dispute*) that were developed with opponents who were *persons* with face-to-face, enduring relationships be successfully applied to battles between homeowners and the electric company or between elderly people and the Social Security Administration? If a modern American dispute is produced when a home-building subsidiary of a multi-national corporation boosts its profit margin by installing dangerous aluminum wiring in several thousand housing units, can we expect to understand the resulting relationship between builder and buyers as a process comparable to either a domestic quarrel in a remote Mexican village or an experiment on the reactions of college sophomores to laboratory games? Is there a dispute when an elderly person freezes to death at home because the gas company cut the supply in order to put pressure on a welfare agency to pay their client's bills? When IBM and Xerox sue each other over a question of patent violation, or when Metropolitan Edison sues Westinghouse for failure to deliver a contracted supply of enriched uranium, should we expect the same emotional climate, the same sense of outrage and demand for justice, as when a Mexican village woman demands land from her father in spite of a norm that land goes first to sons?

Those who make this connection by treating all these cases as disputes are not unaware of the problem. This is why some of them have abandoned the term "dispute settlement" in favor of "dispute processing." This is why they emphasize the variations in dispute processing produced by factors such as disputants' hopes of preserving relations with opponents, prior history of relations with opponents, and ability to endure protracted disputing costs and maneuvers. All of these factors are conclusions which are meant to elaborate the basic analysis of disputes in the face of strains put on the concept by the obvious inequality between individual complainants and giant corporations, and by the depersonalization of conflict between corporations.

However, the buyer of a mass-produced home with defective plumbing and the asbestos-factory worker whose lungs are decaying from asbestosis are not just individuals with unique disputes requiring individualized "dispute processing." They belong to *classes* of persons whose problems stem from the unilaterally imposed policies of bureaucratically organized corporations. Solutions to *their problem* may not produce solutions to *the problem*. The language of disputing tends to divert attention from the mass quality, the political content, of these conflicts by focusing on the individual.

Similarly, a battle between two corporate giants, or between a corporation and a governmental regulatory agency, is not usually an emotion-laden crusade for justice. It is rather a struggle between organized interests in which cold-blooded calculations of strategy are juxtaposed against a background of uncertainty to shape the course of battle. Lawyers working for government regulatory agencies, for example, have no apparent emotional difficulty taking their insider's knowledge and skills along with them when they quit and go to work for the very corporations they have been fighting as regulators.

The current attempt to transfer dispute-processing analysis from non-Western to Western settings may help perpetuate what Abel (1981) sees as a negative characteristic of things legal. Abel argues that when someone's problems have been successfully defined as *legal,* their *political* nature is suppressed because legal ways of dealing with them foreclose political methods. Legalizing an issue depoliticizes it by disaggregating the many instances of the same problem and treating them individually. If we call the struggle between an asbestos producer and one of the company's dying workers a *dispute,* we locate it on the legal side of the law-politics dichotomy. To call a conflict a dispute is to define it as a problem amenable to legal (that is rule-bound and authoritative) treatment. By insisting on its political content, avoiding the connotations of the "disputing" terminology, we instead recognize the key role of power in the development of the conflict.

SOURCES OF DISPUTES

The general approach in the studies we have looked at thus far is to treat the individual as a strategist whose choices are the object of study. As we have seen, many of the studies done on disputing are concerned with identifying the major influences on those individual choices which stem from the nature of the dispute and the characteristics of the method being used to resolve it.

Another approach asks quite different questions about disputes. It involves a search for predictable patterns in the *frequency* and *type* of disputes typically occurring in the societies under study. If such patterns exist, we should be able to identify connections between social conditions and disputing patterns. Unlike game theorists and strategy analysts, who seek understanding of the internal dynamics of the disputing process, this approach focuses on the *external determinants* of *disputing patterns.* It treats the individual as a member of groups or classes which share similar problems and resources, rather than as an isolated strategist making choices in a unique dispute "game."

For example, in chapter 4, we saw the prediction that *avoidance* as a response to disputes ought to be more common in technologically complex, rich societies like the United States than in simple, poor societies like those most often studied by anthropologists (Felstiner, 1974). This approach typifies the interest in linking socioeconomic conditions to particular disputing patterns.

One set of studies has addressed the question of whether or not there is a predictable relationship between increasing industrial development and levels of disputes handled in law courts. Some find a *curvilinear* relationship, while others using the same data find a simple *linear* relationship. In either case, as you will see, there is agreement that industrialization does affect the amount of "trouble" in society.

The curvilinear model refers to evidence in some courts that their caseloads are low at the beginning of industrialization, shoot up rapidly as industrialization accelerates, and then level off or decline as court costs and congestion dampen people's enthusiasm for going to court and as industrial society develops institutional solutions to the disruptions created by industrialization. For example, when two California county courts were compared, researchers found that, from the late nineteenth century onward, judges gradually shifted their attention from adjudication of disputes to routine administration of simple legal formalities (Friedman and Percival, 1976; see also Friedman, 1973). This trend, they said, was evidence of the last stage of the curvilinear relationship between industrialization and disputing. Court work became routine because there was less disputing as time went on.

In support of this curvilinear model, data comparing litigation rates in different regions of Spain show significant differences according to whether or not they were in the midst of rapid industrial growth (Toharia, 1973). Those areas experiencing economic "takeoff" (the rapid entry into industrial forms of production) showed rapid increases in rates of litigation. But the most advanced regions of Spain, areas which were already established industrial zones, did not have high rates of litigation.

Other studies, however, show that there is reason to doubt the curvilinear model. Over the years in United States federal courts, for example, both legal activity and litigation increased in the states that had become the most industrialized (Grossman and Sarat, 1975). But in those states where industrialization was slow, overall legal activity decreased while litigation increased. This pattern is just the opposite of what we would expect from the curvilinear model. Also, a reexamination of the two California county courts produced results contradicting the original curvilinear model because it defined the questions differently (Lempert, 1978). Instead of comparing the amount of routine legal work to the amount of litigation handled in the courts, as was done in the original study, the second study compared the amount of litigation to the size of the populations from which lawsuits could have come. It also compared litigation rates to outside data on the actual number of disputes which could have been brought to court. With these changes, the data showed that litigation had actually *increased* steadily throughout the period. There was no curvilinear decline in litigation. True, the courts had taken on a heavier load of routine work.

But they had not become less involved in the process of dispute settlement. They had actually taken on more work altogether. Court records therefore support a *linear model* (continuous steady increase) of the relationship between industrial development and disputing.

Hence the present state of evidence on the effects of industrialization on litigation is ambiguous. Studies done so far support the general conclusion that socioeconomic development has effects on the kinds of disputes which are generated in a society and that these effects are reflected in data on court use. But we do not yet have conclusive evidence on whether courts play an increasing, steady, or decreasing role in dispute processing as industrial societies mature.

All of these studies share a common problem of interpretation because they rely on court records as their primary source of data. Such records appear at first glance to be a gold mine of information about disputing activity in a society. But those who have worked with such data have found hidden hazards in their use (e.g., see Cartwright, 1975, p. 369). One assumption common to all these studies is that cases filed as lawsuits represent disputes. This leads to the further assumption that if courts record a certain number of lawsuits during a given year, there is a correspondence between that number and the number of disputes which got started or settled during that year.

A closer look shows that we cannot rely on court records as solid evidence of disputing. Looking back in this chapter at the evidence we presented about court uses in India (Kidder, 1973) and the United States (Sarat, 1976; Merry, 1979), we can see that official court statistics may bear little relationship to the actual incidence or history of disputes. In India, one dispute may be expressed in three or four different lawsuits at the same time. The fact that a judge renders a "final decision" in a case may tell us nothing about whether the dispute has been settled or not. Such decisions are often just intermediate mileposts on pathways of conflict which stretch off to the horizon. Cases which should be handled by civil courts as lawsuits show up instead in the statistics of American criminal courts because working-class people find this the only usable route into the legal system. People thus use the courts in diverse ways not necessarily consistent with court record-keeping categories, which are made to fit only the formal legal definitions of what the events in court mean. It may thus be either partially or totally misleading to treat lawsuits as instances of dispute-settling activity in society.

Because of these difficulties, current research is aimed at measuring the "hidden dimension" of disputing in the United States. Until we know more about the history, frequency, and content of disputes which never get to court, as well as those which continue after their appearance as lawsuits, we cannot say whether the courts are inadequate or overdeveloped.

SUMMARY AND CONCLUSION

We began this discussion with a couple of lawsuits to illustrate the widespread interest Americans show in public disputes. We discussed three different research traditions which led investigators down separate paths to many similar destinations. We saw how the laboratory experiments of game theorists and strategy analysts produced predictions and results which often coincided with what anthropologists were discovering in their on-the-spot study of trouble cases. We also saw that the anthropological study of disputes led some anthropologists into questions and perspectives on disputes in modern industrialized societies quite similar to the issues being studied by sociologists and political scientists whose main concern was with the operations of modern courts.

We see here a convergence from different disciplines on a set of shared conclusions. These include statements about the characteristics and effects of different modes of dispute handling (e.g., adjudication uses third parties and relies extensively on the invocation of rules while negotiation is a dyadic relationship in which rules are invoked less often and have less definitive effects on the outcome). They also include statements about the effects of disputants' characteristics on the development of disputes (e.g., where disputants expect to continue interacting with their opponents in the future, their strategies are more likely to include compromise, as compared with disputes between strangers).

However, we have also seen that the convergence of results can be exaggerated. It is difficult, for example, to move from the abstract strategy analysis of the game theorist to the real-world operations of American courts, because the official court definition of the "game" in most lawsuits bears little resemblance to the strategies being pursued by litigants. These strategies are not bounded just by the law and procedures of court. A host of alternative arenas blossoms in the environment of conflict. Procedures often do not result in neat, clear settlements where losses and gains can be accurately weighed. We are finding that the law's answers to disputes are often indistinguishable from the give-and-take of politics, where power operates in an extended process of strategic maneuvering and where "settlements" are no more than temporary accommodations to inequality. We find that we cannot take at face value the claim that law functions to resolve conflicts in society. We are not sure that anything reliably resolves them, and we cannot even be confident that law courts, on the whole, lessen rather than heighten the level of conflict in society.

Rather, our attention has shifted to the study of two major categories of questions: (1) How do disputes get handled? What is the process or the array of alternative processes which begin to operate when disputes emerge as public issues? What are the effects of these processes on the disputants, their immediate social networks, and society as a whole? and (2) What are the major sources of conflict in society? How have changes in these sources affected the ways in which disputes are processed? How does the idea of disputing fit into the processes which produce conflict and affect its development?

APPLYING WHAT YOU KNOW

Every approach we have studied in this chapter takes for granted that when certain conditions arise, a dispute is born. In the case we will examine here, however, that basic assumption cannot be made. This case therefore raises difficult questions of interpretation. Thinking of the issues we have reviewed thus far, see if you can develop a way of fitting the following case into one or more of the analyses in this chapter.

In a town just outside of Atlanta, Georgia, an anthropologist found that there were three distinct groups who used the legal system in very different ways (Greenhouse, 1981). One group, the *newcomers,* relied quite heavily on courts to help them when they had disputes. A second group, the *old-timers,* used the services of lawyers and knew how to make legal threats to get what they wanted. But they rarely went to court, because their strategies usually were effective in making litigation unnecessary. The third group, the *Baptists,* were also old-timers. They had lived in the town as long as the others. In response to disputes, however, they never went to court and never used lawyers.

The focus of attention, then, is on the Baptists. If they never used the law, what did they use? The answer is that they rejected the idea of disputing entirely. To them conflict with others represented *sin.* Anyone unable to avoid conflict with neighbors must be exhibiting one or more kinds of sinful behavior. Therefore, a good Baptist in this town would not even consider taking legal action to pursue a disputed claim.

Theoretically, then, anyone wishing to take advantage of this situation could encroach on the rights of Baptists with impunity. The only response good Baptists would make would be to pray for divine intervention to make their non-Baptist foes see the error of their ways and cease their aggressive behavior. The situation sounds ripe for exploitation. How could these people get along without acknowledging the reality of conflict?

Separation is not the answer. They lived in ordinary homes scattered throughout the town, and they, like most others in town, commuted to Atlanta for their work. They did not practice any form of self-denial which would have made them invulnerable to attack. Their homes were normal American homes with all the ordinary facilities.

Psychologically, however, there was a strong sense of separation. To the Baptists, they were the only people in the world who were following

God's word. Nobody else in town was on the right track, not even other Christians. As a result, the Baptists avoided, as much as possible, having anything to do with non-Baptists. Their time was entirely consumed in matters of family and church. With other members of the church, a person who felt the beginnings of conflict would feel the obligation to retire to prayer and meditation. The church provided no other means for resolving conflicts.

Strangely, however, the sense of separation did not extend to politics. Though Baptists never ran for office in town, they did participate to the extent of voting. So their rejection of "worldly institutions" was not very broad. It extended primarily to the law.

This exclusive hostility to law had its roots in the economic and political history of the town. During the period just before and after the Civil War, relations between different classes in the area underwent changes. Before the war, the town had been surrounded by two rings of farms. The inner ring contained the prosperous plantations of the Presbyterians. The outer ring harbored the less productive lands of the dirt farmers, who were Baptists. The war wiped out the labor force (slaves) of the prosperous farmers, driving many of them out of business and giving the dirt farmers a chance to buy more land and prosper.

These changes produced a period of considerable instability and strife in the Baptist church. The issues of slavery and of support for foreign missions split the church so badly that it nearly disappeared. To revive it, leaders began a campaign of total withdrawal from political participation. They focused particularly on the law because judgeships were the primary political prize handed out by the winning party after an election.

The strategy worked. The church pulled itself together under this policy of nonparticipation, and by 1975 it had a population of around 2,300. The rejection of law and of conflict as anything other than sin continues to be an expression of their strong sense of separation from the "unsaved" balance of the population. Apparently this form of self-denial is sufficient to provide a clear-cut "we-they" feeling, which strengthens the church's hold on its members' loyalty even though they no longer differ from everyone else in the kind of work they do or life-style they lead.

We have, then, a twentieth century population which rejects the proposition that disputes involve issues of justice which can be resolved by human intervention. They will not lift a finger to defend their "rights" because they refuse to think in terms of rights.

How can a group of people in modern American society survive with such a philosophy? Do you think that this example shows that we could drastically reduce all legal services relating to disputing without serious side effects? Does the fact that these people get along without acknowledging the legitimacy of rights mean that everyone could if they were just reeducated to think like these particular Baptists? If everyone took up the Baptist philosophy, what would happen to the group solidarity which the Baptists now have? What method would people use for deciding how to distribute property, or how to allocate blame in the case of accidents, or how to make hiring and promotion decisions in government offices? Finally, what changes would have to be made in the way society works if we were committed to ending our ways of thinking about disputes, conflict, rights, and justice? Could we continue to have "normal" American jobs and lead "normal" American lives as the Baptists appear to be doing in every respect except where law is concerned?

REFERENCES

ABEL, RICHARD   (1979), Western Courts in Non-Western Settings: Patterns of Court Use in Colonial and Neo-Colonial Africa, pp. 167–200 in S. B. Burman and B. Harrell-Bond (eds.), *The Imposition of Law*, New York: Academic Press.

ABEL, RICHARD   (1981), Conservative Conflict and the Reproduction of Capitalism: the Role of Informal Justice. *International Journal of the Sociology of Law*, 9, 2.

AUBERT, VILHELM   (1969), Law as a Way of Resolving Conflicts: The Case of the Small Industrialized Society in L. Nader (ed.), *Law in Culture and Society*, Chicago: Aldine.

BEST, ARTHUR AND ANDREASSEN, ALAN   (1977), Consumer Responses to Unsatisfactory Purchases: A Survey of Perceiving Defects, Voicing Complaints, and Obtaining Redress, *Law and Society Review*, 11, p. 701.

BOHANNAN, PAUL   (1957), *Justice and Judgment Among the Tiv*. London: Oxford University Press.

BOHANNAN, PAUL   (1965), The Differing Realms of Law, *The Ethnography of Law* Supplement to *The American Anthropologist*, 67, Pt. 2, pp. 33–42.

BOULDING, KENNETH   (1963), *The Strategy of Conflict*, Oxford: Oxford University Press.

BOWEN, MURRAY   (1978), *Family Therapy in Clinical Practise*, New York: J. Aronson.

CAPLOW, THEODORE   (1968), *Two Against One*, Englewood Cliffs, N.J.: Prentice-Hall.

CARTWRIGHT, BLISS   (1975), Afterword: Disputes and Reported Cases, *Law and Society Review*, 9 (2), p. 369.

CBS,   *Sixty Minutes*, December 7, 1980.

COHN, BERNARD   (1959), Some Notes on Law and Change in North India, *Economic Development and Cultural Change*, 5, pp. 79–93.

COSER, LEWIS   (1956), *The Functions of Social Conflict*, New York: Free Press.

DANZIG, RICHARD AND LOWY, MICHAEL   (1975), Everyday Disputes and Mediation in the United States: A Reply to Professor Felstiner, *Law and Society Review*, 9 (4), pp. 675–94.

DUBOW, FREDERIC   (1973), *Justice for People: Law and Politics in the Lower Courts of Tanzania*, Doctoral Dissertation, University of California, Berkeley.

ECKHOFF, TORSTEIN   (1966), The Mediator, The Judge and the Administrator in Conflict Resolution, *Acta Sociologica*, 6.

EHRLICH, THOMAS   (1976), Legal Pollution, *New York Times Magazine* 17, February 8.

EPSTEIN, A. L.   (1973), The Reasonable Man Revisited: Some Problems in the Anthropology of Law, *Law and Society Review*, 7 (4), p. 643.

FALLERS, LLOYD   (1969), *Law Without Precedent: Legal Ideas in Action in the Courts of Colonial Busoga*, Chicago: University of Chicago Press.

FEELEY, MALCOLM   (1979), Perspectives on Plea Bargaining, *Law and Society Review* 13 (2), p. 199.

FELSTINER, WILLIAM   (1974), Influences of Social Organization on Dispute Processing, *Law and Society Review*, 9 (1), p. 63.

FELSTINER, WILLIAM; ABEL, RICHARD; AND SARAT, AUSTIN   (1981), The Emergence and Transformation of Disputes: Naming, Blaming, and Claiming, *Law and Society Review*, 15 (3).

FITZGERALD, JEFFREY   (1974), The Contract Buyer's League and the Courts: A Case Study of Poverty Litigation, *Law and Society Review*, 9 (2).

FRIEDMAN, LAWRENCE   (1967), Legal Rules and the Process of Social Change, *Stanford Law Review*, 19 (4), pp. 798–810.

FRIEDMAN, LAWRENCE   (1973), General Theory of Law and Social Change in J. Ziegel (ed.), *Law and Social Change*, Toronto: Osgood Hall Law School, York University.

FRIEDMAN, LAWRENCE AND PERCIVAL, ROBERT   (1976), A Tale of Two Courts: Litigation in Alameda and San Benito Counties, *Law and Society Review*, 10, p. 267.

GALANTER, MARC   (1981), Adjudication, Litigation and Related Phenomena, in Social Science Research Council: *Handbook on Law and Social Science*, Chapter 5.

GLUCKMAN, MAX   (1955), *The Judicial Process among the Barotse of Northern Rhodesia*, Glencoe, Ill.: Free Press.

GREENHOUSE, CAROL   (1981), Diverse Legal Cultures in an American Town. Paper presented at the 1981 Annual Meetings of the Law and Society Association, Amherst, Mass.

GROSSMAN, JOEL AND SARAT, AUSTIN   (1975), Litigation in the Federal Courts: A Comparative Perspective, *Law and Society Review*, 9 (2), p. 321.

GULLIVER, PHILIP   (1969), Dispute Settlement without Courts: The Ndendeuli of Southern Tanzania in L. Nader (ed.), *Law in Culture and Society*, Chicago: Aldine.

GULLIVER, PHILIP   (1979), *Disputes and Negotiations: A Cross-Cultural Perspective*, New York: Academic Press.

HOEBEL, E. ADAMSON   (1954), *The Law of Primitive Man*. Cambridge, Mass.: Harvard University Press.

KIDDER, ROBERT   (1973), Courts and Conflict in an Indian City: A Study in Legal Impact, *Journal of Commonwealth Political Studies*, 11 (2) (July), pp. 121–40.

KLINE, J. ANTHONY   (1978), Curbing California's Colossal Legal Appetite, *Los Angeles Times*, Pt. VI.1 (February, 12).

LEMPERT, RICHARD   (1978), More Tales of Two Courts: Exploring Changes in the Dispute-Settlement Function of Trial Courts, *Law and Society Review*, 13 (1), pp. 91–138.

LLEWELLYN, KARL AND HOEBEL, E. ADAMSON   (1941), *The Cheyenne Way*, Norman, Oklahoma: University of Oklahoma Press.

MACAULAY, STEWART   (1966), *Law and the Balance of Power: The Automobile Manufacturers and Their Dealers*. New York: Russell Sage Foundation.

MALINOWSKI, BRONISLAW   (1926), *Crime and Custom in Savage Society*, London: Routledge and Kegan Paul.

MANNING, BAYLESS   (1979), Hyperplexis: Our National Disease, *Northwestern University Law Review*, 71, p. 767.

MERRY, SALLY   (1979), Going to Court: Strategies of Dispute Management in an American Urban Neighborhood, *Law and Society Review*, 13, p. 891.

NADER, LAURA   (1964), An Analysis of Zapotec Law Cases, *Ethnology*, 3, p. 404.

NADER, LAURA   (1969), Styles of Court Procedure: To Make the Balance, in L. Nader (ed.), *Law in Culture and Society*, Chicago: Aldine.

NADER, LAURA   (1980), *No Access to Law*, New York: Academic Press.

NADER, LAURA AND TODD, HARRY   (1978), Introduction, pp. 1–40 in L. Nader and H. Todd (eds.), *The Disputing Process: Law in Ten Societies*, New York: Columbia University Press.

NBC,   *NBC Magazine with David Brinkley*, December 5, 1980.

PERISTIANY, J. G. (ed.)   (1965), *Honour and Shame: The Values of Mediterranean Society*, London: Weidenfeld and Nicholson.

POSPISIL, LEOPOLD   (1958), *Kapauku Papuans and Their Law*, Yale University Publications in Anthropology, Number 58.

RAPOPORT, ANATOL   (1960), *Fights, Games and Debates*, Ann Arbor: Univeristy of Michigan Press.

RAPOPORT, ANATOL AND CHAMMAH, A. M.   (1965), *Prisoner's Dilemma*, Ann Arbor: University of Michigan Press.

ROSENBERG, MAURICE   (1971), Let's Everybody Litigate? *Texas Law Review*, 50, p. 1349.

ROSS, H. LAWRENCE AND LITTLEFIELD, N. O.   (1978), Complaint as a Problem-Solving Mechanism, *Law and Society Review*, 12, p. 199.

SARAT, AUSTIN   (1976), Alternatives in Dispute Processing: Litigation in Small Claims Courts, *Law and Society Review*, 10 (3), p. 342.

SCHELLING, THOMAS   (1960), *The Strategy of Conflict*, Cambridge, Mass.: Harvard University Press.

STARR, JUNE   (1978), *Dispute Settlement in Rural Turkey*, Leiden, The Netherlands: E. J. Brill.

STERN, PHILIP   (1980), *Lawyers on Trial*, New York: Times Books.

THIBAUT, JOHN AND WALKER, L.   (1975), *Procedural Justice: A Psychological Analysis*, Hillsdale, N.J.: Lawrence Erlbaum Associates.

TOHARIA, JOSE   (1973), Economic Development and Litigation in Spain, Paper presented at the Conference for the Sociology of Law, Center of Interdisciplinary Studies, University of Bielefeld (Germany).

TURK, AUSTIN   (1976), Law as a Weapon of Social Conflict, *Social Problems*, 23, p. 276.

Wall Street Journal, August 6, 1980, p. 1.

YNGVESSON, BARBARA   (1976), Responses to Grievance Behavior: Extended Cases in a Fishing Community, *American Ethnologist*, 3, p. 353.

8

LEGAL COMPLEXITY: PLURALISM, MODERNITY, AND THE SEARCH FOR SIMPLICITY

'Tis a gift to be simple,
'Tis a gift to be free,
'Tis a gift to come down
Where we ought to be.
        (Traditional Shaker Hymn)

Simplicity. Where has it gone in our lives? Why is everything so complicated? In particular, why is our way of dealing with legal problems so complicated?

These are questions we all seem to ask from time to time as we deal with the frustrations of modern existence. Often we compare our own experience with "the good old days," when we assume that life was simpler, experience more direct. Or we look to other parts of our country or the world and marvel at some society's simpler ways of handling problems.

Anthropological studies of law have contributed to this belief in the simplicity of earlier times by showing the swift, direct methods of legal action carried out in "simpler," "premodern," "nonindustrialized" societies. When the !Kung San of the Kalahari desert, for instance, disagree about how to distribute the meat of an animal killed by a hunter's arrow, they gather around and discuss all aspects of the hunt, the people involved, the people needing the meat, and the prospects for future kills (Marshall,

1974). One among them, respected for his hunting prowess and reputation for fairness, helps to direct the conversation so that all in the group will remember their dependence on the continued solidarity of the hunting band. Without that solidarity, they know they would quickly perish. After thorough discussion, the meat is divided up by an elder recommended by the respected hunter. Everyone gets a share that seems fair.

Done. No judges in black robes, no regulatory agency demanding reports in quadruplicate, no expensive lawyers speaking an unknown language, no libraries full of gold-embossed law books, and no computerized, radio-based patrol cars racing to the "scene of the crime" so that professional police can take charge of "the case."

So simple. Why do we need anything more? Why can't people just be people and deal directly with each other? Who needs red tape?

The development of complexity in society and in legal systems has been a central concern of sociology since its birth. Some social scientists speak of this process as *modernization* or *development*. Some call it the development of *pluralism*. Some reject both these terms by arguing that modern society is actually *less* complex than earlier societies. Others reject all of them as expressions of ethnocentrism, a belief in the superiority of one's own culture in contrast to others. Still others see both terms as part of an ideology which helps to justify the inequalities which have developed in Western society.

In this chapter we will compare these different interpretations as they relate to the specific proposal that modern legal institutions should be simplified so that ordinary people can have inexpensive, uncomplicated, effective *access to justice*. In previous chapters, we compared competing views of legal development. Here we will see how those theories relate to a specific set of policy proposals.

There has been a wave of proposals to simplify law throughout the world. These initiatives appear in both "underdeveloped" and highly industrialized societies. In the United States, for example, legislatures have passed laws requiring ordinary, simple language in all contracts, bills of sale, insurance policies and similar legal documents affecting consumers' rights. Across the United States and in many other societies, experiments are tried using minimally trained neighborhood mediators to replace courts and judges as settlers of disputes. Programs for neighborhood mediation, labor mediation, use of the ombudsman, creation of simplified courts, development of independent associations of arbitrators and mediators all reflect a desire to escape the formality and expense of modern law and lawyers, to bring law back down to earth, back "to the people" (e.g., McEwan and Maiman, 1981; Abel, 1982).

Can we turn back the legal clock? Will modern legal problems lend themselves to methods of "simple justice"? What forces work against the simplification of law? And how should we interpret the significance of campaigns in modern industrial societies, as well as in "developing" or "Third World" societies, to establish "grass-roots" methods of law in the final quarter of the twentieth century?

These are the questions considered in this chapter. They are not simple. They require us to investigate the meaning of *modernity*, the legitimacy of calling certain procedures *simple,* and the possibility of bias in the concepts of *progress* and *development.* We will see that it may even be a mistake to equate legal simplicity with turning back the clock. Popular, or grass-roots, justice may become a regular feature of "modern" social orders. But its significance, its *impact,* bears the kind of careful investigation just discussed in chapter 6.

MODERN LAW

Let us begin by clarifying what is usually meant when people speak of modern law. Galanter (1966) has listed the characteristics of legal modernity as follows:

1. *Uniformity* of rules and their application. Law recognizes only functional differences among people, not intrinsic differences. (Example: a woman might be refused a job as a professional football player, but only for being too small or too slow [functional difference], not for being female [intrinsic difference].)

2. *Transactional basis* for rights and duties. People's obligations to each other come from agreements freely negotiated between them, not from unchanging obligations based on personal or group identity. (Example: a person has a right to belong to a union and go on strike because the union has negotiated with management and the person has chosen to work in that place. Membership does not come from being born into the union or having an inherited right to unionize.)

3. *Universalism.* Legal decisions, once made, are kept uniform rather than altered from case to case. This is done to insure predictability.

4. *Hierarchical administrative system.* Authority is distributed downward from higher officials to lower, and appeals of lower-level decisions follow a prescribed route upward "through channels."

5. *Bureaucracy.* This means impersonal procedures ("I don't care who you are— the rules apply to you too") and the use of written rules and records, so that decisions depend on objective application of rules, not personal whim or memory.

6. *Rationality.* Understandable rules are designed to achieve clearly stated goals using demonstrably effective methods.

7. *Professionals.* The system is run by people with objectively demonstrated qualifications, specialized skills which they spend full time applying to legal matters.

8. *Lawyers.* The system includes specially trained persons who act as mediators between the specialists of the system (the bureaucrats and judges) and laypersons who must deal with the system.

9. *Changeability.* The rules and procedures can be modified for the purpose of achieving stated goals. (That is, there is nothing sacred or immutable about the rules. They are treated only as pragmatic solutions to problems, and if they fail, they are changed.)

10. *Politicality.* Modern law exists to serve the purposes of the state (as opposed to systems which serve church, tribe, clan, or some other form of authority).

MODERNITY AS PROGRESS

In chapter 4 we saw in Durkheim's structural-functional analysis of legal development, that one major perspective in sociology sees the trend toward modern law as progress, even though it probably also sees such development as inevitable, given the forces leading to societal complexity. In this section we will see two interpretations of the position that, although modern law is a positive development, it was *not inevitable.* The first of these is Weber's classic statement about the relationship among formality, rationality, and legal progress. The second is a present-day application of cybernetic theory.

Rule, Reason, and Legal Progress

Max Weber, another of the founders of modern sociology, not only presented an analysis of legal development asserting that modern law was not *inevitable,* but also showed that he considered modern law to be progress, an improvement over earlier legal forms. We will see that his vision of modern law would make him skeptical of any project to simplify justice.

One of Weber's major projects was to explain why industrial capitalism developed in the Occident (the West) but not in Africa or Asia. He concluded that legal development played a central role in the transformation of the West (Weber, 1954, 1925). Besides the tremendous scope of his research, Weber stands out in sociology for his insistence on the intervention of *ideas* as shapers of legal and social development. Only where particular ideas and social forces coincided did certain forms of development occur.

Weber divided legal systems into four major types, each determined by its location on two polarities of legal ideas. The first polarity involves the extent to which legal procedures are *rational* or *irrational.* Where irrationality prevails, procedures are not necessarily logical or linked to specified goals. Instead, they are based on general ethical principles or mystical beliefs which we would call "magical" or "religious." By contrast, rational procedures use logic to achieve specific, measurable goals. Such rationality is the basis of modern science, and its application to legal matters means doing law scientifically.

The second polarity distinguishes between *formal* and *substantive* legal thinking. *Formal* law is law which "goes by the book." It means making decisions on the basis of rules made in advance, even if they sometimes seem to be "unfair." *Substantive* law is more flexible. It is influenced by the special features of each case. Written rules are not expected to contain all the answers. Decisions based on substantive law should seem fair within the particular circumstances of each case.

Combining these two polarities, we get the typology of legal thought in table 8.1. The four cells in this table are also four *stages* of legal development. Cell 1, *formal irrationality,* involves legal procedures based on *magic.* They are irrational because nobody tries to understand and clarify why the procedures work. They are formal because they demand strict adherence to the magical procedures. If you use the wrong potion or secret word, you will fail to do justice. The result will be bad. For example, couples in India are forbidden to marry if their horoscopes show that their marriage is ill-fated. In parts of Liberia, suspects are tested for guilt by pressing a hot knife against their skin. If it burns them, their guilt is proven. The innocent are protected by the magical chants and objects which are used to prepare the knife. Formal irrationality is the earliest legal form.

Where *substantive irrationality* prevails (cell 2), law is conducted by respected religious elders, who decide cases according to their own sacred inspiration and their commitment to general ethical principles. The *khadi* (religious judge) uses witness testimony, evidence, and "divine inspiration" in flexible ways to arrive at a just conclusion.

The object of law in cell 3 (*substantive rationality*) is to blend written rules with the specific details of each case in order to produce a just decision. The procedure is rational because the rules are made through the systematic analysis of information gathered in pursuit of logically stated goals. It is *substantive* rationality because the procedure allows the judge to modify the invocation of rules to assure that the results are fair.

To Weber, *formal rationality* (cell 4) is the most advanced (and desirable) form of law. Here the unique features of individual cases are not

TABLE 8.1   Weber's Typology of Legal Thought

	FORMAL	SUBSTANTIVE
IRRATIONAL	*Formal Irrationality* (magical ritual) 1.	*Substantive Irrationality* (rule by religious leaders) 2.
RATIONAL	*Formal Rationality* (modern European codified law) 4.	*Substantive Rationality* (English Common Law) 3.

allowed to interfere with the application of rules. Rules are based on reason. They are thought through so that they will enable authorities to cope with all possible conflicts in the real world. Rules and legal principles are interwoven into a "seamless web" ready to deal with every eventuality.

These four types are not conditions that you would find in *reality* in any society. Each is an *ideal type,* that is, a cluster of characteristics which coheres and tends to push aside elements of any other ideal type. Real societies contain characteristics from more than one type. But the trend of history, says Weber, has been for formality and rationality to crowd out the substantive and irrational side of legal thought.

Weber held that the pressure to develop formal rationality in law came from the unique coincidence of *capitalism* and state *bureaucracy* in the West. Rationality was a fundamental condition making capitalism possible. Rational procedures (including science and technological innovation, systematic bookkeeping, and job specialization) dramatically increased *efficiency* in both industry and business. At the same time, political efforts to consolidate centralized governmental authority produced a growing reliance on *bureaucratic* organization, which has built-in pressures to rationalize procedures. The need to coordinate the activities of widely scattered administrators leads to rationalization.

Because capitalism and bureaucracy coincided in the West, Western law grew increasingly formal and rational. Elsewhere these elements failed to merge, leaving those societies "behind" as the West surged into modernity. China, for example, had bureaucracy very early in history. But it never developed formal rationality in law because it lacked other ingredients necessary to the birth of capitalism. In other parts of Asia there were petty capitalists, but no government ever brought them under centralized bureaucratic control. Only in the West did the combination of bureaucracy and capitalism appear. Hence the "high" level of legal development in the West.

Although Weber considered formal rationality to be the most modern and admirable form of law, he did not see it as the inevitable result of irresistible forces such as population growth and increased complexity (see pp. 63–74). Three major complications can obstruct progress. First, ideas do affect people's actions. If a population fails to develop ideas consistent with formal rationality, then legal progress will be retarded along with economic growth. Second, legal progress produces legal institutions which are autonomous from the rest of society. That autonomy can actually retard further legal progress because it insulates the law from changes occurring in the economy. That is why England, which was one of the earliest industrial economies, has continued to shelter an archaic level of substantive rationality in its law. Third, formal rationality tends toward a rigidity which can generate resistance among the general populace which wants *justice.* This tension will always inhibit the pace of formal rational development.

If this is an accurate account of Weber's analysis, it indicates that he would look on proposals to "simplify" law, to develop popular justice or return authority to "the people" as a step backward. It would mean a retreat from formal rationality and would therefore undermine modern economic institutions which dovetail with that legal form. (Weber's prose was so complex, the translations from his original German sometimes less than perfect, and the content of his work so filled with second thoughts and cautious qualifications that sociologists do not all agree with this view. Some believe that he was both attracted and repelled by formal rationality and the bureaucracy which goes with it, because he did write extensively about the negative aspects of bureaucracy in practice.)

Cybernetics and Legal Progress

If early sociologists were cautiously enthusiastic about legal moderni-zation, later structuralists have been less restrained in their praise. Some see modern law forms as evidence for the support of *cybernetic theory*. The easiest way to understand cybernetics is to think of a thermostat in a cen-trally heated building. It is designed to switch on a furnace when the temperature is too low and to turn the furnace off when a preset tempera-ture is reached. The heating system is *self-regulating*. It is controlled by *information feedback* between furnace and thermostat, so that each responds to the condition of the other.

Applying this cybernetic model to law, theorists see law as having a cybernetic relationship with society's other major institutions (Turner, 1974). Economic, political, educational, kinship, and religious systems are a society's way of meeting four basic needs or "functional imperatives" (Par-sons, 1937) facing all social systems: (1) *adaptation* to the environment, which the economy does; (2) organization for group *goal attainment* which the political system does; (3) *latency*, or the problem of managing tensions within society and reproducing group members so the system will have a future, which education and kinship systems do; and (4) *integration* of the activities of everyone into the system which religion and *law* do.

Each of these systems influences the action of all the others through feedback among them. The law is therefore part of a *feedback loop* with each other system. For example, going back in history to the time when humans first began to produce more than they could immediately consume, we find that surpluses created opportunities for *trade*. This change in the economy created the need for trade *regulation*, just as the increased heat from a furnace signals the thermostat to shut it down.

However, the thermostat analogy is too simple to explain the opera-tion of feedback loops in society. It only involves *negative feedback* where the feedback message helps the system achieve *preset* goals. Cybernetic social systems require *positive feedback*, where the exchange of information leads to the adoption of *new goals* and the development of more complex social forms. In a heating system, this kind of feedback would be something farfetched, such as the furnace responding to the thermostat's messages by developing a humidifier, and the thermostat then learning to measure humidity as well as temperature.

Cybernetic theory says that positive feedback accounts for the development of modern social institutions. For example, when trade relations in Egypt began to develop, the legal system did not respond with negative feedback ("business as usual"). Instead, a set of new courts was developed, and trade was facilitated by the development of a distinction between criminal and tort law. This is positive feedback because it provided the economy with a new institutional context for even more rapid economic development. In China, by contrast, only negative feedback occurred, and economic development was retarded.

Theorists apply this kind of analysis to each of the other major institutions mentioned above. They argue that wherever modernization took place, it was a response of positive feedback between those institutions and law. The general trend of development within each institution is toward increased differentiation and specialization of function and increased centralization of organization.

Modern societies are therefore the latest expressions of ongoing cybernetic processes. Societies which lack modern characteristics, including modern law, are victims of negative feedback. To catch up with the modern world, therefore, "backward" societies need to develop positive feedback relations among their institutions. The reform of legal practices cannot by itself produce modernity. But legal modernization would have to be part of that process.

What does this mean for current proposals to simplify law, to develop grass-roots justice? It means that such policies would be a retreat from modernity, a barrier to progress. The inevitable effects of positive feedback are increased differentiation, specialization, and complexity. Popular justice, therefore, could not succeed unless it could somehow be converted into measures which reinforce the drive toward further societal complexity.

The thrust of the analyses we have looked at so far in this chapter is that legal complexity is modern and necessary to the operation of modern industrial societies. Their practical implication is that we cannot "revert" to simpler forms of law because law forms are an integrated part of the systems which make modern society "work." Because these theories emphasize the *interrelated operation* of social structures and because they treat modernity as evidence of *progress,* we can, for convenience's sake, call their proponents *progressive structuralists.*

In the remainder of this chapter, you will see that progressive structuralism has been strongly challenged by new research and by new interpretations of previous research. Challengers have attacked the accuracy of structuralist analysis and have argued that the inaccuracies arose from the unrecognized influence of structuralists' values.

MODERNITY VS. SIMPLICITY: A FALSE DICHOTOMY?

You may have already detected something wrong with the notion of modern law. As you read through the list of *modern* characteristics earlier in this chapter, you may have felt that it was very idealistic. It is not difficult to show that American law has not freed itself from favoritism, sexism, racism, prejudice, and religious interference, though we know that these things are not *supposed* to happen. In addition, we can find "modern" laws which seem to exist because they express sacred rather than practical goals. These include laws governing morality, such as antipornography, antiprostitution, antiabortion, antihomosexual, and antigambling laws. Furthermore many modern laws are so obscure and complicated that ordinary people cannot follow them. Government has become so "bureaucratic" that it spends most of its time and money processing "red tape" rather than helping people achieve the goals intended by the laws.

If *modern law* means the real operations of present-day legal systems, there appear to be strong forces preventing "modern" societies such as the United States from achieving the "modern" ideal set down in our list.

Approaching this issue from the other side, we find that "backward," premodern, or simple social institutions can contribute to, and fit in with, the development of "modern" economic activities. The "backward" caste system in India has served as a breeding ground for "modern" political involvement. It has also allowed for the consolidation of capital which encourages more productive forms of industry (Rudolph and Rudolph, 1967). The maintenance of "primitive" customary law in Japan may be part of the explanation for Japan's "economic miracle" (Kawashima, 1963).

The term *modernity* is meant to refer to things happening right now. It is supposed to be different from tradition, "backwardness," and simplicity. But we see here that a closer look calls that whole dichotomy into question. If actual American practice regularly deviates from modern legal ideals, why call American law modern? If American law is not modern, what use is left for that term? If "backward" legal practices operate in a "modern" economy, why call them "backward"? Something is wrong with the simple linear model of law and society "progressing" from simple, backward institutions to increasingly complex, modern ones.

Modernity: The Struggle over
Centralized Authority

One answer to this quandary goes by the name *pluralism*. It holds that modernization actually means the increase of centralized authority in any form (Galanter, 1966). In law, modernization means a drive toward total control: modern law "tolerates no rivals." However, no matter how strong this drive for control may be, it is always accompanied by a process which works against centralization.

A key feature of modern societies is that they are not stagnant. Modernity means change. Many major characteristics of such societies are caught up in rapid change. The population grows rapidly. Mobility increases, with major elements of the population changing both their physical locations and their social positions. While such mobility weakens traditional or "backward" patterns of solidarity (clan, tribe, caste, family), people respond to this loss by forming *new associations* which can operate in the unstable environment of rapid mobility.

One important source of these new associations is the growth of new occupational categories. Forty years ago, there were no computer programmers, laser technicians, environmental protection engineers, or television producers. New occupational identities stimulate the growth of new social groupings, as people discover the shared problems and potentials of their specialties.

Such changes challenge the drive for centralized control through law for two reasons. First, they create new problems for which nobody has convincing solutions. The explosive growth of automobile use in the United States flooded the legal system with unprecedented numbers of lawsuits. Existing formal law was unprepared for such an onslaught. So great was the tide of accidents and litigation that the system, in effect, collapsed. It could not provide solutions to the problems created by the automobile (Ross, 1970).

Likewise, technological advances in medicine, and related changes in the structure of the profession, have produced an unprecedented wave of malpractice litigation. In the United States, the delivery of medical services has become the subject of heated debate. Some critics see the whole system in crisis because of skyrocketing costs, including the costs of malpractice action. Again, the law is involved in a storm of social change and is not well-fortified with answers. Similar crises are stirring because of the environmental issues created by post-World War II developments in the chemical industry and because of a copyright crisis created by the development of quick copiers and inexpensive video taping equipment.

Second, rapid changes throw people into situations where older patterns of association must be replaced by new ones. Rural people driven by economic necessity to seek work in the city discover that their family and clan ties no longer help in dealing with the problems they face. Unions begin to form as an alternative. Women entering the work force discover a similar need for association, so they join organizations to combat obstacles to their full participation. Family patterns change with these new patterns of work. As they do, old habits are replaced by new expectations. New patterns of business organization and financial manipulation wipe out older companies and change patterns of production, marketing, and management.

The effect of so much change is that no legal system can gain total control. While modernity in law may mean a drive toward monopolization of authority, it operates in an environment so unstable that monopoly is under constant challenge. Established rules, procedures, and authorities are constantly being circumvented or made irrelevant by new social phenomena. The pace of change is too rapid for any elite to completely control. Hence, even though existing law may express the interests of elites, new law is constantly being created by new groups challenging those elites.

During the First World War, for example, English munitions producers saw the chance to exploit the crisis atmosphere. They wanted to subdue rebellious labor unions which had plagued them for years. They pressured parliament into passing an emergency act outlawing strikes, imposing compulsory arbitration of workplace disputes in munitions factories, punishing violations of work rules laid down by factory owners, banning any union tradition which hindered production, and forcing workers to get written permission from their bosses before going to work elsewhere (Rubin, 1979, p. 258).

In the ensuing struggle, managers tried to use the act, which was supposed to be a temporary wartime measure, to arrange permanent changes in work schedules and working conditions. The unions responded with resistance so formidable that the munitions act collapsed into an ignored backdrop for ordinary labor-management bargaining.

This reassertion of labor's autonomy in English economic relations was echoed years later when government sought to restrict the "alarming" level of trade union autonomy, especially the growing frequency of "wildcat" strikes led by unofficial work-group leaders (Anderman, 1979). Between 1968 and 1974 Britain experimented with various measures to bring unions under greater control. The major legal device used was the Industrial Relations Act, which punished strikers for unauthorized strikes and tried to bring "unofficial" leaders under more official control.

The act failed, largely because official union leaders could not control the unofficial leaders. Unions might be fined and threatened, but only the official leadership could be attacked, and they did not have the power to order a return to work. So in the end, the act was scrapped as unworkable.

These two examples illustrate the argument that modernization produces forces resistant to the total control of "modern" formal law. While there may be forces pushing society in the direction of more centralization, specialization, and formality in law, countervailing trends are unleashed by those same forces. New forms of interest-group solidarity arise to weaken the hold of the center and force accommodations. These new forms may be modern in the sense that they did not exist in earlier societies. But they are not modern in the sense that they conform with the ideals of modernity in law.

MODERNITY, SIMPLICITY, AND INEQUALITY

The position stated in the previous section, that modern society is composed of many competing forces, none of which gains the kind of dominance implied in the idea that legal modernity means authoritative monopoly, is known as *pluralism.* Those who make the pluralistic case recognize the existence of inequality in society. But they focus their attention on the efforts of "have-not" groups to change their status, to resist legal intimidation, and to use the law in promoting their own "progress."

Next, we will see two different kinds of attacks on both pluralism and progressive structuralism. These two positions are variations of the *conflict* perspective which was introduced in chapter 5.

Inequality: The Engine of Legal Evolution

In this section, we will be examining Roberto Unger's theory of legal evolution (1976). His position is that the driving force behind changes in legal systems is the persistent irritant of economic and political inequality.

The history of law as it has evolved over many centuries in Western societies begins with *interactional* (or customary) law. Like law on the Israeli kibbutz (see chapter 4), interactional law is vague, unarticulated, and shared as a set of attitudes by everyone in society. Each person's act ". . . leads a double life: it constitutes conformity or disobedience to custom at the same time that it becomes part of the social process by which custom is defined" (Unger, 1976, p. 49). There are no separate law enforcers (law is *not public,* there is no state). There is no separate body of written rules (law is *not positive,* that is, it is not consciously created with particular control objectives in mind). "To codify them (customs) is to change them" (p. 50).

To work effectively, interactional law depends on the existence of highly integrated community networks. But the *division of labor*—the differentiation of populations into different work specialties—destroys those community networks. So far, then, Unger agrees with progressive structuralists and pluralists. The catch is that differentiation inevitably produces inequality. Specialization does not simply produce a host of persons, each with a special skill, peacefully exchanging the value of his or her expertise for values from other experts. Rather, it produces a social order in which one group dominates others because of its control of material wealth. In other words, the elite is a product of the division of labor.

Once having cornered the wealth of a society, the elite's basic problem is to maintain its position. That position is constantly threatened by the possibility that others will refuse the claim that elite dominance is *legitimate*. The need for legitimacy produces a new form of law—*bureaucratic law*. *Bureaucratic law* expresses the elite's need to make explicit and predictable the rules by which society's other groups are to relate to each other. In a sense, Unger's bureaucratic law is the kind of law you saw Rex the King trying to make in chapter 2 (p. 27).

Bureaucratic law is *public* (it is created by a centralized government and applied to the rest of the population) and *positive* (it consists of explicitly written rules rather than vague principles). It first comes into existence as an agency to perpetuate ". . . the existing social order (i.e., existing patterns of dominance) and . . . the forces committed to it" (p. 60). But it is plagued by a built in paradox: ". . . it must be distinct from any one social group in the system of domination and dependence (so that its authority will *appear* legitimate). Yet it has to draw its staff and its purposes from groups that are part of this system" (p. 61). Since its rules clearly support inequality, it faces the difficulty of establishing its legitimacy as a system of rules to be obeyed. People will not accept dominance unless it is justified. To deal with this problem, bureaucratic law has been "almost invariably accompanied by a body of religious precepts" (p. 65). By itself, bureaucratic law would be an obvious tool of monarchical tyranny. But bureaucratic law was always restrained by two forces: (1) the resistance of subordinate classes who were wedded to their own parochial customs, and (2) the powerful religious establishments which narrowed the range of decisions left under the monarch's control.

Despite these constraints, the bureaucratic state was relatively unrestrained in its ability to promote the interests of the dominant class. All this changed, however, because the original elite became fragmented into competing groups striving for domination. Technological and social change undermined the monolithic structure of earlier societies, resulting in *pluralism*—a social structure with several competing elites in addition to a differentiated group of lower classes.

Bureaucratic law could not prevent this occurrence, because the resistance to inequality is relentless and eventually produces effective challenges. As bureaucratic law broke down, it was replaced by the third major law form—the *liberal legal order* (the rule of law). This legal order came into existence when earlier structures of dominance became disorganized, when competing elites were unable to gain total dominance over each other and had, therefore, to *compromise* with each other.

The legal order did not end inequality. But because it had to accommodate competing power centers, it could not appear to favor any one of them. So it adopted the *appearance* (the ideology) of promoting *equality*. The demise of a single dominant class demolished the older ideology that the monarch (or anyone else in society) has a God-given right to rule.

Because law had to accommodate strong antagonistic interests, it developed *generality* (its commands applied to everyone regardless of class) and *autonomy* (the legal establishment became a separate competing power unbeholden to any single elite). Like bureaucratic law, the legal order was also *public* and *positive*.

As the legal order emerged from earlier bureaucratic law, a new standard of law (*natural law*) came to replace bureaucratic measures of efficiency and conformity to religious doctrine. Like customary law, *natural law* obscured the distinction between facts and values. It was portrayed as originating from some supernatural force or universal philosophical truth rather than from practical administrative considerations. Laws and the operations of legal administrators were now compared against this abstract standard of natural law, so that law would not appear to be the creature or servant of any one interest group (including organized religion). Natural-law ideals can be seen in the United States Bill of Rights, and in the call for protection of "human rights" around the world. Advocates of human rights hold them to be inherent in being born human (i.e., they are natural entities—part of the natural order of things). Since states or other "mere mortals" do not create those rights, they cannot legitimately be taken away. In Western society, natural law became part of the new theologies of Western religion with their emphasis on a single God whose acts of creation must be acknowledged and followed even by governments.

Despite its egalitarian talk, the legal order did nothing to eliminate the inequalities which were an inherent part of economic differentiation. When Myrdal studied racial tensions in the United States, he saw a profound "American Dilemma" in the contradiction between America's professed loyalty to the ideal of equality for all and the persistent lack of equality for blacks (Myrdal, 1944). Unger is extending Myrdal's conclusion to all societies with liberal legal orders, whether they have racial conflicts or not. He is saying that economic differentiation has always resulted in inequality and that the liberal order of law has done nothing to alter that condition.

Since inequalities did not disappear, the attempt to channel conflicts born out of inequality through liberal courts led to a decline in people's belief that the legal system could produce justice. This happened because judges' decisions could not be made only on the basis of preexisting rules (in Weber's terms, they could not be totally *formal*). They had to take into consideration the circumstances of each specific case. Furthermore their procedures produced decisions favoring one party, from one position in the system of unequal power, over another. Liberal legal systems could not achieve conformity with natural-law principles because the cumulative effect of actual judicial decisions was to make the legal system appear to be supporting unequal, unjustifiable privilege. Despite its lofty claims of impartiality, liberal law eventually became seen as "rich man's law."

This is why Western law is now moving away from the liberal model. Unger calls our present social system *postliberal society*. This is not a move toward what is popularly known as conservatism. Rather, it is a move toward the *welfare state, corporatism,* and *communitarianism.*

Welfare state.   Because of the persistence of inequality under the liberal state system, pressure has built to develop state-run ways of eliminating those differences. The welfare state has new legal features which violate the legal standards of the liberal model. For one thing, state bodies (courts, legislatures, administrative agencies) increasingly issue *vague general standards* which maximize the discretion of administrators. Judges are told to prevent business "monopolization," "unjust enrichment," and "unconscionable contracts." More importantly, perhaps, many courts are being stripped of their judging functions and are becoming administrative agencies where judges process routine claims in which there is no contest (see Friedman and Percival, 1976). Administrators of the Occupational Safety and Health Administration are told to make and enforce measures which will guarantee safety and good health to workers. Regulators of the broadcasting industry are told to preserve "the fairness doctrine." Legislators tell various agencies to work to protect "the family farm" from too much big business competition.

In these cases, formal law is minimal and vague. Administrators and judges must figure out what these standards mean in actual cases. The emphasis has shifted from following prescribed rules which protect people because of their "impartiality." Now the law is supposed to "get results," or produce what Weber would call "substantive justice" (Unger, 1976, p. 194). Specific pockets of inequality are to be attacked with whatever it takes to achieve "justice." (Charles Reich [1964] even holds that we ought to think of these government initiatives as rights, a kind of "new property" to which everyone is entitled. Since older forms of property no longer protect people from exploitation by big companies and big government, people should be guaranteed shares in the enormous wealth now controlled by modern welfare states.)

So the new standards by which modern law is measured are those of efficiency (how best to accomplish stated welfare goals) and the layperson's view of justice. We saw in chapter 6 how the question of *legal impact* arose as a reflection of concern over the efficiency with which the law could be used to achieve reform goals. Unger would categorize this concern as a manifestation of the new welfare state, the postliberal system.

Corporatism.   A key characteristic of modern socities is the declining distinction between the state and other organizations. It becomes increasingly difficult to determine whether an area of activity is run by the state or by private institutions, because the public-private split is becoming a myth. Government increasingly penetrates and regulates private organizations. Private organizations develop such power that they rival the state and begin to resemble the state in their structures and operations. Labor federations, multi-national corporations, educational institutions, mass media conglomerates, medical organizations, atomic energy and railroad organizations are all examples of the move toward corporatism. Many such organizations operate as bureaucracies, with all the trappings of formal authority, chain of command, written rules, and promotion for merit which are definitive features of modern Western governmental organizations.

The careers of corporate managers increasingly flow back and forth between governmental and private sector executive positions. There is little noticeable difference between the two sectors in terms of job qualifications, skills used, objectives, or colleagues. The intermingling of governmental and private personnel in industries such as atomic energy, railroads, aircraft production, and in some countries (e.g., Italy, France) automobiles, together with mixed public and private financing and regulation, make it difficult to characterize the activity as public or private.

Corporatism means that people find their lives increasingly controlled by *private governments* which rival the power of the state. This is a trend away from the total centralization of governmental power which was the trend which originally moved societies toward the liberal legal state. But decentralization does not mean that power is being returned to local communal groups so that they can redevelop interactional law. Rather this is a shift to a new form of dominance unchecked by government impartiality. The rise of corporatism and the welfare state reduces the number of groupings to which people belong in society. It makes their involvement in those fewer groups more total.

People's relationships with each other are actually beginning, therefore, to resemble *tribal* social relationships. In tribal society, the individual belongs to only a few *all-inclusive* groups. People feel complete loyalty and safety with members of their own group and see all others as untrustworthy strangers. Inequality *within the group* is accepted as part of the natural order of things. Tribalism vanished in the liberal legal order. People belonged to a host of different groups and felt only partial loyalty and involvement in any one of them. Liberal society was *pluralistic* (as opposed to tribal) because of the large number of interlinked group involvements people had. "Freedom" meant the opportunity to pick and choose one's involvements with different groups, not to be locked into membership in any of them. But corporatism in postliberal society cuts back on those partial involvements and replaces that experience with the experience of loyalty to the corporate group.

Communitarianism.   Another part of the shift to postliberal society is the rise of *communitarianism,* meaning the search for community, or a rebirth of premodern patterns of living. People come to feel that modern society has failed, that it perpetuates unjustifiable patterns of subordination, and therefore is not worth the sacrifice it makes on people's involvements with each other in closer, more personal, more cooperative living. People praise the "good old days" when neighbors helped each other, doors did not need locks, and life was simple. So they support the kinds of "popular justice" programs which we have targeted as the subject of this chapter.

Corporatism and communitarianism have developed together in postliberal society because they both hold out a promise of more intense, total involvement with others whose rules are, for now, perceived as legitimate. They are both, however, simply new ways of organizing inequality. They both, therefore, continue to harbor the seed which will ultimately drive people to seek yet another alternative.

Alternative paths to legal evolution.   Two other kinds of *modern* society exist side-by-side with postliberal society. Though they differ significantly from postliberal society in their histories and forms of organization, they have also developed in response to the same irritant of inequality evident in Western development. One alternative is *traditionalist* society. The other is *revolutionary socialism.* Both are modern societies, but neither exactly resembles postliberal society, because neither went through the stage of liberalism experienced in the West. Japan is *traditionalist.* China represents a *revolutionary socialist* society.

In Japan, corporate loyalties are intense. People who go to work for an industrial manufacturer spend the rest of their lives in that employment. They expect the company to provide totally for their family's welfare. The company provides medical care, wedding expenses, vacation and recreation facilities, housing, stores, and even funerals. In this way, corporate bodies in traditionalist societies capture their members' loyalties, much as tribes did in premodern societies.

Such societies are "traditionalist" because social control is achieved by involving people in groups where traditional values are *selectively exploited to achieve modern goals.* Traditionalistic societies seem odd because they mix "modern" activities with seemingly incompatible traditional practices and beliefs. Since these societies lack some features found in modern liberal or postliberal states, Western observers have mistakenly assumed that the presence of "outdated practices, backward loyalties, and antiquated values" meant that such societies were caught in a struggle between tradition and modernity, between backward and progressive values, between superstition and science. Instead, leaders of traditionalistic societies have used the creative forces and restraints within their traditional heritage to produce unique patterns of modernity. Law in traditionalist societies is usually a mixture of enforced custom (as we saw in the Japanese case in chapter 3, and in British India) and extensive bureaucratic law used to govern economic activity and prevent political challenge to the elite. "Custom" is imposed in ways which transform it into measures of centralized control.

Conflict exists in traditionalist societies, but not between tradition and modernity. Rather, it is the same tension we see in postliberal society between the experience of dependence and the ideal of community. In other words, like postliberal society, traditionalistic society has the "fatal flaw" of inequality, which is bound to generate its major conflicts.

Revolutionary socialistic leaders, such as those in China, differ from traditionalist leaders in the *reasons* they give for the community based, popular justice they promote. But the practical result is the same since both societies use "popular justice" to draw people into centrally governed social and economic activity. A brief description of law in revolutionary China will show you the similarity.

Since the Chinese revolution in 1948, two models of law have vied for dominance, one *internal,* the other *external* (Li, 1971). The *internal* model consists of thousands of local committees consisting of workers, neighbors, students, or soldiers, depending on which local group composes each committee. The committees are responsible for most of the social control functions handled by law in Western democracies. Yet they do it with no formal legal training and no written laws, with informal procedures used on a volunteer basis, and they manage to involve all members of the group in the decision-making process.

In a village, for example, the committee would be chosen from among the villagers. When people have disputes, or when they begin to show signs of behavior which might inhibit the village's well-being or it's ability to be productive as a unit, the committee calls all villagers together, conducts prolonged discussions about all the issues involved, and then proposes some action which will insure that everyone can get back to being productive citizens. Often the political ingredients of the issue are examined, and the "trial" turns into an "educational" meeting where individuals can test their political ideas and the group can decide how best to handle the incident so that it improves their political awareness and action.

Cases of all kinds are handled this way, including divorce, theft, industrial "sabotage" (slowing down production), assault, domestic quarrels, parent-child disputes, and juvenile delinquency. As in the Israeli kibbutz (chapter 4), there is little need to spend time on evidence since people know each other so well from close daily contact. Decisions are swift and inexpensive. Lawyers or other professionals are not involved. This system allows the local group to keep a close eye on the behavior of every member. No one is allowed to stray far from the group's norms before being confronted with pressure to conform.

During the ascendency of this *internal* model, the legal profession in China was being systematically liquidated, either physically or by being forced into other occupations. These moves left the *external* model of law (*bureaucratic law*) with almost no lawbooks and few people able to administer it. Since the death of Chairman Mao, external law has been gradually gaining ascendency over the internal model.

But the key feature of the overall legal strategy in China is that the central government has always maintained some degree of influence over the internal model. Every local committee has always had a party *cadre* to "guide" the people to "correct" political thought. Cadres are not professionals. They are workers, villagers, and others who have demonstrated strong party loyalty. They receive several weeks of training in Beijing (the national capital), and they periodically return there for "reeducation" to insure that the Central Party's "line" is carried out throughout the country.

Unlike traditionalist leaders, China's elite uses "popular justice" for the pursuit of "modern" goals, by persuading people that they are being liberated from the "backward" traditions of the past. Yet the actual operation of law is similar in many ways to ancient ideals laid down by Confucius. And the total effect of revolutionary justice is to produce a legal system which is institutionally similar to the traditionalist one in Japan: few lawyers, infrequent litigation, reliance on local group pressure, and dominance by bureaucratically organized corporate elites.

Wherever socialist governments have promoted "popular justice," local authority has always been leashed by some measure of control from the central government. In most (e.g., Tanzania, the USSR, Cuba and Chile [Tiruchelvam, 1973]), the governments used people's courts as instruments of political education and, at times, mobilization. Government or party representatives always played a key role in "guiding" the local committees or courts to "correct" decisions.

Because both traditionalist and socialist elites share the same basic goal (rapid economic development), they develop similar forms of corporatist political and economic organization. They differ only in their official acceptance or rejection of traditional justifications for inequality. Since economic modernization demands centralized control, socialism contains the same "fatal flaw" as traditionalist and postliberal societies: the contrast between the promise of equality within a local, self-regulating community and the reality of centrally dictated inequality.

As you can see, all three types of modernity (postliberal, traditionalist, and socialist) have encountered, and used, the desire for *simple justice* in their marches toward "progress." In each, the tension between complexity and simplicity is a tension over inequality. In none has that tension been eliminated.

Worldwide Inequality: Dependency Theory

In chapter 5 you saw that dependency theory tells us not to do sociology the way progressive structuralists and pluralists do it. It is a mistake to treat each nation in the world as a separate little experiment in social organization and progressive development, because development everywhere, whether in Paraguay, Jamaica, Kenya, or India, is intimately linked to decisions made by elites in New York, Moscow, London, Tokyo, and Frankfurt. A worldwide system of capitalism has come into existence during the last four hundred years. All societies are therefore "modern" because they all occupy some niche in this worldwide system. "Backwardness" or underdevelopment in any area is a product of this system, not just tardiness in becoming modern.

Underdevelopment, as dependency theorists use the term, refers to the enforced economic and political backwardness or subservience of *peripheral* populations (i.e., people living in areas which furnish raw materials and labor to the manufacturing *centers*). Economies in peripheral areas are distorted, incomplete, and dependent. They serve capitalist centers of manufacture and finance, so their patterns of economic and social organization are shaped to the needs of the centers.

To speak of *modern* versus *traditional* or customary law in such a situation is to misstate the reason for the existence of "simple" methods of justice. They do not exist because of some fundamental human desire for "down-to-earth" justice. Nor do they exist because of *negative feedback*, as cybernetics theory argues.

Informal law methods serve different functions in the modern world system, depending on the relationship between each peripheral population and the center. In some areas "popular justice" deflects the resentment of a population which has been excluded from participation in the capitalist sector. The center promotes popular justice and related traditional institutions as a kind of *social corral*, managing local populations so that they do not develop institutions or organizations which could threaten supplies to the center. Preservation of "tradition" also prevents these populations from developing competing business activities which would divert resources from the center and threaten the center's monopoly over production and marketing.

South Africa's *Bantustan* program is an obvious example of tradition used to corral a people. Blacks not needed in the mines and factories are herded into inland enclaves ruled by "traditional" tribal chiefs (Sachs, 1973). They are encouraged to practice their "ancient" religions and use traditional economic and legal methods. They are totally barred from developing economic or political ties with organizations or governments outside South Africa. Government thus guarantees that they will remain "premodern."

In other peripheral areas, informal law is part of traditionalist methods of mobilizing people to work in the mines and plantations which supply the center while discouraging them from trying to share in the center's system of control (Snyder, 1980, pp. 779–80). Typically, a small local capitalist class dominates the area either because of its intermediate position in the flow of business to the center or because of its control of the local governmental bureaucracy. In either case, the local elite's status is *derivitive:* it exists at the pleasure of the dominant partner in the alliance—the transnational corporation (such as Exxon, United Fruit, Alcoa, Firestone, General Motors) (Evans, 1979).

Law in such areas does not contain the elements of liberalism or pluralism. Political speeches emphasize the need to "sacrifice" civil rights in the pursuit of rapid economic development. Or they contain nativistic praise for local tradition as against "foreign" practices. Both kinds of speeches serve the same purpose: to pacify peripheral populations, making them fit more easily into the role assigned them in the world economic order.

As you can see, dependency theorists distrust proposals by "experts" from central institutions to tinker with law in underdeveloped areas, whether the proposal is to "modernize" legal practices or to bring law "back to the people." In both cases, such policies are implemented only if they increase the dependency of the population. If law is simple, swift, and informal in coal mining communities in West Virginia, or among migrant laborers' families in southern California; or in the slums of Kingston, Jamaica; or in Liberia's villages, this is not because those people refuse to abandon their customs. Rather, it is because the coal mining companies, the California agribusiness operators, and the aluminum and rubber industries find they have better control, fewer problems, and less disruption of their operations if law works simply among the people dependent on them. But that "simple justice" gives those people no power to resist the corporate interests that control their lives. When elites support "simple justice," they do so expecting it to serve their "unsimple" goals (Galanter, 1966; Spence, 1978; Fitzpatrick, 1979; Okoth-Ogendo, 1979).

WHY SIMPLICITY NOW?

I began this chapter by pointing out that there has been a recent surge of interest in the United States in proposals to simplify law. In view of what we have seen so far, the question arises of why those proposals have caught on now. Is it a fad? Or does it arise from more profound roots? Is it a spontaneous upsurge from ordinary people, or a sentiment deliberately encouraged by self-serving elites?

We have already seen that Unger treats this trend as communitarianism and considers it to be a predictable, spontaneous reaction to liberal law's failure to end inequality.

Another answer is that societies vacillate between emphases on formal and informal legal methods (Galanter, 1966). Such cycles can be seen in the changes which have occurred in American methods of handling juvenile crime. Before the passage of child-labor legislation, children were treated as adults in criminal courts (see Platt, 1969). No age distinctions were made. But the reforms of the early twentieth century included the introduction of paternalistic informality into newly created *juvenile courts*. Children were to be treated as innocents by the courts. They were no longer considered capable of committing crimes because they were too young to have criminal intent. Since they were no longer being accused of crime, it was assumed that they would not need lawyers or procedural protections such as those afforded to adults. Adult court formality was therefore abolished, and the accused child stood legally naked before a judge with almost unlimited power.

The abuses resulting from this arrangement were used as political ammunition in the campaign to reinstitute many of the formal procedures which the reforms had abandoned. The Supreme Court acknowledged these needs when it declared, in its *In Re Gault* decision, that children must be allowed to have legal representation in juvenile court. The cycle, therefore, appears to have returned to formalism, on the theory that formal procedures protect the weak.

Critical theorists reject either side of this cycle as capable of protecting the weak. They hold that the consequences of either method are continued inequality, because legal action does not hold the key to developing real equality.

Abel, for example, contrasts *legal* and *political* conflict (1980). In purely political conflict, rules are not standardized, so "anything goes," "might makes right," and, paradoxically therefore, the two sides become more equalized than they ever would in legal conflict. The reason for this inversion of our usual assumptions about legal procedure is that in political combat, no agreements about "acceptable differences or inequalities" are respected. Courts and law make it impossible for subordinate persons or groups to challenge the roots of inequality between themselves and their dominant opponent. Only when they reject all rules and directly challenge those roots can they achieve any measure of equality, though this is no guarantee they will win.

"Simple justice" cannot do any better than formal law in producing equality, because neither kind of law empowers subordinate groups to challenge the roots of dominance.

Then why is "simple justice" so popular just now? The answer, says Abel, is that dominant economic interests in the United States see "simplicity" as a movement that can help them avoid government regulation. The decade of the 1970s saw a number of significant political victories against big business and big government. Laws were passed promoting occupational safety and health, antipollution standards, welfare rights, and restraints on coercive police tactics. Because formal law was beginning to support disadvantaged groups, members of the threatened (or, more accurately, aggravated) elite have been promoting "simple justice." The elite is thus using people's frustrations with "the way things are" to promote delegalization, because it helps to minimize the effects of the welfare-state laws which hurt them.

This interpretation reverses the pluralistic view that the push for simplification comes from below as a way of resisting established monopolies on power. It also gives a peculiar twist to Unger's argument that communitarianism is a common feature of postliberal society, because it interprets the communitarian sentiment as an opportunity for increased elite domination rather than as the basis for a challenge to that domination. Since law, whether formal or informal, is a way of subjecting conflict to rule-bound expression, the movement of any conflict from political to legal expression means the containment of open challenges to the inequalities which underlie it.

CONCLUSION

One experience shared by almost everyone living today is the frustration of dealing with "bureaucrats who don't care." We try to mail an oddly shaped gift to a friend. A postal employee coolly informs us that Post Office regulations won't allow shipment of our package. Our frustration builds as each question we ask about alternative ways to send the gift is met by a heartless reference to Post Office regulations. We try to tell a bill-collection agency to stop dunning us for payments we have already made. But all we get are further threats from a computer. Over and over again, we find ourselves faced with the coldness, insensitivity, and inefficiency of formal rules wielded by rigid bureaucrats.

No wonder that we periodically lash out and try to simplify procedures, to eliminate the "middlemen," to regain control of Frankenstein-like institutions run amok. We want to take some action against the nightmare, so vividly described by Kafka in *The Trial*, of innocent people trapped in endless mazes of unbending rules, and regulators ruining people's lives by insistence on "going by the book."

Unfortunately for these sentiments, the one conclusion shared by all the students of legal modernization presented in this chapter is that "you cannot go home again." That is, there is no hope that the scrapping of formal law in favor of simple justice will reproduce earlier, more responsive and equitable forms of society. As different, and even contradictory, as are the theories we have studied in this chapter, they all conclude that the attempt to simplify justice, to bring law "back to the people," will produce distorted results.

Progressive structuralists say that modern formal law is a necessary element of modern society. A return to informal procedures would be bound to fail because it could not be integrated with the other more differentiated institutions of modernity. Trying to establish "people's courts" in the middle of American society would be like trying to fly a jumbo jet using one of Orville and Wilbur Wright's first airplane engines.

Pluralists see the center as composed of several competing elites. No one elite has total control, and each is restrained by certain limits inherent in the basis of its power. The nature of the battle for legal alternatives is determined by the characteristics of those elites, so there can be no return to legal forms which operated before those elites came into existence. Promoting "simple justice" will not make those elites or their ambitions go away any more than will a hole in the ground shield an ostrich from its enemies. "Popular justice" only arises where elites allow it, and they allow it only if it promises to promote elite interests.

While the rest of the theorists in this chapter reject functionalist reasoning, they agree with the functionalist conclusion. They argue that the progression of technological, economic, and political changes which have produced "modern" society are parts of an irreversible process. These changes have created a reality which is the context within which legal forms have meaning. They have a momentum of their own which is too forceful to be reversed by minor modifications in the machinery of law. Technological innovation has led to more extreme and differentiated forms of inequality because it has created the means for a more complete, far-reaching concentration of power. The theorists we have studied here disagree only over the extent to which that centralized control is unified. They all agree that the law's role in the process is largely derivative—that is, it is a tool used in the struggle for control, rather than a separate force capable of reversing the trend toward centralization.

Their view of campaigns to simplify justice, therefore, is pessimistic. They see such reforms as occurring under the watchful eye of centralized authority. They see simpler justice as being incapable of reversing the dominance of the center. Therefore, to them, wherever "people's justice" is found today, there also will be found the hand of the center.

As the hymn says, "'Tis a gift to be simple." As most sociologists have concluded, simplicity is a gift that is gone from our lives, at least at the level of our institutions. It may still be available to individuals at the psychological or spiritual level. But as long as this planet sustains the level of technological development already achieved, simplicity in law is likely to be little more than a mirage which occasionally proves useful to some political movement as a way of mobilizing sentiment for changes of considerable complexity.

REFERENCES

ABEL, RICHARD   (1979), Delegalization: A Critique of Its Ideology, Manifestations, and Consequences, in E. Blankenberg, E. Klausa, and H. Rottleuthner (eds.), *Alternative Rechtsformen und Alternative zum Recht, 6, Jahrbuch fur Rechtssoziologie und Rechtstheorie*, Epladen, W. Germany: Westdeutcher Verlag.
ABEL, RICHARD   (1980), Informal Alternatives to Courts as a Mode of Legalizing Conflict. Unpublished Mimeo.
ABEL, RICHARD (ed.)   (1981), *The Politics of Informal Justice*, New York: Academic Press.
ANDERMAN, STEVEN   (1979), Attempts to Impose Legal Restrictions on Trade Unions in Britain, 1968–1974, in Sandra Burman and Barbara Harrell-Bond (eds.), *The Imposition of Law*, New York: Academic Press, pp. 237–55.
COHEN, JEROME ALAN   (1967), Chinese Mediation on the Eve of Modernization, in David Buxbaum (ed.), *Traditional and Modern Legal Institutions in Asia and Africa*, Leiden, The Netherlands: E. J. Brill, pp. 54–76.
DOLBEARE, KENNETH AND DAVIS, JAMES   (1968), *Little Groups of Neighbors: The Selective Service System*, Chicago: Markham Pub. Co.
EVANS, PETER   (1979), *Dependent Development: The Alliance of Multinational, State, and Local Capital in Brazil*, Princeton, N.J.: Princeton University Press.
FITZPATRICK, PETER   (1979), The Political Economy of Dispute Settlement in Papua, New Guinea. Presented at the Cambridge Criminology Conference Trinity Hall, University of Cambridge.
FRANK, ANDRE GUNDER   (1967), *Capitalism and Underdevelopment in Latin America: Historical Studies of Chile and Brazil*, New York: Monthly Review Press.
FRANK, ANDRE GUNGER   (1978), *Dependent Accumulation and Underdevelopment*, London and Basingstoke: Macmillan.
FRIEDMAN, LAWRENCE AND PERCIVAL, ROBERT   (1976), A Tale of Two Courts: Litigation in Alameda and San Benito Counties, *Law and Society Review* 10, p. 267.
GALANTER, MARC   (1966), The Modernization of Law, in M. Weiner (ed.), *Modernization*, New York: Basic Books.
GALANTER, MARC   (1974), Why the "Haves" Come out Ahead: Speculations on the Limits of Legal Change, *Law and Society Review*, 9, p. 95.
HUNT, ALAN   (1978), *The Sociological Movement in Law*, Philadelphia: Temple University Press.
KAFKA, FRANZ   (1937), *The Trial*, New York: Alfred A. Knopf.
KAWASHIMA, TAKEYESHI   (1963), Dispute Resolution in Contemporary Japan, in A. T. von Mehren (ed.), *Law in Japan: The Legal Order of a Changing Society*, Cambridge: Harvard University Press, p. 41.
LI, VICTOR   (1971), The Evolution and Development of the Chinese Legal System, in T. Lindbeck (ed.), *China: Management of a Revolutionary Society*, Seattle: University of Washington Press, p. 221.

LI, VICTOR   (1977), *Law without Lawyers*, Stanford: Stanford Alumni Association.
MARSHALL, JOHN K.   (1974), *The Meat Fight* (Film). Documentary Educational Resources, Inc.
McEWAN, CRAIG AND MAIMAN, RICHARD   (1981), Small Claims Mediation in Maine: An Empirical Assessment, in *Maine Law Review* 33, 237–68.
MYRDAL, GUNNAR   (1944), *An American Dilemma*, New York: Harper & Row, Pub.
NEW YORK TIMES, October 26, 1980, p. A-3.
OKOTH-OGENDO, H. W. O.   (1979), The Imposition of Property Law in Kenya, in Sandra Burman and Barbara Harrell-Bond, *The Imposition of Law*, New York: Academic Press, p. 147.
PARSONS, TALCOTT   (1937), *The Structure of Social Action*, New York: McGraw-Hill.
PLATT, ANTHONY   (1969), *The Child Savers: The Invention of Delinquency*, Chicago: University of Chicago Press.
REICH, CHARLES   (1964), The New Property, *Yale Law Journal*, 73, p. 778.
ROSS, H. LAWRENCE   (1970), *Settled out of Court: The Social Process of Insurance Claims Adjustment*, Chicago: Aldine.
RUBIN, G. R.   (1979), Wartime Industrial Relations Legislation and Legal Institutions and Procedures: The British Munitions of War Acts, 1915–1917, in Sandra Burman and Barbara Harrell-Bond (eds.), *The Imposition of Law*, New York: Academic Press.
RUDOLPH, LLOYD AND RUDOLPH, SUZANNE   (1967), *The Modernity of Tradition*, Chicago: University of Chicago Press.
SACHS, ALBIE   (1973), *Justice in South Africa*, Berkeley and Los Angeles: University of California Press.
SANTOS, BOAVENTURA DE SOUSA   (1978), The Law of the Oppressed: The Construction and Reproduction of Legality in Pasargada, *Law and Society Review*, 12, p. 5.
SNYDER, FRANCIS   (1980), Law and Development in the Light of Dependency Theory, *Law and Society Review*, 14, p. 723.
SPENCE, JACK   (1978), Institutionalizing Neighborhood Courts: Two Chilean Experiences, *Law and Society Review*, 13, p. 139.
STOKES, ERIC   (1959), *The English Utilitarians and India*, Oxford: Clarendon Press.
TAO, LUNG-SHENG   (1974), Politics and Law Enforcement in China: 1949–1970, *American Journal of Comparative Law*, 22, p. 713.
TIRUCHELVAM, NEELAN   (1973), The Ideology of Popular Justice. Lecture given at University of Windsor.
TOHARIA, JOSE   (1975), Judicial Independence in an Authoritarian Regime: The Case of Contemporary Spain, *Law and Society Review*, 9, p. 475.
TURNER, JONATHAN   (1974), A Cybernetic Model of Legal Development, *Western Sociological Review*, 5, p. 3.
UNGER, ROBERTO   (1976), *Law in Modern Society*, New York: Free Press.
WEBER, MAX   (1930), *The Protestant Ethic and the Spirit of Capitalism*, London: Allen and Unwin.
WEBER, MAX   (1954, 1925), *On Law in Economy and Society*, New York: Simon & Schuster.
YNGVESSON, BARBARA AND HENNESSEY, PATRICIA   (1975), Small Claims, Complex Disputes, *Laws and Society Review*, 9, p. 219.

9

THE LEGAL PROFESSION

It is no longer difficult to imagine what life would be like without police, fire fighters, teachers, or air traffic controllers. Strikes by the providers of these public services have become so commonplace that we can speak from experience about "what would happen if . . . ?" Nevertheless, we still seem to fear them. During a recent budget crisis in Philadelphia the mayor laid off several hundred police officers. A common response among angry citizens was display of a bumper sticker saying "If you need a cop, call the mayor." Anger and fear were widespread. Images of gangs and rapists running wild in the streets seemed to plague many people.

But how do you suppose they would have reacted if, rather than police, they were suddenly faced with the loss of services provided by *lawyers*? Suppose for example, that there were a lawyers' strike? Would there be a similar outcry? What would be lost, what endangered? Who would even notice?

The comparison is obviously ridiculous. Everyone knows that lawyers are different from police and teachers. They're autonomous, self-employed professionals, and such professionals don't strike. They act as individuals, setting their own fees and working conditions, so how could they strike, and against whom? Nevertheless, as you read further in this chapter, keep in mind this "ridiculous" possibility, both as a way of understanding how legal practice has differed from other occupations in the past, and as a way of conjuring up possible new scenarios of "law work" in the future.

From what surveys tell us about current attitudes toward the legal profession, we can guess that many people would either cheer or not even notice a sudden cessation of lawyers' services. For decades American lawyers have experienced a uniquely ambiguous reputation. Surveys which asked people to rank the prestige of different occupations consistently showed a split. People either revered lawyers as highly prestigious or reviled them as low-grade undesirables (N.O.R.C., 1953; Reiss, 1961; Hodge, Siegel, and Rossi, 1964). Lawyers appear to the public as either a distinguished group of statesmen or a venal hodgepodge of troublemakers. They either impress us with their wisdom, wit, and solidity, or infuriate us as amoral masters splitting hairs, obscuring clear issues, and milking the public of hard-earned wealth by preying on their troubles.

Our literature and art, both popular and classical, abound with comments on the debatable merits of lawyers. One story has it, for example, that a physician, an architect, and a lawyer were arguing over which profession was the oldest. The physician said "You can't beat Adam and Eve, can you? Didn't God take a rib from Adam to create Eve? That's surgery." The architect replied "Sure, but before there were Adam and Eve, there had to be a place for them. That took a designer, someone who could make order out of the chaos." "Aha!" concluded the lawyer, "And who do you think made the chaos?" We find similar opinions more elaborately expressed in Dickens's *Bleak House,* Kafka's *The Trial,* and Daumier's well-known series of wood-block prints.

On the other hand, a lowly assistant prosecutor stands out as a true hero in the film, entitled *Z,* about right-wing political repression in Greece. American prime-time television dramas have continued to carry the mixed message. Some programs show the lawyer as hero (Perry Mason and Petrocelli). They combine expert training, "instincts" for truth, command of the language, and their "cool" under public pressure to free the innocent and expose the guilty. On the other side, however, is the unscrupulous district attorney and other wicked opposing lawyers who twist every truth and bend every ethical rule in their unprincipled drive to win. For them truth and justice are irrelevant. They care only about victory, their own careers, their evil clients, and their pocketbooks.

Few other occupations have so consistently generated a split image matching the legal profession's. Something about lawyers' work, or about the kinds of people who become lawyers, or about the expectations people have of lawyers apparently produces this split. Some see lawyers as responsible for crime waves, since lawyers defend criminals and help put them "back on the streets." When Beatle John Lennon was murdered, this attitude reached extreme levels with people threatening to murder any lawyer who tried to defend the accused. On the other hand, there is probably not a child in the country who has not provoked the comment: "You ought to be a lawyer when you grow up." This seems to occur when the child's argumentativeness or inquisitiveness has finally proven aggravating, or at least entertaining, to the adults. Many of those who object to "scheming lawyers" winning release for "obvious criminals" are also likely to see law school as a prestigious route to respectable status for their sons (and perhaps daughters).

One way to explain these contradictions is to assume that the profession is split between good and bad persons. The good ones, of course, work for justice. The bad ones work for money, power, and injustice. The good ones are respectable and deserve the high regard which people show them. The bad ones are devious, unprincipled imposters who "dirty" the name of the profession and make us think, from time to time, about banning lawyers from the law.

Unfortunately for this theory, reasonable people disagree over who the good and bad lawyers are. That disagreement goes to the very heart of the position of lawyers in society. Take, for example, the case of native American tribes trying to win back lands and resources taken from them in past centuries. Lawyers for their cause may look like heroes to them and their supporters. Many work on a volunteer basis (Medcalf, 1978), and all of them face time-consuming struggles to excavate ancient treaties and propose legal arguments which the courts may never before have considered. To white landowners, mine operators, and business people whose ownership is being challenged, these lawyers may look like unprincipled "publicity seekers." Their efforts to win tribal rights look like an unrestrained attack on innocent victims. The "law" which they claim to be discovering in ancient treaties may look like a crafty collection of doubletalk and lies. Their own lawyers are the heroes. Only their skill protects their clients from economic ruin. But to their native American adversaries, they are perpetrators of the long, terrible tradition of white oppression of Indians. Their defense of white ownership looks like the same old scheme which drove the tribes from their lands in the first place.

Unless you already have a strong bias concerning the issues in such a debate, you can easily see one reason for ambivalence about lawyers. It is the nature of much of their work that they are found on both sides of conflicts brewing in our society. Their appearances will win for those lawyers a comfortable standard of living. If the lawyers are on your side, you applaud their genius at protecting your interests, though you may feel that you need them only because of the devilish activities of lawyers on the other side.

In this chapter, we will first look more closely at law jobs to see what they have in common. We saw in chapter 2 that it is no easy task to define law. What about lawyers? What is the practice of law? How does it differ from what other people do? How did it come to be what it is today, and what will it probably be like tomorrow? How does American law work compare with legal practice in other societies or at other times in history?

Then we will deal with a set of interrelated questions concerning a chronic doubt which has beset the profession for years: Do lawyers provide services which are sufficiently honest, fair, competent, and available to justify the profession's lofty position of power and immunity from outside interference and regulation? Do poor or working people get justice in a legal system where lawyers' services are bought and sold on a free-market basis? How true is it that, as lawyers claim, only lawyers can judge whether or not their fellow professionals' services are being adequately and ethically performed? Does modern legal practice conform to the ideal which the organized bar has used to justify its autonomy: the model of a highly trained expert who balances the demands and interests of clients against the restrictions of law in order to moderate conflict and steer opponents toward reasoned, just, equitable, and legal solutions?

As we will see, social scientists look for answers to these questions by investigating the system of *stratification* within the profession and its relationship to stratificational processes in society as a whole. They see the issue of the adequacy of legal services as being tied directly to the arrangements of power, prestige, and influence within the profession and between it and society.

THE PRACTICE OF LAW

Types of Practice: The United States

The legal profession in the United States is large and getting larger rapidly. The present number of practicing lawyers stands around half a million. Law schools continue to be besieged with applicants and they turn out thousands more potential lawyers each year. To ask "What do all these people do?" is not to ask a single question. We must address it at several levels.

At one level, we can simply examine the various images of law work which we have already begun to discuss. There is the lawyer as champion of the weak and innocent, the protector of humane social values. There is also the lawyer as the agent of justice against the guilty—the Perry Mason-type hero who digs for facts and produces dramatic turnabouts in the midst of misguided trials, putting the finger on the "real" culprit.

But heroic courtroom performances are only part of the story. In fact, dramatic trial lawyers are no longer typical in the profession. Another kind of legal practice which is more typical is suggested in a recent book title: *Super Threats: How to Sound Like a Lawyer and Get Your Rights on Your Own* (Striker and Shapiro, 1977). They promise to ". . . teach you a method, a *modus operandi*, for taking a firm grip on your rights and wielding them as a club over the heads of scoundrels" (p. 17). Their thesis is that lawyers get things done by saying the right things with a sufficiently belligerent tone to project an image of authority, know-how, and determination. If you know the right words and adopt the same tone, you should be able to accomplish most of the same things.

This is not the lawyer striding back and forth in front of a jury. This lawyer practices in an office, mostly by telephone or typewriter. This is the practice of law as negotiation, the lawyer bargaining on behalf of a client because the client's ignorance of law and of bargaining strategy puts him or her in a vulnerable position which the lawyer can strengthen.

There is also the kind of lawyer you may have seen in the novel and television series, *The Associates* (Osborne, 1979). This is the attorney-specialist who works in a large metropolitan law firm drafting contracts, negotiating them on behalf of corporate clients, arranging corporate mergers, smoothing over relations between corporations and government regulatory agencies, inventing new tax shelters, and researching volumes on statutes and court cases to strengthen the hand of a corporate client locked in prolonged litigation against a corporate rival. Such lawyers may never see the inside of a courtroom. They may never argue a case before a judge. They are specialists, members of law teams which service the never-ending legal needs of large corporations.

A related kind of practice involves the *house counsel*. These are attorneys who work for corporate or government clients on a permanent basis. They are employees. They review proposals, contracts, correspondence, replies to complaints, public announcements, and any other actions which might have "legal ramifications" for the organization. Their job is to make sure that the action will not get the client into legal trouble. At IBM, for example, Stern reports that 243 in-house lawyers augment the company's occasional reliance on a Wall Street law firm (1980, p. 26). When CBS makes program changes, it calls on its own lawyers to review them for possible legal complications (such as libel, obscenity, or violation of Federal Communications Commission rules). Great newspapers such as the *New York Times* and the *Washington Post* consult their own lawyers before publishing controversial stories (Halberstam, 1979, pp. 789–99). Each department of the United States government (State, Labor, Defense, Commerce, etc.) has its own staff of attorneys playing the same kind of role.

Recent studies have shown that the house counsel in many corporations have become more than just passive commentators on legal questions put by corporate management (Slovak, 1980). They have increasingly become involved in policy planning, helping to devise new economic strategies through the use of previously undeveloped interpretations of law.

As this quick summary shows, just within the American legal profession there are significant differences in the way the job is done, the nature of the work done, and the type of client served. The great variety of roles played by American lawyers could cause confusion if we took literally the law's demand that only licensed lawyers may "practice law." With lawyers doing so many different kinds of tasks, where do we draw the line? If a classmate of yours is ordered to appear before a college disciplinary committee because of an alleged infraction of dormitory rules, would you be "practicing law" if you went with your friend and helped prepare a defense? If two of your neighbors cannot resolve an argument, are you practicing law if you step in and act as mediator between them? If a friend at work asks you to sign a document, as a witness, so that it will be legal, are you "practicing law"?

In theory, we could answer these questions only by agreeing on a final answer to the question posed in chapter 2: What is law? In practice, however, the answer is that you may do any of those things so long as no group of lawyers considers your action to be a threat to their livelihood. The "practice of law" is actually a cluster of related occupations which, as we will see later, has developed along particular lines of unique historical selection. These developments have varied widely from one country to another producing a worldwide hodgepodge of activities all labeled "the practice of law." If we look back in history, or if we examine other societies in our search for the essence of lawyering, we find that the American pattern is quite unusual.

Types of Practice: Around the World

In England, the profession of law is split and stratified between *barristers* and *solicitors* (Abel-Smith and Stevens, 1967). Barristers specialize in making courtroom appearances. They are experts at oratory and the presentation of arguments. Traditionally, they are accorded higher prestige in the profession than are solicitors. Solicitors do not make court appearances in those courts served by barristers. Instead solicitors make first contacts with clients, listen to their problems, dole out legal advice, prepare legal documents, and, if necessary, refer them to barristers who take over cases which will go into court.

There is no split like this in the American bar. Some American lawyers specialize in trial work and others specialize in advice giving and document preparation. But lawyers from one specialty are not barred by tradition or law from taking up other kinds of specialties, as they are in England.

In Japan, the practice of law is not actually one profession (Henderson, 1969). Jobs which American lawyers combine as normal aspects of their work are split up among several mutually exclusive occupational categories. To begin with, extremely restrictive standards allow only about 4 percent of those who take the bar exams to pass and become lawyers. The number of lawyers is therefore extremely low, and most of their time is spent in trial work. Other kinds of legal work are handled by a variety of "less qualified" specialists. They cannot "practice law" in court, but they are licensed for practice in their own narrow specialty. Patent agents, for example, need not be lawyers. They are licensed to handle all aspects of litigation over patent issues. Judicial scriveners cannot represent clients in court, but they help draft and register documents, and they prepare paper work for clients who go to court without a lawyer. Administrative scriveners are severely restricted to the drafting of documents not done by all the other specialists. Hence they aid mainly small business operators whose legal business is not lucrative enough for other specialists. Other categories of specialists include notaries, certified public accountants, tax agents, and law-trained corporate employees (who studied law, failed the bar examinations, and therefore cannot represent their employers in court).

In India, the profession is almost entirely composed of trial lawyers. Their work consists almost wholly of representing clients in court lawsuits or in hearings between government administrative tribunals. They rarely spend time preparing contracts, arranging business transactions, or advising clients on issues such as inheritance, family trust funds, or major purchases such as land or a house. Where they do give such advice, it is usually to friends and relatives, and it is not considered work: that is, they are not, and do not expect to be, paid for advice. Such advice is, of course, a major aspect of the paid work done by American lawyers. In India, such advice is given by people from all walks of life, laymen as well as lawyers.

Studies of India's lawyer-client relationships have revealed a whole host of nonprofessionals who serve as "putt lawyers" (little lawyers) (Kidder, 1969; Morrison, 1969). Experienced litigants, for example, become known as "experts" in their village, and people flock to them for all sorts of legal services. Village headmen often develop similar reputations. Literate men in illiterate villages are asked to store precious legal documents, and villagers rely on them to explain what the documents say. Such central village figures become "touts," taking money from both lawyers and villagers for performing the service of bringing new clients to lawyers. Men who work around the courts pick up experience and become legal advisers to those who cannot afford a real lawyer's fee. These include lawyers' clerks, court typists, stenographers, and stamp sellers who vend legal stamps required on all legal documents.

Notice that much of what, in America, is done by lawyers as part of the "authorized practice of law" is done in India by people whose *social position*, not specialized training or licensing, makes them marketable as aides in the doing of legal work. Many Americans, of course, have similar social positions, and some of them perform services like those I have described in India. In Chicago, for example, police officers have sometimes acted as "touts," taking money from lawyers who specialize in narcotics cases for directing drug arrestees to their offices (Sanders, 1975). Bailiffs, court clerks, and others whose jobs give them regular information about the personnel and routines around courts also sometimes perform such "services." Such activities are, however, officially unethical and in some cases illegal because the American legal profession, much more than the lawyers in India, has successfully gained a monopoly over the performance of most legal services.

In the previous sentence I used the word *monopoly* in reference to legal services in the United States. This picture of the profession's position involves the assertion that legal assistance performed for pay has been treated as a separate specialty only under certain circumstances. It means that such services in the past (and in some societies even today) were available to people even though there was no legal "profession." It means that the autonomy and market monopoly which American lawyers have today is not a "natural" way to organize the provision of these services. It means that the rise of the legal profession *as a profession* was the result of a deliberate strategy to capture and control the marketplace for legal services. In the next section, we will see what that strategy was, who developed and pursued it, and what some of its effects have been, besides the creation of the profession as it is today.

STRATIFICATION AND AUTONOMY

Hierarchy in the American Profession

A conspicuous feature of the legal profession in the United States and other industrialized nations is the stratification of power, prestige, and wealth between different levels within the profession, and between lawyers and others in society. Studies of the American profession show that these status distinctions have their roots solidly planted in American history. We will begin here by looking in some detail at the facts of stratification within the profession. Then, in the next section, we will consider alternative explanations of the origins of this hierarchy. Finally, we will deal with questions about the effects of this stratification on the quality of legal services available to people in American society and the ability of a legal system dominated by a stratified profession to meet the needs of people for justice.

A detailed study of the legal profession in New York City was designed to investigate the effects of professional stratification on the willingness and ability of lawyers to either conform with or break the rules of the profession's code of ethics (Carlin, 1966). Law practice in New York falls into very clear-cut categories of status. Factors which determine status include the background characteristics of lawyers, the types of clients they serve, their level of income, and their conformity with the code of ethics. These factors are all intermingled in a stable system of status differentiation.

At the top are the Wall Street lawyers in large law firms. They come mostly from WASP (White, Anglo-Saxon, Protestant) backgrounds. They are almost all male. Most of them attended law school at either Harvard, Yale, or Columbia University, graduating in the top 10 percent of their classes.

The narrowness of this background is the product of restrictions which arise from the rarefied pressures of big business in America. Wall Street law firms serve large, wealthy corporations almost exclusively. They rarely handle cases for individuals. Their specialty is the kind of law helpful to large corporations. The corporate executives who work with the lawyers and must decide whether or not to employ them come from backgrounds very similar to those described in the previous paragraph. Law firms hire the kinds of people they do in order to put their best-paying clientele at ease. They maintain an intimate network of contacts with professors at the three "best" law schools in order to insure their own access to the "best legal minds" in the country, knowing that those "minds" will also know how to behave in the company of corporate clients.

The practice conducted by such lawyers almost never takes them into courtrooms. They work long hours and sacrifice almost all private life to furnish top-grade service to the firm's corporate clients. Eight years of practice as a kind of apprentice in the firm is followed by either promotion to the rank of junior associate or polite hints that the person should leave and find employment elsewhere. Salaries are very high, even for beginners, in these firms and rise very rapidly for those who succeed.

These, then, are the people at the top in New York's legal profession. They are a small percentage of the total, but they dominate the profession's organizations, the bar associations, which regulate all lawyers in New York.

The lower two-thirds of the professional pyramid involves lawyers whose lives, both before entering the profession, and as working lawyers, are very different from those of the lawyers on Wall Street. These "lesser" lawyers are *solo practitioners*. They practice alone, seeking out their own clients, maintaining their own offices, and facing their own uncertain futures alone. Most are either Jewish or Catholic, and their family background fits the category "ethnic." They attended "second- or third-rate" law schools and were not among the top 10 percent in their classes. Older lawyers in this category may not have attended law school at all, or they may have casually picked up a degree from some "evening school" taught by part-time faculties and having no law libraries.

Although solo practitioners usually specialize in one area of law (divorce or personal injury, for example), they have difficulty getting clients. As a result, they often resort to a hidden population of illegal "assistants" to bring them business. These include "ambulance chasers" posing as lawyer's aides, tow-truck drivers, ambulance drivers, bail bondsmen, doctors, police, and pharmacists. Paying for such services is illegal, but common.

Clients of solo practitioners are generally of lower status than the Wall Street lawyers', and their problems usually require their lawyer to be in contact with the lower ranks of those who work in the justice system. They must routinely seek the cooperation of court clerks, stenographers, bailiffs, record keepers, judges, and other attorneys who affect the daily routines of court. Therefore, says Carlin, they are much more likely than the Wall Street lawyers to have to deal with the petty rackets, the bribery, the favor-trading, and the corruption which are part of the routines of these offices. For the solo practitioner, a bribe may be the only way to get a court hearing for a client soon enough to make the hearing worth waiting for.

To make matters worse, solo practitioners tend to get business only from individuals, and specifically from those individuals whose needs are for a one-shot encounter with the services of lawyers. Therefore there is reduced incentive for the lawyer to invest heavily in any single case. Moreover, among those individuals who do find it necessary to contact a lawyer on more than one occasion, there is a strong tendency to seek out a new lawyer (Curran, 1977, p. 191).

Professional stratification reflects distinctions which extend throughout American society. High finance and big industry nurture a class of legal specialists whose skills are totally dedicated to the solving of corporate problems. Such lawyers are therefore beyond the economic reach of ordinary citizens. Yet it is this professional elite which has used its power and influence within the centers of American economic and political leadership to win autonomy for the profession. Because of these efforts, the *Code of Ethics* for lawyers now has the force of law, even though its enforcement is left almost entirely in the hands of the lawyers' own bar associations. As a result, the training and professional conduct of even the solo practitioners is controlled by organizations created and run by elite corporate-law specialists.

This research concluded that the Code of Ethics places unrealistic restrictions on solo practitioners who practice in large metropolitan areas. The code is couched in outmoded terms and prescribes conduct appropriate only for lawyers practicing in small cities or rural areas (see Handler, 1967). Like rural lawyers, Wall Street professionals never encounter the difficulties faced by urban solo practitioners. Country and corporate lawyers both share the advantage that their clients come to them through contacts within an established community. For them, it is sufficient to rely on reputation and the cultivation of relationships among potential clients.

The urban solo practitioner faces an entirely different business situation. Few stable communities exist in metropolitan areas, so lawyers cannot count on contact networks as a basis for business. Advertising would be a logical alternative for solo practitioners, but the Code of Ethics forbade all advertising until the Supreme Court's recent decision rejecting that rule. Fee competition would have been another alternative. But again, until the Supreme Court rejected it, the Code of Ethics helped the bar associations enforce fixed-fee schedules for all standard legal services. Such services were precisely those most likely to come from solo practitioners.

In sum, the Wall Street elite, by dominating the rule-making process for the whole profession, has protected its own self-serving practices while outlawing those practices which would have helped solo practitioners. The "good old, down home" country values enshrined in the Code fit conveniently with the nature of corporate law practice and helped to legitimize the profession's insistence that nonprofessionals should be kept out of the business of regulating lawyers' conduct.

We will see later in this chapter that this pattern of dominance has consequences which extend well beyond the confines of lawyers' offices. The Code's restrictions distort the free-market availability of legal services and thereby create limits on people's access to justice. Professional stratification is therefore more than just a reflection of general social stratification. The stature which corporate practice gives the Wall Street lawyer within the profession may actually reduce the role of the law in rectifying the injustices of inequality in American society.

Origins of Professional Stratification

One way to explain the position of prominence and power which the profession's elite enjoy today is to say that it is the end product of separate successes of many individuals competing in a free marketplace. This position leads to the judgment that the profession has become what it is because it meets certain needs in society. It is the application of structural-functionalism (see chapter 4) to the analysis of occupational differentiation.

A very different way to explain the existing structure of the profession is to argue that it is the product of a collective campaign by an existing elite to preserve its power and privilege in the face of status-threatening social changes. This second kind of thesis reflects a conflict perspective (see chapter 5).

Free market vs. controlled development. The free enterprise thesis can be seen in an attempt to explain the differences between the American and German legal professions (Rueschemeyer, 1973). In Germany, neither lawyers nor judges ever achieve the wide repute of some American lawyers and judges. The individual lawyer or judge rarely becomes a "household word" in Germany.

Their much lower profile bespeaks their less central role in the administration of justice. Both lawyers and judges become fixed in their separate careers by their choices of specialized training in law school. There is rarely any crossing between the two positions once legal training has been completed. Their careers are set by the curriculum they follow and the examinations they take. German law practice is therefore more dominated by routine than is American practice.

For most German lawyers, trial work is only a small part of their work. In those trials, moreover, lawyers play a much less active role than do American lawyers. German civil-law procedures place most of the burden of questioning and interpretation on the judge. The lawyer's role is mainly to advise the client and insure that the client knows what to expect and how to cooperate with the authorities.

Much of the German lawyer's work is done outside of court. Unlike prominent American corporate lawyers, however, the German's practice is not usually confined to one specialty. German lawyers do not usually join together in large law firms, and they rarely become wealthy from law practice.

All of these differences are associated with the out-of-court responsibilities which distinguish German from American corporate lawyers. Outside of court, German lawyers play a role in managing the relationships between their clients and the various branches of government. The centralized nature of German government and the active role traditionally played by government in promoting and controlling economic and social development put a premium on knowing how to deal with the bureaucracy. That knowledge is the lawyer's forte in Germany.

The thesis here is that the differences between American and German legal practice stem from the different ways in which the two nations became modern. In the United States, economic development was a decentralized, unrestrained project of private entrepreneurs. The marketplace regulated the pace and direction of development. This environment of free-trade and laissez-faire economics encouraged the development of a legal profession concerned especially with the conduct of commercial relationships. In this free-for-all commercial environment, conflict and adversarial relations were normal, and the law developed in the direction of serving to curb the excesses of competition. Hence American law, and the practice of law, became organized around the adversary model of legal procedure. The adversary model puts the lawyer squarely in the middle of the battle, and law develops mainly as referee in the contest.

In Germany, by contrast, development was a conscious policy of government. It was a goal to be pursued by plan. The purpose of law was to ensure the success of the plan. The practice of law was therefore oriented more around the relations between individuals and policy administrators than around the conflict business interests might have with each other. Government was much more intrusive in the lives of individuals than it was in the United States. Courts were more centrally controlled from the beginning because political power was centrally consolidated very early in Germany's move toward modernity.

The freewheeling commercial environment in the United States meant that lawyers could become involved in the building of private fortunes in industry and commerce. The relative absence of restraint on their actions meant that they could pursue careers which occasionally produced fame and fortune. They could combine law work with other economic activities (banking, investments) to help themselves to a share in the fortunes they were helping to build for clients.

German lawyers, by contrast, were always kept on a tighter leash. In a sense, they were conceived of as bureaucrats—just another set of specialists helping to administer the government's plans. As bureaucrats, their options were more limited and the scope for expression of their imaginations was more restricted. Like other bureaucrats, they felt pressure to "fit in" rather than "stand out" like American lawyers. And as bureaucrats, they have typically shared the general social status of bureaucrats rather than members of the business elite.

To sum up the structural-functional thesis of this analysis, American lawyers have achieved a prominent, powerful position because they were able to make themselves useful to the free-enterprise developers of American business. In the atmosphere of free enterprise which prevailed, individual American lawyers could seize opportunities as they came along, just like other ambitious entrepreneurs.

The continuity of elite dominance.   Studies from a conflict perspective treat professional stratification differently. One, which we will consider in detail here, describes the American profession's development as an example of a *mobility project* (Sarfatti Larson, 1977). The "mobility project" thesis differs from the functionalist view in that it holds that lawyers won their prestigious positions by collectively working *against* free-market competition in their specialty. Like other professions, the legal profession is a creation of monopolistic strategies which have undergone several stages of growth to establish the current level of organized occupational dominance.

The "mobility project" among lawyers was part of a larger pattern of changes in American class structure. These changes were the result of the industrial revolution, that accelerating shift from an agrarian economy to industrial capitalism. In preindustrial society, lawyers were usually employed by wealthy families who supported them as patrons, much in the way they would have their own private physicians, musicians, and artists. With the rise of industrialism and the gradual eclipse of its supportive aristocracy, new market conditions and ideologies created new opportunities in legal practice. A forceful tide of democratic reform swept the country during the "Age of Jackson," making it particularly difficult for lawyers to justify their elitist claims that they alone should control the market for lawyers' services. Their argument that only "qualified" practitioners should be allowed to conduct law work fared badly against the egalitarianism of the Jacksonian era. During this period, therefore, the practice of law became a decentralized, well-diversified activity. Law practice became widespread and inexpensive, making the law an affordable reality for ordinary people. Only in the larger cities were lawyers able to fend off this challenge to their elite status.

Leaders of the bar, especially those in the booming urban centers, embarked on their "mobility project" in order to monopolize the market for legal services under the new market conditions of industrial capitalism. To meet these new conditions, the project had to conform with the new ideologies of capitalism. Specifically, capitalism demanded *scientific rationality* and the promotion of persons on the basis of merit (i.e., their ability to "get the job done" rather than their connections with influential families).

In forming nationwide associations, lawyers demanded, and ultimately won, *autonomy*—the exclusive right to control entry into the practice of law and to regulate the ethics and quality of service. They did this by successfully promoting two ideas: (1) only other lawyers could judge the quality of legal work being offered to the public, since "legal thinking" and language are too complex for the layman; and (2) without autonomy, lawyers would become totally partisan advocates of their clients and lose the ability to temper client demands by invoking the law. Since the "quality of the product" or the "efficiency of the producer" (both of these being measures elevated to prime importance by industrial capitalism) in law work is difficult to measure objectively, elite lawyers realized that they could not justify the control they sought by simply pointing to their output. So they promoted the idea that what set them apart was their *training*, their specialized knowledge. To back this up, they persistently pushed for stricter and more prolonged programs in legal education as prerequisites for practice. This campaign led finally to the total autonomy over legal education and admission to the bar which the profession now enjoys.

As America emerged from the Jacksonian era (following the Civil War), a shift became noticeable in the nature of law practice. Previously the work had involved courtroom argumentation, work on litigation. Oratorical and debating skills made some lawyers famous and others envious, since courtroom drama was the backbone of most lawyers' incomes. As industrial development accelerated, the new industries began to use lawyers as negotiators, people with "important contacts," people who could help the business avoid litigation and legal traps by arranging good contracts and out-of-court settlements. Those lawyers who were already in the most powerful positions in the profession took over this kind of work, leaving the courtrooms to the "riffraff" whose lower-status social origins prevented them from establishing the kinds of "contacts" needed to enter the more lucrative practice of corporate law.

Overall, then, the elite of the preindustrial era transferred their status to successors who worked to defend it by engaging in a "mobility project." Since elite lawyers were active in helping aggressive capitalists drive their competitors into bankruptcy, they felt a need to clothe themselves in democratic legitimacy. They did this by developing the theory of law practice as a form of nonpartisan *expertise* which could only be guaranteed by closely supervised learning.

It was this theory of expertise which became the foundation of the modern image of professionalism. It justified the lawyers' ever-expanding demands for autonomy, restraint on entry into practice, ethical rules which preserved their high incomes, and defense of fellow lawyers against charges of incompetence or dishonesty. It was the key to control, both of the marketplace in general and of the individual client whose potential for interference with, and critical judgment of, the lawyer's work always posed a threat to the stability and size of lawyers' incomes. (Rosenthal's 1974 study of lawyer-client relations in the early 1970s showed that many lawyers normally do whatever they can to hide from their clients what is happening to their cases. When they say "Just leave everything to me," they try to gain complete control over their own work schedules, strategy decisions, information about setbacks or mistakes affecting the case, and interpretations of the often ambiguous outcomes of clients' cases. Rosenthal showed that when clients refused to accept the passive role set for them by their lawyers, when they interfered, asked questions, and insisted on an active decision-making role in their cases, they achieved better results for themselves and felt more satisfied with the outcomes. But many lawyers work hard to prevent such "interference" by insisting on the superiority of their expertise.)

Once the legal elite had established a new basis of security and influence in the booming world of industrial capitalism, it consolidated this control by promoting "democratic" reforms in legal education. These reforms consisted of changes in the curriculum at Harvard Law School, the establishment of full-time law faculties at other schools, and the spread of the Harvard curriculum to other schools as the only valid method of legal education. These changes were used to justify the demand that only those who had received a Harvard-type education could be allowed to practice.

These reforms gave the appearance of opening the profession to anyone smart enough to get through the rigors of professional training. In practice, however, the "rigors" were used with deliberate selectivity to defend the "ethnic purity," political conservatism, and elite standing of the profession (Auerbach, 1976). "Ethnic purity" was the real agenda behind the mobility project in the profession. One hundred and fifty years of "unequal justice" resulted from the exclusiveness and political conservatism of those who controlled the bar. Each immigrant or other minority group which began to knock at the profession's door was confronted with a stone wall of elite strategies designed to keep it out of the profession. Irish, Italians, Eastern Europeans and especially Jews, blacks and women all experienced the creative methods of exclusion invented by this elite. Even if they managed to gain entry to law school, and pass, and even pass the prejudicially graded bar examinations (which were supposed to measure only merit, but which were used to exclude whole ethnic groups), often they were still kept out of practice by being branded as lacking proper "moral character."

Restraints on entry into legal practice were thus part of a deliberate elitist strategy to protect and enhance the profession's status. Such monopolistic control makes legal services more costly and less responsive to the needs of ordinary people than they would be in a less regulated market. Though the strategies have varied with changes in the political environment, the elite has met every move to "open" the profession, to expand its services, to give people greater access to justice with ingenious campaigns of exclusion disguised as ways to "insure high-quality, ethical legal practice."

Notice that analyses which emphasize *collective* strategies to regulate the provision of legal services contradict the functionalist view that the prominence of American lawyers stems from their *individual* successes at discovering people's needs and filling them.

As we weigh additional evidence for these two opposing positions, keep in mind that the "mobility-project" thesis is a conflict theory approach, while the free-market thesis is a functionalist perspective.

Assessing the Critical Perspective

You should be warned that critical theories, such as the "mobility-project" thesis, can be convincing for the wrong reasons. Whether they support the critical perspective or not, sociologists do not dispute the overwhelming evidence that there are large status differences among lawyers and that some lawyers occupy very influential positions in American society. The fact of stratification alone, however, does not prove the validity of the conflict perspective, although in a culture which so strongly emphasizes equality of opportunity, the discovery of stable class differences can make the critical perspective seductively convincing. Like any set of claims, the conflict perspective should be scrutinized for its ability to deal with hard evidence from detailed research.

Does autonomy equal power?   Conflict theorists studying the legal profession clearly suggest that autonomy and professional elitism arise from, and reinforce, the profession's intimate connections with the economic and political leadership of society. In this view, *autonomy* is part of the strategy by which lawyers have promoted their rise to power.

However, some studies suggest that autonomy and elitism can cost the profession dearly in terms of its relevance to, and influence over, the ruling circles of a society. In both England and Spain the legal profession has become increasingly impotent because of its autonomy.

English lawyers are often regarded as the model of what law in Western societies is all about. While often portrayed as paragons of scholarly erudition, even-handedness, and legal brilliance, they have not adjusted successfully to the changes brought about by capitalism.

Abel-Smith and Stevens's history of the English legal profession from the eighteenth century onward shows that a kind of stagnation has increasingly excluded lawyers from participation in major social and economic developments (1967).

The English profession grew up around the hodgepodge of courts which developed in a decentralized way over several centuries in Britain. Because English government was weak and decentralized, different governmental branches, along with other organized groups (e.g., the church and merchant groups), set up their own courts and developed their own traditions, practices, and patterns of organization. Some lawyers practiced in London at the "more important" courts (including the appeals courts which heard cases brought from elsewhere in the country). They developed their own restrictions on entry into practice before those courts. It was they who became the *barristers,* and their practice was organized and controlled by the Inns of Court, which became their own separate professional association.

Elsewhere in England, groups of lawyers formed around the lower courts (e.g., county courts and the circuit courts which were in session only during the few weeks when judges from London were in residence before they moved to other towns on the circuit). These "country" lawyers were excluded from practice in London by rules laid down by the barristers. If "country" clients needed to bring a case into the London courts, their lawyers had to refer them to London barristers who would present the cases in court. Gradually these "lesser" lawyers formed their own professional association (The Law Society) and established their own restrictions on practice so that, for example, barristers from London could not move in on their "turf." These lesser lawyers became known as *solicitors* and they now constitute the larger, though generally less prestigious and less wealthy, portion of today's profession.

As in the United States, there were occasional reform campaigns to "upgrade" the educational level of the profession. Other reforms were supposed to reduce the cost of legal services so that law would not serve only the rich. Barristers, for example, qualified for apprenticeship primarily by reason of their graduating from Oxford or Cambridge, even though most had studied no law. This restriction had meant that most barristers came from aristocratic families. Reforms were supposed to open the profession to other classes. Throughout most of the nineteenth century, however, neither solicitors nor barristers made much of an attempt to disguise the fact that the restrictions they placed on entry into practice were designed primarily to protect their incomes by keeping their numbers small and raising court-enforced fees for their services. Somehow, no matter how a reform movement got started, it had the effect of keeping the club small and the fees high. Reform commissions repeatedly pointed to the development of law schooling in the United States and other countries as a model that the English profession should follow. But even into the twentieth century, English lawyers resisted these measures, arguing that the only way to learn law was by apprenticing to a senior practitioner and then setting out on one's own.

Compared with the profession of law in the United States, then, the English profession must be viewed as never having executed a successful "mobility project" in response to industrialization. The absence of strong democratic political pressures, such as the American profession experienced during the Jacksonian era, allowed the English profession to remain comfortably stuck in its aristocratic niche, able to defend its privileges and exclusiveness but unresponsive to the major social and economic changes being wrought by capitalism.

The autonomy, isolation, and antiquated procedures which these traditions preserved resulted in a legal profession whose services became increasingly irrelevant to ambitious, impatient, innovation-seeking leaders of industry and commerce. The expense and delay of litigation, caused by the insistence of lawyers on maintaining traditional procedures, produced a court process which business leaders increasingly found ways to avoid. As a result, the English profession never became central to the major transactions, negotiations, and agreements of modern business in England. English business leaders have come to rely on such devices as commercial arbitration run by nonlawyers in order to get things done. Meanwhile the legal profession becomes increasingly peripheral to English society and remains too expensive to ordinary citizens.

Spain's experience with the dictatorial rule of Generalissimo Franco gives us another example of the limits of professional autonomy. Lawyers and judges during Franco's rule were, as a group, not only strong believers in liberal political values. They were also outspoken opponents of Franco's repressive political tactics (Toharia, 1975). As a group, the Spanish legal profession had a high level of autonomy. They governed their own professional organizations, applied their own code of ethics, and felt free to openly criticize the government.

But the autonomy they enjoyed as professionals made them powerless to prevent the totalitarian practices which they opposed. Franco knew of their liberal ideals and their open criticism. So whenever he took action to silence political dissidents, "Communists," or other citizens who displeased him, he simply tried them in special military tribunals which bypassed the legal profession, the regular courts, and their liberal judges. Political trials were thereby placed beyond the reach of the autonomous legal profession. Yet their autonomy and their outspoken, but unpunished, criticism of the government helped Franco pose as a tolerant, benevolent dictator rather than a tyrant.

In both England and Spain, then, the development and preservation of autonomy has been associated with the loss of power and influence. The autonomy which in the United States was an essential ingredient of the profession's "mobility project" can have just the opposite effect: the isolation and bypassing of an entire occupational group. We find relevance and autonomy at odds with each other in England and Spain, rather than complementing each other, as in the United States. How do we decide which of these relationships is the right one?

We may have an answer in Sarfatti Larson's discussion of the American profession's experiences in more recent times (1977). As she points out, the "myth" of autonomy was formed around the model of a single lawyer serving a single client. Autonomy is supposed to help the lawyer promote the "legitimate" claims of clients while deflecting their extravagances.

However, the autonomy myth has persisted as an ideology even where lawyers work for large bureaucracies (government or industry) in which their position of autonomous neutrality becomes clearly untenable. In a bureaucracy the "autonomous" lawyer becomes an employee. Even-handedness and disinterested expert advice get squeezed out by organizational pressures to promote the client-organization's interests. The organization is the lawyer's only employer, a fact which greatly reduces any readiness to temper the client's demands with appeals for restraint. The reality of autonomy has thus receded even farther into the land of mythology.

Nevertheless, it remains a useful myth. By invoking it, organizations can wash their hands of responsibility for the quality or ethical content of the work done by their own lawyer-employees. If their actions prove to be legally unacceptable, managers can shift the blame to their own certified legal "experts," even if it was their own managerial initiative which pressured the lawyers into playing along "with the team." On the other hand, lawyers in these situations cling to the myth of their own autonomy because it is their last remaining defense against the kind of subordination to authority which all other employees of the organization experience.

Is law just another profession?   We have now seen that one vulnerability of the conflict perspective of the legal profession is its unjustified assumption that power and autonomy necessarily go hand in hand. A second possible weakness lies in the tendency to treat the legal profession as just one of several professions sharing the same characteristics. Both functionalists and conflict theorists tend to lump lawyers together with doctors as birds of a feather in the mobility-project business. The implication is that the differences between law and medicine are less important than their shared histories as leaders of professionalization.

But what are those differences? Are they really so insignificant? For one thing, lawyers for rich clients must practice a different kind of law from those serving ordinary individuals. In medicine this is not usually the case. Even a poor patient can have an interesting, complicated medical problem which will attract the "best medical minds." In law, challenging, intellectually stimulating, career-enhancing cases are much more likely to involve corporations or wealthy individuals whose "affairs" involve many interrelated legal problems and arrangements. Where the doctor ". . . decides when the patient needs an appendectomy, . . . the client decides when the client needs a divorce" (Heinz and Laumann, 1979, p. 1138). If this is true, then lawyers have substantially less control over the market for their services than do doctors.

Another significant difference is that ". . . the role of the lawyer is to mediate conflict . . ." Because this role "presupposes an adversary," a lawyer's services ". . . are valuable only if they are roughly equal, in quality and quantity, to the services possessed by adversaries" (Abel, 1981). Such balancing is not even contemplated in medicine. There it is easier to support the belief that the profession provides at least adequate care even for those who cannot afford the best doctors in the business. But a client paying minimum fees to a marginal lawyer may be purchasing disaster if the opponent has the resources to pay for "the best in the business."

A third major difference between law and other professions is that lawyers must routinely face public challenges to their own claim to expertise by others with equally valid credentials. While all professionals must deal with the problem of proving themselves to their clients, most can at least expect support from their fellow professionals. In medicine, for example, nothing about the nature of the task of healing requires doctors to try to prove the incompetence of their colleagues. With conflict at the core of its task, the legal profession does pit lawyers against each other in this way. They know that the slightest mistake can be not only exposed but also greatly exaggerated by opposing lawyers. They know also that unless they arrange more cooperative working relationships with these colleagues, the structure of incentives in law work will surely produce a frenzy of attacks and counterattacks between professionals vying for the business of clients.

This special vulnerability of lawyers can be seen more vividly in societies where lawyers have not yet developed a successful "mobility project." In India, for example, easy entry into the profession, along with lively competition from nonprofessionals, reflects the general failure of the profession to corner the law-work market. As I mentioned earlier, practically the only law work available to lawyers is in lawsuits by clients who are already convinced that they must sue. Indian lawyers thus work in an atmosphere of keen public competition. Should clients become dissatisfied with their lawyers' work, many other lawyers eagerly await their business. The uncompromising adversarial atmosphere of litigation also increases the likelihood that a lawyer's clients will be told by self-serving parties that they can get better legal advice elsewhere.

The problem of establishing a stable career, of getting and keeping clients, in this environment becomes the overwhelming obsession of most aspiring lawyers. Since no "mobility project" shields them from the consequences of working in the business of conflict, they adopt ingenious strategies to sustain their business. "Stage props" help their offices to look serious. Bookshelves loaded with weighty (though often obsolete and irrelevant) law books announce the lawyer's literacy and expertise. The lawyer usually sits on a chair raised above the places for clients by a small platform, so that his status of dominance over the client is physically reinforced. Lawyers demand conspicuous displays of deference from their clients (e.g., following the lawyer at ten paces when walking together at court, carrying the lawyer's briefcase, fetching refreshments for the lawyer's guests). These gestures are worth the risk of offending clients because they help to reinforce the lawyer's image as one who is capable of making things happen.

In court, speaking style and long-winded arguments are vital. Such theatrics rarely impress judges or other lawyers, since they often have no relevance to the decisions judges must make. But they impress clients, and they are good advertising for others in court who might become clients in the future.

In sharp contrast with the American law school scene, Indian law schools are "easy," both to get into and to finish. They are the "last-resort" choice for young persons whose grades are too low for medical or engineering school. Even successful lawyers try to direct their children away from law as a career because they are so aware of the instability and anxiety which pervade legal careers.

Functionalist theorists argue that facts like these support the validity of claiming that the legal profession is a creature of the characteristics and demands of the clients served by lawyers (Heinz, et al., 1976; Laumann and Heinz, 1977). They claim that market forces have been free to shape the profession, and that law is one profession where a "mobility project" is least likely to explain what we see. Where conflict theorists see a unified monopoly over particular services in the United States, functionalist research reveals ". . . a profession so riven by conflict—reflecting the conflicting interests of its clients—that the bar can reach a consensus only on inconsequential issues or on symbolic issues that permit the professions' differences to be 'papered over' " (Heinz and Laumann, 1979, p. 1141).

Here are some of the market differences which split the profession into cliques with dissimilar attitudes and conflicting interests.

1. Corporate lawyers serve organizations, while solo practitioners must deal face-to-face with individuals.
2. Some specialties involve "symbol manipulation" (e.g., work on complex documents such as contracts and reports to government regulatory agencies), while others involve "people persuasion" (e.g., negotiating a settlement in a personal injury case).
3. Some specialties involve work centering on governmental statutes and regulations, whereas others focus on issues in the older common law. Lawyers need more formal training to handle governmental law.
4. Some specialties (e.g., divorce, accident claims, immigration) involve servicing large numbers of individual clients in courts designed for mass processing. Other specialties involve the lawyer in complex, unique, time-consuming actions. Typically, wealthy clients are involved in the latter, while clients who lack money usually get routine treatment.

In fact, each of the four contrasts listed above is also a contrast between law practice with rich versus poor clients.

Cautious functionalists do not go so far as to claim that the legal profession is now, or ever has been, willing and able to satisfy all of American society's legal needs. They do, however, oppose conflict-theory explanations about the determining role of elites. To them, the profession is organized (or fragmented) as it is because the diverse interests alive in American society, and composing the dynamic structure of that society, have created the kind of profession they need.

Ironically, one important piece of evidence against the functionalist position turned up in a major functionalist study of the profession. In trying to identify the factors which contributed to the prestige rankings which lawyers themselves gave to the specialties into which their profession is split, Laumann and Heinz found that one feature stood out above all others: the *status of the clients* served by a specialty (1977). Lawyers who serve corporate clients receive more deference from their colleagues than do lawyers who serve individuals. Moreover, this difference is true regardless of the level of other factors which would have been more consistent with functionalist theory, such as intellectual challenge or degree of specialization required for the practice. Lawyers for IBM rate more prestige than those serving individuals fighting IBM.

The results are clear: Power and prestige among lawyers mirror the status of clients served. Fragmentation between different segments of the bar can therefore be explained as a predictable consequence of the class conflicts in society as a whole. Such a conclusion supports the "mobility-project" thesis. Unity, autonomy, and power in the profession were not built by having all lawyers join hands to promote their common interests. The mobility project was undertaken by one small part of an occupational group: elite lawyers who succeeded in their "project" because their status enabled them to infuse the growth of corporate industrial power in America with legal strategies which only they could fathom and successfully manipulate. If market forces or the "needs of the clients" helped shape the profession, as functionalists argue, they did so only in the distorted sense that lawyers serving rich corporate clients successfully structured the practice of law to fit their needs in serving such clients. The Laumann and Heinz data show that lawyers for individuals and the unwealthy are tainted by the status of their clients

These results have special significance for the question addressed in the next section: Can legal services for individuals and the unwealthy be improved by helping them pay for better lawyers? The functionalist argument is that individuals and the unwealthy receive *apparently* inferior legal services (routinized, mass-produced "justice" in which individual differences are ignored) because their needs are simpler and lend themselves to such treatment (e.g., see Mayhew and Reiss, 1969). In other words, legal services for the poor are not really inferior. Rather, poor people have less-complex problems than those of the Dupont Corporation or the Hearst family. However, if the status of lawyers is determined by the status of their clients, then we know that the incentive system in the profession is to avoid low-status clients and pursue the wealthy. If it is true of legal practice that "the cream rises to the top," or in other words that the best lawyers succeed, then the prestige system in the profession robs from the poor to give to the rich.

There are, however, several "ifs" in the preceding argument. We will examine some of them in the following section, since there have been several good studies aimed at assessing the quality of legal services available to the unwealthy.

But first we should examine the possibility that the notion of the mobility project in the legal profession is obsolete, that changes have swept through the profession making the mobility project a thing of the past.

Is the mobility project finished?   Research on the Chicago bar supports the argument that professional autonomy is dying among corporate lawyers (Slovak, 1980). There is, however, an important new twist to the autonomy-power issue. Top-level house counsel are increasingly ". . . playing a strategic or controlling role in the management and execution of corporate legal work" (Slovak, 1980, p. 67). True, they are committed partisans of the companies they serve. But they are not legal automatons blindly executing their bosses' orders. Rather, they are becoming an assertive and influential element in the process of top-level corporate decision making. This trend takes on added significance in view of the fact that house counsel practice has replaced the private law firm as the typical way that corporations now purchase legal advice (Slovak, 1979). Older patterns of reliance on "business generalists" (see Bazelon, 1960; Smigel, 1969) in large, exclusive, costly, private firms have been replaced during the past twenty years with in-house legal departments which place heavy emphasis on specialization and teamwork. Private firms are not dead or even dying. Instead, their role in corporate law has become more narrow and specialized. Now they become involved when in-house lawyers need limited, specialized advice which fills gaps in house-counsel skills and resources. Businesses are decreasingly inclined to simply hand over all their legal work to "good friends" in private firms.

Why is this happening and what does it signify? One theory, which is particularly significant for our assessment of the mobility-project thesis, treats this shift as evidence that we have entered a new, "postliberal" stage of economic and social development (Unger, 1976; Slovak, 1980). We have passed the stage of unchained capitalism which stimulated and supported the professional mobility project.

Postliberal society, in response to excesses in free-market capitalism, contains two major elements which increase business demand for house counsel: (1) business is increasingly pressured by government and the political environment to deemphasize the profit motive in favor of decisions which benefit the general public; and (2) the size and influence of corporate enterprises stimulates increasing insistence that they act like minigovernments, granting full citizenship rights to their members and following established legal procedures for resolving internal conflicts.

Business operates in an increasingly regulated environment. It must respond by learning to live with the regulators. This need has given house legal counsel a much more central role in the making of crucial management decisions (Slovak, 1980). The corporations' need to curry favor with the regulators of air pollution, occupational safety, antitrust, fair employment, and similar "public trust" policies has led to the expansion of house-counsel departments.

At the same time, the predominance of the corporate form as the way of organizing everything from business to education, religion, entertainment, medicine, and even physical exercise has led to increasing pressure to "legalize" the decision-making and conflict-handling processes within large organizations. This trend has been called *corporativism* (Unger, 1976). It transforms the individual into a "citizen" with a growing list of demands for "justice" within the corporate group. Ordinary legal procedures become the models for the creation of due process within the organization. Lawsuits by these "citizens" against violations of established procedures increase the pressure on management to "legalize" its relations with subordinates. Corporations thus become private, or limited, governments within which the processes of law are reproduced. To handle this process effectively, management finds it necessary to hire more persons especially trained in legal matters. Hence, corporativism produces a second source of pressure to expand house-counsel departments. Over the past twenty years, house counsel have taken over a growing share of the problems created by both governmental regulation and corporativism. More recent studies demonstrate that the *internal conflicts* associated with corporativism account for more of the growth in house-counsel departments than does the expansion of governmental regulation (Slovak, 1981).

The rising star of house counsel has had some interesting effects within the profession already, and it holds the potential to produce major changes in the status of legal practitioners and in the equation of legal practice with professional autonomy. Wall Street lawyers, and their equivalents in other major metropolitan areas, look down their noses at house counsel (Laumann and Heinz, 1977). Among lawyers themselves, the consensus is that house counsel is a step below private corporate law practice. The apparent reason for this is the ability of private-firm lawyers to maintain an image of greater autonomy from the wishes of their clients. The paradox which takes some of the edge off their sense of superiority is that they must increasingly rely on house counsel to direct corporate law work their way. Thus the loss of autonomy which comes with the employee status of the house counsel contaminates the reality of the private firms' autonomy.

The rise of "postliberal" society may thus pose a challenge to the privileges and power of today's organized profession much as the earlier emergence of industrial capitalism challenged an earlier elite in the profession. The achievement of a unified, autonomous, professional status with a monopoly over certain service markets may be a passing occupational phase doomed to extinction by the rise of corporativism. Or we may yet see a new mobility project designed to rescue professional integrity by creating a new set of legitimations more consistent with the new social realities. If this does not happen, we may yet see lawyers *on strike,* demanding higher salaries, better working conditions and longer vacations from managers whose ranks may include executives who entered the company as lawyers themselves. After all, how long can top-level house counsel make managerial decisions before their identities as lawyers become blurred if not lost entirely?

SERVING SOCIETY: PRO BONO PUBLICO

Regardless of our choice between functionalist and conflict perspectives in the preceding section, the image of the profession appears to be rather tarnished. Both perspectives seem to accept the notion that talent and skill are more available to the rich than to the poor. Both seem to belie the profession's lofty claims to be serving *all* the people with quality work designed to improve the ability of our legal system to produce justice. Do all lawyers in fact turn their backs on the poor if they can afford to? Do the poor get only those losers in the profession who cannot do any better for themselves because of their backgrounds, ethnic identities, and poor performances on tests?

Answers to these questions apparently depend on where and when you look for alternative patterns. There have, over the past fifteen to twenty years, been a variety of programs and a fluctuating population of lawyers doing work *pro bono publico* (for the good of the public). Even if you have not studied this issue closely, you can probably recall hearing of lawyers bringing lawsuits against major industrial polluters, nuclear power projects, violators of fair housing and equal employment opportunity laws, and in favor of victims of industrial disasters; race, sex and age discrimination; and communities trying to prevent destructive military, industrial, or similarly vast developments from overrunning their quiet way of life. You may have read of native American tribes, religious or racial minorities, or public housing tenants being championed by lawyers.

Where do these lawyers come from? Are they the dregs, the leftovers, the malcontents who just could not succeed on Wall Street? Is their service a flash in the pan, a sop thrown to the poor to keep them quiet? Is there any difference between these activities and those of lawyers who have done free or low-cost favors for friends, relatives and "connections" for years (Lochner, 1975)?

The Pro Bono Movement

In the late 1960s and early 1970s, it began to look as though profound changes were rocking the American legal profession over the issue of "doing good." The federal government, and some state governments, began funding major legal services programs. These were intended to be far more comprehensive and helpful than the limited "legal aid" programs which had served poor persons during previous decades. Some proponents of the new programs saw them as a way to empower disadvantaged groups, to help them work together toward basic social reform.

At the same time, a small but conspicuous percentage of young lawyers just entering the profession showed an atypical commitment to the pursuit of careers helping the poor and powerless. There was evidently a surge of idealism which ran directly against the usual pursuit of "success," lucrative practice, and "important" clients. A wave of reform spirit seemed to have swept through the law schools and into the upper chambers of power within the profession. Some of the best students in the best law schools were beginning to demand "released time" for public interest work as part of their employment agreement with the major law firms who wanted to employ them. These firms found that the only way they could lure "the cream of the crop" for conventional positions in their "shops" was to set aside some of their resources for *pro bono* work. In some cases this meant assigning one or two young attorneys to full-time public interest work. In other cases, several would be granted one or two days a week for such work. Other firms formed public interest committees or departments to organize the work. (See Marks et al., 1972, for a general discussion of these developments.)

These changes appeared to hold the potential for a major reorientation in the firms concerning their responsibilities to the client-public. Corporate clients, it seemed, would now have to compete with ordinary people for the attention of the "best legal minds."

Part of the pressure on the private firms came from government-funded legal services. Begun as a program of the Organization for Economic Opportunity and later transferred to the Legal Services Corporation, the government alternative offered young attorneys a respectable, potentially challenging, way to use and develop their skills by helping poor people and unrepresented middle-income groups instead of big business. At the same time, private monies were becoming available to establish independent public-interest law firms to fight against pollution, discrimination, and for consumer rights and justice in other public-interest issues.

These alternatives allowed some younger attorneys to remain committed to the public-issue work which had led them to study law in the first place or which had developed during the course of their law school experience (Erlanger, 1978; Erlanger and Klegon, 1978). Many of the negative features of serving the poor (lack of intellectual challenge, pettiness of cases, lack of cases around which to build long-term commitment) were for a time, it seemed, reversed because of the new patterns of funding. There was optimistic talk that the entire profession would have to reorient its priorities in the direction of greater equality of service.

Barriers to Success

Resistance from the bar.   As early as 1972, though, a study funded by the American Bar Foundation concluded that reform within large law firms could not be counted on to sustain the drive for public-interest lawyering (Marks, Leswing, and Fortinsky, 1972). The harsh reality was that those firms remained primarily dependent on, and therefore committed to, their large corporate clients. Because of that commitment, they could be expected to treat public-interest work as peripheral, and their decisions about which public interest cases to handle (and how hard to fight them) would continue to be influenced by the preferences and interests of their major corporate clients.

Most evidence on the government-funded legal services programs shows that their fate has been even more decidedly negative. Even as they were beginning to operate, these programs encountered a storm of determined opposition from local groups of lawyers and politicians. In order to sabotage reforms, lawyers won places for themselves on "representative" legal services committees which had been created to insure "citizen input" into program planning. By dominating such committees, lawyers could intimidate "nonexpert" members and redirect programs in order to stifle their reform content (Stumpf, Schroerluke, and Dill, 1971). They also led political movements to alter legislation, in order to gut programs of their ability to attract cases, act collectively, and fight effectively. Their opposition around the country contributed ultimately to the abolition of the OEO program and the weakening of its replacement, the Legal Services Corporation. Like a new chapter in the saga of the mobility project, the story of the fate of legal services reforms leads us to the privileged chambers of the private bar.

> So long as the private attorney plays his customary politico-legal role in the community, he stands as an ominous barrier to the use of the legal system for widespread societal change. His monopoly as gatekeeper to the courts is well-entrenched in custom and heavily armored by his canons of professional ethics which have the force of law and the support of the political system. He shows little or no willingness to share his power with mere laymen, on whose behalf it is said, law exists. (Stumpf, Schroerluke, and Dill, 1971, p. 64) (Used by permission.)

Before we move on, it is worth pointing out here that most studies of professional opposition to legal services reforms show that it did not come from the elite, the corporate lawyers who figure so prominently in the mobility-project report. Rather it seems to have been led by regionally prominent solo practitioners whose practices were more likely to be affected by such programs. If such lawyers did not spearhead the original mobility project, the overall success of the project has apparently placed them in a position from which they can contribute to its further development.

Ideals, poverty, and career goals. Opposition from the organized bar has not been the only threat to these programs. A second major problem has been the distorting effects of eligibility limits. As with most "welfare" programs, legal services projects were created only for people with incomes below certain fixed ceilings. In the case of law, this has meant that legal services lawyers cannot build their careers around promoting the success of specific clients, as do corporate lawyers (Katz, 1978). As soon as "poor" clients achieve any degree of success, they become ineligible for assistance from the very lawyers who may have helped them to get where they are.

Further aggravating this situation is the fact that poor people tend to seek legal assistance only when they are already facing some kind of crisis (e.g., they face eviction, or loss of some item they purchased "on time," or they need a divorce, or they face some kind of financial crisis). Consequently, legal services lawyers rarely get the chance to sit down with a client and carefully plan a legal strategy which can have long-run benefits.

Because of income ceilings, therefore, idealistic young lawyers find their hopes for careers in challenging, pioneering, legal reform work becoming swept aside by a flood of cases which they find they can only deal with as routine, standardized legal matters focused on short-term problems. Such routines are boring, frustrating, career dead ends which have little effect on the major social problems which such lawyers hope to resolve.

Adding insult to these injuries, poor clients are often unprepared for the delay and frustration which their opponents can create for them by manipulating the formalities of law. As a result

> . . . poor people are not always delighted with their lawyer. A great many problems in poverty law can be tolerated if the lawyer can make it with his clients: but there are important problems of style . . . frustrations and anger about failures. . . . The lawyer who wants to help and wants to be accepted, and cannot help or is not accepted will be frustrated . . . (Wexler, 1971, p. 213)

Because of the programmatic limits of legal services programs and the frustrations of the legal experience, therefore, legal services projects have had great difficulty with turnover among lawyers. Programs hire good young attorneys, only to see them leave in order to pursue more rewarding careers. The rewards they seek are not just financial. They include the satisfaction of dealing with challenging legal issues (not just routines) and following through on long-term legal needs of clients.

The turnover problem is not just a case of "burnout" (the loss of idealism or commitment to the use of law to help the poor), and it does not mean that these attorneys are abandoning the poor (Katz, 1978; Erlanger, 1978). Rather it signifies a change in their perceptions of the most effective kinds of activities. As they gain experience, many lawyers become convinced that they can best help by developing "block-busting," reform-oriented lawsuits which hold the promise of improved conditions for whole groups of people. Hence, the turnover problem comes from the desire of an agency's experienced attorneys to take on new challenges which they cannot do in their original positions. Reform litigation keeps these lawyers committed to their original goals. But the tension between the routine and the reform sides of legal services for the poor produces such a high rate of turnover that most legal services offices are constantly being stripped of the experience they need to develop coherent programs.

Disorganizing legal theories. Thus far we have examined two major barriers to the success of campaigns to bring legal services to the poor and powerless: the organized resistance of the bar, and the lack of fit between young lawyers' idealism, restrictions in poverty law programs, and the ability of poor people to endure the strategic maneuvering which legal procedures make possible. These are not, however, the only stumbling blocks faced by the *pro bono* movement. Even where financial support made the work possible, and where the reform stakes were broad enough to hold the attention of capable lawyers, the success of the venture has often been short-circuited by the nature of major assumptions which are an inherent part of American law.

You may recall from chapter 5 that one of the key features of modern law is its focus on the rights of *individuals*. This approach separates issues which may be intimately linked outside the courtroom. One of the early discoveries of *pro bono* or activist lawyers was that the machinery of law which set them apart from their clients as experts and which made them useful also placed severe limits on the kinds of remedies they could pursue for those clients. The desire to help a whole group with the same problem would be met by judges' demands that the needs and rights of each individual be separately identified and processed.

For a time, a promising alternative to these procedures offered hope for real breakthroughs. This alternative was the *class action lawsuit*, an action for relief of every person in a class or category which had suffered some harm (such as all buyers of a defective automobile, or all blacks who had been denied the right to vote through systematic discrimination). Much of the reform momentum built on this procedure slowed after the Supreme Court adopted rules which made it much more difficult and expensive to use.

The result has been the refragmentation of collective issues and movements. If a nuclear power station accident decimates the property values of hundreds of residential lots, public advocacy for all the victims becomes a tedious process of developing the separate cases of each individual. When a mail-order sales operation proves to be a fraud, each victim is treated as a separate case. Such procedures devour the time and resources of public interest lawyers. Costs for copying, phone calls, and postage are multiplied. At a less mundane level, such procedures deny the very collective characteristics which make the cases of "public interest" in the first place.

Co-opting effects of involvement. Now we have considered three quite different barriers to effective *pro bono* law programs. A fourth hurdle lies lurking for those lawyers who overcome the first three. It comes in the form of limits on the fit between law and legal procedure on the one hand and the needs and goals of powerless groups on the other. Involvement in the legal process itself, even if "successful" in conventional legal terms, can work subtle changes on the groups who turn to law for protection. The name for these changes is *co-optation*.

A good example of this can be seen in the work done for native American tribes by sympathetic activist lawyers (Medcalf, 1978). The object of their *pro bono* work was to develop legal protections for the tribes so that they would no longer be vulnerable to interference from white economic and political civilization. Their intentions for their clients were generally altruistic. They worked hard for the cause. They won many impressive gains for the tribes.

On reflection, however, it becomes clear that they could not involve their clients in legal action without producing basic, destructive changes in attitude and interaction among members of the tribes. Involvement in lawsuits forced tribal members to think "like white men." The categories of law which made their cases *justiciable* (i.e., consistent with categories of conflict which judges are authorized to adjudicate) required them to take stands which violated their traditions. They were not accustomed to thinking of themselves as having *rights* against others in an adversarial confrontation. Their tribal ways depended on the sharing of property and the avoidance of leadership status or "standing out" in the group. They preferred collective decisions made by consensus.

None of these patterns was compatible with the strategies which their lawyers devised to get and keep tribal rights. The lawyers therefore saw their task as requiring them to train their clients in new ways of thinking. Because of their professional training and experience, they were generally insensitive to the incompatibility between the lessons they were teaching and the strategies they were developing, on the one hand, and the fundamental social orientations which sustained tribal solidarity on the other.

No matter what happened to their cases in court, therefore, those native Americans who became engaged in the battle emerged with profound changes in their ways of thinking and relating to each other. Paradoxically, successful public interest lawyering was helping to destroy the very social reality which the lawyers were trying to preserve. Each victory for the lawyers and their clients was like another nail in the coffin of tribal culture.

Perhaps this interpretation is too pessimistic. Perhaps to expect more from the law is to demand too much. White society, for example, is a hard reality with which native Americans would have to deal even without law. Are they not better off with the aid of *pro bono* attorneys than they would be trying to go it alone?

Such reasoning is directly attacked by some activist attorneys who have reached the conclusion that their own skills and expertise pose a threat to their clients. One form of the campaign for greater access to justice in the late 1960s and early 1970s was the *law commune*. These were supposed to benefit marginal or radical people whose causes were in political opposition to established institutions. These beneficiaries included opponents of the draft; military deserters; radicals being harassed by the FBI, the Army, and local police "red squads"; young people arrested for drug offenses; homosexuals suffering harassment; and so on. These "movement" people were, of course, the very kind of population who, in the past, had been denied adequate representation because they were so offensive to the professional elite. "Movement" lawyers had a vision of helping to create a world without war, drug arrests, racial and sexual discrimination, and environmental destruction.

What they discovered, however, was that their work as lawyers often did as much to destroy the political movement they wanted to promote as did the more obvious tactics of the police, secret surveillance, big business, and general harassment. As Wasserstrom put it, "when you enter court, you enter a social network in which marketplace values prevail" (1971). Courts are bureaucracies composed of assorted actors (both employees of the courts and partisan "outsiders") bargaining for their own interests. Justice becomes an object of barter. Participants, whether radical or not, are forced to adopt the language, logic, and tactics of this marketplace if they want success. To be skilled in this setting, to be a legal expert, means to be competent in guiding a client through the maze to the arrangement of some mutually satisfactory "deal" with the various other actors.

As movement lawyers discovered, such deals only rescue individuals. They leave intact the oppressive conditions against which "movement" people wanted to work. Freeing one comrade from a drug charge through plea bargaining, for example, does nothing to alter drug laws, enforcement policies, or antidrug ideologies. Successful defense of a draft objector does nothing to end the draft or even to alter the policies of local draft boards which routinely reject the positions taken by objectors.

Movement lawyers thus found that the better they became as lawyers, the more their efforts deflected and defused the political energies they wanted to help mobilize. If they engaged their clients in effective strategies of legal defense, they drew them into ways of thinking and spending time which were irrelevant to their causes. Awareness of, and involvement in, the collective side of a struggle was undermined by the consuming attention to detail demanded by court procedures.

Movement lawyers concluded that their only alternatives were to use the drama of courtroom confrontation (having refused pretrial deals) as a forum for broadcasting their political message, to avoid legal action altogether and forget about their own expertise, or to serve as "insiders" who could wheel and deal within the legal system, using any means available to keep as many "movement" people as possible out of the law's clutches.

The practical side of legal "expertise."   One idea which neither functionalist nor conflict theorists have examined in great depth is the claim that what clients purchase from a lawyer is *expertise*. Both critics and supporters of the profession have usually accepted uncritically the profession's claim that the value of a lawyer lies in the level of his or her grasp of technical legal know-how which laypersons lack. Such acceptance is quite consistent with a functionalist perspective. But it is surprising to see so many critics of the legal system and the profession making this concession to the ideology of professionalism (for example, see Auerbach, 1976; Stern, 1980).

If not expertise, then what is it that lawyers sell? One alternative interpretation undermines the whole idea that we could improve the condition of poor people, that we could count on the law to rectify the injustices of inequality if only we could furnish poor people with the level of expertise available to the rich.

This alternative can be stated as follows: Expertise, such as the information taught in law school or gained by intensive study of law books, has very little to do with the actual practice of law. Law school is a gate-keeping device which keeps the number of lawyers down (to reduce competition) and sustains the myth that lawyers possess special knowledge inaccessible to the rest of us. Every lawyer knows that law school courses ignore the "hard realities" of daily practice.

What lawyers do contribute to their clients is a small margin of technical information (which can be gained by almost any reasonably intelligent person quite quickly if he or she decides to investigate) combined with a major dose of *inside information* and *influential contacts*.

The inside information consists of those facts about legal and governmental organizations which one must know in order to get things done. They are not legal facts. They are organizational. They are comparable to the kinds of lessons you undoubtedly have learned about your college or university (for example, who in the dean's office will be sympathetic to your need for an extension on a course you have not completed in time, how you get into a course that is already "closed" at registration, or which courses are easy and which professors grade on a curve). All organizations have these informal "realities." Lawyers simply exploit the more intimate knowledge they gain about legal organizations from regular involvement with them, to provide an insider's "edge" to clients.

Influential contacts are probably the most important asset most lawyers have. When clients complain "My lawyer just charged me two thousand dollars for making a two-minute phone call," they may not understand that the phone call went to the only person whose action could save the client much more than two thousand dollars. Nor do they realize that, in exchange for that favor, the lawyer now owes a potentially costly favor to the influential party on the other end of that phone call. Similarly, criminal defendants who wonder why they have to pay five hundred dollars to a lawyer who "made a deal" with the prosecutor for a six-month jail sentence, may not realize that without the cozy relationship the lawyer has built up over the years with the prosecutor, the defendant might have faced a fifteen-year prison sentence.

If contacts are important at these lower levels of practice, they are even more so in corporate law. Having "friends in Washington" can make the difference between prolonged, costly legal battles and quick, "gentlemanly" resolutions of conflict over patent infringement, antitrust claims, or pollution control regulations. This is why many lawyers' careers at this level involve periods of service in government regulatory agencies, followed by highly successful careers in prestigious law firms serving the businesses regulated by those agencies. It is not simply that four years in government service make one an expert in regulatory law. Those four years afford young lawyers the opportunity to attend cocktail parties, play golf, attend plays and concerts, and perhaps even to jog with the people who decide who, how, and when to regulate the businesses under their jurisdiction. Such lawyers learn the unannounced priorities governing decision making in these agencies and discover the all-important internal politics of their operations. Lawyers who move from such positions to private firm employment are then well-placed to "make a few calls" for clients and save them from mountains of costly red tape, tactical errors in dealing with the agencies, and unnecessary expenditure on irrelevant precautions.

"Knowing the law" therefore is not like "knowing medicine." The lessons learned in law school are a ticket of admission, but they bear only faint association with the work lawyers actually do most of the time. To build a practice, to create something of value that clients will pay for, a lawyer must build connections, both with the officials who process (and can therefore block or retard) formal legal procedures and among all other persons whose positions in vital social networks make them potentially helpful or obstructive to the clientele the lawyer wishes to develop.

If this version of law work is accurate, then it jeopardizes the hope that poor people can be helped if we can just find the resources to help them pay for "high-quality" legal advice. "Contacts" and "inside information" take time and prolonged involvement to build. They are an "intangible asset" without which a lawyer's expertise (technical knowledge) would be almost worthless. Such relationships are typically built through reciprocity (Here's what I can do for you, so what can you do for me?). Reciprocity is, of course, that process at which poor persons tend to be weakest. What do they have to offer, and therefore what would a lawyer working on their behalf have to offer?

This leaves poor persons with the alternative of fighting without the "insider's edge." Such fights can be waged, but they burden the *pro bono* lawyer with a job where most of the vital tools have been locked away. It is something like a football game where one side has to play barefoot and without any padding. They have a chance, of course. But the few victories such a team might win would be notable mainly because of their rarity.

Some of the critical theorists we have mentioned in this chapter turn a skeptical eye toward the claims of lawyers that their autonomy and power are justified by their expert training and skill. But they fall short of the careful analysis which would back up their skepticism. The summarizing thoughts I have presented here are not "proven fact." Rather they are a hypothetical model which can serve as an alternative to the predominant model of expertise tendered by the legal profession as "the way things are." They extend the critical perspective by providing testable propositions which, if not shown to be false, can lend substance to the critical theorist's skepticism.

We saw in chapter 2 that it is exceedingly difficult to define law. We saw in subsequent chapters that it is sometimes even difficult to defend the proposition that law differs in any significant way from the ordinary processes of society. In our examination of the legal profession, however, we see some evidence that law is indeed a separate social phenomenon which must be studied on its own terms. The ambiguous status of lawyers in the eyes of others, their peculiar history as a separate occupational group, and the differences which distinguish them from other professionals, all announce that the field of law can be usefully studied as a distinct aspect of social process.

SUMMARY

Throughout this chapter we have seen a variety of forms of legal practice and conflicting interpretations of those forms and their origins, history, and consequences for the success or failure of the legal system to furnish its primary product—justice. We have seen that the profession is highly differentiated in the United States according to type of law specialty, type of client served, type of workday experience, and personal background. We have also seen that this differentiation goes hand in hand with stratification: the unequal distribution of prestige, power, and wealth between different ranks of lawyers.

Both functionalist and conflict theorists acknowledge that professional stratification closely parallels patterns of stratification in society as a whole. They disagree over the conflict theorist's conclusion that inequality within the profession has the effect of intensifying the injustices to which poor persons often fall victim. Functionalists see the structure of the profession as a neutral response of people (lawyers) with normal free-market instincts to the hierarchically structured needs of people from different ranks within society. To them, the profession's structure is a result, not a cause, of the unequal distribution of wealth and power in society. To conflict theorists, the lawyer's role is not neutral because the business he deals with is the business of conflict, which means the making and preserving of inequalities. By maintaining tight controls over the number of practitioners and their business practices, the professional elite effectively insures that millions of people receive either no legal advice or inferior service, and that those with more power and wealth are able to purchase services which widen the gap between themselves and the poor.

REFERENCES

ABEL, RICHARD (1981), Legal Services, in Marvin Olsen and Michael Micklin (eds.), *Handbook of Applied Sociology: Frontiers of Contemporary Research*, New York: Praeger.

ABEL-SMITH, BRIAN AND ROBERT STEVENS (1967), *Lawyers and the Courts: A Sociological Study of the English Legal System, 1750–1965*, London: Heinemann.

AUERBACH, JEROLD S. (1976), *Unequal Justice: Lawyers and Social Change in Modern America*, New York: Oxford University Press.

BAZELON, DAVID (1960), Portrait of a Business Generalist, *Commentary*, 24, 277–86.

CARLIN, JEROME (1966), *Lawyers' Ethics: A Survey of the New York City Bar*, New York: Russell Sage Foundation.

CURRAN, BARBARA (1977), *The Legal Needs of the Public: The Final Report of a National Survey*, Chicago: American Bar Foundation.

ERLANGER, HOWARD AND DOUGLAS KLEGON (1978), Socialization Effects of Professional School: The School Experience and Student Orientations to Public Interest Concerns, *Law and Society Review*, 13, 1, pp. 11–35.

ERLANGER, HOWARD (1978), Young Lawyers and Work in the Public Interest, *American Bar Foundation Research Journal*, pp. 83–104.

HALBERSTAM, DAVID (1979), *The Powers that Be*, New York: Dell Pub. Co., Inc.

HANDLER, JOEL (1967), *The Lawyer and His Community: The Practicing Bar in a Middle-Sized City*, Madison: University of Wisconsin Press.

HEINZ, JOHN; EDWARD LAUMANN; CHARLES CAPPELL; TERENCE HALLIDAY; AND MICHAEL SCHAALMAN (1976), Diversity, Representation, and Leadership in an Urban Bar: A First Report on a Survey of the Chicago Bar, *American Bar Foundation Research Journal*, No. 3 (Summer), 717–85.

HEINZ, JOHN AND EDWARD LAUMANN (1979), The Legal Profession: Client Interests, Professional Roles, and Social Hierarchies, *American Bar Foundation* reprint from Michigan Law Review 76, 7, 1111–42.

HENDERSON, DAN FENNO (1969), Japanese Lawyers: Types and Roles in the Legal Profession, *Law and Society Review*, 3, 2 & 3, 411–13.

HODGE, R.; SIEGEL, P. M.; AND ROSSI, P. H. (1964), Occupational Prestige in the United States, 1925–1963. *American Journal of Sociology*, 70: 286–302.

KATZ, JACK (1978), Lawyers for the Poor in Transition: Involvement, Reform, and the Turnover Problem in the Legal Services Program, *Law and Society Review*, 12, 2, pp. 275–300.

KIDDER, ROBERT (1969), Report of the Conference on the Comparative Study of the Legal Profession with Special Reference to India, *Law and Society Review*, 3, 2 & 3.

LAUMANN, EDWARD AND JOHN HEINZ (1977), Specialization and Prestige in the Legal Profession: The Structure of Deference, *American Bar Foundation Research Journal*, No. 1 (Winter), 155–216.

LOCHNER, PHILIP, JR. (1975), The No-Fee and Low Fee Legal Practice of Private Attorneys, *Law and Society Review* 9, 3, 431–73.

MARKS, F. RAYMOND WITH KIRK LESWING AND BARBARA FORTINSKY   (1972), *The Lawyer, The Public, and Professional Responsibility*, Chicago: American Bar Foundation.

MAYHEW, LEON AND ALBERT REISS, JR.   (1969), The Social Organization of Legal Contacts, *American Journal of Sociology*, 34 (June), 309–19.

MEDCALF, LINDA   (1978), *Law and Identity: Lawyers, Native Americans and Legal Practice*. Beverly Hills, Calif.: Sage Publications, Inc.

MORRISON, CHARLES   (1969), Lawyers and Litigants in a North Indian District: Notes on Informal Aspects of the Legal System, *Law and Society Review*, 3, 2–3, 301–302.

N.O.R.C. (NATIONAL OPINION RESEARCH CENTER)   (1953), Jobs and Occupations: A Popular Evaluation, in R. Bendix and S. M. Lipset (eds.), *Class, Status, and Power: A Reader in Social Stratification*, New York: Free Press.

OSBORNE, J. J.   (1979), *The Associates*, Boston: Houghton-Mifflin.

REISS, A. J.   (1961), *Occupations and Social Status*, New York: Free Press.

ROSENTHAL, DOUGLAS   (1974), *Lawyer and Client: Who's in Charge?* New York: Russell Sage Foundation.

RUESCHEMEYER, DIETRICH   (1973), *Lawyers and Their Society: A Comparative Study of the Legal Profession in Germany and the United States*. Cambridge, Mass.: Harvard University Press.

SANDERS, CLINTON   (1975), Caught in the Con-Game: The Young, White Drug User's Contact with the Legal System, *Law and Society Review*, 9, 2, 197–217.

SARFATTI LARSON, MAGALI   (1977), *The Rise of Professionalism: A Sociological Analysis*. Berkeley, Calif.: University of California Press.

SLOVAK, JEFFREY   (1979), Working for Corporate Actors: Social Change and Elite Attorneys in Chicago, *American Bar Foundation Research Journal*, No. 3 (Summer), 465–500.

SLOVAK, JEFFREY   (1980), Giving and Getting Respect: Prestige and Stratification in a Legal Elite, *American Bar Foundation Research Journal*, No. 1, (Winter), 31–68.

SLOVAK, JEFFREY   (1981), Lawyers in American Industry: Structural Determinants of Professional Expansion. Paper presented at 1981 Annual Meetings of the American Sociological Association, Toronto, Ontario.

SMIGEL, ERWIN   (1969), *The Wall Street Lawyer: Professional Organization Man?* Bloomington, Ind.: Indiana University Press.

STERN, PHILIP   (1980), *Lawyers on Trial*, New York: Times Books.

STRIKER, JOHN AND ANDREW SHAPIRO   (1977), *Super Threats: How to Sound Like a Lawyer and Get Your Rights on Your Own*, New York: Dell Publ. Co., Inc.

STUMPF, HARRY; HENRY SCHROERLUKE; AND FORREST DILL   (1971), The Legal Profession and Legal Services: Explorations in Local Bar Politics, *Law and Society Review*, 6, 1, 47–67.

TOHARIA, JOSE   (1975), Judicial Independence in an Authoritarian Regime: The Case of Contemporary Spain, *Law and Society Review*, 9, 3, 475–96.

UNGER, ROBERTO MANGABEIRA   (1976), *Law in Modern Society*, New York: Free Press.

WASSERSTROM, RICHARD   (1971), Lawyers and Revolution, in J. Black, (ed.), *Radical Lawyers*, New York: Avon Books, 74–83.

WEXLER, STEPHEN   (1971), The Poverty Lawyer as Radical, in J. Black, (ed.), *Radical Lawyers*, New York: Avon Books, 209–231.

10

MORALITY AND JUSTICE: IS THERE A PSYCHOLOGICAL BASIS FOR LAW?

INTRODUCTION

How do you react when you hear that some well-known professional athlete has just signed a contract guaranteeing more than $1 million per year salary? Does the question of fairness ever cross your mind when you reflect that the newscaster you watch each day on television gets paid more each year than you may earn in a lifetime?

Is it fair for whites and males to make special sacrifices so that blacks and females can gain access to jobs or places in medical school?

If you know that out of the 4 billion people now populating the earth, nearly three-fourths of them are undernourished, how can you feel comfortable with yourself when you go to your well-stocked refrigerator for a snack? What do you feel as you pass from store to store doing your Christmas shopping and you must step over or around a disheveled old derelict sprawled in his own vomit?

Looking to your own future, what if world energy and raw materials become exhausted? How will your friends and neighbors react? How will Americans treat each other, not to mention people from other lands? How much deprivation would you be willing to accept before you decided to support a "law of the jungle" justification for war?

My purpose here is not to thrash you with guilt. Each of these questions deals with the issue of fairness or justice, though they come from many different kinds of situations. They are variations on a set of issues which social psychologists have recently been involved in developing.

Some sociologists do not think that such questions have any place in the scientific study of society. Questions of value cannot be answered scientifically (e.g., see Black, 1973). Therefore some who use this book will probably feel that the material presented in this chapter belongs in a book on theology or philosophy.

But social psychologists who have done research in this area argue that they can develop a general psychological theory which explains why people obey rules, share things, help each other, try to be fair to each other, or, in short, act "civilized." Their success in this venture would be significant to most of the issues raised elsewhere in this book, because they could then explain patterns of legal development and the operations of legal institutions as being logical consequences of predictable psychological processes. A confirmed general theory would give us an explanation of legal practices not only in our own culture but also in all other cultures, because it would identify universal factors about human behavior, factors which operate in the same way wherever humans live in social contact with each other.

In this chapter, we will review some of these theories, the evidence which has been gathered in their defense, and their implications for some of the basic issues we have examined from nonpsychological perspectives elsewhere in this book. We will also see that a serious challenge to these social psychological theories has begun to arise among some social psychologists who question the entire enterprise of developing a general thory of human psychology. We will see that within psychology itself, a move is afoot to reorient theory to make it more consistent with sociology's critical theory (chapter 5). Within psychology, as within sociology, the challenge is to fit theory with the evidence of conflict, the effects of power differentials, and the dynamics of collective action.

STAGES OF COGNITIVE DEVELOPMENT

Where do we get our ideas about morality and justice? How do we come to know that one choice we might make is "right" and the other "wrong"? Do we learn these attitudes in the same way as learning arithmetic, or how to drive, or the geography of Asia?

One approach to such questions is to theorize that our ideas about morality and justice develop in regular, predictable stages as we pass through the various developmental stages of childhood. The idea is that interaction with others, combined with our "readiness to learn" (which is determined by our maturation and by our having achieved previous levels of development), produces a sequence of beliefs or attitudes about (1) what happens if a rule is obeyed, as opposed to the outcome of rule breaking, and (2) what kind of distribution of scarce resources would be *fair*. Each belief *stage* is a prerequisite to the next, much as a college curriculum is built on the assumption that you must take lower-level courses before you are ready for advanced ones.

The Development of Moral Judgment

The Swiss psychologist, Jean Piaget, pioneered this *cognitive* perspective (1965) in his studies of the development of moral judgment among children. He patiently watched children at play and periodically asked them to explain the rules of their games. He observed that their answers could be reliably classified and that each child's answer could usually be predicted by knowing the child's age. Younger children gave answers which Piaget classified as showing *heteronomous morality*, while older children displayed *autonomous morality*.

Heteronomous morality is a set of beliefs which lead a person to strict obedience of the *fear of punishment* or other externally imposed bad outcomes. In very young children, for example, there is often not even the recognition that a rule *can* be disobeyed. For them, a rule such as "Stop at all red lights" is so absolute that they would think it physically impossible to go through a red light. Rules, in other words, have the same absolute reality for them as a brick wall. The world they see does not permit any behavior besides rule compliance. When Piaget questioned children about what would happen if they broke a rule in a game of marbles in order to get a better shot, the youngest could not even imagine such an act. All they could do was repeat the rule, showing that they saw no choice in the situation.

A child at this stage typically chooses pain-inflicting punishments as the only way to treat rule violators. Such *expiational* punishments reflect the child's egocentric orientation, in which avoidance of pain is the main reason for obedience. The *effect* of an act, rather than the actor's *intent*, is the criterion such children use to evaluate good and bad: They would punish you even if you ". . . didn't mean it."

At the opposite extreme in Piaget's typology is *autonomous morality*. Children at this level obey rules because they recognize that the rules best serve the interests of all those involved in a moral-choice situation. These children would explain stopping at a red light as a reasonable choice because of the dangers to everybody when the rule is violated. They see the rule as a practical compromise and therefore as a directive which can, and sometimes should, be changed or ignored if circumstances change. If you suggested violating the rules of a marbles game, these children might consider doing so, but only if they did not care about continuing to play with the other child thus cheated, or if the suggested violation were adopted by all players as a new way to make the game more interesting.

In response to rule violations, children who have achieved autonomous morality reject expiational punishments in favor of *restitutive* actions. Their purpose is to restore the harmony which the rules were designed to protect. Such restitutive choices show that these older children have learned to see their own behavior in a wider social context, to put themselves "in the shoes" of others and recognize the need to treat others fairly. Because they have learned this art of empathizing with others, they also place more emphasis on a person's intentions. If you harmed someone "accidentally," they would consider milder punishment for you than if you did it "on purpose."

Between the extremes of heteronomous and autonomous morality as described above are several transitional stages which involve modifications of the extreme forms. For example, the child who cannot distinguish between moral and physical rules gradually learns that rules can be violated, but that when they are, someone older and bigger than they punishes them. Their obedience is still heteronomous because it is still produced by conditions *outside* themselves. Their decision about whether to obey or disobey a rule becomes dependent on whether or not they expect to "get caught." Only when they *internalize* rules, recognizing them as patterns which they want to follow because they choose to, do they begin to possess autonomous morality.

Piaget argued that the constancy of this pattern among children was the combined result of maturation and their experiences with rule making. Very young children typically learn to play games from older children. They usually do not help to make the rules. Therefore they experience rules as edicts handed down or imposed on them. They gain little or no understanding of the reasons for the rules. As they grow older, however, becoming the elders in the play group, they begin to have the experience of making up their own rules for games they invent or modify on an *ad hoc* basis. In bargaining with their peers over the structure of their play, they gain firsthand understanding of the purposes behind the rules they invent. They discover that without certain rules of restraint, for example, competition in their games may become so lopsided that it becomes boring and friends become unwilling to play. It is this discovery that rules are made by people, made for purposes, and changeable which forms the basis of moral maturation. To the extent that the child is able to generalize from the use of rules in games to the wider world of rules in general, that child achieves the highest level of moral development.

Piaget thus built a general theory of rule-learning from his "simple" observations of children's games. Children learn most of society's rules

from adults. Because adults are authority figures, who can insist on obedience and impose sanctions in case of violations, adult teaching of morality
is likely to produce only heteronomous morality. Moral maturation, then, is
not usually something parents or other adults can directly teach, whatever
they might like to think about their role in steering children in the right
direction. Moral maturity can only flower in interaction with peers, persons
of equal status who can neither impose their will nor be bossed around
against their will. Only if they abandon their superior position of power
over children, can adults play any role in bringing about the full moral
maturation of children.

Later psychologists have supported Piaget's developmental model
with some systematic research (Hoffman, 1970). More recent studies have
shown, however, that some of the more "mature" forms of thought may
appear in children at a much earlier age than Piaget suspected (Surber,
1977; Wellman, Larkey, and Somerville, 1979).

Some psychologists took Piaget's basic theory and expanded it with a
more elaborate set of stages. A substantial body of research now supports a
six-stage theory (Kohlberg, 1963). The first two are basically the same as
Piaget's heteronomous and autonomous morality. The other four are
"higher" levels of development which we can find among older children if
we present them with hypothetical moral dilemmas and listen to them
reasoning out a solution. Most children, and many adults, never mature
beyond the second stage. Some do achieve the more advanced levels, but
very few ever reach level six.

Let us pause for a moment to begin thinking how such findings might
relate to some of the sociological issues raised earlier in this book. We have
examined different explanations for the origins of law, for example. How
might we revise our understanding of law's origins if we knew that there
were orderly, universal patterns of moral development in all humans and
that research can reveal the conditions which produce that development?
One implication of such a position is that every society's methods of social
control would have to contain certain characteristics compatible with patterns of moral maturation in order to survive. If people learn the most
advanced forms of moral orientation through *participation* in judgmental or
conflict resolving situations, rather than by rote memorization of some list
of rules taught by authorities, then legal systems which deny participation
to their citizens should produce people with stunted moral development.
Such people would obey only those rules which they could not "get away
with" breaking. Surveillance and punishment would have to be widespread
because such a population would lack any inner commitment to laws. A
legal heritage may thus be a burden to people if they have not participated
in giving meaning and shape to it. Most Americans, for example, do not
recognize the major statements in the Bill of Rights. Unless told that the
statements come from that "sacred" legal document, they typically reject
Thomas Jefferson's masterpiece as a bunch of dangerous radical nonsense.

Perhaps only those who directly experienced and helped overthrow an onerous political tyranny can fully understand and identify with the legal principles which emerge from such experiences.

The Development of Justice Reasoning

Perhaps the connection between psychology and sociology will be clearer if we now shift our attention to a cognitive theory about the development of *justice* thinking. The approach used in moral-judgment research has been modified to study the ways in which children develop attitudes toward questions of what is fair. If a group of children, for example, spend an afternoon washing cars for neighbors, how does each child evaluate the fairness of the different ways to divide the proceeds? Should each child get an equal share? What about those who worked faster or who did the most disagreeable parts of the job—a larger share for them? What about giving more to the child who never has any money because his parents are poor? Should bigger children get more than smaller ones? These are all questions of *distributive justice*. They involve different issues from those studied in research on moral judgment. You can see that such questions lie at the heart of most law business.

Theoretically, maturation of ideas about distributive justice ought to mean increasingly complex reasoning which moves away from egocentric choices toward choices which take into account the complexities of group life (Damon, 1981). Following this reasoning, research indicates the existence of six stages of development:

1. Around age four—children say they alone should get as much as they want "because I want it"
2. Ages four to five—children say they should get the largest share because of some arbitrary, external, self-serving reason (e.g., "because we're boys")
3. Ages five to seven—everyone should get exactly the same share; no difference justifies different shares
4. Ages six to nine—people should get what they *deserve* according to how much they contributed or how well they behaved
5. Ages seven to ten—there are several valid, but competing justifications for claims to a share, necessitating compromise
6. Ages eight to twelve—as in level 5, there are alternatives, but the solution does not necessarily lie in some easy quantitative formula. The choices are hard and require tailor-made solutions.

In experiments with children who had to make distributional choices which would affect what they received, the results showed that the older the children, the more likely it was that they would make choices based on the more mature levels of justice thinking. Even more striking is the finding that maturation in justice thinking is even more closely associated with maturation in other areas of thought than it is with age alone. Apparently, ideas about justice develop in "clumps" along with other ideas (such as an understanding of money, competence in spatial orientation, the distinction between dreams and reality, and the relationships of different parts of the body). Thinking progresses through *wholistic* shifts from one mode to another, such as the shift away from egocentrism to awareness of the needs of others.

There is some evidence, then, that justice thinking develops in stages, along with other forms of thought, moving children away from egocentrism toward a more realistic recognition of their places in society. Other research brings out some complications in this model. If you consider the lot of younger children, for example, you might conclude that their choices are no more egocentric than those of older children. After all, they would not fare well if they had to abide by level four reasoning (you get out what you put in), since their youth makes them less able to contribute an equal share to a group venture. For older children to invoke the merit principle may be to take a stand that is to their advantage because of greater skill. In general, older children may look more "mature" simply because they have adopted positions which are to their advantage.

In a comparison of children's *imaginary* distributions of rewards (candy bars) with their *actual* distributions after they had completed group projects, about half of the children studied made the same choices in both real and imaginary situations (Damon, 1981). The other half regressed to less mature levels of reasoning as they moved from imaginary to real choices. They stated higher ideals of justice in theory than they actually practiced.

This could be a simple case of immaturity among the backsliders. But the evidence supported another interpretation: in real choice-making situations, a person's behavior is usually some compromise between justice and self-interest. Even the backsliders gave at least one candy bar (out of ten allotted to each experimental group) to the youngest and least competent members of each group. None of the older children reverted to the lowest levels of reasoning. Most fell, if at all, only one or two levels below their imaginary distribution choices.

Therefore justice reasoning does not displace self-interest. Rather, older children (and adults) find other more complicated ways of expressing their self-interest by the justice choices they make. Acting fairly does not mean making totally selfless choices. It does mean finding solutions which balance self-interest with the need to be fair.

Problems in the Use of Stage Analysis

Further research in this direction raises serious questions about the ability of psychological research alone to explain people's justice-related behavior. If we know that all people move through these different stages of cognitive development, and if we know that all the children in a particular group are older and more mature in their thinking, then we should be able to predict that their choices of distribution within their group will be made according to their high levels of maturity. Instead such children usually backslide toward the principle of *equality* when faced with real choices. (Damon, 1981.) They do better than groups of younger children in the sense that they can always arrive at an agreement about distribution, while younger groups often stalemate. Nevertheless, settlements apparently require people to suspend their most mature patterns of thought. The equality (or *parity*) principle evidently is a lowest common denominator and is, therefore, best-suited for promoting compromise.

Compare this finding with our discussion of dispute processing in chapter 7. There we saw that even in the most formal arenas of justice, litigation often follows the path of compromise through negotiation. Could these courtroom patterns be the result of psychological processes which operate wherever humans live and work together?

Or is there another reason more damaging to social psychological theory? Perhaps what the psychologist calls "more mature" justice thinking is simply the use of ideas with which the psychologist agrees? If equality is the principle which enables groups to distribute things fairly in the eyes of most group members, other "more mature" justice principles could be viewed as bargaining positions which individuals invoke when (1) they stand to gain from an alternative to the equality principle, (2) they have enough experience to know when to use alternative principles, and (3) they have enough power in a given situation to take what they want on the grounds of those alternative principles. "Maturation" may not be a process of learning "higher" forms of just reasoning. Older children may simply have had more opportunity to learn a larger repertoire of justifications for bidding on their share in distributional situations.

These theories of cognitive maturation, like many theories in social psychology, are based on the belief that experimental research can show us truths about all people at all times in all societies. Often this is an unstated assumption. Sometimes psychologists do not even recognize that they are making such claims. But they can be seen, for example, in Piaget's title *The Moral Judgment of the Child*. Though his study involved only urban Swiss children, he speaks of *the* child, by which we must assume that he means any child. Do his theories apply to Japanese children in the sixteenth century, to urban Columbian street children who have no families, or to Cheyenne children growing up to be buffalo hunters in the nineteenth century?

We may risk misclassifying a whole culture of people as "immature" in their thinking if their approach to distributive reasoning is different from our own. Several studies have shown that the same stages of development can be found in a wide variety of cultures, and even between different social classes (Kohlberg, 1969; Kohlberg and Kramer, 1969; Tapp and

Kohlberg, 1971; Turiel, Edwards, and Kohlberg, 1978). But they also show so much variation in the extent to which these populations had "achieved higher levels of moral maturity" that researchers have had to develop an explanation for moral underdevelopment in these cultures. They concluded that cross-cultural variations must be the result of variations in the wealth or poverty of people's experiences in role-taking situations which would increase maturity. "Culture may accelerate or retard movement through the stages but not the quality or order of these different modes of thinking" (Tapp and Kohlberg, 1971, p. 67). Some populations, in other words, are childlike because of their general lack of experience.

Does it make sense to portray such persons as childlike? We would have to say yes if we acknowledged no possible cross-cultural variations in the meaning of "moral maturity." But if we think of the tremendous diversity in class structures, religious systems, legal and political philosophies, and other major aspects of social differentiation, we must wonder about the wisdom of labeling some thought and behavior pattern "immature" simply because it differs from our middle-class American notions of maturity. The risk some psychologists apparently do not recognize is that, in trying to be "scientific," psychologists may fail to recognize their own cultural biases. Such biases then produce culture-bound measurements of the behaviors and attitudes of people whose social systems the psychologist misunderstands. It is a much different problem to develop a metric for moral judgment or justice reasoning across cultures. This latter kind of venture is riddled with variations of meaning derived from social diversity. Theories of cognitive development are particularly vulnerable to this kind of criticism.

JUSTICE AND COGNITIVE BALANCE

All the previously discussed theories in this chapter are *developmental*. They explain moral or justice reasoning as being the product of cognitive growth or maturation. A competing perspective is to treat people's thinking as the product of a need for inner *balance*. Here, instead of expecting different behaviors of people with different mental "ages," we concentrate on the demands of each choice-making situation in which justice is an issue, because we expect people's choices to reflect a need for balance or fairness *regardless* of their level of maturity.

Theories of this kind, for example, predict that you would object if your professor approached you midway through a course saying that he was going to give you the only A grade in the class because he liked you. Such favoritism would make you uncomfortable (Austin and Walster, 1974) even though it would obviously be to your advantage. Balance theories say that you would take some kind of action to bring either your behavior, the professor's behavior, or your own thinking into balance. You might argue for equal treatment of others in the class. You might try to organize a protest of the professor's decision or take the matter to the dean. But if such actions were infeasible or ineffective, a shift would probably take place in your own thinking about the fairness of the situation. You might work a bit harder in order to "deserve" the advantage, or you might begin to favor lurking suspicions that you actually are better than everyone else in the class. You might even shift the focus entirely by concluding that this particular windfall makes up for unfairly low grades you got from other professors. You try, in short, to restore either actual or psychological balance, because imbalance means high anxiety (Walster, Walster, and Berscheid, 1978).

Balance theorists assert that people cannot endure the feeling of injustice, the imbalance of it, and that the actions they take, including their adjustment of internal thought patterns, conform with the predicted need to redress the balance. Balance theorists disagree over the mechanisms which produce the drive for balance, and this disagreement produces differences in their predictions about where and how balance points get chosen. We will compare two balance theories here: (1) *equity theory*, which says that the balancing process centers on a universal drive to maintain ratios (balance) between the actor's *inputs* and their rewards, and (2) *justice-motive theory* which says that the motive to seek justice for everyone in society comes from a person's learned desire to view the world as a place where people get what they deserve. These two theories are related, since justice-motive theory evolved in part from equity theory. But they make quite different predictions about how people will behave in situations where their choices raise questions about fairness.

Equity as Justice

According to equity theorists, we view a situation as fair when we believe that our treatment has been *proportional* to our *inputs*. If a group of children is given a project to do and there is variation in the amount of the task completed by each child, each child should identify as *fair* any system of reward distributions which balances his or her own self-interest (give it all to me) with notions about how much each child contributed (Leventhal and Anderson, 1970). In one experiment of this type, children who saw their own work as roughly equal to others' chose equal shares. If they thought they did more, they took larger shares, though none tried to take the whole prize even in experiments where no experimenter or group member could stop them. If they did less than others, they tended to choose a nearly equal share (thus showing that the equity principle competes with self-interest motives in influencing choices).

Why do people act equitably instead of selfishly? Because they learn that it is in their own self-interest to do so. People share because they are selfish. They learn that when they do not share they are often punished or lose their own share along with everything else because others also want a share. People act equitably so long as they think that is the way to maximize their outcomes (Walster, Walster, and Berscheid, 1978, p. 16).

Balance is the key to equity theory. But it is not a balance based on equality. The theory holds that equal distribution will seem fair only when people feel they all contributed an equal share. What must be balanced is not people's needs. Rather, distributional outcomes should be proportional to the efforts and value which each participant puts into the joint enterprise.

The Justice Motive

Victim derogation: "Getting what they deserve."   Suppose you are chosen as a paid volunteer to help in a research project on your campus. You and several other students are to act as prison guards or prisoners for the next two weeks. Prisoners will be "arrested" by real police officers, photographed, fingerprinted, and locked in basement rooms of a campus building for the duration of the experiment. Guards will live a normal life except while on duty. You and the others draw straws to see who will play which part. You become a guard.

How would you behave in that role? When experimenters tried this (Zimbardo, 1972), they had to end the experiment after only six days to prevent further deterioration in both guard and prisoner behavior. Within that short time, the guards became increasingly sadistic and abusive, and the prisoners became self-destructively passive. Guards tormented prisoners, and prisoners began making "deals" with guards to betray fellow prisoners in exchange for preferential treatment.

Anyone reading these accounts or seeing the filmed record of this experiment finds it difficult to remember that these were just college students who had been assigned to their roles *by chance.* Why does this happen? Is it just a freak occurrence, contrived by clever scientists? Did they just happen to pick sadistic students for guards? Can you confidently say you would have behaved differently?

According to justice-motive theory, you would behave in the same way. Research on such behavior and reasoning has led to the discovery of a widespread tendency to "derogate the victim" (Lerner and Simmons, 1966; Lerner and Matthews, 1967). When someone is harmed, either by other people or by nature, we may outwardly show sympathy, but we often say to ourselves, "It's too bad, but he probably deserved it." We selectively scan the situation in order to bolster our belief that it was deserved. We react this way especially when we can do nothing to help the victim (when the harm is irreversible or our resources are too meager or remote to be of aid or comfort [Berscheid and Walster, 1967]).

For example, rape victims often get little sympathy from those around them. People make insinuations about the victim's "sexy clothes" or "careless" manner or "seductiveness." We hear people saying "Of course she got raped. What else could she expect walking around there at that hour!" In some societies husbands abandon raped wives. Some cultures even put rape victims to death, on the assumption that their rape was evidence of their sinfulness.

Bystanders sometimes just watch while victims are beaten, robbed, or otherwise brutalized in public places (Piliavin, Rodin, and Piliavin, 1969; Piliavin and Walster, 1972). Part of their indifference stems from the stranger status of both victim and attacker. The bystander cannot be sure that the attack is unjustified—maybe the victim has a history of harming the attacker. Who knows? The bystander's own personal fear of attack motivates him or her to see the victim as one who may deserve the attack. Justice-motive theory adds that even without that personal fear, the bystander's strong motive to see the world as a just place in which to live produces victim derogation (Chaikes and Darley, 1973).

Looking at the "prison" experiment, we can see that both guard and prisoner behavior may be a result of the strong motive to believe in a just world where people get what they deserve. The guards became brutal because their role in the experiment arbitrarily gave them privileges which the prisoners were denied. In order to continue to accept such privilege without the painful anxiety of feeling undeserving, they had to adjust their view of the prisoners (they were not given the option of switching places with prisoners). They began to see the prisoners as really different from guards, inferior to them, and undeserving. Similarly, the prisoners in some cases began to think of themselves as guilty in some vague way, and therefore deserving of the real torment inflicted on them. When the experiment was over, their answers to questions showed that both guards and prisoners had adopted interpretations of the situation which "made sense" of the real differences in privilege they experienced.

To the balance theorist, the conclusion is that it would have been too painful for either guard or prisoner to endure the inequality without derogating the victim (the prisoner), because we all have a strong need to believe that the world is just, that we all have good reason to expect fair treatment, and that prolonged unfair treatment must actually be fair.

We should also notice that in the prison situation, derogating the victim produced a vicious cycle: the more the guards abused the prisoners, the stronger their motive to view the prisoners as sneaky, dishonest, weak, or in other words deserving of scorn and punishment. Conversely, the more they were abused, the more the prisoners adopted passive responses instead of resisting the guards' outrageous actions. Their passivity reinforced the guards' view that prisoners deserved harsh treatment, while the harsh treatment itself created the need (and justification) for even harsher treatment.

It is tempting to conclude that the law, like the scientists in this experiment, steps in to protect us not only from being victims but from becoming victimizers. In earlier chapters of this book, we considered three sociological explanations for the origins of law and legal systems: (1) custom, (2) structure, and (3) conflict. Does psychology have a more basic explanation? Perhaps we have come to recognize the serious threat to justice inherent in our own psychological plasticity. Perhaps we build legal structures as a way to insure actual, rather than psychological, justice, since we have learned how freely our minds can wander into psychological self-justification. Certainly the language and public posture of our legal systems pay a great deal of attention to preventing victimization, and some to compensating victims (Macaulay and Walster, 1971).

However, both sociological and psychological limits seem to be constantly thwarting this high objective. Because of limits on institutional capacity, judges usually encourage lawyers to accept a solution based on compromise. In these negotiations, the aim is to guard against a wrongdoer's worst possible actions rather than to achieve a complete restoration of balance between wrongdoer and victim. Practical as this may be, it creates the impression that the legal system agrees that the victim "deserves" some loss, since compromises officially sanction solutions in which the victim is not totally vindicated or compensated (Friedman and Macaulay, 1969, p. 182). Limits in our institutions thus reinforce, rather than eliminate, our psychologically fluid tendency to derogate the victim.

Even worse, our legal institutions normally put power into the hands of a few individuals, just as the prison experiment empowered the guards. Even legal institutions must, for "practical" reasons, delegate authority. Research evidence indicates that a major hazard of such power is the development, in the mind of power holders, of the idea that they are "better" than less powerful persons, who are unworthy and despicable (Kipnis, 1972). Because they reason with the same need for balance as we do, the people we invest with the power to protect us from our own psychological plasticity become our exploiters and we their willing victims.

Is there a justice motive?   The attempt to make sense of the paradox that people so often derogate victims led a number of social psychologists to look for a broader context within which to understand it. This effort led first to the "just-world hypothesis" (Lerner and Simmons, 1966) and thence to justice-motive theory. The theory explains not only why people derogate victims, but how this apparently cruel, some might even say barbaric, behavior fits in with the strong beliefs people have about justice and their willingness to act generously, to share, to be polite, to be patient, to be considerate—in short, to act "civilized."

The justice motive is not inborn. It grows out of a simpler self-interested motive to control one's environment so as to find pleasure and avoid pain. To this point, therefore, justice-motive theory resembles equity theory. But whereas equity theory hangs all justice reasoning on this basic selfishness, justice-motive theory tells us that basic selfishness, in its confrontation with the demands of others, becomes transformed into a variety of modes of justice reasoning. These modes have a wholistic quality, that is, they act as templates shaping our thoughts and actions in several different kinds of relationships. By *template* we mean a preformed pattern which arranges the elements of a process into repeatable final products. The electronic pathways wired into a computer are examples of templates, as are the pattern boards used in automatic weaving machines to determine which pattern of cloth will be woven. Programmed cylinders used to make music in player pianos and mechanical music boxes are also templates. Special features of each kind of relationship lead to the formation of the different justice templates. The result is that mature adults do not constantly revert to actions or thoughts based on simple "what's in it for me" reasoning. Instead they invoke that wholistic cluster of justifications (the justice template) which they have come to "feel" is appropriate for the particular relationship in which justice has become an issue.

How does this "feeling" for the right kind of justice arise? It comes from the development of the *personal contract* (Lerner, 1981). As children begin to experience the environment, they find that some experiences repeat themselves. A cry brings someone to change a wet diaper or it summons a source of food. A fire brings a feeling of heat. Too much of it produces pain. Later, certain words like "please" and "thank you" bring praise and smiles from important adults. These examples are only a glimpse of the countless instances where the environment can begin to seem *stable* to the child. The repetition of an event or a person's actions begins to be expected. From being expected it becomes a *right* in some sense, because its occurrence assures the child that the environment is stable enough to be able to make reliable choices about action. The *personal contract* is the "deal" we make with our environment in which we take action, assuming that we have a right to expect certain results. We feel angry and cheated if we do not get those results.

Children who grow up in stable environments are more likely to develop the ability to *defer gratification* than children from chaotic, unstable environments, because gratification deferral is one of those choices we make when our expectations have been repeatedly fulfilled. If, when you "save your pennies," you learn that you can count on them being there when you need them, you are more likely to save than if you experience robberies, fires, frauds, thefts, inflation, or other disasters (instability in the environment) which repeatedly wipe out your savings. You make similar decisions about whether or not to be polite, generous, helpful, cooperative, and, most important here, fair in your dealings with others. Unstable environments stunt the development of trust and the assumption that the world is a just place where you get what you deserve.

If there is enough stability, then trust does develop and the child becomes committed to a *personal contract* (Lerner, 1981). The personal contract means postponing immediate gratification of desires in the expectation of even better long-run rewards. We speak of this expectation in terms of getting what we *deserve*. It is this personal theory of deserving which supports the act of deferring gratification. The child's reasoning would be, "I could have eaten the candy right away (or cheated in the game, or hogged the swing, or butted ahead in line, or copied from a classmate's test), but I waited, so now I *deserve* a reward (a whole box of candy, or fair play in the game, or a share of time on the swing, or a guaranteed place in line, or a good grade from the teacher)."

As the personal contract becomes established, it begins to become more generalized. The child learns that others also have similar expectations and that in order to get along with them, their personal contracts must be respected. Learning the importance of accommodating the personal contracts of others leads to the development of the *social contract*. By *social contract* we mean the willingness of people to abide by rules and to act with restraint in pursuit of their own interests. The social contract is the agreement to act civilized, but it is "signed" or endorsed by people because of their desire to maintain their own personal contracts—the stable patterns to which they have come to feel entitled.

This theory of a *justice motive* produced by the experience of living in a stable environment represents a major departure from previous ways of explaining why and how people learn to obey rules and become socialized members of society. It differs because it reverses the order of appearance of the social contract. The conventional notion has been that society and its rules are already there when we are born into this world and our learning consists of learning those rules and being disciplined to follow them. The social contract, in other words, is usually treated as a *fait accompli* (something already fixed with obligatory rights and duties) facing each new person entering society.

Justice-motive theory says that the opposite happens: Children develop the personal contract, the psychology of *deserving*, even in the absence of existing rules if stability in their environment leads them to expect certain outcomes. Expectancy gives the child a sense of entitlement, or deserving, even if nobody has taught the child such ideas. Society's rules may say one thing, but if people regularly experience the violation of those rules, they feel entitled to the conditions produced by rule violation. Conversely, if rule following consistently produces predictable outcomes, people develop a sense of entitlement to those outcomes, not because society endorses those rules, but because expectations are repeatedly validated by experience.

Therefore the social contract is not threatened by inadequately socialized young savages who need more lessons in proper behavior. Rather it is threatened by adults whose responses to children are inconsistent, unstable, or contradictory. By failing to provide a stable environment for children, we force them into the only alternative to "civilized behavior," namely the "jungle" attitude of taking whatever they can get whenever and however they can, because they never know what tomorrow may bring. Children begin to support the social contract only if they have developed a motive for protecting a general theory of deservedness which produces deserved outcomes.

This theory differs from equity theory because it says that the equity principle is only one of several justice standards which we learn to invoke selectively, depending on the situation. The standards we use differ from each other because of the different kinds of relationships we have with others. If we identify totally with another person (as we might, for example, with a best friend, a sibling, or a parent), we tend to feel very secure about that person's willingness and ability to support our expectations. We feel less certain about someone less close (such as a fellow employee, classmate, or fellow trumpeter in the marching band).

We adopt different norms of justice to fit our assessments of the quality of relationship involved. Besides equity justice, which we use in only one kind of situation, we also sometimes rely on

1. The justice of *needs* (as expressed in the Marxian phrase, "From each according to his abilities, to each according to his needs"). Here it does not matter how hard you worked or how much value you invested in a joint project. Your "share" is determined by what you need.
2. The justice of *parity*, which means that all participants get an equal share regardless of their needs or inputs.
3. *Legal* justice (Lerner groups this together with Darwinian justice), which allocates rewards to those who *win* them in either regulated or unregulated competition. Rewards are deserved because "the best person won," but the outcome must be backed by force because the loser is usually bitter.
4. The justice of *entitlement* (involving social obligations and contract) where allocation of rewards is deserved because the person occupying a certain social position is entitled *by right of social position* to those rewards (e.g., the "divine right of kings," "rank has its privileges," "let the buyer beware").
5. The justice of *justified self-interest*, where rewards are distributed on a competitive basis, but where the outcome is not challenged by the loser because the competition is accepted as a fair contest.

We can predict the predominance of each type of justice reasoning if we know the type of relationship involved. Two key factors determine which mode of reasoning will prevail: (1) whether the relationship in which rewards are being distributed is perceived by a participant as *personal* or *positional*, and (2) how *closely* the participant is involved with others in the relationship.

The *person-position* difference refers to our perceptions of others as either unique individuals who remain the same in different situations (*person*) or as occupants of social positions which can be filled by any number of qualified persons (*position*). Lerner lists three degrees of *closeness* in relationships: (1) *identity*—a relationship so close that we feel empathy for the other; (2) *unit*—a cooperative relationship where we see certain others as belonging to the same "team" or unit, and therefore as pursuing shared goals; and (3) *nonunit*—we see others as different or as having separate goals and therefore in competition with us. Any nonunit relationship is a competitive or conflictful one, though competition and conflict can arise in identity and unit relationships if the mode of justice most relevant for that relationship is violated.

How do the relationships and the modes of justice fit together? Table 10.1 shows the connections thus far supported by the results of experiments. Read this table as showing the way one individual (to simplify discussion, we will call this person *ego*) evaluates the fairness of his or her relationships with others in six kinds of distributive-justice situations. Notice first that equity justice fits in only one cell (cell 5). In this case, ego perceives the other person as being a position holder rather than as a unique individual, and as being different from ego but involved in some cooperative venture. The relationship between ground control engineers and space shuttle astronauts during a flight would be an example of this relationship. In the closest relationship (cell 1, person-identity), the justice of needs predominates. Here, ego has a lasting relationship with someone and is willing to sacrifice anything to meet the needs of the other because ego feels the other's needs as if they were ego's. Romeo and Juliet may not have fulfilled each other's needs very well, but they fit this category. They felt each other's needs so totally that suicide was their only option when they thought their beloved was dead. On the other hand, if ego identifies with someone else because they occupy the same *position* (e.g., both are teenagers, or pipefitters, or Catholics, or Chicanos), then ego will insist on getting (or assigning to those others) what people in those shared positions are *entitled to* (cell 4, entitlement justice).

Cells 3 and 6 concern conflictful or competitive relationships. Where, for example, two families have been feuding with each other for years, members of each family would look on any damage they could do to the other side as just, whether they did it through law or through any other means (Darwinian "survival of the fittest" justice). The conflict is personalized. Justice to them means defeat of an opponent. Hence it fits in cell 3. Cell 6 is well-illustrated in the tension students usually feel when taking

TABLE 10.1 The Effects of Relationship Differences on Ego's Justice Preferences

Other as Person or Position Holder	DEGREE OF EGO'S IDENTITY WITH OTHER		
	IDENTITY	UNIT	NONUNIT
PERSON	1. NEEDS* (Perception of other as self)	2. PARITY* (Perception of similarity belonging with other)	3. LAW, DARWINIAN JUSTICE* (Perceptions of contesting interests and personal differences related to claims)
POSITION	4. SOCIAL OBLIGATION AND CONTRACT* (Perception of self in other's circumstances of need)	5. EQUITY* (Perception of equivalence with other)	6. JUSTIFIED SELF-INTEREST* (Scarce resources, with equally legitimate claims within the "rules")

*The form of justice preferred by ego under these relational circumstances.
Source: Melvin Lerner, 1975, p. 15.

"standardized" tests, such as IQ, college, or professional school entrance examinations, where scores are determined by how well they perform compared with all others who took the test. They usually hold no personal animosity toward others taking the test. But access to scarce resources (places in the entering classes of colleges or professional schools) hangs in the balance. People around them may be facing the destruction of their dreams. But they will feel fairly treated if they score well and go on to their "reward." Assuming there was no cheating, and no computer scoring error, their feeling about those who fail will be "That's the breaks."

The assignment of justice types to these categories is not based on intuition. It is the result of experiments on groups of children doing jobs and then deciding how to distribute the rewards. Each child was told that a child in the next room was doing the same task. When the other child was identified as a member of the subject child's *team*, thus making the final product a team product, subject children usually decided that the reward should be equally shared with the other child regardless of who produced more. But when the child was told that the other child was simply another person doing the same job (*position* relationship rather than *personal*), most children gave themselves more than half the reward if they were told they had produced more than the other child, and less than half if they were told they had produced less.

Similar experiments support the rest of this typology, particularly where it goes beyond equity theory in explaining the determinants of justice-related actions. Equity theory does not acknowledge differences among kinds of justice thinking. It says that in all of these relationships, ego should react according to a strict weighing of inputs and outputs along with other motives such as pure self-interest. Justice-motive theory says that self-interest does not enter as a separate motive, but rather plays a role in giving birth to the various forms of justice reasoning we see in table 10.1. It says for example, that ego will be as upset when given more than a fair share of rewards as when given less. Equity theory, in contrast, predicts that there will be greater distress when ego comes out on the short end of the stick than when he or she comes out ahead, because the self-interest motive will produce variation even though the equity motive does not. Experiments showing the predominance of parity over equity justice in "person-unit" relationships (cell 2 in table 10.1) support the proposition that people do not start new encounters from scratch, with a set of mental scales and looking for equity. Rather they approach relationships with a developed concept of the type of justice appropriate to that type of relationship.

By locating *legal* justice in the category of *person-nonunit* relationships (cell 3), research has exposed the very limited circumstances under which purely legal methods of dealing with a conflict will produce the *feeling* that justice has been done. Strict adherence to legal rules and procedures is not meant, nor is it able, to produce the justices of parity, equity, needs, or even social obligation (a proposition which should raise eyebrows among those legal scholars who try to formulate formal theories of particular laws to justify the decisions of judges). Where courts take these other feelings of justice into consideration, they do so by "bending" formal rules, by considering "extenuating circumstances," or "public policy," or "community standards." Accusations against judges for "making laws instead of interpreting them" arise from just such attempts to accommodate alternative models of justice reasoning.

MACROJUSTICE: BEYOND THE INDIVIDUAL

All the material we have discussed so far focuses on the individual. Moral judgment and issues of justice have been treated by psychologists as conditions or tendencies developed *within each person* because of the interaction between characteristics we all have at birth and social facts we all face. For many social psychologists, the dominant research agenda has been to identify those universal human qualities which shape our responses to our environment.

Recently, however, a move away from this agenda has begun to gather some momentum, though it is by no means a flood tide as yet. Some social psychologists have begun to question whether it is possible to find universal human qualities uninfluenced by the specific variations of time and place in which people live (Riegel, 1976; Rosnow, 1978; Gergen, 1978; Sampson, 1977, 1978, 1981; Smith, 1978). They believe that "basic" motives, such as equity or the justice motive, are not basic at all. Motives seem basic only because the language used to describe them strongly dominates the thinking and teaching of particular societies at particular times in history. The problem is that psychology is dominated by a natural-science paradigm which cannot accommodate itself to cultural-historical relativity and which is therefore inappropriate for psychology. Culture and history affect the thinking and behavior of both the scientists' subjects and the scientists themselves. The natural-science paradigm which most psychologists accept blinds them to many of the limits and biases in their own thought.

When we look at the literature on equity theory and justice-motive theory, for example, we find most of the research focused on the choices made by individuals in contrived experimental situations. The individualistic results obtained in these experiments are produced in part by the limited concept of justice held by the researchers (Brickman, 1981). They deal only with *microjustice* (ideas of justice applied only to the actions, choices, and outcomes of individuals) and typically ignore *macrojustice* (a concept of what is fair for a group *as a whole*).

For example, in the contrived experiment, it is possible to arrange the rewards within a group so that people, when questioned about the payoff to each individual, will say that each payoff is fair because it fits with each person's inputs into whatever project the experimenter had them do. If we then ask about the overall pattern of rewards between subgroups of that population, the very same respondents may call it unfair because it is too unequal (Brickman, 1975; Brickman and Bryan, 1975, 1976). In other words, when people set their sights only on the question of justice for one individual at a time, they apply a different standard of justice (microjustice) from the one they use to look at all of the outcomes taken together (macro-justice). The whole is greater than the sum of its parts. Twenty justices can add up to one big injustice.

Merit (to each according to his or her contribution) is a microjustice standard because it examines only the inputs and outcomes of individuals. Equality is the purest form of macrojustice because it says that the *overall pattern* of distribution determines whether or not justice has been done. Standards of limited inequality (e.g., no one shall receive more than twice what anyone else receives) are also macrojustice standards because attention is on the overall distribution rather than the outcome of any one individual.

In concrete cases, macrojustice and microjustice principles may be in conflict. The *Bakke* case (1978) is a good example. A white student sued for entry into a medical school on the grounds that the school's affirmative-action policies gave preference to black applicants with lower test scores. School officials did not deny that it gave such preference (a violation of microjustice principles of merit), but argued that such practices were needed to reverse the unfair treatment of blacks which had gone on for hundreds of years (a macrojustice preference for balance in the overall pattern of race relationships).

Sensitivity to macrojustice principles varies according to people's experiences with learning different social roles. Women are more likely to endorse macrojustice principles than are men (Brickman, 1981). Social-science majors more often favor macrojustice than do physical-science majors. Democrats show more acceptance of macrojustice than do Republicans. In general, the difference apparently turns on the person's sensitivity to the needs of groups as opposed to those of individuals.

The type of justice reasoning people use can also be affected by the circumstances under which they must explain themselves. Several studies have shown, for example, that males usually choose equity (merit) as the basis for allocating rewards, while females choose equality (parity) (Levanthal et al., 1973). Related research has shown that women, more often than men, seek accommodative solutions to problems of distribution or reward (Uesugi and Vinacke, 1963; Levanthal and Lane, 1970; Benton, 1971; Mikula, 1974). Yet when women and men were questioned *anonymously* about their justice preferences in a reward allocation situation, their choices were the *reverse* of those shown in all previous research (Kidder, Bellettirie, and Cohn, 1977). Students who had done group projects were asked whether they would share credit points (affecting their grades) with group members who had gotten fewer points because of lower input into the group project. When they thought their answers were anonymous, women refused to share, while men said they would share. When they thought their answers were not anonymous, both women and men said just the opposite.

These results show how closely justice reasoning may be tied to social roles. In American society, women are expected to be accommodative, and men to be aggressive and competitive. In public, therefore, their reactions to distributive justice dilemmas should, and do, conform with these general role expectations. Equity is a more assertive, "masculine" position, while equality is softer, more self-denying (under the conditions of this experiment). The reversal of positions under the anonymous condition shows that a person's "preference" for a particular mode of justice is only a preference posture tailored to the expectations of given audiences. Women clearly understand equity reasoning, and in fact often prefer it "in private," though their public posture salutes equality. Men publically drum up the virtues of equity while their private gestures may be much more generous.

These two sets of research, on macrojustice and on sex roles, directly challenge the proposition that our ideas about justice are universal, that they stem from some process or tendency which we all either have at birth or acquire because of an imperative governing all social interaction. Some people in some situations clearly prefer macrojustice. Many people assert justice positions because they "fit" those persons' social roles. In both cases, we see that some thinking about justice comes from peoples' acceptance of an overall *pattern* or *norm* which does not spontaneously develop within them because of some universally shared human experience. Some peoples' responses, in other words, are determined by their exposure to, and acceptance of, justifications which exist and have a life of their own outside the individual, in the group.

Justifications of this sort are sometimes called *ideologies*. The most important feature of an ideology for our discussion is that it is a set of beliefs which is typical of particular groups at particular points in history. The beliefs are not permanent. Rather we find them changing as the economic and political circumstances of group life change. If some forms of thinking about justice are ideological, then we should find them present among some groups and absent among others. Then we would have grounds for rejecting the idea that human existence uniformly produces particular modes of thinking about justice.

From this perspective, for example, we would see both equity theory and the just-world hypothesis as being the products of a particular civilization (Western Europe) during one phase of its evolution (the Enlightenment—see Sampson, 1981, p. 120). To impose such concepts on the analysis of behavior or thought in a premodern peasant society or a non-Western autocracy, therefore, would be to prejudge and probably bias our understanding of what justice means to such people. The tremendous variation in law-related behavior we have seen in earlier chapters of this book ought, if nothing else, to caution us against easy acceptance of claims that particular thought patterns exist everywhere.

What is justice, then, if it is not a basic internally generated human motive? One answer to this question is that there are many conceptions of justice and that each represents a potential position we can adopt as a means of thinking about, and negotiating for, our own interests (Sampson, 1981, pp. 107–112). ". . . justice is a way in which people's actions become intelligible to and may be evaluated by themselves and others; it does not refer to an internal state of need" (Sampson, 1981, p. 108). Any mode of justice is a set of ideas which, if you understand them, can help you see the possibilities for cooperation and conflict in your relationship with someone else. Your interaction with that person will be conducted through a "vocabulary of motives,"* including the motive of justice. You will bargain with each other, using phrases which you both understand, which "make sense" to both of you, because you both have been taught the meanings of those phrases.

Looking at justice this way, we see that whenever the question of justice arises, the fairness of the outcome cannot be predicted, and we cannot even predict what the participants will consider a fair outcome unless we know their socio-cultural backgrounds and which "vocabularies of justice" they have probably learned. Justice will be constructed "on the spot" through the bargaining which goes on as each side promotes that concept of justice which best supports its interests.

This does not mean the triumph of unrestrained self-interest, the law of the jungle, or what Lerner calls "Darwinian justice." The vocabulary of motives sets limits on the actions and justifications a person can adopt and still retain *self*-respect. If you insist on a share which everyone else considers unfair, you may be unable to justify your actions even to yourself, since your self-image is largely a product of the way you think other people perceive you. You would suffer from your "greed" if your actions impressed others as being "greedy." Only if you can find a justice theory which supports your claim and is endorsed as reasonable by others whose

---

*This expression *vocabulary of motives* refers to the explanations people give each other for their actions. Within given areas of activity, some kinds of explanations are acceptable while others are not. Scientists cannot explain their experiments by saying that the holy spirit told them the answer to a problem. Saints, on the other hand, cannot give the scientists' explanation that logic and empirical data led them to reject worldly ways and perform miracles. Part of learning to live successfully in society involves learning the correct vocabulary of motives which is acceptable within the area of activity that a person wants to join.

opinions matter to you will you find the support you need to sustain self-respect.

This approach to justice departs quite drastically from experimental research traditions which have dominated social psychology for several decades and which continue to guide many social psychologists. By locating justice in the context of social interaction rather than basic human motives, some social psychologists are calling for a new approach to the study of psychology. The new approach says that research results are at best true only in their time and place, not for all people everywhere. It says that the content of justice reasoning varies from society to society and era to era. It therefore opens psychology to the study of ideology and brings it closer to the study of questions we have addressed in the earlier chapters of this book. If ideas about justice shift over time, vary from society to society or between different classes in complex societies, then, as in our discussion of macrojustice, we can link the psychologists' highly detailed study of variations in people's justice thinking to the sociologists' more broadly based study of the social and economic conditions which produce shifts from one ideology to another.

SUMMARY

Social psychology has been engaged in a search for the roots of that area of behavior and thought which we usually identify as morality and justice. The connection between morality, justice, and law is "obvious" to people raised in modern Western social systems. Therefore, it is not surprising that psychologists see their work on these issues as a process of uncovering universal psychological processes which limit and give shape to the processes of law. The two major perspectives we have considered in this chapter are cognitive-developmental theories and theories based on the principle of balance.

Developmental theories identify stages of both morality and justice reasoning. They tell us that the *order* in which these stages appear in a person's thinking is invariant. Everyone goes from one stage to the next because each stage is a cognitive springboard from which it becomes possible to "leap" to the next higher developmental stage. Not everyone moves up through all the stages to the top—some remain "childlike" because of their own personal limits or the restrictive features of their social worlds. But nobody skips stages.

Balance theories differ from developmental in that they see justice as arising out of an inner *need* for balance. When beliefs, values, and actions are inconsistent with each other (as, for example, they would be if a person thought he or she was unprejudiced but then realized that some of his or her behavior was resulting in racial discrimination), the lack of fit produces high anxiety. Equity theory says that all justice reasoning (and, therefore, behavior that is fair) is based on attempts to reconcile inputs (one's investments of time, energy, skill, or resources) with outcomes, and to apply that equation to others' outcomes also.

Justice-motive theory sees the balance principle as having a different origin and effect. It says that the need for balance becomes converted into a basic need to see the world as a just place—a place where one gets what one deserves. If we could not see the world this way (whether it is just in an objective sense does not matter), we would be in a constant state of anxiety about what might happen next to us and others we care about. Our actions would be paralyzed, because we would lack the necessary confidence that our acts would lead to predictable outcomes. We adopt different modes of justice reasoning depending on the amount and kind of trust we feel we can invest in different kinds of relationships. Several quite distinct justice "templates" develop in our thinking and action and we selectively apply them as each situation requires.

While these several theories are fascinating in the richness of their implications for questions we have discussed earlier in this book, their applicability to those issues is debatable. Other social psychologists dispute the possibility of finding universal psychological processes which explain morality or justice thinking. They hold that these theories, and the methods used to test them, have ignored the influence of cultural and historical variation to a dangerous degree. Even if there were universal features of human existence which lead to the modes of moral or justice reasoning we adopt, their effects would be so modified by cultural, structural, and historical factors that we would never be able to find them through laboratory experiments. The questions social psychological experimenters ask, and the concepts they use to form their questions, predestine their results to imprisonment within the walls of their own social environment.

We have seen throughout this book that legal forms are not universal, that societies vary greatly in the rules, procedures, and structures they adopt for the frequently conflicting purposes contending for survival and dominance in most societies. It is not necessarily conservative, liberal, or radical to say that all humans hunger for justice. Such an assumption can be found in the philosophies of both left and right. But the great differences between societies, and even between different strata within complex societies, mask any such universal hunger. The attempt to short-circuit those cultural differences by the use of "pure research" in "controlled laboratory experiments" has left several social psychologists unconvinced that what results is basic human reasoning uncontaminated by local variation.

Their alternative, which is sometimes called an *interactionist* perspective, sees justice not as a condition which people try to create, either in fact or in their imaginations. Justice is, rather, a linguistic abstraction, a "vocabulary of motives," which people learn to manipulate in pursuit of their own interests. Such a vocabulary is stable, internally consistent, and relevant only as long as people in competition or conflict with each other find such stability useful. We could expect cultures to differ in the vocabularies they develop, without concluding that the absence of some moral or justice mode signifies cognitive immaturity. We would even expect some cultures to produce vocabularies of motive which do not include what we recognize as the concept of justice.

Such variations in systems of justification are the stuff of the sociologist's interest in ideology and its relationship to social processes. If bridges can be built between psychology and other social sciences interested in law, an interactionist perspective combined with the analysis of ideology is a prime candidate for linkage.

APPLYING WHAT YOU KNOW

A good way to strengthen your understanding of the issues in this chapter is to try your hand at assessing the fit of psychological theories in a social setting very different from your own.

Behold, then, the Nandiwallas of India. Nandiwallas are a nomadic caste of bull trainers and traders (Hayden, 1981). They travel from town to town within zones assigned to them by the ancient traditions of their caste. Their work consists of performing with their bulls for money wherever they can gather an interested crowd, the way snake charmers do. They also make money buying and selling bulls.

Like nomads in many urbanized countries (e.g., gypsies and circus performers) Nandiwallas are not trusted by police and government officials. Returning the compliment, they avoid officials (police, courts, administrators) whenever possible. The official court system is therefore unavailable to them for settling disputes or enforcing caste rules.

Once every three years, therefore, they leave their scattered territories and converge on a summer encampment in order to reestablish their bonds as a separate caste group, arrange marriages, perform special religious ceremonies, and settle disputes which have grown up during the previous three years. Quarrels stem from such offenses as poisoning, failure to live up to the terms of arranged marriages (which always involve considerable exchange of property between two extended families), and gross insults of caste members.

The method for handling these disputes is to gather all adult males in the community together and carry on a long, disorderly discussion until consensus is reached on "fines" to be imposed on wrongdoers. When they cannot reach consensus, they often call on their hereditary Brahmin (high caste) *guru* to decide the fine. The guru is a nonnomadic, educated city dweller. He meets with the Nandiwallas only during these encampments and keeps half of all fines as compensation for having to live in a hot tent for several months. The other half of all fines is kept until the end of the encampment and then distributed equally among all caste families, including those of persons who paid fines in the first place.

The most obvious difference between this process and Western legal procedures is that the issue of justice is never raised. According to Hayden, Nandiwallas do not perceive disputes as problems of equity or parity or any other form of justice (1981). Instead, they see the entire problem as one of *ritual pollution* which threatens the purity of the caste as a whole. The council almost always treats disputes which come before it as incidents which automatically excommunicate the guilty from their caste. Excommunication is not permanent, and it is not imposed as a form of justice by agents of the caste. Nandiwallas believe, rather, that certain acts automatically pollute, and therefore automatically excommunicate, the polluted person in the same way that you might think of a person as polluted if he or she had just received a heavy dose of radiation or had just been pulled from a cesspool. Imposing the fine therefore has nothing to do with justice. The council's job is to find out who is polluted. The fine is paid as a way of *expiating* the polluting sin so that the entire caste's purity may be preserved. Until the fine is paid and the pollution is thus cleansed, caste people must protect themselves by avoiding contact with the polluted person.

For Nandiwallas, as for other Hindus in India, it pays to avoid caste excommunication. Without caste, one cannot marry or have one's children married. This ban means that one's entire family can face financial ruin, because marriages are a fundamental mechanism for redistributing wealth among caste members. Under excommunication, one cannot do business with caste members or dine with them. If one dies while excommunicated, funeral rites will not be allowed. To a Hindu this is like dying without life insurance. Among Nandiwallas, a man's exclusive right to do business in a particular zone is a caste-protected right. So excommunication threatens even the means of earning a living. In other words, the entire fabric of a person's life is interwoven with the supports and obligations of caste. There is, therefore, strong incentive to avoid or terminate a state of pollution and preserve one's caste status.

The fines imposed on people are not large. It is more important that the offender make the gesture of seeking purification than that the fine be made painful, because the fine is only secondarily a form of punishment.

In this way, the Nandiwallas manage their own affairs, maintain their solidarity, and validate the rules of caste.

Now try applying some of the ideas we have examined in this chapter to the case of the Nandiwallas. Begin with the developmental theories.

What kind of "moral judgment" development would you expect to find among these people? Would they display the "maturity" of judgment which Piaget and Kohlberg expect of "developed adults" if they believe that misbehavior produces instant pollution? If they are morally "immature," how do they manage to survive as a group without outside help or supervision?

Where would equity theory fit here? It is not obvious on the surface, since these people deny that their procedures have anything to do with justice. But could the equity principle be lurking below the surface? In their disputes, for example, and in their council's actions, the result of the process is often the restoration of severed or disrupted relationships. Doesn't that sound very much like "restoring the balance," which we discussed in chapter 4? Isn't the idea of equity a fundamental expression of the balance principle? Can relationships be restored without making participants feel that they are being "fairly" treated? Among Nandiwallas, although pollution, not justice, is the issue, a failure to make fines equitable can cause the council to end in a confusion of shouts and recriminations. But once fines are set, they are not changed, however unfair they may seem.

Again, if justice is not the issue on the surface, does this case damage the credibility of justice-motive theory? Suppose that, instead of looking for the language of justice, you consider the view of the world which the Nandiwallas apparently hold. Does it not fit with the "just-world hypothesis," which says that you get what you deserve? Automatic pollution could be considered an instant form of justice, something like Darwinian justice, because it fits with the idea that the world is stable and impartial, not capricious and arbitrary. But is it useful to apply the term justice to events which are thought of as inevitable, beyond our control, comparable to the law of gravity?

The elaborate system of caste obligations suggests that ideas of caste and pollution place the Nandiwalla legal system in the category of *obligational* or *contractual* justice (*identity-position* relationships in table 10.1). But given the scattered nature of their occupation and life-style, and the strong sense of in-group-out-group distinctions between caste members and outsiders, caste affiliation looks more like a *unit-position* relationship, in which case table 10.1 tells us to expect *equity* justice. If you were an anthropologist trying to test justice-motive theory in their situation, what would you need to ask a Nandiwalla informant?

Does the Nandiwalla case perhaps support the interactionist assertion that justifications are parts of vocabularies of motives? Is caste and the idea of pollution another example of ideology, showing us that people living under different circumstances from our own really do think differently from us? Or do the differences mask an underlying similarity in the way all people react?

REFERENCES

AUSTIN, W. AND WALSTER, E. (1974), Reactions to Confirmations and Disconfirmations of Expectancies of Equity and Inequity, *Journal of Personality and Social Psychology*, 30: 208–216.

BENTON, A. A. (1971), Productivity, Distributive Justice, and Bargaining among Children, *Journal of Personality and Social Psychology*, 18: 68–78.

BERSCHEID, E. AND WALSTER, E. (1967), When Does a Harmdoer Compensate a Victim? *Journal of Personality and Social Psychology*, 6: 435–41.

BLACK, D. (1973), The Boundaries of Legal Sociology, in Donald Black and Maureen Mileski (eds.), *The Social Organization of Law*, New York: Seminar Press.

BRICKMAN, P. (1981), Microjustice and Macrojustice, in Melvin and Sally Lerner, (eds.), *The Justice Motive in Social Behavior*, New York: Plenum, pp. 173–203.

BRICKMAN, P. (1975), Adaptation-Level Determinants of Satisfaction with Equal and Unequal Outcome Distributions in Skill and Chance Situations, *Journal of Personality and Social Psychology*, 32: 191–98.

BRICKMAN, P. AND BRYAN, J. (1975), Moral Judgment of Theft, Charity and Third-Party Transfers that Increase or Decrease Equity, *Journal of Personality and Social Psychology*, 32: 156–61.

BRICKMAN, P. AND BRYAN, J. (1976), Equity versus Equality as Factors in Children's Moral Judgments of Thefts, Charity, and Third-Party Transfers, *Journal of Personality and Social Psychology*, 25: 268–76.

CHAIKES, A. AND DARLEY, J. (1973), Victim or Perpetrator: Defensive Attribution and the Need for Order and Justice, *Journal of Personality and Social Psychology*, 25: 268–76.

DAMON, W. (1981), The Development of Justice and Self-Interest during Childhood, in Melvin and Sally Lerner, (eds.), *The Justice Motive in Social Behavior*, New York: Plenum, pp. 57–72.

EDWARDS, C. (1975), Society Complexity and Moral Development: A Kenyan Study, *Ethos*, pp. 505–527.

FRIEDMAN, L. AND MACAULAY, S. (1969), *Law and the Behavioral Sciences*, Indianapolis: Bobbs-Merrill.

GERGEN, K. (1978), Toward Generative Theory, *Journal of Personality and Social Psychology*, 36: 1344–1360.

HAYDEN, ROBERT (1981), *No One Is Stronger than the Caste: Arguing Dispute Cases in a Caste Panchayat*. Ph.D. Dissertation, Department of Anthropology, S.U.N.Y. at Buffalo.

HOFFMAN, M. (1970), Moral Development, in P. Mussen, (ed.), *Carmichael's Manual of Child Psychology*, New York: John Wiley.

KIDDER, L.; BELLETTIRIE, G.; AND COHN, E. (1977), Secret Ambitions and Public Performances, *Journal of Experimental Social Psychology*, 13: 70–80.

KIPNIS, D. (1972), Does Power Corrupt? *Journal of Personality and Social Psychology*, 24: 33–41.

KOHLBERG, L. (1963), The Development of Children's Orientations toward a Moral Order, *Vita Humana*, 6: 11–33.

KOHLBERG, L. (1969), Stage and Sequence: The Cognitive-Developmental Approach to Socialization, In D. Goslin, (eds.), *Handbook of Socialization Theory and Research*, Chicago: Rand-McNally.

KOHLBERG, L. AND KRAMER, R. (1969), Continuities and Discontinuities in Childhood and Adult Moral Development, *Human Development*, 12: 93–120.

LERNER, M. (1981), The Justice Motive in Human Relations: Some Thoughts on

What We Know and Need to Know about Justice, in Melvin and Sally Lerner, (eds.), *The Justice-Motive in Human Behavior*, New York: Plenum, pp. 11–36.

LERNER, M. (1975), The Justice Motive in Social Behavior: Introduction, *Journal of Social Issues*, 31: pp. 1–19.

LERNER, M. AND MATHEWS (1967), Reaction to the Suffering of Others Under Conditions of Indirect Responsibility, *Journal of Personality and Social Psychology*, 5: pp. 319–25.

LERNER, M. AND SIMMONS, C. (1966), The Observer's Reaction to the 'Innocent Victim': Compassion or Rejection? *Journal of Personality and Social Psychology*, 4: 203–10.

LEVANTHAL, G.; POPP, A.; AND SAWYER, L. (1973), Equity or Equality in Children's Allocation of Reward to Other Persons? *Child Development*, 44: 753–63.

LEVANTHAL, G. AND ANDERSON, D. (1970), Self-Interest and the Maintenance of Equity, *Journal of Personality and Social Psychology*, 15: 312–16.

LEVANTHAL, G. S. AND LANE, D. (1970), Sex, Age and Equity Behavior, *Journal of Personality and Social Psychology*, 15, 312–16.

MACAULAY, S. AND WALSTER, E. (1971), Legal Structures and Restoring Equity, *Journal of Social Issues*, 23: 173–88.

MIKULA, G. (1974), Nationality, Performance and Sex as Determinants of Reward Allocation, *Journal of Personality and Social Psychology*, 29: 435–40.

PIAGET, J. (1965), *The Moral Judgment of the Child*, New York: Free Press.

PILIAVIN, I.; RODIN, J.; AND PILIAVIN, J. (1969), Good Samaritanism: An Underground Phenomenon? *Journal of Personality and Social Psychology*, 13: 289–99.

PILIAVIN, J. AND WALSTER, E. (1972), Equity and the Innocent Bystander, *Journal of Social Issues*, 28: 165–89.

RIEGEL, K. (1976), From Traits and Equilibrium toward Developmental Dialectics, in J. Arnold, (ed.), *Nebraska Symposium on Motivation*, Lincoln, Nebr.: University of Nebraska Press.

ROSNOW, R. (1978), The Prophetic Vision of Giambattista Vico: Implications for the State of Social Psychology, *Journal of Personality and Social Psychology*, 36: 1322–31.

SAMPSON, E. (1981), Social Change and the Contexts of Justice Motivation, In Melvin and Sally Lerner, (eds.), *The Justice Motive in Social Behavior*, New York: Plenum, pp. 97–124.

SAMPSON, E. (1978), Scientific Paradigms and Social Values: Wanted—A Scientific Revolution, *Journal of Personality and Social Psychology*, 36: 1332–43.

SAMPSON, E. (1977), Psychology and the American Ideal, *Journal of Personality and Social Psychology*, 35: 767–82.

SMITH, M. (1978), Perspectives of Selfhood, *American Psychologist*, 33: 1053–63.

SURBER, C. (1977), Developmental Processes in Social Inference: Averaging of Intentions and Consequences in Moral Judgment, *Developmental Psychology*, 13: 654–65.

TAPP, J. AND KOHLBERG, L. (1971), Developing Senses of Law and Legal Justice, *Journal of Social Issues*, 27: 65–91.

TURIEL, E.; EDWARDS, C.; AND KOHLBERG, L. (1978), Moral Development in Turkish Children, Adolescents and Young Adults, *Journal of Cross-Cultural Psychology*, 9: 75–85.

UESUGI, T. AND VINACKE, W. (1963), Strategy in a Feminine Game, *Sociometry*, 26: 75–88.

WALSTER, E.; WALSTER, G.; AND BERSCHEID, E. (1978), *Equity: Theory and Research*, Boston: Allyn & Bacon.

WELLMAN, H.; LARKEY, C.; AND SOMERVILLE, S.   (1979), The Early Development
   of Moral Criteria, *Child Development,* 50: 869–73.
ZIMBARDO, P.   (1972), Pathology and Imprisonment, *Society,* 9: 4–8.

CASES CITED

Regents of the University of California v. *Bakke,* SC 76-811, 1978.

INDEX

AUTHOR INDEX

A

Abel, R., 148, 153, 172, 174, 180, 184, 204, 205, 207, 228, 244
Abel-Smith, B., 214, 225, 226, 244
Althussar, L., 94, 110
Anderman, S., 193, 207
Anderson, D., 255, 274
Andreassen, A., 180
Aubert, V., 154, 180
Auerbach, J., 223, 241, 244
Austin, W., 254, 274

B

Balibar, E., 94, 110
Ball, H., 120, 121, 143–145
Bayley, D., 97, 110
Bazelon, D., 232, 244
Becker, H. S., 42, 56, 118, 137, 143
Becker, T., 132, 143
Bellettirie, G., 267, 274

Benedict, R., 108, 110
Benton, A. A., 266, 274
Berscheid, E., 255, 256, 257, 274, 275
Best, A., 180
Beutel, F., 127, 144
Black, D., 20, 22, 24, 33, 34, 35, 71, 81, 247, 274
Bohannan, P., 30, 31–35, 37, 40, 42, 44, 56, 87, 102, 149, 161, 180
Boulding, K., 154, 155, 180
Bowen, M., 153, 180
Braverman, H., 105, 110
Brickman, P., 265, 266, 274
Brinkley, D., 147
Bryan, J., 266, 274

C

Campbell, D. T., 23, 35, 43, 56, 126, 144
Canon, B., 132, 133, 144
Caplow, T., 152, 180
Cappell, C., 244
Carlin, J., 216, 217, 218, 244
Cartwright, B., 176, 180

Wellman, H., 250, 275
Wexler, S., 237, 245
Weyrauch, W., 13, 35
Williams, G., 35
Woodworth, J. R., 129, 145

Y

Yamamura, D., 144, 145
Yancey, W., 125, 146

Yinger, J. M., 80, 82
Yngvesson, B., 69, 82, 135, 146, 163, 182, 208

Z

Zimbardo, P., 256, 275
Zinn, H., 28, 29, 33–35

SUBJECT INDEX

A

Abortion, 114, 137, 140, 191
Access to Law, Justice, 74, 164–168,
    171–174, 184, 212, 219, 224, 231,
    234, 244
Adjudication, 162, 170, 171, 175, 177
Affirmative Action, 26
American Bar Foundation, 235
Apartheid, 94, 95
Autonomous Morality, 248–250
Autonomy 188, 196, 212, 216, 218,
    222–227, 228, 231, 233
Avoidance, 72, 154, 174

B

Bakke, 266, 276
Balance, Cognitive, 254–258, 269, 273
Bar Association, 217–219, 222–224, 230
Barristers, 214, 215, 225, 226
Berkeley School, 25–28, 33–34

Bill of Rights, 196, 250
Black Acts, 84–87, 93
Brazil, 139, 140
British Empire, 40–42, 49, 50, 78, 79, 92,
    100–103, 137, 200
Brown v. Board of Education, 3, 10, 116,
    118, 119, 124, 125, 139
Bureaucracy, 185, 186, 191, 195, 196,
    198, 201, 203, 205, 220, 221, 227

C

Camp David Accords, 153, 164
Child Labor, 95, 96, 139, 204
Chile, 26, 201
China, 67, 188, 190, 199–202
Civil Law, 133, 220, 221
Class Action, 238
Code of Ethics, 218, 219, 223, 226
Cognitive Dissonance, 119
Columbia Broadcasting System, 147, 180,
    213
Common Law, 17, 41, 133, 187, 230
Communitarianism, 197–202, 204, 205